Barbs, Bullets, and Blood

The 1880s Texas Barbed Wire Wars

Harold D. Jobes

University of North Texas Press
Denton, Texas

© 2025 Harold D. Jobes

All rights reserved.
Printed in the United States of America.

10 9 8 7 6 5 4 3 2 1

Permissions:
University of North Texas Press
1155 Union Circle #311336
Denton, TX 76203-5017

The paper used in this book meets the minimum requirements of the American National Standard for Permanence of Paper for Printed Library Materials, z39.48.1984. Binding materials have been chosen for durability.

Chapter 9 is based on an earlier article, "Fence Cutting and a Ranger Shootout at Green Lake," published in the October 2009 issue of the *Wild West History Association Journal*.

Library of Congress Cataloging-in-Publication Data is available from the Library of Congress.

ISBN 978-1-57441-964-1 (cloth)
ISBN 978-1-57441-971-9 (ebook)

The electronic edition of this book was made possible by the support of the Vick Family Foundation.

Typeset by vPrompt eServices.

In memory of my beloved wife Cheryl Smith Jobes, who with love and uncomplaining devotion pushed me to finish this book.

September 19, 1947–February 22, 2024

No greater misfortune could possibly befall a people than to lack a historian properly to set down their annals; one who with faithful zeal will guard, treasure, and perpetuate all those events which if left to the frail memory of man and to the mercy of the passing years will be sacrificed upon the altar of time.

—**Gaspar Pérez de Villagrá**, captain and legal officer in the Juan de Oñate expedition that first colonized Santa Fe de Nuevo México in 1598

Contents

	List of Illustrations	vii
	Preface	ix
	Prologue	1
Chapter 1	The First Barbed Wire War Was in Austin	3
Chapter 2	Barbed Wire, a Yankee's Invention, Comes to Texas	11
Chapter 3	Cheap Land, Cheap Wire, and Expensive Cattle	27
Chapter 4	Cowhands Kill a Fence Cutter in Clay County	41
Chapter 5	Settlers and Barbed Wire Come to Brown County	63
Chapter 6	Governor Ireland Calls a Special Legislative Session, and Representative Odom Explains the Problem	81
Chapter 7	Fence Cutters Assassinate Ranger Benjamin Warren in Sweetwater	105
Chapter 8	Rangers Kill a Fence-Cutting Constable in Brown County	127
Chapter 9	Three Assassination Attempts on the Farmer Who Snitched	151
Chapter 10	Hell Breaks Loose in Coleman, and a Widow Suffers Fence Cutting	173

	Photo Gallery	
Chapter 11	Ranger Wounded, Cutter Killed at Green Lake, Edwards County	193
Chapter 12	Lawmen Stop Medina's Fence Cutting but Suffer Revenge	207
Chapter 13	Tragedy and Death on a Clay County Fence Line	241
Chapter 14	Menard Fence Cutter Sent to the Penitentiary	255
Chapter 15	Ranger Has a Dynamite Solution for Navarro County	265
	Epilogue	285
	Acknowledgments	293
	Appendix 1	297
	Appendix 2	301
	Endnotes	303
	Bibliography	357
	Index	373

List of Illustrations

1. An 1860 Stake-and-Rider Fence near Austin
2. John Grinninger Historical Marker
3. Henry B. Sanborn, Barbed Wire Salesman
4. Early King Ranch Fence Staples
5. Joseph Glidden Barbed Wire
6. Jacob Haish Barbed Wire
7. Barbed Wires in Texas
8. Long-Handled Wire Cutting Tool
9. Cedar Rail Fence
10. Stacked Rock Fence
11. Henry B. Sanborn, Horseman
12. Monument to Shanghai Pierce, a South Texas Cattleman
13. Judge William Bedford Plemons and Wife Mary Elizabeth
14. Thomas L. Odom, Cattleman and State Representative
15. Fence Cutters' Note to Representative Odom
16. Garland G. Odom, Fort Chadbourne Cattleman
17. Governor John Ireland
18. Adjutant General Wilburn Hill King
19. Ranger Benjamin Warren, Undercover Ranger
20. Runnels County Sheriff John Formwalt and Wife Eppie
21. Nolan County Sheriff H. G. Bardwell
22. Meeting of Fence Cutters and Citizens in Brownwood
23. Coggin Brothers' Commercial Building and Opera House
24. The Coggin, Ford, and Martin Bank
25. Samuel R. Coggin and Wife Mattie
26. Levin Powell Baugh, Brown County Rancher
27. Brown County Sheriff William N. Adams
28. Captain James T. Gillespie, Ranger Company E
29. W. A. Pinkerton Letter to Quartermaster John O. Johnson

30. William W. Collier, Young Ranger Working Undercover
31. Ranger Ira Aten, Young Ranger Working Undercover
32. Captain William Scott and Ranger Company F
33. Captain George Heinrich Schmitt and Ranger Company C
34. William Henry Day, Coleman County Cattleman
35. Mable Day Lea with Her Family
36. Green Lake in Edwards County
37. Willian Joseph Greer on Horseback
38. Ranger Oscar D. Baker
39. Ranger Phillip C. Baird
40. Rock Fence, a Fortress for Fence Cutters
41. William Joseph Greer, Rancher, Banker, and Gentleman
42. Old Medina County Courthouse in Castroville
43. Cattleman John Lytle, a Force for Law and Order
44. Clay County Sheriff George Cooper Wright
45. Menard County Sheriff Richard R. "Dick" Russell
46. A. W. Moursund, District Judge, Thirty-Third Judicial District
47. Ira Aten's Dynamite Boom for Navarro County Fence Cutters
48. Ira Aten, Undercover Man in Navarro County
49. Captain Lamar P. Sieker, Frontier Battalion Quartermaster
50. Five Texas Ranger Captains and a Lieutenant

Preface

Fences have had an important place in the history of civilized people for the past five or six centuries. They delivered the profit of owning land with the guarantee of exclusive possession. Fencing enters into the laws of all our states and territories and is firmly established as a principle in the statutes of our oldest states.

The United States' earliest fences were made of rails from timber, or often stone when it could be found, or by planting and growing thorny hedges as a barrier. Pickets or rails were used to construct stake-and-rider fences, or to build zigzag worm fences. But the worm fence and the stake-and-rider fence took up extra land when constructed. These wood-rail fences soon rotted and were often blown down. The type of fence a landowner built was usually determined by materials available. Honey locust or Osage orange (bois d'arc) were grown as thorny hedge rows for fence in Midwestern states and parts of Texas. Several Texas businesses developed harvesting and processing bois d'arc seed and sold their product to farmers in the Midwestern states. But the thorny hedge fences were slow growing and not very effective.

The 1816 Memoirs of the Philadelphia Agriculture Society note that iron wire was being used as fence material. It demonstrated a cost savings for the farmer. Plain, smooth iron wire was an improvement and useful to some, but it had problems too. It stretched and sagged in the summer heat and broke in the cold of the winter. Cattle had no fear of smooth wire and would press through to reach the farmers' crops. Still, plain, smooth wire fences were used by many. There were all types of fences in our nation. The United States Board of Agriculture in 1871 claimed the total value of fences in the United States was over $1 trillion, with an annual outlay for repair of $93,963,187.[1]

The United States' first patent for a fence wire was numbered 10211 and issued November 8, 1853, to William H. Meriwether of New Braunfels, Texas. Meriwether wire was a smooth wire, a barbless, snake-shaped strand that spiraled to allow for expansion and contraction. We are told this wire would not deter cattle, but neighbors used it for fencing yards and gardens. Four years later, in 1857, John Grinninger, a blacksmith living fifty miles north of New Braunfels in Austin, fabricated a vicious hoop iron fence material. Grinninger's fence was very effective in keeping livestock off his property. Grinninger never patented his fence material and was later murdered.[2]

On April 2, 1867, the first patent to arm a fence with points or barbs was issued to Alphonso Dabb. His patent described arming a picket with sharp points to keep intruders from scaling or crossing a barrier. Using this device as a deterrent to livestock had not occurred to Dabb and was not mentioned in his patent. Lucien B. Smith was granted a patent on June 25, 1867, for a wire with spools defensively armed with sharp protruding nails. The spools were free to revolve upon the fence wire. They were held in position laterally and of such size that they were plainly visible to livestock. William D. Hunt was granted a patent on July 23, 1867, for arming a plain wire fence with rotating spurs made from sheet metal, noting that "animals are deterred from pushing against the fence or attempting to break over it."

Michael Kelly of New York received a patent on February 11, 1868, then manufactured a more practical prickly wire than those previously mentioned. His wire was made with small sheet iron points projecting in different directions. Kelly's main improvement was laying another wire alongside the wire with barbs to hold the points in place. He called this wire a thorny wire and his company was later known as the Thorn Wire Hedge Company.

Six years followed with several more patents for prickly fence material granted. Then in the year of 1874, three men of DeKalb, Illinois, received patents for what we now know as barbed wire. Jacob Haish, Isaac Ellwood, and Joseph F. Glidden were each issued patents, and Glidden and Ellwood soon became business partners. Of the three men and their patents, Glidden's patent no. 157,124, granted November 24, 1874, was the winner over the years and the nation's bestselling barbed wire. These three men from the town of DeKalb began manufacturing their barbed wire, and their production grew. Express and freight trains created danger and hazardous conditions along unfenced tracks, and the railroads were being held responsible for damages. Barbed wire quickly met their need; a rail carload of spooled barbed wire would fence twenty miles of track. In Texas the land and cattle business needed a cheap fence material.[3]

When the Republic of Texas became a state in the Union, the United States was brought into the war with Mexico. When the war ended, the United States and Texas were in a dispute over the boundary of lands taken from Mexico. This dispute was settled in 1850. Texas kept roughly 170 million acres of land and ceded 67 million acres of territory to the United States. The relinquished acreage includes parts of what are now Colorado, Kansas, Oklahoma, New Mexico, and Wyoming. Texas came out of this settlement with a vast and boundless acreage of range land. In the years that followed, the Texas legislature began parceling this land out in development grants for roads and canals, in donations to its veterans, as set-asides for education, as land for railroads constructed, and for homesteads. The state sold land, and cheap. Land was dirt cheap after the legislature passed the Fifty Cent Act and sold land for fifty cents an acre.[4]

The cattle business had helped Texas recover after the Civil War and through the dark days of Reconstruction. The Texas cattle industry prospered in the 1870s. Those were the years of the famous cattle drives, and Texas led the nation in beef production. Refrigeration was a new technology, and slaughtered beef was being shipped to Europe. Profits from Texas beef were strong, and the Britain cattlemen's aristocracy feared their competition. British wealth formed syndicates and came to Texas with large sums of money to buy large tracts of land plus cattle and horses. Some of the Texas cattlemen, who had survived the early years of ranching and prospered, saw this as an opportunity. They sold their large ranches and cattle to the Brits and then bought even more land. Texas land was cheap, and it was selling rapidly.

During this period of strong and rapid growth in Texas, Joseph Glidden, Isaac Ellwood, and Jacob Haish from Illinois began manufacturing and selling barbed wire. Joseph Glidden employed Henry B. Sanborn, a young horse trader, as their company's sales representative. Glidden gave Sanborn exclusive rights for sale of Glidden Barbed Wire in Texas. Sanborn's horse-trading partner, Judson P. Warner, joined him to work the Texas barbed wire sales. Sanborn sold the first ten spools of barbed wire to Cleaves & Fletcher Hardware Company in Gainesville, Texas. Judson Warner traveled south and sold the first carload of barbed wire to implement dealers John A. Webb and Brother in Austin, Texas. Their sales of barbed wire in Texas grew rapidly. Across the United States, sales of barbed wire vaulted from 10,000 pounds sold in 1874 to 120 million pounds in 1881. Railroads and farmers across the nation were buying barbed wire, and a great amount of the new fence material was sold to Texas cattlemen.[5]

As barbed wire was now manufactured, sales of Texas land was brisk and the cattle market was strong. The first order of business after purchasing large land tracts was buying barbed wire, then fencing the new purchased property. Emigrant farmers were now migrating to Texas and homesteading on the frontier. They cleared land, raised small crops, and may have had a milk cow and a few heads of livestock, but few settlers had the money for wire fences.

By the early 1880s, barbed wire fences were causing problems across Texas, and the barbed wire war had its beginning. In the years past, cattlemen and sheepmen grazed their livestock free on the vast millions of acres of open, unfenced state public domain and the open railroad lands. The state's land sales and the new, cheap barbed fencing material changed this arrangement. In a broad sense, the war that followed was between two adversaries—the free-range men and the pasture men. The free-range men were the stock raisers who benefited from free grazing and now refused or weren't able to buy land and build fences. The pasture men were those buying land and building barbed wire fences to enclose their livestock and protect their investment. Open-range land for free grazing of livestock was rapidly disappearing.

Now homesteaders and small farms were often surrounded by pasture fences with no gates for entrance or exit. New barbed wire fences were built across roads and obstructed public travel. Cattle trails were closed by barbed wire, and cattle drives halted in parts of the state. By 1883 the fencing of Texas was almost complete. Citizens had difficulty adjusting and now they rebelled. Fence cutting became epidemic and a revolt began. Fences were cut, fenced pastures were burned, and pasture men's cattle and sheep were killed. Often the lives of the pasture men were threatened. The two classes of stock raisers, the pasture men who owned fenced land and the free-range men who opposed fencing, were in bitter conflicts. When the barbed wire war began, the free-range interests were supported by a majority of the public, who opposed the changes fences had brought and despised the intrusion of big money investors and foreigners.

Will S. James, an old cowboy turned preacher, wrote a book in 1893 titled *27 Years a Maverick, or Life on a Texas Range*. In this book about his cowboy years, James describes the barbed wire war:

> The advent of barbed wire in Texas brought with it a reign of lawlessness and terror, such as has no parallel in the State's eventful history. There were decidedly two classes, free grass, and pasture men, and never in any land has there been greater bitterness and eternal hatred than existed between these two factions. It was to be heard on the range, at home, round the fireside, in the courts, in the legislative halls, every election was carried or lost on the issue, the best men in the country were on one side or the other side of this question. If a man was a pasture man, he was favoring the wealthy, if a free grass man, he was branded a wire cutter, when in reality neither charge was necessarily true.[6]

By 1883 fence cutting was occurring in over half of the 171 Texas organized counties. The most destructive and frequent occurrences were on the state's frontier edge, running from Clay County in North Texas down through Brown and Coleman, on to Medina, Frio, Gonzales and south to Wilson and Bee Counties.[7]

The fence cutters in many areas worked as teams and were well organized; some belonged to clandestine groups with names such as the Owls, Hatchet Company, Javelinas, and Blue Devils. These groups had passwords and secret signs. But there were also lone individuals cutting fences; some clipped wire to get in and out of their own property.

When fence cutting started, local lawmen across the state failed to stop the perpetrators of the crime. Lawmen were overwhelmed by the job and local politics played a part. The sheriff was elected, serving at the will of the people, and the majority of the people opposed barbed wire. His constituents were angered by the invasion of the syndicates, the corporations, and wealthy cattlemen buying and fencing the land with barbed wire. Cutting a fence was a misdemeanor offense and almost always performed at night. So why would the sheriff work at night to try to arrest a fence cutter, charge him, then have a jury refuse to indict him? Other crimes were of greater public concern, therefore they were the sheriff's priority.

The fence-cutting problem grew rapidly, and there was little interest or effort of the public to stop it. Fence cutters wrote threatening notes to the fence builder and nailed them on fence posts and cattle pens and tacked signs on the sides of buildings. Coffins and ropes with hangmen nooses were left along destroyed fences, warning the owner not to rebuild. As fence cutting and lawlessness intensified, the Texas economy was crushed. Fence cutting had a major impact on the state. The land and cattle prices plummeted, and farmers could not farm and produce. Immigrant farmers and homesteaders stopped coming to the state. Some who had come and established homesteads loaded their belongings in their wagons and left Texas.

With a crushed economy and increasing violence, fence cutting finally lost its public support. But now local officials acknowledged their inability to stop the clandestine fence cutting and its related atrocities. Local officials and the citizens across the state sought help from the state government in Austin. There was a call on the governor and the adjutant general to send the Texas Rangers to stop fence cutting. The Ranger's Frontier Battalion was established as a military unit in 1874 to confront the Indians and violent crime on the frontier. Recently the state's Ranger Force had been reduced in size and lost most of its funding. They were not prepared for the task and little help was forthcoming. The governor lacked statutory authority to provide decisive help. He could only offer small rewards for apprehension and conviction of the fence cutters, and such happening was rare. Stockmen and property owners took matters into their own hands; shootouts and killings occurred on fence lines across the state.

There was a crying need for legislation to enhance law enforcement and deal with the fence-cutting causes. In October of 1883, Governor John Ireland called a special session of the Eighteenth Texas Legislature. His charge to the legislative body was, "Consider and provide a remedy for the wanton destruction of fences."

Preface

The legislature convened in Austin on January 8, 1884, receiving an outpouring of sentiment from the public on the fence-cutting issue. Legislators were swamped with letters, memorials, and petitions and met with citizens and community leaders from the state's distressed counties. The members introduced a mass of bills in the house and senate. Proposed legislation introduced covered a broad spectrum of cures for fence cutting, ranging from bills making it a justifiable homicide to shoot and kill a fence cutter to instituting a statewide herd law. A herd law would require livestock owners to keep their animals on land they owned or leased by fencing or other means. Such a law would end free grazing of the state's remaining open-range land and was feared by the free-range men.

As the session was underway, newspapers quoted Senator A. L. Matlock saying the state loss in tax valuation was estimated at $50 million. State Representative T. L. Odom claimed the state of Texas suffered $100 million in damages to fences, other property, and the state's economy. Cattle that once sold for $30 a head now sold for $5. Horace R. Starkweather, an aged banker and rancher who lost his ranch during the barbed wire war, spoke of the economic disaster years later. He said virtually all the free-range cattlemen went broke and $90 million in loans from eastern banks were called on livestock loans in Texas.[8]

Following contentious debates, new laws were passed by the legislature to remedy fence cutting, stop the fencing of land not owned, and open public roads obstructed by barbed wire fences. Cutting fences and burning pastures were made a felony with mandatory time in prison. The Texas legislature appropriated funds for use by the governor to employ detectives and to pay rewards for fence cutters captured and convicted. The legislature adjourned and went home on February 6, 1884.

The new laws were constructive and over time brought an end to fence cutting in Texas. Commercial detectives were employed, and Texas Rangers stepped in and aided the local lawmen. Some of the fence cutters were captured, prosecuted under new criminal statutes, and sent to the state's prison. Time in the penitentiary served as a warning to others who now recognized there were teeth in the state's new fence laws.

Still, there were counties where clandestine groups ignored the new laws and battles followed. During encounters across the state, blood was shed with the killing of fence cutters. But lawmen didn't escape the bloodletting. On the cold winter night in February of 1885, Ranger Benjamin Warren was in the lobby of a Sweetwater hotel, sitting in front of a woodburning stove. He was smoking a pipe, with his hands in his overcoat pockets. A shot was fired through the hotel window, striking Warren below the left eye and exiting by his right ear. He fell from the chair with blood spurting from his face. Another Ranger was wounded in a shootout with fence cutters on a fence line. Detectives of the Ferrell and Pinkerton Agencies employed by the governor and working undercover fled the state to save their lives. A former sheriff who led a fence-cutter roundup was killed by the new sheriff elected by the fence cutters. The Texas barbed wire war was short but bitter and violent. Most of the violence was in 1883, 1884, and 1885 and then came to an end in the later years of the 1880s. Sheriffs and Texas Rangers did a commendable job of enforcing new laws, and district courts also did their part. The county commissioners used new powers to solve the road issues.

Most fence cutters in this book, and in other written histories, are characterized as villains who violated the law, committed violent acts, and wrecked the state's economy. Some of these men were truly malicious and dangerous. A criminal element was involved, but many cutters were small stockmen rebelling against what they saw as the evil of the time, a sinister force taking away free grass and water, their bountiful gift from God on this earth.

Several outstanding books and publications on barbed wire and its history have been written over the years. My favorite is Henry and Frances McCallum's *The Wire That Fenced the West*. The *Panhandle-Plains Historical Review* published C. Boone McClure's "History of the Manufacture of Barbed Wire." This is an excellent history of barbed wire development and the many patents granted. Harold L. Hagemeier's *Barbed Wire Identification Encyclopedia* is an indispensable guide for barbed wire collectors across the nation. Hagemeier's book is truly an encyclopedia. It lists and describes close to five hundred types of barbed wire produced since its invention.

Several of today's writers of the Wild West's history have written about incidents and dustups caused by men cutting fences when barbed wire came to Texas. But the story of the barbed wire war in Texas is fragmented and incomplete. This book is an attempt to put the pieces together. I have drawn heavily on court records, old newspapers, the state's adjutant general files, and other primary source material. I also used writings of contemporary authors and historians, filling in around and adding to their stories. In doing so I have made a serious effort to cite my sources with endnotes for the historian, future writers, and genealogists. Barbed wire changed ranching in Texas forever. These difficult times of change for the early stockmen and their battles over barbed wire fences are the stories that follow.

Prologue

The Runnels County District Court convened on May 9, 1884, and the grand jury heard testimony on fence cutting from Texas Ranger Benjamin Warren. Warren, a young cowhand from San Saba, had enlisted in Captain J. T. Gillespie's Ranger Company E. He was working as an undercover operative on the state's contentious fence-cutting problem. The young Ranger did a commendable job. The Runnels District Court's grand jury delivered twenty-four indictments on fourteen men charged with fence cutting.

The week before the Runnels County fence cutter's trial was to begin, Ranger Ben Warren, the state's key witness, was in Nolan County, Runnels's neighboring county to the north. The winter night was freezing cold, and Warren was in the Sweetwater Central Hotel's lobby with State Representative Thomas L. Odom. Warren and Odom were sitting around a large woodstove, carrying on a conversation with a man who had come to Nolan County and engaged in the business of poisoning prairie dogs for the ranchers. C. F. Powell, W. S. Lester, and a Mr. Dabney from Austin were sitting around the woodstove listening to the discussion. Representative Odom, four feet from Ranger Warren, leaned forward, punching up the fire in the woodstove. Warren, sitting near the stove, was smoking his pipe with his hands in his overcoat pockets. There was the loud crack of rifle fire. A shot was fired through the glass pane of the office window from an alley that ran past the hotel. The bullet struck Warren in the head, entering below his left eye and exiting below his right ear. The shot barely missed Representative Odom, who later testified that he felt a concussion in the air as the bullet passed his head and struck Warren. Odom sprang through the door to the hotel dining room and, looking back, saw Warren still in the chair with blood spurting from his face. In a matter of seconds the state of Texas had lost it key witness in the Runnels County fence-cutting trial. This incident was neither the first nor last bloodletting that barbed wire brought to Texas. Violence followed the destruction of fences as the cattlemen rapidly fenced more land.

Chapter 1

The First Barbed Wire War Was in Austin

> Another Murder—we are again called upon to record one of the most cruel and bloodthirsty murders that has ever disgraced our usually orderly city.
> —*The State Gazette* (Austin) 1862

In the communities of early Texas, there was the need to grow food crops for the citizenry, whether it be grains, vegetables, fruits, or nuts. Food crops were grown by families in gardens and orchards and often shared or sold to neighbors and others. In those days, gardening was often a challenge. Roaming hogs, cattle, horses, and other livestock roamed freely through villages and could be a real nuisance. Construction of rail, picket, or rock fences was used to solve this problem. Such was the case in Austin, Texas, where cedar pickets were cheap and stake-and-rider fences were common in the early years.

In January of 1839, the Texas Congress selected the Austin site for the new republic's capital. Austin's town, originally named Waterloo, was laid out on the Colorado River between Waller and Shoal Creek, with a broad avenue and streets sectioned in a square shape. President Mirabeau Lamar appointed Edwin Waller, a Virginian and a veteran of Texas's fight for freedom, as the agent to divide 640 acres of land into lots. The survey and construction crew located their camp on Waller Creek but were unprepared for an Indian attack. Indians came, and two of the workmen were killed and scalped.

Eighteen years afterward Texas had become a state, and Austin was finally the permanent state capital. In 1857 the buildings had evolved from log cabins to several elegant homes. Austin's population was 3,034 people and had its share of lawyers; there were sixty listed. One of those individuals, Alexander W. Terrell, would gain prominence as an attorney, judge, and later a powerful state senator representing his Austin district. Terrell as a senator was noted for drafting legislation that created the Texas Railroad Commission, developed early Texas election laws, and pledged a million acres of land to the Chicago syndicate for constructing a new state capitol building.[1]

In 1857 a German (or Swede) named John Grinninger, who lived alone, worked in an ironworks or blacksmith shop near the state capital. Grinninger also had an income from a small orchard and vegetable garden by his home near Waller Creek. He owned four lots on block number eleven, according to an 1853 map of Austin. There is little history of his life or business left behind today. Austin residents claimed the old immigrant had a quick temper and poor command of the English language. He was difficult to understand when he talked, and his loud voice, sharp tongue, and brogue scared and unnerved people. Grinninger had threatened several of his neighbors who owned roaming livestock that broke through his cedar-rail fence that protected his orchard and vegetable garden.[2]

To remedy this livestock problem, Grinninger devised a mechanical solution to stop roaming animals from entering and destroying his garden crops. Using his ironworking skills, he developed what was later considered a forerunner of barbed wire, which would be patented, manufactured, and sold to cattlemen and farmers years later. As remembered by Austin's old-timers, the fence Grinninger built around his garden and the orchard was a unique rail or picket fence. It was topped with the ironworker's novel invention—long strings of twisted wires laced with vicious sharp spikes made of hoop iron, resembling barbs of the barbed wire in use today. The iron barbs, however, were larger and sharpened to a point.

Grinninger nailed these lengthy strings of wire laced with hoop iron points above the top of the rail fence to upright cedar posts set in the ground. His invention proved to be quite adequate but was extremely vicious; it injured his neighbor's roaming livestock. His barbed device also tore clothing and injured children who were climbing over the fence and stealing melons and other produce. In later years, during the deposing of Austin witnesses for barbed wire patent litigation, Ben Thompson, the noted gambler, gunman, and later city marshal of Austin, testified that as a boy he stole fruit from the old gardener. Thompson shot a companion when about 13; Ben Thompson would have been about 14 in 1857 when Grinninger's fencing was gaining notoriety. He said he had to leave the garden in a hurry on one occasion, and the sharp barbs on the fence had played "hell" with his pants.[3]

Children and their parents learned from these bad experiences, and kids avoided Grinninger's fence, but the livestock didn't seem to learn. The severe injury of a neighbor's horse cut up by the barbed fence inflamed the community and resulted in threats. The concerns and anger caused by damages inflicted by Grinninger fencing continued to grow. There followed an attempt to remove him from the neighborhood. This hostility toward the old immigrant, and his fence, was the first opposition to barbed wire to appear in Texas. Some claim the conclusion of Austin's barbed wire war came with the injury to livestock on Waller Creek and caused the murder of John Grinninger.[4]

The records, however, tell a different story. On April 26, 1862, there was more news about Grinninger. The *State Gazette* of Austin printed the following tale.

> Another Murder—We are again called upon to record one of the most cruel and bloodthirsty murders that has ever disgraced our usually orderly city. The residence of Mr. John Grinninger, (a native of Sweden, 75 years of age and a gardener by occupation, a sober and industrious man and a good citizen), was entered Saturday, in broad daylight between 1 and 2 o'clock, and his life taken in a most brutal and inhumane manner. On an evening the same day, someone visited his place and found him lying on the floor with his head frightfully mangled. Mr. Grinninger was a bachelor and lived by himself, and doubtless supposed by the murderer to have money. The authorities were at once informed. A coroner's inquest was held and returned a

verdict following the facts stating the deceased met his death from an ax's blows. George, a slave of Mr. W. R. Lount, was examined before the Mayor and committed to jail to await his trial, which will occur the first Monday in June. Much praise is due our city authorities for their vigilance in ferreting out the perpetrator of this insult to the laws. Let this be a warning to evil doers in the future. Our authorities are determined that due respect shall be paid to the law, and all violators made to suffer its penalties.[5]

On April 20 John Grinninger had been found dead inside his house. He was lying on the hearthstone, and his head had been split open by a heavy, sharp instrument. At the time of the murder, by growing and selling vegetables and saving his money, Grinninger had accumulated a small sum. His customers knew that he had money, but his money wasn't found when a search was done. Excitement reigned with neighbors, and numerous other persons searched for clues to this brutal murder.

James B. Barron, one of Austin's citizens, followed footprints from Grinninger's home to an old frame house adjoining Grinninger's lot. Under the house Barron found an ax thrown on the ground under the floor. When he inspected the ax, he found the sharp blade covered with clotted blood and human hair. Here was the first clue in the ax murder.

On the day of the murder, an elderly Black man named Uncle Jim Dieterich, employed by the Avenue Hotel to chop wood, lost his ax. Another Black man, a slave and sort of a body servant owned by a Mr. W. R. Lount, a boarder residing at the Avenue Hotel, visited Uncle Jim while he was cutting wood. This slave carried his owner's name and was known as George Lount. Uncle Jim asked George to chop some more wood during a brief conversation while he loaded the wood already cut into a wheelbarrow and delivered it. He left his ax at the woodpile. When Dieterich returned to the woodpile, George and his ax were gone.

On the same morning, a Black woman who lived with and cooked for Dr. Rentfro and his family saw George pass their home at Second and Neches Streets with an ax on his shoulder going toward Grinninger's house and garden. Another witness saw the slave with the ax near Waller Creek, traveling in the same direction. Other witnesses testified they saw George spending money the night of the murder. For George Lount, having money to spend was unusual. He was apprehended and placed in jail to await trial.

During the murder trial in district court, Dr. Rentfro's Black cook became sick and couldn't attend court. Her testimony was essential to complete the chain of evidence. District Attorney Thomas Sneed, the prosecutor, submitted a motion that Judge Alexander Terrell eventually granted after the proper showing. With sufficient time and preparation, Judge Terrell, District Attorney Sneed, the defendant, his counsel Major C. S. West, Sheriff Thomas C. Collins, clerk Frank Brown, and the jury of twelve men went to the residence of Dr. Rentfro. The prosecution and defense closely questioned the doctor's cook on direct cross-examination. All the facts she was aware of were brought out while she was lying in bed. She testified clearly and sincerely, completing the chain of circumstantial evidence, which was heard by the jury.

After returning to the courtroom and hearing arguments of counsel and Judge Terrell's charge, the jury brought in their verdict finding the defendant guilty and assessed George Lount punishment by death. In the past George Lount had been sent to Grinninger's garden to purchase vegetables. On this occasion, when Grinninger pulled out his sack of money to make change, George was found to have been overcome by temptation. He committed the violent murder with the ax.[6]

Sheriff Thomas Collins erected a temporary gallows west of Shoal Creek. Before his execution, the condemned man confessed his guilt. The public hanging of George Lount for the murder of John Grinninger took place on July 25, 1862.[7]

John Grinninger had been brutally slain and his murderer executed. At this point the Grinninger murder and his barbed fence became just another footnote in the history of Austin. Years later a new invention called barbed wire swept across the western states, having a major impact on Texas, adding a new chapter to the state's ranching history. The subject of Austin's early barbed fence came up again, receiving national attention. John Grinninger's barbed fence wasn't forgotten.

Eighteen years after Grinninger's fence was built, a lawsuit began in US federal court between two large barbed wire manufacturers. The 1874 litigation over barbed wire patents was filed by Jacob Haish and the Barbed Wire Union over Glidden Barbed Wire Patents owned by the I. L. Ellwood and the Washburn & Moen Company. In one of the twenty-eight lawsuits filed, Grinninger's fence was the charge, alleging prior use of barbed fences before the dates I. L. Ellwood and Washburn & Moen's barbed wire patents had been granted. Lawyers representing the Barbed Wire Union and Haish's company came to Austin to gather evidence and prove that Grinninger invented and used barbed wire in the years before the contested Glidden patents were issued. To build the prosecution's case, the plaintiffs hired Austin lawyers Carleton and Chandler to assist. They rented a room over one of Austin's livery stables for an office and went out into the community, searching for witnesses who had seen Grinninger's fence. Some residents of Austin were glad to testify; others were not and were subpoenaed.

Texas Ranger Walter M. Robertson had seen Grinninger's fence and had watched the hanging of George Lount. The lawyers subpoenaed Robertson, but the Ranger found business out of town and never provided testimony. Old-timers with memories of Grinninger's fence were escorted to the livery stable. Their minds were refreshed. Then their recollections and descriptions of the barbed fence were transcribed for the record. Based on their memories, a fence replica was constructed, photographed, and carried back east with the transcribed testimony.[8]

Historian Walter Prescott Webb's father-in-law, Mr. W. J. Oliphant, owned an Austin photo gallery when Jacob Haish's legal team was in Austin trying to document Grinninger's barbed fence. The lawyers employed Oliphant to make photographs of a reconstructed Grinninger fence for use in their court proceedings. Oliphant's photographs of the reconstructed fence, and transcribed testimony from old-timers who had seen the original fence, went to Chicago for the trial. The defendants, the Washburn & Moen Company, presented strong testimony building a case against Grinninger's wire fence being prior-use barbed wire. In 1880 the Circuit Court of the Northern District of Illinois ruled in favor of the Washburn & Moen Company. Presiding Judge C. J. Drummond said the court didn't find false swearing of the plaintiff's Austin witnesses, but proof of prior use of barbed wire was based almost totally on the recollection of witnesses after the passage of many years.[9]

The First Barbed Wire War Was in Austin   9

The Grinninger case wasn't the end of legal battles between the two large wire manufacturers. Jacob Haish and his Beat Em All Barbed Wire Company and the Washburn & Moen Company battled in court with appeals, reversals, and continuing litigation, all of which finally ended in 1892 in the United States Supreme Court. The Washburn & Moen Company, the owner of the Glidden patents, came out the winner. By the time this legal battle ended, Austin, Travis County, and virtually all of Texas had fences built with barbed wire. Once again, John Grinninger's name and the vicious barbed fence he built faded from memory and became just another footnote in Austin's history.[10]

Chapter 2

Barbed Wire, a Yankee's Invention, Comes to Texas

> Be it resolved by the Commissioners Court of San Saba County, that our members of the Legislature be requested to use their endeavors to prevent the passage of any law making such fences (barbed wire) legal, and to secure the passage of a law making it a penal offense for anyone to use or own any such fence.
>
> —San Saba County Commissioners Court, February 11, 1879

The first fences in early Texas were built to keep ranging livestock out of fields and gardens rather than to enclose the stock. Exceptions might have been small pastures or traps, as they were called, built to keep horses, mules, or a milk cow close by the settler's home. Much of the state's settled part had plenty of timber, and settlers built rail or picket fences. The stake-and-rider fence was common across most of the state in the early years. In Texas's central parts, German pioneers built fence with cedar pickets or posts, or of rock gathered when clearing land and working fields. In Mason County native stone was used to build field fences but also some pasture fences. Several of these pastures were quite large. A stacked rock fence enclosed a large pasture owned by Heinrich Friedrich (Fritz) Kothmann, an early Mason

County stockman. Kothmann fenced a large land tract near Loyal Valley, remembered today as the Premier Ranch. His rock fence was built by German workers from San Antonio and was under construction from 1873 to 1877 before barbed wire was common in Texas. Some of the men performing this back-breaking labor were Schumaker Burghardt, Otto Kollet, John Klassig, and Kohler, Saeger, and William Kammellah. Another large tract of Mason County ranch land with fences of rock was the Ranck Pasture, operating as the W. P. Lockhart Company. The Ranck Pasture contains close to seventeen thousand acres, and based on old survey notes, much of their fence was built with stacked rocks. Grace Davenport, a historian from Mason, said the decade of the 1870s was the decade of rock fence. Today the old picket fences are gone, but remnants of rock fences still stand on many Texas ranches.[1]

North Texas and some of the Texas coastal areas used thorny hedge fences grown from bois d'arc, also known as Osage orange. Between 1850 and the 1880s, gathering bois d'arc apples and drying them, then chopping and washing their seed became a thriving business in Texas. At one time bois d'arc seeds found a good market in Illinois. Texas farmers were processing bois d'arc seed, then selling them and profiting from their labor. Doctor Walter Prescott Webb describes the bois d'arc fences in his book *The Great Plains* and tells of William H. Mann, who lived on Bois d'arc Creek in Fannin County. Mann heard that bois d'arc seed was selling for eighty dollars a bushel in Peoria, Illinois. Expecting to make a fortune, he processed and washed thirty bushels of seed, loaded them in his farm wagon, and traveled to Illinois. On arrival he discovered the bottom had fallen out of the market and sold his seed on credit for twenty dollars a bushel, a price he had refused in Texas. Bois d'arc hedges, grown for fencing, were advertised as being "horse high, bull strong and pig tight," but when a fence was needed, they were slow growing, and most farmers claimed they were ineffective.[2]

Before barbed wire was invented, some early South Texas cattlemen along the Texas coast were trying to upgrade their Longhorn cattle, grazing on the free, open range. To accomplish this upgrade, these men began building fences using lumber and smooth wire to confine and protect purebred stock brought to Texas. This first smooth wire used for fences was manufactured in Belgium and brought to the United States as ballast on ships carrying immigrants. The cattlemen brought cypress posts and creosoted lumber from Louisiana. As early as 1868, Captain Mifflin Kenedy built a fence across the throat of a peninsula on the Texas Gulf Coast, enclosing a tract of land known as the Laureles Grant. This short fence created a pasture that consisted of 131,000 acres. The fence was constructed with heavy posts and three planks and created the first fenced pasture of such enormous size west of the Mississippi. After fencing this tract, Kenedy built about one hundred miles of fence using six-inch by six-inch by eight-foot cypress fence posts set three feet deep and coated with tar or creosote. Posts were placed twenty feet apart and had five smooth wire strands running through each post with a plank across the top. Kenedy invented winches, which were placed one-fourth mile apart along his fence and tightened the wires when they became slack. One of Kenedy's earlier pastures, fenced with creosoted posts and lumber from Louisiana, had cost an estimated $500 to $1,000 per mile. Imported lumber was expensive. Captain Richard King, Captain Mifflin Kenedy's former partner and neighbor, soon followed Kenedy and built fences. Both men were upgrading their cattle herds. King had imported one hundred head of Durham cattle, mostly bulls used with his better range cows.[3]

Captain King's Santa Gertrudis tract contained seventy-eight thousand acres, with sixty-five thousand fenced acres of grazing land and a fence about forty miles in length. This pasture's fence was built with mesquite fence posts of a large diameter cut from his property and set deep in the ground. King had pine planks and smooth wire freighted to the ranch. The pine planks were six inches wide, an inch and a quarter thick, and twenty-four feet in length. They were attached to the mesquite post with wrought-iron spikes manufactured for that purpose. Three strands of smooth nine-gauge wire were also fastened to the posts using specially made iron staples driven into the posts. There was another pine board nailed along the top. King claimed his fence was "perfectly secure, and . . . more than useless for stock to attempt to either get in or get out." King's new fenced pasture had six gates guarded by men employed to ensure his breeding stock's further protection.[4]

The Coleman, Mathis, and Fulton Cattle Company, with headquarters in Rockport, was another massive ranching operation on the South Texas Coast. The Mathises came to Texas in 1859. After the Civil War, they built a profitable business slaughtering cattle and shipping tallow, hides, and bone east in their steamboat, the Prince Albert. At the peak of their operation, the company controlled 265,000 acres of land west of Rockport. Before barbed wire arrived in Texas, the company built their fences with smooth wire and lumber.[5]

In the years between 1850 and 1870, it was estimated that America's agriculture used 350,000 miles of plain, smooth iron wire for fencing purposes. The smooth wire was cheap and quickly erected and provided some degree of relief for the farmers. Unfortunately, the fences were not feared or avoided; livestock frequently pushed and broke through smooth-wire fences. The first early smooth wire was brittle. It broke when the weather was cold and sagged when the weather was hot. Despite smooth wire's shortcomings, its use grew for want of better fence material.[6]

Following the Civil War, inventors familiar with the farmer's fence problems began filing patents for new fence material. In 1867, exactly ten years after John Grinninger built his barbed wire fence in Austin, patents were filed by Lucien B. Smith and William D. Hunt for fence material armed with sharp points or barbs. Michael Kelly filed for a fence patent in 1868, and another was filed in 1871 by Lyman P. Judson. These men lacked financial means for the manufacturing and sale of their barbed fence material. A large manufacturing company purchased their patents for what was known in the years that followed as an armored fence.[7]

On May 13, 1873, Henry M. Rose of Waterman Station, Illinois, was issued a patent for a prickly device. His invention wasn't a fence wire. It was a device to be hung on smooth wire fences or maybe nailed to fence posts. His product was a deterrent to livestock that might try to go through a fence and was considered armored fencing. His patent number 138763, as issued, described the device as "a strip of board one-inch square or any convenient size, to which are secured or inserted metallic points six or eight more or less inches apart. The points are made of wire, cut obliquely at any desired angle, form sharp points, and may be long to pass through the strip and project on both sides, or maybe made short so as to project on one side only." After Rose patented his invention, he traveled to the neighboring town of De Kalb and displayed his product at the De Kalb County Fair. As part of his product demonstration, Rose armed a smooth wire corral fence with his newly patented devices. A farmer penned cattle in the corral, and the cows could not be driven through the fence by heel-nipping dogs. The county fair demonstration drew the attention of three men from De Kalb—Joseph Farwell Glidden, Isaac Leonard Ellwood, and Jacob Haish. All three men examined Rose's display and soon would patent, manufacture, and begin selling armored fence material later known as barbed wire.[8]

Jacob Haish, a prosperous German lumberman, understood the needs of farmers for fencing material. In past years Haish had purchased, then marketed Bois d'arc seeds to farmers to grow the thorny shrub as a fence barrier. Isaac Ellwood was a merchant with a hardware business in De Kalb. He, too, understood the farmer's needs; they were his customers. His community store supplied farmers' needs and was where farmers gathered, visited, and traded. The third man, Joseph Glidden, was born in New Hampshire in 1813, and on becoming an adult, he was a schoolteacher. At the age of 29 he began farming and soon came west, working the grain fields with two threshing machines. He arrived in De Kalb, Illinois, in 1844, where he made his home and purchased farmland. He was elected sheriff in 1852. As a farmer and sheriff, Glidden had to deal with the inadequacies of rail and smooth-wire fences. He experienced fencing problems and saw others with issues, prompting his efforts to apply Rose's idea of a prickly fence to smooth wire.

Following an interesting course of inventiveness and development, Joseph Glidden filed his first barbed wire patent application on October 27, 1873. His patent was numbered 157124. He invented the wire with sticky points, made by hand, and used it on his farm. His neighbor, Jacobs Haish, came to view and evaluate Glidden's wire fence. After seeing the fence, Jacob Haish filed patent applications in 1873. His third application, numbered 167,240 for his famous S barb wire, was filed on June 17, 1874, roughly eight months after Glidden's patent application. On June 25, 1874, seeing Glidden's barbed wire's superior nature, Haish filed interference documents with the US Patent Office against Glidden. His maneuver succeeded in holding up the issuance of Glidden's patent. Still, it also delayed his third S barb patent until August 31, 1875. The patent office finally issued Joseph Glidden's patent for barbed wire on November 24, 1874, beating Haish's S barb patent by about nine months

The De Kalb store owner and merchant Isaac Ellwood also filed a patent application, but on seeing Glidden's wire being superior to all others, he visited with his old farmer friend. His visit's outgrowth was the purchase of half interest in Glidden's barbed wire business and in the pending patent for a price of $265. Ellwood's acquisition was consummated four months before Glidden received his barbed wire patent. The two partners named their new business the Barbed Fence Company. They were soon manufacturing barbed wire in a rented building in De Kalb and selling the wire at Ellwood's hardware store. Jacob Haish also began manufacturing and selling his barbed wire in De Kalb.

As Glidden, Ellwood, and Haish began making and selling barbed wire, their increased orders of wire feedstock, used in the manufacturing process, stoked the interest of their supplier, the Washburn & Moen Manufacturing Company of Massachusetts. In February 1876 Charles Francis Washburn, the company's vice president, traveled to De Kalb, Illinois, to learn more about these barbed wire manufacturing businesses and visited with Jacob Haish. After viewing his operation and discussing his patents, Washburn offered to buy Haish's barbed wire business. Perhaps with arrogance, or maybe expecting a counteroffer from the wealthy manufacturer, Haish priced his small business at $200,000. Charles Washburn, the Massachusetts manufacturer, made no counter to Haish's offer, packed up, and traveled back to Massachusetts.

Charles Washburn was also aware of Joseph Glidden's barbed wire invention, which was now manufactured and offered to farmers for fifteen cents per pound (the original price of Glidden's wire). Washburn soon returned to De Kalb to visit with Glidden and Ellwood at their manufacturing shop, the Barbed Fence Company. The meeting was cordial and informative and went well. The Massachusetts industrialist was impressed with what he saw and heard from Glidden. After his visit Washburn offered to buy the Barbed Fence Company and patents, along with several of the older patents they had acquired. Joseph Glidden worked hard all of his life, had aged, and was interested in selling the business. However, Ellwood, his partner, wanted to keep and manage the business. The discussion ended but would continue later. In May Charles Washburn returned and again proceeded to negotiate with the two men. The men reached a sales agreement. With Joseph Glidden selling his half interest in the fence company, a contract was signed with Washburn & Moen. His share of the patents and business was purchased for $80,000, with a royalty of twenty-five cents per hundred pounds of all manufactured barbed wire they produced.

Isaac Ellwood, the De Kalb merchant, was an astute businessman, younger than Glidden. He had a grand vision of barbed wire's future and wanted to develop and grow the barbed wire business. He chose to keep his share of the company and entered into a partnership with Washburn & Moen. The Barbed Fence Company became the I. L. Ellwood Company of De Kalb, with Ellwood the designated sales agent for the Southwest. The Washburn & Moen Manufacturing Company of Worchester, Massachusetts, was listed as agents in the east and south. Charles Washburn became the silent partner of the combined operation. The larger company's heft, and legal knowledge, was indispensable from that time forward.[9]

There was a surge in the production of barbed wire in De Kalb, Illinois, with competition between Glidden's wire and Haish's barbed wire. Hard feelings and rivalry began and had grown from the day Haish filed his interference papers against Glidden with the US Patent Office. Competition and bitter feelings would result in more than $1 million in patent litigation over the years to follow.

Jacob Haish and his Beat 'Em All Barbed Wire Company and the Washburn & Moen Company battled in courts with appeals, reversals, and continuing litigation. The litigation finally ended in 1892 in the United States Supreme Court. Washburn & Moen and Ellwood came out the winner.[10]

Henry B. Sanborn, a young man who had grown up in New York, came to De Kalb, Illinois, seeking employment in the summer of 1864. He stayed a short while, boarding in Joseph Glidden farm home. Glidden may have briefly employed him. He soon left and went to work for an uncle with a lumber milling business in Minnesota. A year later the young Sanborn returned to De Kalb, selling wooden eave troughs. Again he lived and boarded with Glidden, and on February 20, 1868, he married Miss Ellen M. Wheeler, Joseph Glidden's niece.

In 1872 Henry Sanborn made a sizeable profit on two loads of horses purchased in Illinois and sold in Colorado. He gave up his business selling wood eave troughs and entered a partnership with a friend, Judson P. Warner, buying and selling horses and mules. He was now a horse and mule trader. Sanborn would buy horses in Illinois and then send them to Denver, Colorado, by rail, where Judson would sell them at his horse and mule barn. Their horse and mule business had become a profitable venture, but there was an interruption.

On November 24, 1874, the day Joseph Glidden received his barbed wire patent no. 157,124, the old farmer wrote a letter to Henry Sanborn, his friend and now relative by marriage, asking for help. Glidden wrote, "I cannot say definitely what we would like to do. We should very much like to have you interested in the fence business. It promises to be a big thing and needs deliberation. The patent issues today, and we are progressing nicely with the old patents, and, if our counsel is reliable, we should be able to monopolize the wire barb business."[11]

As an outgrowth of Glidden's request for assistance, Sanborn and his partner Judson Warner entered into a contract with Glidden and Isaac Ellwood to sell their barbed wire production exclusively for two years. Sanborn sold his first reels of wire in Rochelle, west of De Kalb, and other small sales of Glidden's barbed wire followed. Judson Warner closed the horse and mule business in Denver and joined Sanborn to sell barbed wire in Texas.[12]

After the devastation caused by the Civil War, men from the Southern states were trying to recover. Many of these men and their families migrated to Texas to start anew and establish farms on cheap land. The large cattlemen in Texas with Longhorn stock were trying to upgrade their range cattle herds. Both the farmers and cattlemen were potential buyers for Glidden's barbed wire. Sanborn traveled to Texas to assess the prospects for wire sales and talk to merchants, farmers, and cattlemen. He visited the famous South Texas cattleman Abel H. Pierce (Shanghai Pierce), who operated in Wharton County. Sanborn talked with Pierce and asked his opinion of barbed wire. Shanghai told him bluntly, in his usual foul-mouthed language, that here has been cleaned up: "It will never do; cattle and horses would run into the wire, and cut themselves to pieces, and all die of screwworms." Sanborn also quickly discovered there was a healthy distrust of Yankees in Texas. Many farmers and cattlemen had memories of the Civil War and were suspicious of barbed wire; it was one of those Yankee inventions. Some called it "Yankee fake fence" and saw it as another attempt of the northern industry to get in their pockets and take their money.[13]

Sanborn observed the cattlemen's sentiment against barbed wire. Still, he also saw a crying need for cheap fencing material in Texas. He knew he could sell barbed wire to the farmers because it would keep cattle out of their fields. He was also confident that he could convince the cattlemen of barbed wire's merits. Sanborn returned to Illinois satisfied he could succeed and that barbed wire sale in Texas would become a profitable venture.

Near the end of the year, Sanborn was on a train in Sedalia, Missouri, traveling back to Texas, when he met and befriended John F. Evans, a gentleman who claimed to be a professional traveler. Sanborn showed his new friend a sample panel of the Glidden barbed wire and explained he was on his way to Texas to sell this new fence material to Texas stockmen. That was a lucky day for Sanborn. In years past Evans had traveled through Texas as a saddlery salesman and was now invested in the Texas cattle industry. The two men rode the train into Denison together and in the years that followed became close friends and associates. John Evans knew the North Texas cattlemen and cattle country. He and Sanborn traveled the range together in a horse-drawn buggy, because few towns had railroads in those days. John Evans knew the merchants in most of the communities they visited. Taking Evans's advice, Sanborn selected a merchant in each town visited, made his sales pitch, and left a spool of wire as they traveled through. Years later John F. (Spade) Evans became the first president of the Panhandle and Southwestern Stockman's Association and was the association's lobbyist in Austin. Henry Sanborn and Judson Warner both made Sherman, Texas, their headquarters, and the Sherman Merchant and Planter Bank handling their accounts. For the first years in Texas, Sanborn had wire orders shipped to Sherman.[14]

Henry Sanborn made his first Texas barbed wire sale in Gainesville. He sold ten spools of wire to the Cleaves & Fletcher Hardware Company.

Sanborn and Evans made an eleven-day trip along rough roads and cattle trails to towns such as Decatur, Pilot Point, and Denton, where he managed to sell sixty spools of wire. Sanborn's business partner Judson Warner arrived in Texas and worked the counties west of Dallas and down to Austin. On reaching Austin Judson Warner sold the first carload of Glidden Barbed wire to John A. Webb and Brother, implement dealers located on Pecan Street (today Austin's East Sixth Street). Soon the Webb brothers were advertising Glidden's barbed wire in the town's newspapers. Anticipating more future sales, Sanborn ordered four carloads of Glidden wire, one each for Austin, Sherman, Dallas, and San Antonio.[15]

San Antonio was known in those early days as the Cow Capital of Texas. Sanborn traveled to San Antonio in the late summer of 1875 to sell his barbed wire to South Texas cattlemen. Norton & Dentz, one of the city's prominent hardware dealers, was receptive to Sanborn's sales pitch, became a dealer, and began advertising Glidden's barbed wire in the San Antonio newspapers. Soon a satirical story appeared in the *San Antonio Daily Herald*, poking fun at smooth-wire fences used in South Texas. The spoof on smooth wire read, "When it comes to keeping out cattle, it's like the constitutional convention, those who pay for it become discouraged, and want their money back . . . the [smooth] wire fence is a perpetual source of amusement to cattle. They will travel for miles to have a chance to unravel a wire fence and sit down on their haunches and bellow with disappointment when they have got through with all the fence in the neighborhood." The story ended with the statement, "This Glidden Barbed Fence is exactly the thing our hardy frontiersmen have been sighing for."[16] The same issue of the newspaper featured a Glidden barbed wire advertisement on another page. In his 1931 historical masterpiece *The Great Plains*, historian Walter Prescott Webb says that it was reported that Sanborn set up a demonstration of a fence on Alamo Plaza in San Antonio for ranchmen and farmers from the surrounding country.

In San Antonio Sanborn found the South Texas market promising, and he urged the Barbed Fence Company to reduce their price from eighteen to thirteen cents a pound when a carload lot was purchased. The Barbed Fence Company approved his request in a letter dated October 22, 1875, saying,

"Your proposal to sell in Texas to wholesale dealers at 13, is approved, but we shall not entertain proposals for a less price than that. Think probably in South Texas, where lumber is reported dearer, the wire would probably sell for more."

From San Antonio Sanborn traveled by horse and buggy to the large South Texas ranches. On one of his visits with cattlemen, he sold an entire carload of Glidden's barbed wire directly to a consumer, the Coleman, Mathis, and Fulton Cattle Company. This partnership had built in years past miles and miles of fences using smooth wire.

Another cattleman buying wire from Sanborn was Frank Skidmore. Frank grew up in San Patricio County, where his dad was sheriff. During Texas's Reconstruction period following the Civil War, Frank was almost killed by Captain Jack Helm and his Regulators. He suffered seventeen bullet wounds, most from a shotgun blast. Frank Skidmore survived Reconstruction, became a prominent South Texas cattleman, bought barbed wire, and began fencing. He eventually fenced thirty-five thousand acres in Bee, San Patricio, and Live Oak Counties.[17]

In the years that followed, national barbed wire production and sales increased rapidly, with much of the wire going to Texas. In 1875 the nation's barbed wire sales were around 600,000 pounds. By 1880 sales had grown to 80,500,000 pounds. Barbed wire sales in Texas, even with growing public opposition, gained momentum. As Texas was selling off large tracts of cheap land, most of it was immediately fenced.[18]

The first few years of barbed wire production, hardware merchants and their customers were skeptical of this newfangled fence material. They didn't know how to handle the new barbed fence material. The Washburn & Moen (i.e., Ellwood Company) employed and sent agents to the Plains states to teach hardware merchants and landowners how to build a barbed wire fence. One of the agents is reported to have been a man named John Warne Gates.

In a letter to historian Walter Webb, W. H. Richardson described how his father, owner of a hardware store in Mexia, was introduced to the new fence material by John Gates in the 1880s. After hearing Gates's pitch and seeing samples of the barbed wire, Richardson's father ordered a carload. In due time a railroad car of the barbed wire arrived. This wire had four dangerous barbs, was painted a sticky black, and was unevenly wound on wooden spools (probably what was known as moonshine wire). No one knew how to handle it, and no one would unload the wire.[19]

According to W. H. Richardson, "Father built a chute up to the car door and secured the services of several venturesome cowboys, some of whom were put in the car and others at the end of the incline, and the unloading started. . . . One of the spools got away, or jumped the chute, struck one of the cowboys on the leg, and tore half of his boot off. They all struck and went to a nearby saloon and were only persuaded to return when their spirits were attuned with those found inside." Richardson's father then demonstrated a barbed wire fence's construction along a road on his property. People came from miles away to watch his father build the fence. Posts were set, the wire was unrolled, and preparations were made to stretch the wire using a wagon wheel. One wire end was fastened to a well-anchored fence post, and the wagon was stopped and braced several hundred yards from the post. The wagon's rear wheel was jacked up, and the strand of wire was fastened around the hub. As the wheel was turned and the wire wound taut, the wire was attached to the posts with staples.[20]

John Gates, one of the agents sent to Texas to demonstrate barbed wire, was said to have built a barbed wire fence on Military Plaza in San Antonio and produced a rodeo or carnival of sorts for the cattlemen. As the story goes, at dark, following festive activities, Gates's cowhands drove wild Longhorn steers into Military Plaza, which was enclosed with barbed wire. Then a Mexican cowhand rode in and choused the steers around with a flaming torch. Even with the excitement, none of the steers broke through the barbed wire fence. This story has grown into a legend and today is folded into Texas history.[21]

Several sources say that after a short time of promoting barbed wire in Texas, Gates returned to De Kalb and tried to buy into Isaacs Ellwood's part of the wire company. If this occurred, Ellwood refused Gates's offer. On January 1, 1877, Ellwood and the Washburn Moen Manufacturing Company renewed Henry Sanborn and Judson Warner's contract and again gave them the exclusive right to sell Glidden barbed wire in Texas. John Gates was soon in St. Louis, where he began manufacturing and selling moonshine wire. Moonshine wire was barbed wire manufactured that violated US patents. Litigation followed Gates. From that time on, Gates had numerous skirmishes with the law over his moonshine wire and was in constant conflict and litigation with Isaac Ellwood and the Washburn & Moen Manufacturing Company. John Warner Gates's real claim to fame was founding United States Steel, being one of the founders of the Texas Company (later Texaco), and being the father of Port Arthur, Texas. Gates was a risk-taker and a big-time gambler, acquiring the nickname "Bet a Million Gates."[22]

By 1877 Sanborn and Warner's barbed wire sales were bringing in a massive flow of money. Sanborn invested his profits in two thousand acres of land twelve miles west of Sherman. His new ranch was fenced with Glidden wire using bois d'arc fence posts. He stocked the ranch with quality running horses, trotting horses, Percheron draft horses, French coach horses, and Missouri Jacks. He also began raising purebred Durham Shorthorn bulls. He built barns and a two-story home on this Grayson County ranch, created a showplace, and continued to buy land adjacent or near this property, eventually owning about 10,300 acres. In 1884 the *Galveston Daily News* published an article giving a glowing description of Sanborn's Sherman ranch and describing it as "the finest ranch of its kind in Texas."[23]

After Joseph Glidden sold his interest in the Barbed Fence Company to Washburn & Moen, the giant company produced vast barbed wire quantities. Sales increased and in 1877 Sanborn moved his main barbed wire warehouse and sales office to Houston. The newly manufactured wire was transported by ship to the port city. Sanborn also established two branch depots in North Texas, one managed by R. V. Tompkins in Dallas and the other with the Bayer Brothers and located in Sherman. The *Galveston Daily News* reported that from August 1882 to August 1883, Sanborn and Warner handled $1 million worth of barbed wire sales from their new Houston headquarters.[24]

Henry Sanborn and Judson Warner were the first barbed wire salesmen in Texas, bringing in Glidden's barbed wire. Many other wire salesmen came to Texas in the years that followed, selling other manufacturers' barbed wire. Sam Baker was the Texas agent selling Allis Buckthorn wire. His headquarters was in Waco. His Buckthorn Ribbon wire took first place for fencing material at an annual fair in Austin. Out of Dallas, the Mitchell and Scruggs Partnership advertised and sold the Kelly Steel barbed wire statewide. W. A. Huffman of Fort Worth was the Northwest Texas agent selling Scutt's Cable Laid wire, commonly known as Scutt's Horse wire. Jacobs Haish's S barb wire was present and was popular. John Gates and other parties manufactured moonshine wire, and it too was sold in Texas. Still, the Glidden wire was advertised as the best-selling wire in Texas, with sales reported to be five times that of all other barbed wire combined, and Sanborn and Warner had the Glidden wire franchise.[25]

By 1879 fencing land with barbed wire had spread throughout the east, the Midwestern states, and Texas. Railroads became significant users of barbed wire along their tracks. It was also in 1879 that opposition and protests against barbed wire showed up. The opposition was strong in the eastern states. The general public had concerns about barbed wire's vicious nature and cruelty to livestock. In Texas, aside from barbed wire's injurious effect on livestock, it was becoming an impediment to livestock grazing the open, free range and to driving cattle to markets, and began obstructing roadway travel. In Connecticut, Vermont, New Hampshire, and Colorado, state legislation was filed to restrict or prohibit barbed wire fencing. Washburn & Moen, the large wire manufacturing company, entered the battle and used its financial heft and legal resources to protect its product. They pursued an aggressive program, with their lawyers appearing at legislative hearings and countering damaging testimony about their wire. Materials with talking points on the merits and benefits of their products to agriculture were printed by the company and distributed to barbed wire merchants, public media, and legislative bodies.[26]

The first strong opposition to barbed wire fences in Texas also began in 1879. Legislation was introduced to halt the use of barbed wire and to make barbed wire fences illegal. On February 11, 1879, the commissioners court of San Saba County adopted a resolution opposing barbed wire. Their resolution was to be delivered to Senator L. J. Story and Representative J. M. Moore at the state capital in Austin.

More protests came in from across the state. One group of cattlemen from Nolan and neighboring Fisher County petitioned the Sixteenth Texas

Legislature to ban fences west of the one hundredth meridian, saying the line's land was not suitable for farming, only for grazing.[27]

When the Sixteenth Texas Legislature convened on January 14, 1879, barbed wire fences were a hot political issue. There is no record of Ellwood or Washburn & Moen lawyer's appearing to testify in Texas. But Henry Sanborn and Judson Warner, the company's Texas men, were probably busy working the capital during this legislative session. Legislators filed several bills that would affect barbed wire fencing, but the legislature refused to outlaw the new barbed wire. In the end, a new law required that blinds (wood boards) be placed on a barbed wire fence as visual protection for livestock. A bill introduced on March 26, 1879, provided that a lawful barbed wire fence has "three barbed wires or two strands of barbed wire," and when building a barbed wire fence, "the owner of the fence shall be required to fasten a board not less than four inches wide and one half inch thick between wires." The bill was amended on April 18, adding more detail for a sturdy fence: "three strands of barbed wire, with posts no further apart than 15 feet, with a board not less than four inches wide and one half inch thick hung to the top wire; or two strands of barbed wire and a board not less than five inches wide and one inch thick." This state law requiring blinds on fences existed for many years, but the law was later ignored by most who built barbed wire fences. In some instances stockmen would substitute wood staves or pickets for the board blinds required on fences.[28]

When barbed wire came to Texas, livestock grazed the state's land free, cattle were plentiful and selling for good prices in the east, and Texas's great cattle drives reached their peak. A few years later, the barbed wire would write a new chapter in Texas history and change ranching in Texas forever.

Chapter 3

Cheap Land, Cheap Wire, and Expensive Cattle

> Herds passing up the trail since the drives commenced are shipped by rail from all parts of Texas at Wichita Falls, as it is no longer possible to bring a herd through the State on account of the fences.
> —*Galveston Daily News*, June 4, 1883

Texas land was cheap in 1875 when barbed wire arrived in the young state; cattle grazed free on state land, and cattle sold for high prices in the northeastern states if the cattlemen were able to get their stock to market. The United States had annexed the Texas Republic in 1845, bringing it into the Union as the twenty-eighth state. When Texas entered the Union in 1845, the articles of annexation stated Texas would be liable for its public debts. Since the Union didn't assume the public debt, Texas kept ownership of its public lands and its debts. In 1850 the state ceded 67 million acres to the United States to settle a boundary dispute and in return received $10 million of federal bonds to pay off its debts. In the trade Texas gave up territory including parts of present-day Colorado, Kansas, Oklahoma, New Mexico, and Wyoming. But even with this land transaction, the new state of Texas retained approximately 170 million acres of land.

In the years following, tracts of Texas land were parceled out as grants for canals, road construction, and industrial development. Settlers' preemption and homesteaded tracts were provided, and donations were made to veterans of Texas wars. As early as 1839, the Texas Republic's congress appropriated three leagues of land to each county to establish public schools. In 1854 the state set aside land to reimburse railroads for constructing rail tracks across the state to promote growth. Railroads were granted sixteen sections of land for each mile of rail track built. For each 640-acre section of land received, the railroad was required to survey an adjoining section set aside for the state's public schools. If viewed from above, these surveyed tracts of railroad and school land would have the appearance of a checkerboard and covered most of the western parts of Texas. In 1856 the legislature appropriated 410,600 acres of land for the state mental asylum, the institute for the blind, the institute for the deaf and dumb, and the state's orphan home. Later this land was sold under the state's various land sale acts, with terms like the school lands sold. In 1876 the state constitution granted public schools one half of the unappropriated public domain. This land's sale proceeds were to go to the Texas Permanent School Fund.

The Texas State University System was credited with over 2.3 million acres of appropriated land, some donated by the Republic of Texas congress. First appropriations to the university system were sold, but two million acres granted in 1876 and 1883 were held in solid blocks and leased for grazing. That land today is still owned by the Texas State University System. It produces a fortune in oil and gas revenue.[1]

Texas land laws changed so often it was difficult to follow them. By an act of the Fourteenth Texas Legislature, dedicated school land was offered for sale at $1.50 an acre. It could be purchased only by settlers. A purchaser was allowed a maximum of 160 acres and was required to settle on the land within twelve months. Later, this land law of 1874 was repealed. The legislature passed a new land act on July 8, 1879, which provided for the sale of the railroad surveyed school lands at $1.00 an acre. This time sales weren't limited to settlers. It permitted the purchase of one section of land classified as agriculture land and the purchase of two sections of land classified as pastureland. One-tenth of the purchase price was required down, with the balance paid in nine annual installments at 10 percent interest.

A few days later, in this same session, the legislature passed another land law. This act placed the unappropriated public domain of land on the market for fifty cents an acre. Sales receipts were to be used to pay the state's bond debt and augment the available school fund. The act was referred to as the Fifty Cent Act and created rampant land speculation.

An article in the *Marlin Ball*, a local newspaper, described how the new land law was working. The paper's story read,

> Mr. K. Aycock stopped over Monday on his way to Austin, where he goes to pay into the treasury $14,000 on the account of lands purchased from the State. We are pleased to know that Dock has made a snug fortune in land speculations. He purchased 30,000 acres of 50 cent land put on the market by the last legislature, had six months to pay it in, but resold it to third parties, making a profit of $15,000 in the transaction. He retained 3000 acres of the land, however, which he will convert into a sheep ranch, and says he would not take $5 an acre for it.[2]

Passage of the new state land laws and the massive sales of public land occurred as the barbed wire arrived and provided a new fence material. Barbed wire was replacing pickets and rock fence material and hastened the construction of wire fences when land sold. Now a landowner had a cheap, durable, readily available fence material to build fences and protect his water, grass, and purebred cattle from the encroachment of roaming cattle belonging to the free-range men. Now barbed wire was available as the least expensive fence material in Texas and hastened the construction of wire fences as the land sold. Though not recognized at the time by the citizens, cheap barbed wire and the cheap land would have a colossal impact on the state of Texas.

Texas land was dirt cheap as barbed wire arrived in the state, and the cattle market was strong. Large tracts of land were purchased by the wealthy Texas cattlemen, eastern capitalists, and European syndicates. They moved in, buying up and fencing land with barbed wire at a rapid pace. Many Texas cattlemen with a vision, expecting to see the end of state land's free grazing for livestock, were notable purchasers. Despite the rapid land sales, some cattlemen made fun of those buying cheap land, arguing, "Why buy land grazed for free, for nada, while an owner has to pay taxes on his land?"

One old-timer with a vision of the future, a time when there would be no free grazing, was old cattleman Tomas O'Connor, who came to Texas from Wofford, Ireland, as a boy. People thought Tomas O'Connor had lost his mind when he sold his cattle and bought more land. He systematically built one of the largest ranches in South Texas and the first barbed wire fence in Refugio County. O'Conner continued to buy land and build fences until he owned over half a million acres.

William Day, a young cattleman from Hays County invested every dollar he could borrow, buying and fencing land in Coleman County, then stocking it with cattle. Before his early death, Day acquired over 77,500 acres of ranch land. His brother-in-law and sometimes business partner, Jesse Lincoln Driskill, was one of the state's prominent cattlemen refusing to buy land. Driskill grazed his cattle on the state's lands free. Senator Alexander Terrell of Austin, in a speech before the Texas legislature, lectured on the wrongs of free grazing of open state land and the loss of state revenue. Terrell cited Jesse Driskill as an example of what was occurring. "Mr. Driskill of my town authorized me to say that eleven years ago, he owned 800 head of cattle and now is worth $800,000, every dollar of which was made from cattle raised on free school land. He never was even called on to pay one dollar of taxes." Jesse Driskill made a fortune in the cattle business and built the famous Driskill Hotel, still an Austin landmark. But Jesse had failed to invest in land; he lost the fortune he made in cattle after free-range grazing ended. Later he lost the Driskill Hotel and died a broke man.[3]

The robust sale of state land continued until the Eighteenth Regular Session of the Texas Legislature convened in Austin in January 1883. Legislators took note of the public's anger over the sale of large tracts of state land and land speculation. They came to Austin to correct the land sale problem. On January 22, 1883, the legislature suspended all laws authorizing the sale of public land. Bills were introduced and debated, some favoring leasing state land, others favoring its sale. After three months of wrangling, the new Land Act of April 12, 1883, was passed and signed into law by Governor John Ireland.

This act established a new system for classifying, selling, and leasing public land. Changes were made in pricing land and the amount that could be purchased. Provisions were now made for leasing the state's land for pasturage. The most significant feature of this new law was creation of the State Land Board composed of the governor, attorney general, comptroller, treasurer, and the General Land Office's commissioner. The State Land Board was now in charge of the administration of the public land and took their responsibility seriously—too seriously, complained the influential cattlemen. New land prices were set, and the land board rules were put in place. Agricultural land could be sold to those buyers declaring by affidavit their intent to settle within six months. A settlement was required before the sale could be perfected. The Land Board now began leasing the state's surveyed lands by competitive bidding, with a minimum bid of four cents an acre. Leases could not exceed ten years and would be paid in advance each year.

One of the problems suffered by the cattlemen who leased large tracts of state land was a provision in the law making leases subject to small tracts being sold to settlers within a lease boundary. An immigrant or newcomer could buy a choice section of land out of a substantial lease and move in on the lessor with his own livestock. Cases on record show buyers who purchased a 640-acre section of land under lease, wouldn't build fences, and then would bring in as many cattle as they desired without restrictions. In one case this was close to three thousand heads of cattle. The Land Board now favored the small settler and farmers, rather than the prominent stockmen and land speculators. As state land was sold and fenced with barbed wire, the demand for cattle to stock the fenced pastures increased.[4]

The United States western cattle industry had its beginning in the early years in what is now Texas but at the time was part of Mexico. The Texas cattle population grew. Before the Civil War, the United States Eighth Agricultural Census listed Texas as having a cattle population of 3,533,786 head. The year following the war should have been profitable for the Texas cattlemen, but it wasn't. Stockmen drove an estimated 260,000 head of cattle north, but few reached a good market. These drives were plagued with problems; some were disastrous. In spite of hardships, the cattlemen's drives continued and new trails were opened. The years between 1870 and 1880 were a period of transition and growth for the Texas cattle industry. With new cattle trails opened to the Kansas cattle markets, rail transportation from Kansas provided delivery of beef to the northeastern population centers, creating a lucrative market for the Texas cattlemen.[5]

Profits from the Texas cattle trade didn't go unnoticed. General James S. Brisbin, a Union officer during the Civil War, penned a bestselling book titled *The Beef Bonanza, or How to Get Rich on the Plains*. Brisbin's book described huge cattle profits. His book and the weekly market reports in the nation's newspapers stoked eastern investors' interest, and money from the east began flowing into Texas.[6]

With the advance in refrigeration technology in 1875, American's dressed beef was refrigerated and shipped to England. Along with an increase in live cattle shipped, the shipments of chilled beef set off an alarm among British farmers; they feared a drop in European beef prices. A Scottish newspaper, *The Scotsman*, sent a man to the United States to study this profitable cattle industry. He reported back in 1877 that the shipment of beef to the United Kingdom was 6,016,200 pounds, six times the amount reported in 1876. Two members of the British Parliament came to America to investigate the booming cattle industry in 1880. They reported that profits of 33.5 percent could be made annually ranching and raising cattle. Soon large sums of British money began flowing into the Texas land and cattle industry.[7]

The Texas legislature appropriated 3,050,000 acres of land in 1879 to cover costs for the construction of the new Texas State Capitol building. The land was in one block, beginning in the Texas Panhandle's northwest corner and running along the New Mexico border, and covered all or part of ten counties. An eastern syndicate was formed by a group of Chicago capitalists. They offered to construct a state capitol building and take payment in three million acres of land. The syndicate then turned to the British for capital, and the Capitol Freehold Land and Investment Company was registered. The Marquess of Tweeddale, governor of the Commercial Bank of Scotland, was made chairman. The new ranch owned by Americans and British would be known as the XIT Ranch. Fence building began on a large scale. The syndicate's fencing project was the largest in the nation, with 781 miles of barbed wire fence enclosing all but 35,000 acres of the ranch.

Materials used in fence construction were estimated to be 6,000 miles of barbed wire, 100,000 fence posts, five carloads of staves, and one carload of staples. There were so many gates that management ordered a carload of gate hinges.[8]

For Great Britain and the east's investors, buying into the Texas land and cattle business was a challenge. They needed counsel and help and often partnered with Texas cattlemen. Such was the case with the New York banker who entered into a partnership with the loud, boisterous Shanghai Pierce, who ranched on Matagorda Bay. Traveling to New York, Pierce entered the 120 Broadway Bank building, hoping to meet and discuss financing with the famous banker Augustus Kountze. The tall six-foot, five-inch cattleman, who considered himself the Webster on Cattle, walked through the door of the elegant New York bank. Looking around, he bellowed out in his usual loud voice, "By God, sirs! I want to see Augustus Kountze." Almost instantly a tranquil but stern older man emerged from an interior office, bowed, and said, "Come this way, Mr. Pierce."

Shanghai followed the gentlemen into his office and then exclaimed again in his booming voice, "My God, Brother Kountze! How in the hell did you know it was me, Sir?" Kountze, the courteous banker, replied, "O, you carry your introduction with you." Shanghai departed New York confident there would be a future partnership, and there was. Soon Kountze furnished the capital to purchase 200,000 acres of land and 12,000 yearling calves, giving Shanghai Pierce one-sixth interest in the cattle's profits. It was no surprise their partnership turned out to be a rocky relationship. Yet it was a profitable venture for both of the partners. Shanghai had earlier opposed barbed wire when Henry Sanborn brought the first Glidden wire to Texas. Now he purchased a flat wire with barbs from the Lambert & Bishop Wire Fence Company of Joliet, Illinois, and fenced Kountze new range to protect the grass and their cattle. Soon after building the partnership's fence, fence cutters cut the barbed wire between each post for nineteen miles. Shanghai put fence riders armed with Winchesters on the fence lines and traveled to Austin to lobby the governor for new fence-cutting laws.[9]

Early British investors formed the Scottish American Mortgage Company, which then created the Prairie Cattle Company. The company was registered in 1880 with a capitalization of $1 million and was chaired by the Eighth Earl of Airlie, who took an active role in management. They paid a 20.5 percent dividend in 1883, and one report claims they had 150,000 head of cattle.[10]

The Texas rancher Mifflin Kenedy sold his South Texas Los Laureles Ranch in 1882 for $1.1 million in cash to a Dundee Scotland syndicate known as the Texas Land and Cattle Company, Ltd. This sale was of 242,000 fenced acres with 50,000 head of cattle and 5,000 horses, and mules. But Mifflin Kenedy didn't leave the ranching business. Following the sale Kenedy purchased the La Parra, or Grapevine Ranch, fencing all of 400,000 acres, doubling his South Texas operation's size.[11]

The Spur Ranch, whose corporate name was the Espuela Land and Cattle Company Ltd., was registered in London. Their initial purchase consisted of 378 sections of land with 40,000 head of cattle. Later they acquired additional school land.[12]

British investors demanded supervision unheard of in the Texas cattle businesses and called for frequent records and reports. They asked questions that produced frustration and scorn by Texans working for them. The Brits had little or no knowledge of the Texas cattle trade and didn't understand the customs of Texas cattlemen or the problems they soon encountered.[13]

One of the British investments that illustrates their difficulties is the Rocking Chair Ranch. The Rocking Chair Ranch owned and leased 300,800 acres in Collingsworth and Wheeler Counties in the Texas Panhandle. In 1883 cattlemen John T. Lytle and A. Conkle bought and then sold 235 sections of railroad land to Early W. Spencer and J. John Drew, an Englishman. Drew traveled to London and organized the Rocking Chair Ranch Syndicate. Sir Dudley Coutts Majoribanks, First Baron of Tweedmouth, financed the operation for his eldest son, Sir Dudley Edward Majoribanks, and son-in-law John Campbell Hamilton Gordon, the Seventh Earl of Aberdeen. Sir Dudley's youngest son, Archibald John Majoribanks, and John Drew were made comanagers of this ranching operation.[14]

When Archibald John arrived in Texas and traveled to the ranch, he introduced himself to the cowhands as Sir Archibald Majoribanks. From that day on, the cowboys called him Marshie. Archibald didn't adapt well to the Texas ranch business. He spent most of his time indoors at the ranch headquarters, preparing business reports, writing letters, keeping the books, and ordering supplies. John Drew left the bookkeeping to Archie and handled the cow business and the cowhands. Archie did manage to spend quite a bit of time in the Mobeetie bars, wearing his scissor-tail coat. He wore English boots, boot pants, and a riding jacket with his cap back at the ranch. Archie wouldn't ride the ranch cow horses. He had his own horses the cowhands called old pecker neck, and he rode an English saddle. His actions and demeanor convinced the cowboys that not only was this man a tenderfoot and snob, but he also considered himself better than they were. Archie's feeling toward the cowhands was comparable. He shared the sentiment of the British diplomat Victor Drummond, who wrote home complaining about Texas, "The country is unfit for the English settlers of the better class."[15]

The Rocking Chair Ranch suffered many problems caused by homesteaders and small farmers with bitter feelings toward large ranches. When Rocking Chair's ranch hands built new pasture fences, homesteaders would sneak in during the dark of night and steal two of the four strands of the new barbed wire fence for their use. Over the ten years that Archie and John Drew managed the ranch, the operation suffered from fence cutting, pasture burning, burning of the ranch pens, and burning the livestock feed. There were also shootouts on the ranch. But no record was found of a killing.[16]

The Matador Cattle Company, Ltd. was one of the few long-term successes of Britain's investors. It was organized in 1882, by a Scottish group headquartered in Dundee. They started with ownership of 100,000 acres and grazing privileges on 1.5 million acres. The Matador Ranch grew and suffered all of the big ranch problems but survived the most years. It wasn't broken up until 1951.[17]

From 1875 to 1883, millions of acres of Texas grassland had been purchased and fenced with barbed wire. Barbed wire was strung from South Texas to the Red River Country, blocking cattle trails and changing the face of Texas rangeland. In May of 1883, the *Cheyenne Transponder*, a newspaper from Fort Reno in Indian Territory, commented on barbed wire fences and problems barbed wire was causing the Texas cattle drives. The paper reported, "Herds passing up the trail since the drives commenced are shipped by rail from all parts of Texas to Wichita Falls, as it is no longer possible to bring a herd through the state on account of the fences." After reaching Wichita Falls by rail, cattle were unloaded and put back on the trail, and drovers trailed them on north to the Kansas markets. The *Galveston Daily News* reported on June 4, 1883, that large drives of cattle were moving up the trail from South Texas and reaching Taylorville (renamed Taylor in 1892), being loaded and sent by train and rail to Wichita Falls, and then being put back on the trail. Taylorsville was on the Great Northern Railroad. Barbed wire made the town a major shipping point for South Texas Cattle. The *Texas Livestock Journal* reported that there were hundreds of carloads of horses shipped up to Wichita Falls; the land and trails traveled in the previous years were fenced with barbed wire.[18]

As the state's land was sold and fenced, resentment against pasture men grew. Free grazing of cattle and sheep on public land had provided a livelihood for Texans for many years. New landowners fencing the choice grasslands and their fences also enclosed primary water sources. Watered land was always the first land purchased, and permanent bodies of water used by the public were enclosed and no longer accessible. Windmills and well drilling had not yet arrived in Texas.

When large land purchases were fenced, they often surrounded small farms and homesteads. These fences separated the homesteaders from the nearest town, courthouse, post office, stores, and churches. In years past the settler could follow a road or trail directly to his destination. Pasture fences now blocked those routes. A trip that once had been a mile became a day's journey to get around or to get out of an enclosing pasture. Aggrieved parties begged county commissioners for help opening roads. Under state law the commissioners' power to resolve road problems was limited. A traveler's problem with a fence across a road was soon solved with a set of wire cutters. An offense was committed, but the route to the traveler's destination was shortened.

Five years of drought began in the early 1880s and spread across Texas. Cattle prices were good when the drought started; profits were expected. In the hot dry summer of 1883, cattlemen overstocked and overgrazed the remaining open, free range. Lack of water in the droughty summer caused free-ranging cattle in certain counties to die off. The land became bare, and the turf was destroyed. Some of the pasture men aggravated the situation by grazing their cattle on the free range during spring and summer, saving their fenced pasture's grass. When cold weather arrived, they drove their stock back into their fenced pastures for winter grazing, leaving no grass for the free-range man's cattle.

In 1883 another problem was discovered and caused universal outrage. Newspapers reported pasture men were fencing land they hadn't purchased or leased. Because the public domain had been surveyed into alternating 640-acre sections, creating a checkerboard of railroad-owned and school land, buyers of large tracts were often unable to consolidate their property through purchases. They would buy a large block of school land made up of many 640-acre sections, then try to purchase or lease the railroad sections of land between their blocks on this checkerboard of real estate. Rarely was this possible. Consequently, railroad-owned blocks of land that had been available for free grazing were now enclosed in large, fenced pastures. Fencing of this free grazing land by the pasture men became a volatile issue.[19]

Citizens' anger over land sales and barbed wire fences festered, then erupted in the hot, dry summer of 1883. Fences were destroyed across Texas, with fence cutting reported in over half of the state's 171 organized counties. The most frequent and blatant cases were on the state's frontier, starting in Clay County on the Red River, then down through Brown and Coleman Counties, through Lampasas and on to Frio, Medina, and Gonzales Counties. Fence cutting spread, and soon pasture burnings and livestock killings began. Sheepmen and their herds were frequent victims of deadly midnight raids. Even the farmers with small, enclosed fields had their fences destroyed. Picket fences still in use were burned, and some of the old rock fences were pushed over.[20]

The general public, and even some of the local lawmen, conscious of their constituent's feelings, ignored or supported the fence cutters. In parts of the state, it was impossible to impanel a jury that would indict and prosecute a fence cutter, even if he were captured. Early juries were sympathetic, but by the fall of 1883, jurors failed to act because they were intimidated. They feared retaliation by the cutters' criminal element. The justice system was broken.

Late in 1883 the extreme violence and the impact of the fence cutting on the state's economy caused a shift in the public's sentiment. Cattle prices fell from thirty dollars to less than five dollars per head, and virtually all of the state's free-grazing men were broke. Big investors and cattlemen who borrowed money to buy land suffered. Texas cattlemen had close to $90 million borrowed, and the banks were calling in most of this money. Citizens who supported the fence cutters were now affected by the lawlessness and violence and by the impact on the local and state economies.[21]

The citizens called on Governor John Ireland for help, but little help was forthcoming. The governor's ability to deal with the fence-cutting problem was limited by a lack of state laws and funding. Few means were available for dealing with such an extraordinary emergency. The state's adjutant general, W. H. King, advised the public that under state law Texas Rangers had no more power than the county sheriff had.

> Citizens believe their county's peace officers are powerless because these outrages are done in the dark of night, but would indicate a belief that the Rangers possess some power other officials and men don't have. It appears the citizens believe Rangers have a foreknowledge of when and where a probable crime will be committed or that Rangers can be found to stand guard day and night around all the pastures of the state. Neither is possible. As long as fence cutting is carried out by the present methods and finds apparent support among so many otherwise law-abiding citizens, thousands of Rangers cannot stop fence cutting.[22]

Citizens and local officials called for detectives, but the governor had no authority under the law to hire detectives nor funds to pay them. Fence cutting was a misdemeanor offense, with a fine of maybe ten, twenty, or thirty dollars if a person was caught, prosecuted, and found guilty. Governor Ireland offered a thirty-dollar reward for apprehension and conviction of a fence cutter, with the reward bearing some proportion of the misdemeanor punishment possible under the law. Then he increased the reward to fifty dollars, and by the late summer, the reward was raised to one hundred dollars. Rewards were of no benefit, and rarely was one collected. In December 1883 the governor issued a proclamation revoking all rewards.[23]

The *Galveston Daily News*, one of the state's widely read newspapers, criticized Governor Ireland. A burst of condemnation of Ireland read, "The flagitious feebleness of the government of Texas can no longer be hidden from view. No amount of sophistry and no quantity of excuses and apology can remove the naked fact that the Executive of the State is unequal to the suppression of lawlessness."

Soon after this criticism, the *Galveston Daily News* Austin reporter tried to interview the governor and received his indignant reply: "What, recognize that contemptible sheet? No. It's a disgrace to any man to be connected with it."

Recoiling and taken aback, the reporter responded, saying, "The *News* was not fighting John Ireland but the Executive."

Ireland responded, "The character of the attack admits no distinction." The reporter then threatened to publish a letter the governor had written to the *Galveston News* thanking the paper for its services during his last campaign.

Ireland responded, "Publish It! The course of the *News* last year was such a surprise to everybody that I thought it proper to thank it for the same."

The governor unceremoniously booted out the reporter and continued his denouncement of the Galveston newspaper. This battle between the *Galveston Daily News* and John Ireland was described with much hilarity in the competing newspapers, the *Austin Statesman* and the *Fort Worth Daily Gazette*.[24]

Chapter 4

Cowhands Kill a Fence Cutter in Clay County

> A story was circulated about a traveling man going through Clay County. He suddenly came upon a large band of men cutting a barbed wire fence. The surprised man exclaimed, "Hard at it, I see." "Oh yes," responded one of the wire cutters. "Get down and take a hand in the game." The traveler pleaded that he had urgent business demanding his immediate attention elsewhere. "Ah! But you must try a whack or two just to see how easy 'tis done." Reluctantly the traveling man was forced to dismount and clip a few spans of barbed wire.
> —An incident reported in the *Albany Echo*, September 8, 1883

When the Civil War began, the US Army posts in Texas were surrendered to the Confederates, and the federal troops left Texas. Following the US troops' departure, Indian raids and atrocities increased in North Texas. Hearing pleas from its citizens for protection on the frontier, the Texas legislature authorized a line of defense from the Red River to the Rio Grande River. Still, the Civil War effort limited state troops, and little or no protection was available for North Texas. The period between 1863 and 1872 was the most devastating period of Indian atrocities.

Clay County was organized in 1860 but was disorganized and abandoned in 1862 because of the Indians. Neighboring Young County was virtually depopulated. In Young County there were 500 whites and 92 enslaved Blacks listed in the 1860 US Census, but the population dropped to 135 citizens in 1870. Settlers left their homes and fled to safety back east. In Clay County the town of Henrietta was vacated, and the Indians burned some of the buildings. During those years of Indian trouble, many North Texas cattlemen never gave up their pursuit of cattle raising in the Red River Country, but some of the men and their employees paid with their lives. In 1860 sixty-four cattlemen were grazing cattle in Jack County. Ten years later, in 1870, only twenty-one had managed to hold on.[1]

Getting their cattle to the eastern market was critical for the Texans, but eastern Kansas was off-limits with a farmer's blockade. The farmers feared a disease later identified as Texas tick fever that was carried by longhorn cattle. Some drovers tried the Goodnight-Loving Trail, but Oliver Loving of Jack County was shot by Indians while moving cattle up the trail and died at Fort Sumner in the fall of 1867. South and Central Texas cattlemen searching for a route to the eastern markets tried driving through the Indian Territory. At considerable risk cattlemen drove herds north past Decatur and up through Montague County. They crossed the Red River into Indian Territory at Red River Station and drove north through Indian country to Abilene, Kansas.

Here was the beginning of the Chisholm Trail, named for Jesse Chisholm, a freighter and Indian trader. In 1867 Joseph McCoy built cattle shipping pens at the small community of Abilene, Kansas, on the new Kansas Pacific Railway. Texas cattle were then shipped from Abilene. The number doubled each year until the cattle market broke when a glut of cattle moved out of Texas in 1871. Years later the Chisholm Trail would be closed by barbed wire.[2]

From the early days, cattle raising was carried on in Red River Country, but Indian depredations stopped farmers and their families and the advance of head-right settlements. Cattlemen were different. They generally were absentee owners who would come in, establish a headquarter camp on a freshwater stream, and move their cattle out on the free range to graze and reproduce. Their only investment was cattle and the small tract of land that became the cow camp headquarters. They might have a couple of cowhands employed as line riders during the year; these men worked at considerable risk from the Indians. These cattle grazed the free range, and the cattlemen claimed grazing rights of an area; this was the unwritten cowman's custom of the day. Cattlemen would gather and worked their stock in the fall and spring of the year with the cooperative help of other cattlemen.

These first North Texas cattlemen wore names such as Oliver and James Loving, C. C. Slaughter, J. C. Carpenter, William Benjamin Worsham, William Sude Ikard, C. L. (Kit) Carter, Glenn Halsell, and John Belcher. They were grazing cattle in North Texas, suffering some losses but still turning a profit. Dan Waggoner established a cattle operation in Clay County as early as 1866, then later moved farther west. The cattle market was profitable in those years, and most of the men who survived prospered and were later known as the Cattle Kings.

In 1871 Henry Warren, a prominent businessman and government contractor, moved to Weatherford and established his freighting headquarters. He had been a state senator from El Paso in 1866. In May of 1871, a band of about 150 Kiowa and Comanche left the Indian reservation at Fort Sill and attacked Henry Warren's wagon train in Young County, west of Jacksboro. Six of his teamsters and the wagon master were killed, scalped, and mutilated.

General William Tecumseh Sherman, who was in Texas at the time, had the chiefs who led the raid arrested when they returned to Fort Sill. They were tried in civil court in Jacksboro, Texas. After the wagon train massacre, Col. Ranald Mackenzie was directed to begin an offensive against Indians that left the reservation. His aggressive activity became known as the Red River War. Following Mackenzie's successful operation, the frequent Indian raids ceased in North Texas.[3]

Cattlemen and farmers both large and small returned, bringing more cattle and the farmers plowing the sod. In August of 1873, Clay County was reorganized at the community of Cambridge, and citizens voted in a new slate of county officials. Later, after a heated competition, Henrietta beat out Cambridge for the county seat of Clay.

Soon after Clay County was reorganized, Joseph Glidden patented his famous barbed wire, began manufacturing this new fence material, and employed Henry B. Sanborn as his salesman. Sanborn began sales of Glidden wire in North Texas. His partner Judson Warner arrived in Texas and was selling barbed wire south of Dallas. Wire sale looked promising.[4]

While traveling and selling barbed wire, Clay County was visited and crisscrossed on many occasions. Sanborn admired its excellent grassland. Later years he returned to Clay County and purchased 17,337 acres of prime land located in the fork of the Little Wichita and the Red River. He grazed 3,000 head of steers on this tract of land that were purchased as yearlings, grown out, and sold at maturity.[5]

Before Glidden's barbed wire arrived in Texas, farmers depended on native rock and wood rails for building fences, but times were changing. As soon as the first barbed wire arrived in North Texas, cattlemen put it to use. One of the early cattlemen in Red River Country to fence a large tract of land was Captain Peter B. Keyser, a veteran of the Civil War. Captain Keyser imported a carload of Durham cattle and a Denmark stallion, expecting to establish a herd of fine blooded cattle and horses. About the same time, another Clay County cattleman, William Sude Ikard, also brought in Durham cattle. Ikard later switched to purebred Herefords.[6]

To separate their imported breeding stock from the common range cattle and keep their purebloods pure, both men fenced their land with the new barbed wire. It was reported that Keyser's new barbed wire fences were not well received; his fences were probably some of the first cut in Texas. Keyser became a frequent target for fence cutters. At one point fence cutters killed five of his quality purebred calves within sight of his house.[7]

Farmers who had financial means were also fencing with the new barbed wire to keep livestock from destroying their crops. One early incident following the cutting of a farmer's fence in Clay County resulted in a shooting. Several families from Virginia migrated to Clay County in the 1870s, found good land, homesteaded, and plowed the fertile soil near the Buffalo Springs community. J. B. Young and his family were one of these early arrivals. There's a note in Clay County's museum files identifying this man as Brigham Young, but the record notes he wasn't the Mormon leader. In June 1880 Young, his wife, and a young daughter were neighbors of George Cooper Wright and Charles L. Dinwiddie, also Virginians. Cooper Wright was born at Boones Mill, Virginia, about 1851 and grew up working his father's tobacco fields. On arriving in Clay County, Wright made an agreement with Young to farm his land as a sharecropper. Their farming arrangement worked well until Young the landowner suffered some of Clay County's early fence cutting. Details of fence cutting on Young's farm have been lost over the years, but the Wright family history tells of Young and Wright's problem with the cutters. When Young's fences were cut, Wright and his companion Charles Dinwiddie intervened on Young's behalf; a shootout followed. The cutters were of a family named Lamb, and several men were shot. The 1880 US Census lists quite a number of farmers in Clay and Montague Counties with the name Lamb. Following the shootout Wright traded his share of the farm crop he grew for a fast horse and was preparing to leave the country. Family history says Wright was planning to run from the law. He may, however, have been more concerned with retribution by the Lamb family and their fence-cutting friends.

The cattlemen of the area had no sympathy for either fence cutters or farmers. They saw an opportunity to bring a good man with a gun over to their side. The cattlemen convinced Wright to stay in Clay County and found him a job in a mercantile store in Henrietta. He also worked as a night watchman. Then, most certainly with the cattlemen's support, Wright ran for the county sheriff's office. On November 2, 1880, Cooper Wright the farmer was elected Clay County's sheriff and then reelected six more terms, serving a total of fourteen years, the longest in Clay County history. Sheriff Wright carried out an ongoing battle against fence cutters and cattle thieves during those years in office.[8]

By 1883 Clay, Jack, and Montague Counties had experienced changes, and more were coming. Barbed wire fences closed routes for cattle drives up the Chisholm Trail and through the Indian Territory to Kansas. Red River Station in Montague had been the main river crossing out of Texas on the Chisholm Trail. By 1883 cattle crossing at Red River Station was history; drovers had moved herds farther west and up the Western Trail to avoid the barbed wire fences. Another change occurred in 1883 when the Texas legislature passed a bill known as the Leasing Act. This legislation authorized the state to lease the Texas state school land's vast acreage for ten years with a minimum price of four cents an acre. When they leased it, stockmen fenced segments of this land with barbed wire.[9]

Moneyed interests from the Midwest, the northeastern United States, and Britain were investing money in land and cattle. Cattlemen in Red River Country who built their wealth on the free range during the early years were also rapidly buying or leasing land and building fences. For them purchasing land and building fences was a necessity but a big gamble. When borrowing money, they paid interest at rates of 18 to 24 percent. Most, however, had the foresight to see that the days of free grazing in the public domain were ending. Still, many cattlemen large and small were unable to borrow money or simply refused to buy land. They didn't believe free grazing of the open public land would end. Opportunity passed them by. Soon landless cattlemen began agitating against barbed wire fences. Many of these landless cattlemen supported and some even paid fence cutters. In the late years of his life, the old frontiersman and rancher Charles Goodnight spoke of this in his correspondence to a friend:

> There is no question but what the wire cutting originated among the cattlemen, a class of holder who did not want to lease land or buy land and hence did not want anyone else to, their aim to keep the range open and free. I understand this is not generally known, but it's the truth, just the same. It was done generally by men hiring irresponsible people who had no interest on either side.[10]

A drought began in 1883, bringing more stress to this period of Texas history. It eased some but extended for several years. The open, free range was overgrazed, and hardly a sprig of grass was left for cattle belonging to men who owned no land. There was no rain. By 1883 cattlemen and farmers had fenced permanent watering sites with barbed wire fences. The few wet weather watering sites on the open, free range dried up.[11]

New fences were causing travel problems for the small landowner. Homesteaders and farmers were being enclosed inside and surrounded by the larger fenced tracts. Fences with no gates were built across roads. Entering, leaving, or traveling for miles around large, enclosed pastures became a serious problem.

An enterprising young man named Samuel E. Sherwood appeared, and he was an astute trader. He managed to purchase the O brand and the sizable herd of cattle wearing the brand in Jack County in 1881 for $45,000. Sherwood sold the cattle for $65,000 and invested his profits in 35,000 acres of land in Clay County, paying $1.75 an acre. He immediately enclosed the property with a new barbed wire fence. In March 1883 he sold the property for $3.50 an acre to the Red River Land and Cattle Company.[12]

The Red River Land and Cattle Company had been organized in 1880 by Frank Houston, W. R. Bourland, and R. M. Bourland of St. Louis, Missouri. Frank Houston was president, and W. R. Bourland was the secretary-treasurer. The Red River Land and Cattle Company registered its brand, the ISI, and the brand was placed on the right side of their cattle.[13]

The company grew rapidly, with their agent traveling the region, visiting cattlemen, and promoting and selling company stock. The Red River Land and Cattle Company's stock often was exchanged for land and cattle, bringing cattlemen into the company. In a short time, the Red River Land and Cattle Company owned, leased, or controlled over 110,000 acres of land in Clay, Jack, and Montague Counties. Most of this land was soon fenced. Samuel Sherwood invested in the Red River Land and Cattle Company, owning capital stock in 1883. Believing this investment was a profitable venture, he also brought his mother and brother, Bink Sherwood, in as stockholders. Sam Sherwood's troubles began here.[14]

Land that Sherwood had placed in the Red River Land and Cattle Company was located mainly in Clay County but appeared to have spilled into Jack and the eastern part of Montague County. There was an agreement made between Sherwood and the Red River Land and Cattle Company, and Sherwood continued to manage the land and the cattle in southern Clay County. Other large cattlemen who were Sherwood's neighbors did not have an interest in or own stock in the Red River Land and Cattle Company. Stanford Wilson, Nub White, Sammy McGraw, Charley Burch, and S. B. Harrison had land and cattle in south Clay County. Two brothers, Ben and W. F. (Babe) Cobb, established a massive cattle operation before 1880 in southern Clay County, now on the west boundary of the Red River Land and Cattle Company property. The Cobb brothers fenced their ranch, and their operation was known as the Cobb Land and Cattle Company.[15]

The Fort Worth and Denver Railway reached Clay County in 1882, bringing more new settlers to the area. Southern Clay County had good soil. Prime farmland and small tracts were preempted or homesteaded by a surge of farmers migrating to the range. Many small farms were located around the settlements of Fannintown (later Joy), Prospect, Newport, Buffalo Springs, and Postoak. Farmers were moving farther west and out into the open-range country.

William Benjamin Worsham began his early years in the cattle business as a trail boss and came to Clay County in 1868. He established his ranch headquarters eight miles southeast of Henrietta. Worsham's ranch eventually totaled over 60,600 acres, and he owned land and cattle in several other counties. Late one evening two of his cowhands rode into headquarters, and during the discussion of their day's work, reported that several small farms had recently moved onto the free range. The cowhand told Worsham that the small farmer's dwellings, viewed from a distance, appeared as a bunch of bird nests. After this discussion with his cowhands, Worsham always referred to the small farmers and homesteaders as nesters. The name spread and was used by cattlemen throughout the Southwest when referring to the small farmers.[16]

Three or four nesters were located inside the Red River Land and Cattle Company's large, fenced pastures. Sam Sherwood claimed these farmers preferred to be surrounded by a fence because the fences kept their cows from drifting off when the cold winds of winter northers blew through. Their few cows also benefited from good grass year-round. There was a homesteader named J. W. Butler among the farmers who lived on the land with his wife and four small children. According to Sherwood this man owned not one foot of the area and lived on a school land claim. He appeared to have no means of support other than his wife, who milked several of Sherwood's cows, churned, and sold butter. Butler, it seemed, was satisfied to be fenced in. Sherwood built gates where needed and worked to accommodate Butler and the needs of the other fenced-in farmers.

Keeping these enclosed homesteaders happy, however, did not improve relations with farmers or with cattlemen with livestock grazing outside of the cattle company's pastures. These stockmen believed they had a right to free grazing, and no one could fence and close off the land, regardless of who owned it. Most of the Red River Land and Cattle Company's fenced property was purchased and some of tracts were leased. It also appeared that some of the Red River Land and Cattle Company's fenced land may have belonged to the state or was railroad land and wasn't owned or leased. A dangerous storm was brewing over fences in the southern part of Clay County. Southern Clay and Jack Counties experienced a severe flare-up of fence cutting in 1883, when summer heat and drought conditions arrived. The *Jacksboro Citizen* reported, "More wire cut last night. We have not learned the full extent of fences cut, but a considerable portion of Sherwood's was cut. Our town's J. C. Lindsey had three miles cut on his ranch, north of the West Fork and adjoining Sherwood's. The work was done effectually, the wire being cut twice between each post."

More fence-cutting incidents followed throughout Clay and spilled into adjoining counties. A man from Illinois came to Clay, purchased a 640-acre tract, fenced the land, bought cattle, and stocked it. He went back to Illinois to get his family. When he returned he found his fences cut to shreds. He put the land on the market, sold out, and returned to Illinois.

Miss Newcomb, a longtime resident of Clay County, built a fence around her tract and made it known that she owned every foot of the land. She left a road forty feet wide around the ranch and offered to put a sixty-foot lane through the center. A petition was filed with the commissioners court calling for her to build gates. She constructed gates at various points where requested. In return for her effort to accommodate neighbors, her fences were cut.

A man named Shelly owned and fenced a 1,000-acre pasture in Clay and Jack Counties and had his fence cut. His neighbor, a Mr. Ball, owned a small 160-acre farm, and his fence was also cut. Fence cutting quickly spread throughout Clay County and was no longer limited to the county's southern part. G. H. Gowan, a rancher owning 4,000 to 5,000 acres near Henrietta, had his fences cut. The cutters destroyed Gowan's fence and proceeded to cut the fence on an adjoining ranch, which enclosed only a few hundred acres and belonged to Chris Sanzenberger, who was a sick man. He was in bed and unable to rebuild or repair his fence. His livestock was running at large. B. F. Albin ranched and farmed southwest of Henrietta, owned about

1,000 acres, and had his fences cut. His neighbor, a man named Brown, and several other neighbors, each holding 320 acres, had fences cut.[17]

The *Albany Echo* reported an incident in late August 1883, saying, "Wire fence cutters in Clay County were so bold in their work of devilry that in one instance, about 30 or 40 of them being overtaken by daylight while engaged in cutting a fence, held a caucus to decide whether they should proceed with their work or postpone it until another night. Determined to finish, they went ahead with the cutting right before the eyes of employees of the property owner. A gentleman passing along was forced to dismount and take a hand in the cutting himself."[18]

The story circulated in Clay about this traveling man riding through the county when he unexpectedly came up on the large band of men cutting a barbed wire fence. "The surprised man exclaimed, 'Hard at it, I see.' 'Oh yes,' responded one of the wire cutters, 'Get down and take a hand in the game.' The traveler pleaded that he had urgent business demanding his immediate attention elsewhere. 'Ah! But you must try a whack or two just to see how easy 'tis done.' Reluctantly, the traveling man was forced to dismount and clip a few spans of barbed wire."[19]

As Clay County's fences were being destroyed, a newspaper editor interviewed state Representative Allen K. Swan, who traveled through Fort Worth to Austin to meet with Governor John Ireland and discuss the fence-cutting issue. Swan lived in Henrietta, and his district consisted of Clay and Montague Counties. The representative told the newspaper editor that Governor Ireland wrote a letter to the Clay County attorney asking why he didn't prosecute the cutters. Swan said the answer to the governor's question was short and simple: the state's law wasn't sufficient. "Men who had paid for their property did not care to stay up three or four nights to catch a fence cutter then spend money to prosecute him, only to get ten or twelve dollars out of him when he had damaged them more than a thousand dollars. Better to have his house burned down than his fence ruined, as it was easier to rebuild." Fence cutting was only a misdemeanor offense under state law in 1883. Representative Swan pushed for legislation to make fence cutting a felony and for making the killing of a fence cutter justifiable homicide. Later, in addressing the House Conference Committee, he bitterly denounced the fence cutter and his sympathizers. He labeled the crime as atrocious and would have the fence cutters shot without the benefit of clergy.[20]

Clay County's newspaper, the *Henrietta Shield*, reported another incident in September that warned of violence to come. A large band of men went to the home of a Mr. McElroy during the night and awoke him. They told McElroy they were informed he had announced his intention to shoot anyone seen cutting his pastures fences. The band leader explained that they were the fence cutters, and if he was now prepared, the shooting should begin at once. The cutters told McElroy they intended to cut the fences of the Cobb brothers' pasture near the community of Antelope. While they preferred peace, they were ready for war, for the fences had to go. They left McElroy's home that night, and the next day one and a half miles of Cobb's fence had disappeared.[21]

Free grass meetings were held in the communities by the fence cutters and their supporters. The pasture men held indignation meetings. Clay and Jack Counties were now like a powder keg with a short fuse burning. Several shootings occurred between pasture men and fence cutters, but details have been lost over time. One incident, however, is noted by historians and still talked about by some ranchers in Clay County today. The affray occurred in a fenced pasture belonging to the Red River Land and Cattle Company.

Samuel Sherwood was burdened with problems and had been reporting fence-cutting incidents to Frank Houston, the head man of the Red River Land and Cattle Company in St. Louis, Missouri. Company President Houston was now concerned about the fence-cutting losses and decided to come to Texas and check on matters. Before Houston left Missouri, a large band of men cut gaps in almost every standing fence in southern Clay County in one night. Following this fence-cutting onslaught, the news spread that the cutters would finish the job soon. Sherwood armed his cowhands and prepared to see that no more of the cattle company's fences were cut. Cowhands would ride the fence lines performing nighttime guard duty and carrying Winchester rifles ready for action. The night of September 14, fence cutters struck the Red River Cattle Company's property again, and one old-timer reported, "They run up against a circumstance." As the band of the cutters came down a line of fence clipping fence wire, they encountered a rain of bullets from the cowhand's Winchesters. Rumors among the area residents were many. Some said the shooting was done by the fence riders, but others said the cutters had a free-for-all fight among their own. Those knowledgeable about the occurrence agreed excitement was intense and there was shooting by both fence riders and the fence cutters.

Houston, traveling from St. Louis, Missouri, arrived in Fort Worth the afternoon before the gun battle occurred. On arrival Houston learned a pending confrontation and trouble was expected that night on their Clay County ranch. The ranch was over a hundred miles northwest of Fort Worth, so he rushed to the train depot, ordered a special train to Henrietta, and telegraphed ahead to have a team of horses with a buggy waiting. Houston arrived in Henrietta, then drove twenty miles to the ranch with as much speed as possible, traveling over rough roads in his buggy. By the time Houston arrived, the shootout had already occurred. He immediately called in the armed ranch hands. An old-timer speculated that more men would have been killed in pitched battles with cutters had he not called in the cowhands. Frank Houston had come to Texas and seen the fence-cutting problems firsthand. Two weeks later, on September 27, the *Fort Worth Daily Gazette* noted that F. K. Houston, president of the Red River Land and Cattle Company, passed through the city in route back to St. Louis. Houston had terrible news to share with his Missouri stockholders. From several reports of the incident, the main casualty of the fray was J. W. Butler, the homesteader who lived with his family inside the Red River Land and Cattle Company's pastures. He was shot twenty times, according to one source.[22]

Several weeks after the shootout, Charles De Morse, editor of the *Clarksville Standard,* caught up with Sam Sherwood the ranch manager for an interview. Sherwood said he and his ranch hands had been patrolling the area since the incident on the fence line. He told De Morse that he and his associates fenced 75,000 acres in Clay County and 50,000 acres in another county. In the pasture in Clay County, where the assault occurred, the cattle company owned all the land. An exception was one tract that was in litigation. J. W. Butler didn't own a foot of land or a cow. His wife milked Sherwood's cows, then churned the milk and sold the butter.

Sherwood had talked with Butler's wife several days after the shootout. She feared that they would move the cattle. Sherwood assured her he would not move them; she could milk more cows if she wished, and if she needed anything, he would get it for her. Sherwood told De Morse that he was unable to elicit information from the widow whose husband had been killed regarding her husband's motives. The wife said she tried to prevent her husband from riding away that night; his death left four small children for her to maintain. Many believed that Butler was being paid for the fence cutting by free-range cattlemen.[23]

At least two fence cutters besides Butler were shot during the shootout by the cattle company's ranch hands. Newt Jones was a cowhand working on the adjoining Cobb Brothers ranch near where the shooting occurred, and he claimed that two more men were killed. Sam Sherwood reported two men were wounded, and others said two wounded men had left the country. One wounded fence cutter who left the country appears to have been Linton Manning Cutter. During the 1880 US Census, Linton Cutter lived in Precinct 4 of Jack County. His birthplace was Michigan, he was 21 years old, and his occupation was listed as a cowboy. After the shootout Linton Cutter left Clay or Jack County and, in years afterward, resided in Lebanon, Missouri.[24]

The name and the fate of a third man shot by the fence guards hasn't been found. If he lived, he probably left the country, or he may have died, as reported by Newt Jones, and been buried in an unmarked grave. J. W. Butler, the homesteader killed, is buried in the Prospect Cemetery in southern Clay County.[25]

The years that followed the shootout were not kind to the Red River Land and Cattle Company's stockholders. The company went bankrupt, and owners were reported to have lost all they invested. Some said fence cutting broke the company. Fence cutting was undoubtedly a contributing factor, but so were high interest rates, the drought, and the nation's cattle market's disastrous collapse that soon followed. In 1909 Lucian Walton Parrish, an early Clay County historian, summed up the matter, saying, "The Cattle Company failed by the weight of their own cumbersomeness." Other cattlemen who refused to join in with the Red River Land and Cattle Company took advantage of the forced sales and purchased the land when it was sold to settle its debt.

The small farmers operating inside the company's pastures were not affected by the failure.[26]

When the Red River Land and Cattle Company collapsed, Samuel Sherwood traded his stock for a ranch and livestock in Kaufman County. But he was a signer on the Red River Land and Cattle Company notes. Sherwood lost his Kaufman ranch and moved his cattle to Indian Territory in 1885. Later he was back in Clay and Montague Counties with five of his children attending school at Belcherville.[27]

The killing of J. W. Butler on the Red River Land and Cattle Company's fence line brought an immediate countywide effort to settle the fence-cutting war in Clay County. The residents and the prominent cattlemen noted the plight of Butler's wife and his four small children. Assistance for their needs came quickly from Clay County residents and prominent cattlemen. The shock from the killing led to talks between the pasture men and the free grass faction. An agreement was reached; each group would elect two delegates. The representatives would then meet and develop a peace treaty of a sort. A fifth man would be jointly selected by this group of four to mediate.

A correspondent for the *Fort Worth Daily Gazette* in Bowie, Texas, reported that the farmers and free-range men held their meeting at New Bart (Newport) in Clay County. The meeting was of great interest, with several hundred men attending. Resolutions were adopted strongly condemning wire fences and instructing delegates to tell the stockmen that the wire fences were to come down if they were to prevent anarchy and avoid bloodshed. *The Gazette* reported that after their meeting, the group waited with interest and solitude for the outcome of the pasture men's conference in Henrietta.[28]

The pasture men's faction made up of cattlemen, a few farmers, and the local officials met in Henrietta the same day, September 24, 1883. Many of Clay County's prominent citizens were in attendance. A. S. Mercer, the editor of the *Henrietta Shield*, called the meeting to order in the morning. Judge William B. Plemons was elected chairman and adjourned the session until one o'clock. The group reconvened that afternoon, and J. M. Booth, the editor of the *Decatur Tribune*, delivered a strong appeal for peace and enforcement of the law.[29]

A committee made up of J. M. Hudman, B. L. Frost, and B. T. Jones was appointed to draft a resolution concerning differences between the Red River Land and Cattle Company and the farmers obstructed by their fences. The following resolution was adopted by a unanimous vote:

> Resolve, that it is the sense of this convention that we believe it is nothing but proper and right that men should have the right to fence their land but no more.
>
> Resolve further, that we believe that if the pasture men will fence no more land than is owned, or in some way controlled by them, that there will be a cessation of the troubles now on us by wire cutting.
>
> Resolve further, that public roads be unobstructed, provided still further, that while stockmen may have done wrong in fencing land not owned by them, we do not approve of wire cutting nor in any way the destruction of personal property.
>
> Respectfully submitted and signed,
J. M. Hudman, B. L. Frost, B. T. Jones

The convention in Henrietta adjourned at five o'clock, with remarks and a prayer by Reverend Proctor. Judge W. B. Plemons of Henrietta and Joe Harris of Cooke County were appointed to meet with the farmers and free grass representatives the following month on October 4.[30]

The meeting between the two factions that followed was in Postoak, a community roughly two miles across the county line from Clay, in Jack County. Joe Harris and W. B. Plemons represented the pasture men, and R. W. Handley and W. A. Slover served the people of southern Clay and northern Jack Counties. No fifth person, as initially proposed, was present. After reviewing the fence-cutting issues at hand, the following points were negotiated and agreed on by the group:

1. That the pasture men shall take down and remove any wire fences that they may have erected around the land, not their own or controlled by them as shown by public record.
2. That pasture men shall leave open and not obstruct any public roads.
3. No citizen, who lives and owns land inside a pasture, shall be fenced up without his consent.
4. Where there is no public road leading in the direction sought to be traveled in the neighborhood to church, school, or mill, it shall be the

duty of the pasture men to construct gates for persons to pass through when requested to do so.
5. Pasture men will erect blinds (boards attached to the top fence wires) that stock can see along all the lanes which public roads pass.
6. Pasture men shall also build blinds on any part of their fence when requested to do so by any person whose stock runs in the vicinity and are liable to be affected by said wire fence.
7. It is agreed that pasture men shall have a reasonable time in which to make the changes as above agreed to and that all wire cutting or destruction of private property of all persons shall cease.
8. The Committee urgently requests all men of whatsoever calling or business, to observe and abide by this agreement and to aid all good men in settling the existing troubles.

Committee of; J.T. Harris, R.W. Handley,
W.A. Slover, W.B. Plemons[31]

Governor John Ireland sent Adjutant General Wilburn King to North Texas to review this volatile situation. Because of the Clay County shootout, the killing, and continuing fence cutting, Rangers were sent to Clay and Jack Counties. The Rangers arrested several men in Jack charged with fence cutting. But there were protests from some of the most prominent citizens of Jack County, and the Rangers were ordered out. But Ranger presence in Clay was well received, and the adjutant general claimed they helped stop fence cutting and a personal feud over fences. While King was in North Texas, he was contacted by Governor Ireland and directed to go immediately to another hot spot. Fence cutting was rampant in Brown and Coleman Counties and anticipated bloodshed was expected. With haste King traveled to Coleman, followed by Captain McMurry and Rangers from Company B. After surveying the situation and visiting with the Coleman officials, King returned to Austin and briefed the governor on his findings. In his annual report to the governor that soon followed, he addressed fence cutting and made some general comments for the Texas legislature.[32]

Fence cutting across the state had become Governor John Ireland's biggest problem. Having receiving Adjutant General King's report and hundreds of communications from across the state, the governor issued a call for a special session of the Eighteenth Texas Legislature. The special session would convene in Austin on January 8, 1884.

Fence cutting stopped in southern Clay County after the cattle company's fence-line shootout, the Rangers' presence, and the peace agreement signing at Postoak. But fence cutting continued in adjoining counties. Early 1884 fences were cut on the large Dawson Pasture in the northeast part of Clay County, and fence cutting continued in the counties adjoining Clay. The *Fort Worth Daily Gazette* noted that even fences around the graves in Montague County were shown no mercy. The paper reported that in the eastern agricultural counties, "fences of farmers went down as did the fences of the cattlemen," and noted, "The wanton destruction of farmer's fences in purely agricultural sections has probably dissipated the absurd notion that this thing was a war between farmers and stockmen."[33]

Giles J. Gordon was a member of a well-known frontier family in Montague County. The Gordon Family settled in Montague during the county's early years and refused to be run off by the Indians. Gordon was a teenager in 1859 when he met up with Indians who were afoot, searching for horses to steal. A foot race followed between Gordon and one of the Indians who chased him home, a distance of four or five miles. Giles being fleet on his feet, outran the Indian, reaching the safety of his home. Years later, in 1867, he had another encounter with Indians while horseback and wasn't as lucky. There was a horse race home; his horse wasn't as fast as the Indian's horses, and he was shot seven times with arrows tipped with steel points. His father, Albion Gordon, removed the arrows, but three steel points came off the arrow shafts and stayed in Giles. Ten years later, after suffering great pain, a doctor removed one of the steel points from Giles's back. The other two points stayed with him for the rest of his life.[34]

In 1884 Giles Gordon was a prosperous farmer operating near the Saint Jo Community in Montague County. When Governor Ireland's special legislative session began, a dispatch dated January 19 from Gainesville appeared in newspapers reporting that Giles Gordon of Montague County had cut the fence of Joe Harris in adjoining Cooke County. Joe Harris was the cattleman chosen at the Henrietta Convention to represent pasture men at the peacemakers' meeting held at Postoak. Four months earlier Harris helped negotiate the South Clay County Agreement. This incident of fence cutting by Giles Gordon was apparently a matter of revenge.[35]

Gordon was jailed in Cooke County, where his victim, Joe Harris, was a prominent and well-known citizen. A *San Antonio Light* correspondent from Gainesville reported, "Giles Gordon has been in jail for several days, lives in Montague County and had no cause whatever for doing the deed. If the legislature doesn't do something soon to stop the cutting of fences, cattlemen will stop it by the use of shotgun and Winchester Rifle."

Following Gordon's arrest, strong support for his defense came from Montague, his home county. Seventy citizens published a certificate of good character for Giles Gordon. When he cut Joe Harris's fence, the crime of fence cutting was still a misdemeanor; the legislature had not yet made it a felony. Thus the case was prosecuted as malicious mischief. Misdemeanor convictions usually drew a fine of ten, twenty, or maybe as much as thirty dollars. Recently a fence cutter was captured in Jack County and the governor had paid a thirty-dollar reward for his arrest and conviction. The Jack County cutter went to court, was convicted, and paid a fine of only ten dollars. Gordon's fence-cutting case was different; the Cooke County Court showed no sympathy for him. Although his attorney argued that he only cut the fence in two or three places, during the daytime, and with a hatchet, Gordon received a stiff three-month jail sentence with a fifty-dollar fine for the offense. Such severe punishment for fence cutting under the old statute was unheard of, especially for such a prominent citizen.[36]

Clay County Citizens met in Henrietta to draft a memorial to the legislature with recommendations for solving fence-cutting problems. The memorial had signatures of 173 Clay County residents, many of whom were prominent citizens. They asked for the passage of a law making it a felony to destroy fences and called for legislation to stop the fencing of land not owned. They also requested that the discretion of the commissioners court for managing public roads not be disturbed. This memorial was carried to Austin and read before the legislature by Clay County's Representative Allen K. Swan.[37]

Buffalo Springs is in southeastern Clay County about fifteen miles from Henrietta and was known as the fence cutter's community. Citizens of Buffalo Springs and the county's free-range fence-cutting faction followed the citizens' lead in Henrietta, held a meeting, and drafted their own memorial to the legislature. A newspaper said their memorial was printed as a pamphlet and referred to it as the *Fence Cutters Memorial*. Wilbur Fisk Hogan had come from Alabama, was about 41 years of age, and had a wife and two small sons. He was the postmaster for Buffalo Springs and proprietor of a small store. Following their meeting citizens called on Hogan to deliver the memorial to Austin and to explain their problems to the legislature and governor.[38]

Other than one newspaper account, little information is found to tell us about Hogan's visit to the state capital to plead the farmers' and fence cutters' case. When Hogan arrived in Austin, the free grass faction had lost most of their support in the special legislative session. Most committees and the legislature's leadership were siding with the pasture men's interests. The *Galveston Daily News* reported that Wilbur Hogan arrived in Austin with his pamphlets containing the fence cutters memorial; an excerpt from the memorial he delivered follows:

> We, the subscribers, positively assert that a corporation known as the Red River Cattle Company have wired in a large section of our county lying north and west; also another large section just west of the Red River Cattle Company's enclosure has been wired in by Messer's Ben Cable [Cobb] and brother, and that freeholders, neighbors and communities have been wired in without their consent; that much land of non-residents, as well as some lands of residents, have also been enclosed by wire of said corporation and brothers; that perhaps many as far as we know, the humbler citizens, feeling keenly the effects of the encroachment, backed by capital, and that all the commons that they once enjoyed swept so suddenly away from them, and so many of their rights, liberties and privileges being so suddenly abridged by their highways being closed by gates, drawbars and wire fixtures, and their byways being in many instances wired across, completely rendering them useless between neighbors. Neighborhoods and communities led by unscrupulous parties' have summarily used violence to address their real as well as imaginary wrongs, which continue from bad to worse until armed squads representing the extremists of both sides roam over the neighborhood, and surrounding country, soon culminating in a deadly conflict, in which one of the freeholders in the Red River Cattle Company's enclosures lost his life, leaving a wife and four small children, but be it said, to the credit of both factions, they are willing to contribute bountifully

to their present wants, while the fractured laws of this great commonwealth go unsatisfied and unexecuted, which in some cases, above all others, should be executed to the letter.

There were 150 names on the Buffalo Springs Memorial. On arriving at the state capital, Hogan received a hearing of a sort by members from both the house and senate. According to the *Galveston Daily News*, the meeting was more of a kangaroo court. Hogan made a serious effort to describe his community's problems in a three-hour speech. He was reported to have read several resolutions prepared by the fence cutters of his area and repeated a portion of a statement made by Governor Ireland, which he said partially excused fence cutting. The *Galveston Daily News*, with an obvious bias, reported that Hogan made several good hits. Still, the great body of his presentation was unadulterated rot and was undoubtedly the best entertainment of the session. Wilbur Hogan, the Buffalo Springs merchant, gave the small farmers and his community his best effort, then returned home to Clay County.[39]

When the legislature's special session adjourned, parts of their package addressing the Buffalo Springs community's problems passed. Most barbed wire fences stayed in place, but there were now gates for the persons fenced in, and there were substantial penalties for the pasture man who fenced another's land illegally. Occasional fence-cutting incidents occurred in the years that followed in Clay and the other north Texas counties. Still, it was unusual to find a newspaper story about the fence cutting that was so common in the past. The vast number of farmers or nesters, having suffered the power of pasture men and big money interests, resolved to take a new approach to address their problems and protect their interests. They organized and went to the ballot box for relief.

Farmers in North Texas were active in Patrons of Husbandry, the Texas State Grange, and the Farmers' Alliance. The alliance, however, refrained from entering politics, and their refusal disappointed many of its members. Because of the alliance's reluctance to engage in politics in 1884, southern Clay and Jack Counties' farmers organized a new political body known as the Common Wealth Immigration Society. Their campaign promotion was an appeal on behalf of the man of small means. The editor of the *Rural Citizen*, a Jacksboro newspaper, asked questions of the organization's central committee. What legislation did they propose, and how would it encourage immigration? The committee responded, "By electing members of the State Legislature, who will pass a law prohibiting foreign syndicates and corporation bullionaires [sic] from gobbling up the public domain of Texas, thereby saying to the poor man or man of small means, you must go elsewhere for a home, as this country has been sold to Lord Jumbo, president of the Montezuma Cattle Company, on which to graze his hundred thousand Scottish Poled and Hereford Thorough Bloods." When questioned about the best man for offices, the central committee responded, "The Organization favors men for office who will administer the law, according to law; to Jews and Gentile, rich and poor, purple pomp and tattered raiment, alike. Men who will deliver to Caesar the things that are Caesar's, and unto God the things that are God's." When the November 1884 elections were held and votes counted, the Common Wealth Immigration Society had done quite well. Three of their candidates were elected to offices in Jack County. Pledger Jones was elected county judge, John D. Rains was elected sheriff, and William L. Garvin was elected county treasurer. Rains was reelected and served as sheriff until 1888, when he was killed in a shootout on the Jack County's courthouse square by W. W. Terrell, his brother-in-law.[40]

In 1890 James S. Hogg, a Democrat reformer, ran for Texas governor and was elected with strong support from the small farmers. Hogg's actions battling the railroads and big corporations, and his passage of an alien land law to prohibit land investment by foreigners, were bound to have pleased the men of small means. (Hogg's alien land law was later declared unconstitutional.) The Red River Country's free-range days ended and would never return. Land selling and fence building continued, but now the farmers were the dominant force in Red River Country. By 1890 power was in the hands of the farmer and men of small means, many of whom had been fence cutters. Though not openly admitted, it was painfully evident.

Chapter 5

Settlers and Barbed Wire Come to Brown County

> Those yellow Fish Brand Slickers and the rugged men wearing them made quite an impression on Brownwood's citizens that day. In later years, one old-timer who was present and knew some of the fence cutters affirmed the fact that "only those slickers were yellow, the men wearing them weren't, they came to town looking for a fight.
>
> —Comment of one of Brownwood's old-timers

The Texas legislature created eighteen new counties on its western frontier in 1856, which is when Brown County came into existence. Settlers organized Brown's county government in May 1858, but less than five hundred residents arrived during the county's first ten years of life. J. H. Fowler drove the first cattle to the county in 1856. W. Chandler arrived with slave labor and began farming rich bottomland on Pecan Bayou. Samuel R. Coggin visited the area with Fowler and Chandler before 1854, and he was so impressed with the grasslands that he and his brother Modie Coggin drove cattle to Brown County in 1857. In the 1860s W. F. Brown, Israel Clements, and Brooks W. Lee Sr. arrived and began farming. They produced wheat, corn, and sorghum, but they hauled their wheat to Comanche or San Saba to be milled. Most of the corn and sorghum raised was for livestock feed.

The increase in the cattle population after 1860 was significant, and by 1870 there were twelve large cattle operations with stock grazing on the free range in and around Brown County. Settlers in Brown had migrated from the South, and when the Civil War began, their loyalties were with the Confederacy. Most able-bodied men of Brown County enlisted and served the South. The two Coggin brothers, Samuel and Modi enlisted in Colonel R. T. Allen's 17th Texas Infantry, attached to Henry McCullough's division. After the Civil War, the Coggin brothers partnered with William C. Parks and grazed cattle in Brown County and on open-range country in the west.[1]

In 1869 the Coggin brothers and Parks raised cattle but also contracted cattle trailing, delivering other men's herds to the northern markets. Their partnership grew to be one of the more extensive cattle operations in Texas. It was in the same league as their better-known contemporaries John Chisum, G. W. Slaughter, D. W. Waggoner, and Charles Goodnight.

Indian raids became a regular occurrence after the Civil War, and the cattle business suffered. In 1871 the Coggins suffered huge losses of cattle from Indian depredation. Their cattle grazed on the open range and their herd grew to 25,000 head. In July of that year, the partnership suffered a staggering blow; they lost 7,000 head of cattle to Indians. Looking for protection from the federal government, they moved most of their livestock closer to Fort Concho. Government troops were of little help; they lost over 6,000 head of cattle on Christmas Day. Comanche had a lucrative business supplying the Comanchero trade in New Mexico and decimated their cattle operation. It was reported that as many as 300 Indians were in Texas on one of these raids.

The Coggins recovered by restarting their cattle trailing business. Again, they were buying and selling, rebuilding their herd, and their wealth grew. Anticipating the end of free-range days, they now began buying land along rivers and streams. They soon moved into the banking and mercantile business in Brownwood.[2]

The Hanna family also settled early in Brown County. David, John, James, and R. M. Hanna arrived in 1856 and settled on the Colorado River. They were the first to bring sheep to Brown County. David Hanna was active in community affairs and one of the first four county commissioners elected in Brown. He also served on the county's first grand jury. David joined the Rangers and served under a friend, Captain John Williams. Indians killed Williams in a fight in 1863 at Babyhead Mountain in northern Llano County.[3]

Brooks W. Lee Sr. was a leader among the first settlers and arrived in Brown with his wife in 1858. The county was organized that year, and Lee built a cabin and settled on Pecan Bayou. When the state organized a body of Rangers to offer protection from Indians, Brooks was placed in charge of the small Brown County force and was involved in several Indian fights. He was also with the Confederates at the Dove Creek Indian Fight, where Confederate troops and a Texan militia attacked a band of Kickapoo Indians leaving Texas for Mexico. The Texans were soundly defeated, losing over twenty men in the battle that followed.[4]

Another pioneer family that came to Brown County was the Baughs. David Baugh, the elder, was a Mississippi farmer who fathered fourteen children, ten of whom reached maturity. He left Mississippi, moving his family to Kaufman County, Texas, in 1844, then moved to Brown County before the election in 1858, when the county's organization took place. He became one of the early successful cattlemen of the area. Two of his sons, Levin (Lev) Powell Baugh and Washington Morgan (Morg) Baugh, would make their mark and become legends in Brown County as farmers, cattlemen, Indian fighters, and upholders of the law. The brothers were in several scrapes with Comanche raiders, horse and cattle thieves, and later the fence cutters.

Lev, the older Baugh brother, was part of a frontier defense unit during the Civil War. He was rounding up cattle with cowhands in Comanche County south of Brown County in 1865. A rider came into the cow camp notifying the men that Indians had murdered a family in neighboring Hamilton County. Eleven cattlemen picked up the Indians' trail and pursued the raiding party north, assuming they were Comanche traveling back to their reservation on the headwaters of the Brazos. Gaining on the raiders, they spotted two Indian men and a woman in the distance. The cowhands spurred their horses and rushed toward the Indians, but they approached a large ravine separating them and their prey. The gorge delayed the charge, causing the men to search for a place to cross the chasm. Lev however, riding hell for leather, raced ahead and his horse jumped across a narrow stretch of the ravine.

With an Enfield rifle and brace of pistols, Lev's rapid approach surprised the Indians. As he closed and was within range, he fired his Enfield and killed one of the men instantly. Lev dismounted, firing at the other man with his pistols. The first shot hit him, Lev's second shot missed, and a third shot hit the man again. The Indian clung to his horse, which carried him out of range of Lev's pistols. Remounting, Lev decided to rope the woman. Taking down his rope he spurred his horse. As the chase began, the main body of about twenty-five Indian braves traveling in advance heard the shots and looped back to see what was happening. As the braves returned, the cowhands had crossed the ravine. The fight was about to begin when the Indians spotted one of the cowhands off in the distance. The cowhand had finally found a place his horse could cross the deep ravine and was racing toward the Indians, waving his gun. The Indians saw him and, believing another party of white men were entering the battle, fled. When the dust settled, Lev took the equipment and gear of the Indian he killed. His trophies consisted of a bow, a well-tanned buckskin arrow case with arrows, a rawhide shield, a pocketknife, and a pair of silver tweezers. Lev had a keen interest in Indian artifacts. An old-timer from Brownwood who knew him said he carried the dead Indian's possessions home, and his souvenirs immediately infested the house with lice.[5]

Lev started his cattle herd when he was 16. In 1870 he added farming to his cattle business and prospered. By 1880 Lev added hogs to his livestock interests. He built a rock fence on a tract of his bottomland where there was an abundance of pecans and acorns for hog feed. By 1884 he was raising mules for the market on a large scale. His farming operation produced all he needed to sustain the family and carry on his diverse livestock operation.[6]

Lev's brother, Morg, established a homestead on fertile lands that is now covered by Lake Brownwood. He soon was raising a family and moved their home into Brownwood to be nearer to schools and college. Morg's son, Harvey J. Baugh, benefited from a good education, entered the legal profession, and served on the state's Third Court of Civil Appeals. While living in town, Morg served two terms on the Brownwood City Council. In his early years as a cowhand, Morg worked cattle over Central and West Texas, building his herd. He was one of the first cattlemen in the area to upgrade his herd with

Hereford breeding stock. Over the years he contributed to a better grade of cattle in his part of the state. As his cattle business prospered, he began to buy prime land with good water. Like his brother, Morg began farming and raised wheat, oats, and feed for his livestock.[7]

The Baugh brothers, the Coggins, and the other families formed the bedrock and foundation of Brown County. They braved the elements, fought Indians, and opened the country for growth and settlement by others. Through hard work and perseverance, they gained wealth by Texas standards of the time. As Brown County's rapid growth began, they would fight battles of a different type, trying to preserve what they had acquired. Their future conflicts would be known as Brown County's Barbed Wire War.

During the Civil War, immigration to Texas virtually stopped, then started again at the war's end. However, the massive migration of settlers to Texas occurred after the United States military's campaign brought the Comanche's decisive defeat. Growth then surged. Over 400,000 people immigrated to Texas in 1876. Settlers came by wagon, horseback, and, after 1881, by train. Between June 1876 and June 1878, close to 5 million acres of state land were taken up under the state land laws. The immigrants settled in various sections east of the 100th meridian. Those area's most densely settled were along the line of frontier counties from Cooke, Montague, and Clay, down through Comanche, Brown, and Miles Counties. Many immigrant farmers arrive in Brown County, preempting land, and began plowing their fields. Farmers brought their milk cow, some purchasing small herds of cattle, and others began raising sheep. The few who had pockets full of money bought larger tracts of land, which they considered a bargain. During this surge of migrants, Henry Sanborn, representing the Barbed Fence Company of Illinois, was in Texas selling barbed wire. In only a few years, this new barbed fence material brought a change to ranching in Texas and had a brutal impact on Brown County.[8]

One of these immigrants coming to Brown County was Robert Cypret Parrack. Born in Oregon County, Missouri, in 1852, he grew up among Missouri relatives who fought on both the Union and the Confederate sides in the Civil War. Parrack became a drifter at an early age, hiring on and riding as a jockey for two gamblers traveling through Missouri. These men paid him a small sum for riding and caring for their horses, and he got to keep all he won wagering. Parrack knew which horse to bet on because the gamblers rigged many of the races.

Leaving horse racing and his gambling friends in Missouri, Parrack traveled to Texas. He arrived about 1873 and worked as a drover, trailing cattle to the northern market. He also worked on a Brown County farm owned by Mrs. James Earp, a widow. Her husband, James, had come to Brown County in 1863, settling on Pecan Bayou above the mouth of Jim Ned Creek. James Earp and J. M. Johnson cleared and were farming 100 acres of land in 1870. When James died he left his property to his wife, who managed the farm and raised a daughter named Mary.[9]

Parrack worked on the farm for Mrs. Earp following her husband's death. It wasn't long, though, before Parrack found more alluring and profitable employment with the Causey brothers and their buffalo hunting outfit operating out of Brownwood. His job with the Causeys was a skinner, earning him twenty-five cents for each hide he peeled off a buffalo.

By the winter of 1875, Parrack left the Causey brothers and joined with a larger outfit owned by Russell and Dalison. Their main camp was fifteen miles from Fort Concho. Working with this group of hunters, Parrack became a shooter and earned forty-five dollars a month killing buffalo. Parrack used a rifle with a smaller bore than most buffalo hunters, a .45-caliber Sharp. He preferred the .45 caliber over the big .50s that many of the hunters were using. By 1878 Parrack had worked for four buffalo hunting outfits. During the spring and summer, he found employment working cattle trailing jobs. Buffalo hides were at their prime during the winter months, so when springtime arrived and the cattle drives north began, he hired on as a drover, trailing cattle to Kansas. Parrack relates that on one of his trips to Abilene, the outfit's cowhands were attacked at night by the town's crooks. Parrack said there was a shootout in the dark of night, and he shot at the flash from the enemy's gun. When the battle was over, a large number of men were dead. The law didn't know who the shooters were, so no charges were filed.[10]

In 1882 Parrack returned to Brown County where he married Mary Earp. After his marriage Parrack tried to settle down. He owned about two hundred head of cattle grazing on the free range and purchased a 160-acre farm on

Jim Ned Creek. This tract of land had an old cabin and a few improvements. The newlywed couple began to farm and planned to grow their cattle business. Soon, their free-range cattle business encountered trouble; barbed wire fencing arrived and was being strung across Brown County.[11]

When Parrack first arrived in Brown County, he developed a close friendship with the Lovell family. David Franklin Lovell, the elder, was born in Alabama and years later came to Texas. His arrival date isn't found, but David and his wife Sarah Jane were in Brown County the year after the Civil War began. Their son James B. Lovell was born in 1862. The following year, a daughter, Sue Ellen, was born, and Sarah Jane died after childbirth. James grew up in Brown County on his dad's farm and was known as Jim by neighbors and friends. In 1880 James still lived with his father and farmed near Byrds Store, north of Brownwood. The 1880 United States Census lists him as a laborer.[12]

At the age of 22, James Lovell moved to the community of Thrifty, a short distance down the road from Byrds Store. It was there he was elected constable of Precinct No. 6 and became an officer of the law with as much authority as the county's sheriff in his precinct. As a lawman, James was able to legally carry a handgun, a privilege Texas state law stripped from other citizens in 1871.

Other friends of Parrack's were the three Mathews brothers—Asa, Thomas, and John. Family and neighbors called Asa Samuel Mathews "Ace." Ace Mathews was elected justice of the peace in the nearby town of Thrifty. In 1875 he married Georgia Ann Lovell, James Lovell's half-sister, and became the brother-in-law of the constable from Byrds Store.[13]

William Amos Roberts, who grew up in Brown County, was another friend of Bob Parrack. Amos's father Archibald came to Brown from Shelby County, Texas, in 1860, bringing Amos and his family with him. Census records show that Amos and his brother Thomas grew up to be cattlemen. Archibald's occupation was listed as "farming" in the 1870 US Census, but Thomas, the older son, was listed as "raising cattle" and Amos as "driving cattle." The brothers made their living as cattlemen during the strong cattle markets and grazed their herd free on the state's open range. Their cattle business was probably devastated when barbed wire and the drought arrived. Most of Brown County's land with water was sold and fenced.[14]

In the 1880s land sales and fencing with barbed wire became major issues. The large land sales and fence building brought several activist organizations to Brown County. The Farmer's Alliance was founded in nearby Lampasas County. In 1883 one of the local alliances was organized in Brown County and is said to have had a fence cutter's wing.[15]

Another Brown County activist group organized was known as the Texas Land League. In December 1883 the *Austin Weekly Statesman* reported two men were shot, then another narrowly escaped being stabbed at Cross Cut, a tough little community just north of Byrds Store in Brown County. The newspaper's same story closed saying that Saturday night a body of men at Cross Cut, antagonistic to large pastures, organized themselves into a Texas Land League Society. This organization adopted a petition, and their secretary, J. M. Perry Jr., mailed copies to the legislature, newspapers, and other counties. The Land League was opposed to a herd law, wanted no gates on any class of public roads, and wanted public access to streams and rivers on demand. They defined their version of a lawful fence, and they demanded a penalty for those who did not comply. They wanted severe punishment for any fence owner who enclosed land not his or under his control. They urged citizens to meet in their communities and express their views to prevent the land monopoly. Following its creation, the Land League held its meetings at the Brown County Courthouse. This Brown County organization, referred to by some as the Fence-Cutters Association, never grew or gained prominence. Their existence and presence showed up, however, in North Texas when the fence-cutting war flared in Clay, Jack, and Montague Counties.[16]

No record tells with certainty when barbed wire first arrived in Brown County. Some of the county's immigrant farmers were probably using barbed wire in the late 1870s. One source says that Lev Baugh was an innovative farmer and the first to introduce barbed wire in Brown County, but there are no details or documentation. Several local histories mention barbed wire in neighboring Coleman County, first used in 1876 by Clark Mann on Jim Ned Creek. Jim Ned Creek flows across the county line into northwestern Brown County. Mann fenced 640 acres of land with barbed wire. Lee Mobley, an old-timer, said Mann purchased this first barbed wire in Fort Worth at seven dollars per hundred pounds.[17]

In 1879 cattleman William Day enclosed a large pasture in Coleman County with barbed wire. Day purchased 7,200 acres of Brazoria County School Land, freighted in barbed wire and cedar post from Austin, and employed twenty men to build his four-strand fence. As Day was building his fence, Brownwood's Coggin brothers started fencing land owned in Coleman and Brown counties.[18]

Free-range men in the Brown and the surrounding area opposed the fencing of the open range. The San Saba Commissioners Court petitioned the Texas legislature in 1879, to make it unlawful to fence with barbed wire or own a barbed wire fence. Of course that never occurred.[19]

In 1880, there were still 64,000 acres of unappropriated school land scattered across Brown County but soon this land was occupied and fenced. The county's population grew from 544 residents in 1870 to 8414 in 1880, and small farms' development was rapid. Wool became an important commodity in the county, and more sheepmen arrived and built fences. By 1883, barbed wire was in use throughout Brown County, with more fences built each day.[20]

The Coggin brothers acquired and enclosed a large land tract along Clear Creek in 1880, about twelve miles from Brownwood. They established the Mesquite Ranch on this fertile tract of land. The ranch was first used for pasturing purebred Durham cattle, but later much of the ranch was farmed and producing wheat. As the Coggin brothers started building fences in Brown County, Brooks Lee Sr. began building fences. In late 1883 large tracts of land in the county had been purchased by investors, divided, fenced, and rented to sharecroppers. Small farms were surrounded by barbed wire, and farm residents were having problems. Roads were fenced across. Entering and leaving properties became difficult, and small landowners lost access to their water sources and free grazing for their livestock.[21]

The first fence cutting recorded in the area was in the spring of 1883 when fence cutters destroyed a stretch of fencing on the vast Coggin Ranch and destroyed fences on Brooks Lee's ranch in southwest Brown County. By the summer of 1883, pastures all across Brown and the adjoining counties were experiencing fence-cutting problems. Thurmond and Houston had four miles of their fence cut. Their ranch covered 2,300 acres of land, with the fences being cut on three occasions. In August another cattle operation, Hardeman and Taylor, fenced over 2,000 acres of pasture, and their fences were cut. E. J. Brewer's pasture enclosed 1,280 fenced acres. He made an effort to accommodate his neighbors by placing gates wherever requested. Brewer's fences were cut twice. The third time, many of the gates and a large number of his posts and rails were burned.[22]

Pioneer David Baugh acquired close to 4,000 acres of land when he came to Brown County in 1858, and his widow, Mrs. Pencey Baugh, now managed the ranch. Her fences were cut twice during the summer of 1883. Her older son Lev owned close to 2,000 acres near the junction of Jim Ned Creek and Pecan Bayou and built a fence on the upper side of this land. The fence wasn't an enclosure but a drift fence. The drift fence stretched above the valley and repelled strays and wintering cattle drifting down from the northern counties that grazed on his property. Lev's drift fence was cut and fence posts and staves burned. By midsummer of 1883, Brown County's fence-cutting war had begun.[23]

There was a large and growing population of sheep in Brown County in 1883, and the Coggin brothers were active in marketing sheep and buying and shipping wool; 780,000 pounds of wool was produced and shipped from the county the previous year. Sheep were profitable, but a recent state law forced the sheepmen to buy land and build fence. This law, promoted by free-range cattlemen, was passed and made it illegal to graze sheep on land not owned or leased. Sheepmen were now buying and fencing all the grazing land they could finance. Brown County's well-to-do cattlemen weren't the only ones suffering. The free-range cattlemen and fence cutters despised sheep and their owners. The sheepmen's fences were cut, their grass and buildings burned, and their sheep killed.[24]

Late in the summer of 1883, Lev Baugh and his brother fenced a large pasture on Jim Ned Creek and Pecan Bayou, north of Brownwood. While riding this new fence line, Lev found a note nailed on one of the fence posts that read, "Mr. Baugh, take down this fence; if you don't, we will cut it, and if we cut it and a drop of cutters blood is spilled, your life will pay the forfeit."

Settlers and Barbed Wire Come to Brown County 73

Lev Baugh fought Indians and cattle thieves during his younger life and was as tough as a boot. He wasn't intimidated by the note. He scribbled a response that read, "You cowardly cur, this is my fence, and you let it alone." He signed his name on the note and nailed it back on the post. The following month, Lev Baugh's fence was cut between each post by eight to thirty men, depending on the newspaper account you read. The fence cutter's note to Lev, and his note to the man he called a cowardly cur, was the beginning of an episode of fence-cutting actions and a feud. Bitter feelings, and continuing fence cutting, would later lead to a killing.

Soon after Lev found the note, he had an encounter with wire cutters on his fence line. The *Fort Worth Daily Gazette* dated November 10 reported, "Mr. L. P. Baugh caught eight men cutting his pasture fence last Wednesday night, four of whom he recognized. He called out to them to stop, and they fired some twenty or thirty shots at him."

This incident was also reported in the *Galveston Daily News*, saying the cutters were trying to kill Baugh for fear of exposure. The Galveston paper said the following day that Lev Baugh was in Brownwood carrying his shotgun. Citizens and the newspaper expected there would be further trouble and a killing. The next week there was another report in a San Antonio paper saying cutters came in on the night of November 13. They cut six miles of the Baugh's fence.

A group of businessmen, prominent cattlemen, and merchants called a meeting for all interested parties in Brownwood the following Saturday. The meeting was to discuss the wire fence problems, land issues, and try to bring peace. The mass meeting took place in Brownwood, and close to two hundred citizens gathered to discuss the fence problem. They drafted and debated resolutions; some were adopted. Most agreed that the state's land policies, adopted in the past by the legislature, were wrong. They acknowledged that just weeks before this meeting, Governor John Ireland had announced his call of a special legislative session to deal with the fence-cutting crisis, which was now statewide. Citizens at the meeting disapproved of the destruction of property. They resolved no more fences were to be cut, nor would large pastures be fenced before the called legislative session. All main roads should be declared first-class roads and would not be obstructed by fences. New pastures fenced would be limited to 640 acres, but existing enclosures already fenced would be exempt. Blinds of plank, or rail, would be placed on all barbed wire fences. The legislature would be asked to make cutting a pasture fence enclosing less than 640 acres a felony. Many at the meeting wanted a repeal of the general corporation law and no charter given to corporations. They wanted no state-owned land sold to aliens. Members of an appointed committee presented a majority report. A minority report was presented and proposed protection only for those who owned the land they fenced, and compensation was to be paid to owners that took down their fences. No person would be allowed to fence or retain any property in his pasture he did not own. Those at the meeting adopted the majority report.

Brown County citizens expected this meeting would give them a reprieve from the destruction and the violence occurring, but no reprieve was to happen. A few days following the mass meeting, a newspaper reported the cutting of Mr. Driskill, Mr. Glass, and Mr. Burch's fences. This incident caused surprise and astonishment in the community. The *Galveston Daily News* reported communism was the basis of the trouble there. "The wire cutters frequently say no man has the right to improve land to rent to others, and water and grass are the free gifts of God, and thus free to man."[25]

Several cattlemen gave up fencing their pastures in Brown County. Captain S. H. Woods and J. W. Driskill took down their pasture fences and rolled up the wire to save. A sixty-acre pasture owned by Col. William Martin, a Brownwood banker, was soon cut to shreds. A Mr. Dunman's rail fence enclosing three hundred acres was destroyed, and a rail was hung in a tree near his house as a warning not to rebuild.[26]

On the night of November 28, 1883, freighters traveling north from Brownwood stopped and pitched camp near Byrds Store. As darkness set in, a band of about forty men rode into their camp. They warned the freighters they should keep quiet, as the group had some fence business to attend to and they didn't want any interference. They rode out of the freighters' camp, and the next morning George T. Graham's 640-acre pasture fence near Byrds Store was cut to pieces. Graham's pasture enclosed the 640 acres, described as reasonable by the resolution drafted at the November 17 meeting

Settlers and Barbed Wire Come to Brown County

in Brownwood. Soon after word arrived of the cutting of Graham's fence, more news of destruction reached Brownwood. The town's citizens learned the tenant houses on ex-congressman G. W. Jones's farm were burned and that Colonel Bustin's farm, which was also rented to tenants farmers, had his tenant houses burned to the ground during the night.[27]

In those troubled days of 1883, there was resentment of the wealthy class by many Brown County citizens. Brothers Samuel R. and Modie J. Coggin undoubtedly were representatives of the wealthy class in Brown County. The brothers owned large landholdings in and out of the county. By the 1880s they had expanded from land and cattle into commercial businesses in Brownwood. They founded one of the first banks in Brownwood, the Coggin Brothers & Company. The bank grew and they formed a partnership opening a general merchandise and dry goods business, known as the Howards, Wooten & Coggin Company. This company sold fancy goods, clothing, hats, caps, ladies and gents furnishing goods, staple goods, groceries, Queens Ware, and everything found in a first-class general merchandise store. They sold a line of Old Hickory wagons and bought and freighted cotton, wool, and pecans. The brothers also owned an old flour mill built years past on the outskirts of Brownwood.

The Coggin brothers and Claiborne Parks, their partner in the cattle business, built a large two-story rock commercial building known as the Coggins-Parks Building. It was on the corner of North Center and Broadway. Except for their flour mill and the wagon yard, the Coggin brothers' Brownwood businesses operated out of this rock structure. Being community leaders and philanthropists, the Coggins constructed the upper floor of this large rock building as the Brownwood Opera House. Their opera house provided a dual venue of entertainment for the community. Inmates had burned the Brown County Courthouse and jail. Due to inadequacies of a leased temporary courthouse building, the county rented the Coggins' opera house and used the large room at the top of the Coggins-Parks Building as their temporary courtroom. There were cultural productions for the cultured citizens and district court activities as entertainment for the rest of the interested local population. Despite the growth of the Coggins' commercial interests in Brownwood, those businesses did not replace the brothers' land and livestock business.[28]

At the beginning of December 1883, an employee from the Coggins' Mesquite Ranch came rushing into Brownwood. The ranch hand told Sheriff William Adams and the brothers that a large band of fence cutters were gathering at the Mesquite Ranch. They intended to cut the fences in broad daylight. Sheriff Adams gathered a posse of about thirty armed men made up of merchants and men off the street. The posse rode to the Coggins ranch, where they overawed and scattered the fence cutters. This encounter at the Mesquite Ranch didn't stifle the cutters' malicious destruction. Soon after this encounter, the Coggins' flour mill burned, and a school located on the Coggins ranch was closed.[29]

Ranchers and business owners of Brown County decided it was time to take decisive action to stop this property destruction. Stockmen of the county, referred to as the Citizens Committee, met with Sheriff William Adams. Reluctantly, Adams agreed to travel as the spokesman for a group and warn suspected cutters and friends that their destructive activities must stop. Friday morning, December 7, 1883, a party of twenty-six men, composed of merchants and stockmen, rode out of Brownwood to the county's rural areas armed with rifles and shotguns. They traveled across Brown County, visiting homes of known fence cutters and persons suspected of being cutters. The Fort Worth newspaper published an account sent in by their Brownwood correspondent describing what occurred: "Merchants and cattlemen of this town and County mounted their horses and shotguns in hand rode all over the county and saw men who had been suspected of fence cutting. They visited the homes of five or six men. They notified the owners that they had been accused of burning houses and destroying the fences. The good law-abiding citizens of the county wanted the thing stopped. These men were also informed that the party had been appointed as a committee, to wait on them, that if further depredations were committed, they would be held responsible therefor."[30]

Members of the Citizens Committee described in the newspapers were not identified. Still, it's a sure bet that Sam and Modie Coggin, Lev and Morg Baugh, and others suffering the destruction wrought on Brown County rode at the front of the party. Lev Baugh, the old Indian fighter, was a salty character, tough as rawhide. He and his family had suffered multiple fence cuttings, and he was shot at when he discovered cutters on his fence line. In years past Lev had gained a reputation of dealing a rough hand to cattle and horse thieves when the formal justice system wasn't working. John Henry Brown in his 1890 volume titled *Indian Wars and Pioneers of Texas*, described Levin Baugh: "He was often called on to run down lawless characters. Mr. Baugh always insisted on allowing the law to take its way unless the personal security of a citizen was threatened, but when this was the case, he became an advocate for those important adjuncts of the court, the rope, and the six-shooter."[31]

Assuming Lev rode at the head of the group and spoke for the committee, you can imagine his warning to those who were visited. And there were surely vile threats from other party members, who suffered fence cutting and arson by those they visited. The *Brownwood Bulletin*, the county's local newspaper, came closer to the truth of their messages. The paper said the word was delivered to the fence cutters "if any more wire fences were cut, the parties who were visited would pay the penalty with their lives whether guilty or not and without a trial at law."[32]

After two days of traveling across the county, visiting homes of fence cutters and of individuals suspected of pasture burning, the Citizens Committee returned to Brownwood Saturday night. Newspapers noted that the dry, droughty conditions the rangeland suffered enjoyed a reprieve as the men returned to their home. There was rain across Brown County. The committee assumed they now had the fence cutters' attention and accomplished their mission with a feeling of satisfaction. They did have the fence cutters' attention—much more attention than they expected.

On Monday morning, well before daylight, word came that fence cutters were on their way to Brownwood to lay the town in ashes and kill particular residents. Word spread that as many as two hundred fence cutters were traveling to Brownwood. Local businesspeople and the cattlemen who lived in Brownwood grabbed their firearms and prepared to make a stand. The citizens established their base with a secure vantage point for a shootout. One group gathered upstairs in the opera house, on the second floor of the Coggins large stone building. The opera house was soon an arsenal. Couriers went out to the country, and men were coming in to join the town's defense. Reinforcements arrived, and by midmorning armed men ready for the fence-cutters' assault numbered about fifty. One author speaking of this encounter said that morning Joseph Weakley's hardware store sold every gun and round of ammunition in stock. Sharpshooters with rifles found vantage points on top of the town's commercial buildings. A newspaper claimed that several men professing to be neutral rode out to meet the fence cutters as they approached the town and made an effort to compromise the trouble, but their attempt failed.[33]

On that rainy Monday morning, about eleven o'clock, thirty-seven men or more, depending on the newspaper reports, most wearing the famous cowboy's yellow slickers, rode into Brownwood. They and their leader, a one-armed man named J. B. Scruggin (Scoggin), dismounted with their rifles and were met by Sheriff William Adams. The sheriff ordered the group to stack arms, but they insisted the men in the opera house stack their arms. After violent threats and much bluster, the fence cutters surrendered their firearms to the sheriff. He led them into Brown County's temporary courthouse.[34]

That morning was the grand opening of what has been referred to over the years as Brownwood's Fence Cutters Convention. Inside the courthouse the men who rode into Brownwood opened their meeting with a barrage of inflammatory speeches. After blustering and threats, the fence cutters sent a delegation to talk with the men in the opera house. The fence cutters demanded those inside the Coggin Building stack arms and apologize for their past week's visits and threatening actions. Those men barricaded in the opera house refused to surrender their weapons. They sent the fence-cutters' representatives back to the courthouse with a message telling the group they could go to hell.

Later the cutters sent another message to the opera house saying they wanted assurance and protection from mob law. Receiving this request, a team of negotiators from the opera house made up of J. S. Cleveland, Henry Ford, Judge Charles H. Jenkins, and County Attorney William H. Mayes went to the temporary courthouse. Negotiations were heated, but these men conveyed that the committee making the visits the past week had gone out in the interest of good government and wanted nothing more than the country's good.

Settlers and Barbed Wire Come to Brown County

They meant to harm no one, but they wanted the destruction of property and fence cutting stopped. They intended to give aid enforcing the law. A second team, Sheriff William Adams, A. D. McCullough, and Pierce McKinney, was designated to get a written statement from both groups for publication. The team drafted a statement that afternoon. The *Brownwood Banner* was the first to report the meeting, but they couldn't get a copy of the group's written statement for publication. The paper reported the substance of the agreement reading:

> The first party [committee of cattlemen] desired peace and good order in the county; that by their action they intended only the good of the country and did not intend or desire to do anyone harm, and did not want anyone punished for any offense except by the due course of law; that they were opposed to mob law and that no violence was done to any person on who they called, and would assure them that no one, here-to-fore or hereafter accused of any crime whatever, should be punished without a fair and impartial trial. They further asked the cooperation of the second party [fence cutters] in the enforcement of the law and the suppression of the lawlessness. This was accepted as a good and sufficient explanation, and they [the cutters] agreed to give their assistance in the cause of law and order, and further agreed for the parties to go to their respective homes with good feelings toward each other and assurance that no one would be molested.[35]

Late in the afternoon, when the final agreement was reached, the fence cutters gathered their arms, mounted their horses, and rode out of Brownwood, again wearing their yellow slickers. Those yellow Fish Brand Slickers and the rugged men wearing them made quite an impression on Brownwood's citizens that day. In later years one old-timer who was present and knew some of the fence cutters affirmed that "only those slickers were yellow, the men wearing them weren't, they came to town looking for a fight."

That evening as darkness set in, Brownwood's large stone flour mill, belonging to J. D. Kinnebrew, was in flames, and was a total loss in less than an hour. The damage was estimated at $15,500. The adjoining building housing McCloud's grocery store was also on fire, but citizens were able to salvage many of the grocery store's goods.[36]

The Austin newspaper reported the Brownwood telegraph was out of order. However, word of the fence cutters' visit to Brownwood reached the state capital. The telegraph was put back in working order and Governor John Ireland sent a telegram to Brown County Sheriff William Adams. The governor inquired about the trouble between the fence cutters and citizens and offered assistance from the state. Sheriff Adams telegraphed a short reply back to the governor saying, "Everything is quiet, and no assistance is needed at the present."

Adams was reluctant to bring Rangers into Brown County; many of his constituents supported the fence cutters. Receiving the sheriff's response, Governor Ireland met with Adjutant General Wilburn King and instructed him to immediately dispatched Rangers to Brown if the troubles revived.

Fence cutters were a party to an agreement at the mass meeting in Brownwood, November 17, 1883, then another meeting and another agreement in December. These two agreements didn't stop the cutters' destructive work, but fence cutting did slow as winter came. Bitter cold, freezing weather from the north came blowing down into Brown County, lasting through the winter months. The *Austin Weekly Statesman* reported that livestock in Brown County suffered greatly due to the drought, the cold, and the scarcity of grass on the range. This newspaper's story closed by commenting, "The fence troubles in this county have ceased. The cause of this is that there are no more pastures at present in the county to cut. The people of this county are awaiting the action of the legislature on fence cutting troubles with much anxiety."[37]

Chapter 6

Governor Ireland Calls a Special Legislative Session, and Representative Odom Explains the Problem

> There are now $10,000,000 in fences destroyed by the nippers and property damages to the amount of $100,000,000 to the state by these ragtag and bobbed tailed ruffians, these hell-hounds of Texas who go around at nighttime cutting and destroying the property of their neighbors.
> —Representative T. L. Odom, addressing an attempt to reduce penalties in a fence-cutting bill

Thomas Lawson Odom came to Bexar County, Texas, from Conechu County, Alabama, in 1853 with his family. He settled northwest of San Antonio near where Bandera stands today and owned a shingle-making business and sawmill. Odom enlisted as a private in the Confederate Service in 1863, joining J. O. Adams's company of the cavalry. His unit patrolled the Third Frontier District around Fredericksburg, arresting deserters and enforcing conscription laws.[1]

When the Civil War ended, the South Texas cattle business became profitable and was growing. T. L. Odom moved his investments into cattle and the cattle trailing industry. Thomas L. Odom, now respectfully called Colonel, and Garland G. Odom his oldest son were now cattlemen. By 1876 the Odoms had cattle grazing in Tom Green and Runnels Counties. In 1877 Colonel Odom and son Garland drove four thousand head of cattle from South Texas to Runnels and adjacent counties to graze the strong native grass. T. L. Odom purchased land near Fort Chadbourne as early as 1874, but much of the grasslands his cattle grazed were land owned by the state of Texas and railroads. But the Odoms' free grazing business soon changed. Other cattlemen were buying land and building fence. Robert K. Wylie, another Runnels County cattleman, began fencing and enclosed twelve sections by 1879. Seeing free grazing was ending, T. L. Odom changed his operation, buying more land and barbed wire.[2]

As the Odoms were moving cattle to this prime Runnels County grassland, another cattleman, John McEwen Formwalt, moved to Runnels. He also brought cattle to Runnels in 1874, joining his brother Coke H. Formwalt. John Formwalt was grazing cattle in Runnels in 1879 when he was elected Runnels County's first sheriff. As sheriff he served the county along with T. L. Odom, who was by then one of the Runnels County commissioners. John Formwalt, the tall and lanky cattleman, stood six foot, four inches and served as the county's sheriff for twelve turbulent years. John M. Formwalt became a lifelong friend of the Odom family. In the years that followed, he joined Colonel Odom and his son Garland in their battle with fence cutters. Some of Formwalt's encounters with the cutters were brutal clashes.[3]

Samuel A. Maverick owned the old Fort Chadbourne and the surrounding property. While Odom and his family lived in Bexar County, there was a social, or possibly a business, connection between the prominent Maverick family and the Odom family. Samuel died in 1870, and in 1877 his wife Mary Maverick sold the Fort Chadbourne buildings and tract of land to Odom's wife Lucinda for $500 in gold coins. With the land purchase and the old fort's buildings, Fort Chadbourne became the Odom's O-D Ranch headquarters. Now with the old fort their residence and headquarters, Odom's land purchases in the area accelerated, and he acquired ranch land in what today are Runnels, Coke, Nolan, and Taylor Counties. Colonel Odom and son Garland organized the Odom-Luckett Land & Livestock Company in 1879, and Garland Odom became the general manager. The Colonel brought Henry H. Luckett, his son-in-law, into the ranching enterprise.

As the Odoms were buying and leasing more land, settlers were arriving in the Fish Creek area, north of the Odoms' ranch. The settlers preempted small tracts, farmed, and were grazing cattle and sheep on the railroad and state-owned lands.[4]

By 1882 T. L. Odom was a director of an Abilene bank, which later became the First National Bank of Abilene, and was the commissioner of Precinct 3 in Runnels County. He was elected as the state representative for House District Seventy-Eight on November 7, 1882. Odom's legislative district covered Runnels, Llano, Concho, McCullough, and Coleman Counties, and he served on the powerful Stock Raising Committee, chaired by Representative J. N. Browning from Clarendon. Odom had common interests with J. N. Browning and other Texas Panhandle big cattlemen. He also had strong relations with the cattlemen in South Texas, developed during his years in Bexar and Medina Counties. He was a strong advocate for law and order. In the 1883 regular legislative session, there was an attempt to reduce the adjutant general's appropriation and cut the Frontier Battalion's Ranger budget to what the newspapers claimed would be a level of inefficiency. Odom and J. N. Browning took on the issue, fought a budget battle, and maintained the funding level the Appropriation Committee had recommended for the Rangers.[5]

The Odoms had acquired forty-two thousand acres of ranch land by 1883. Their holdings of purchased and leased grassland continued to grow to over ninety thousand acres. Some of the Odom's properties were purchased through delinquent tax sales conducted by his friend, Runnels County Sheriff John Formwalt. When the Odoms purchased ranch land, they usually bought land with water, and much of the property acquired was in the Fish Creek, Oak Creek, and Valley Creek watersheds.[6]

Robert K. Wylie of Ballinger was the first cattleman to construct a barbed wire fence when barbed wire arrived in the area. Wiley had acquired land on both sides of the Colorado River in the 1870s, out of tracts deeded to Germans in the Fisher Miller Grant. By 1879 Robert Wylie fenced in ten or twelve sections of prime cattle country and brought in Durham bulls to upgrade his cattle. His barbed wire fence was one of the first wire fences of any consequence built in this western part of Texas.[7]

After Wylie fenced his land, the Odoms saw the many benefits and began fencing their growing ranch. By the 1880s open-range grasslands were overstocked and overgrazed. Drought conditions had set in, and Colonel Odom built more fences to protect his grass. One such fence was a drift fence stretching across the Oak Creek and Fish Creek watersheds. This long drift fence reached all the way to the community of Silver in the northwest part of what is now Coke County. The drift fence restricted free grazing and watering of livestock owned by small cattlemen and homesteaders north of the Odoms' O-D Ranch and quickly caused anger and bitter feelings. With the drought, short grass, and lack of stock water, there was soon fence cutting, causing a war between a group later known as the Fish Creek Gang and the Odom family. With their cattle fenced off from grass and water, the settlers began cutting Odom's fences, with damages quickly multiplying.[8]

In late 1883 drought conditions pushed fence-cutting problems to their peak with fence cutting occurring in over half of Texas counties. Runnels County suffered from the destruction, with the vast Odom O-D Ranch being the main target of the Fish Creek Gang. The fence cutters cut long gaps out of Odom's forty miles of drift fence. As would be expected, Representative T. L. Odom was in frequent contact with Governor John Ireland on his fence-cutting problems. Soon violence and killings over fence cutting was occurring in other parts of the state.

The shootout between cowhands and fence cutters up in Clay County was only one case of a fence cutter death; there were more across the state in 1883. Adjutant General Wilburn King traveled to North Texas to meet with citizens and learn more about causes of fence cutting and the violent acts that occurred. This epidemic of fence cutting, violence, and destruction of property was causing great damage to the state's economy. Clay County's Representative A. K. Swan, Representative T. L. Odom from Runnels, and Representative N. R. Lindsey representing Comanche and Brown Counties were all pleading with Governor John Ireland for help with fence cutting. Adjutant General Wilburn King returned from his trip and reported to the governor.

Governor John Ireland issued a proclamation on October 15, 1883, calling for a special session of the Eighteenth Texas Legislature to meet

Governor Ireland Calls a Special Legislative Session

in Austin and begin on January 8, 1884. Several issues besides fence cutting were in the governor's call, but the main charge was "To consider, and provide a remedy for wanton destruction of fences." In December of 1883, the month before the legislature was to convene, Representative Odom was preparing to fence seventeen sections of land. He purchased and freighted to his ranch wagonloads of barbed wire, fence posts, and staves for the project.[9]

Weeks before the representative left his ranch for the special legislative session in Austin, fence cutters struck another blow to Odom's Ranch. W. G. Hunt related the story of Representative Odom's misfortune while in Nashville. Hunt had traveled to Nashville, Tennessee, buying liquor for his wholesale business in Abilene. His story was first published in the *Nashville American*, then followed in the *San Antonio Light* and other Texas newspapers: "Mr. Odom, the representative from Mr. Hunt's district, bought about $12,000 worth of posts and wire to fence 17 square miles of land. A large force of cowboys collected together, brought all the posts to one place, made an immense funeral pyre, upon which they placed the valuable coils of wire, and fired the whole as a burnt offering to the days that were fast passing by when they were lords of all they surveyed."[10]

As if this destructive act failed to convey the fence cutter's message, they hung a fence post in a tree near Odom's home with a penciled note nailed to the post that read, "Notice. . . . Here you hang shot, and if you don't spool your wire and stop this fence you will get just what this fence post got. We mean business. We don't intend to let any fences in this country stand, and if you think we don't mean business go on with your fence. Your Friends."

The *Fort Worth Daily Gazette* reported a similar incident occurring on a fence-building project at the L. B. Harris ranch, south of Odom's ranch on the Colorado River. Odom's neighbor, Leasial B. Harris, had brought cattle to this grassland in 1872 and by 1880 had established a massive cattle operation in what is now Coke County. Twelve thousand cedar posts and staves with twenty thousand pounds of barbed wire were stacked and burned on the Harris Ranch. Smoke was seen nine miles away. Governor Ireland responded to these two criminal atrocities and published a special notice over his seal in prominent state newspapers. Ireland offered a $500 reward for the arrest and conviction of the offenders and cited these cases of burning the fence materials as felony offenses subject to confinement in the penitentiary.[11]

Representative Odom placed his fence building and ranch work on hold and prepared to go to Austin and represent House District Seventy-Eight in the legislature's special session. Governor Ireland's charge to the session was to find a solution to the state's fence-cutting problem. The house and senate were to convene on January 8, 1884, and Representative Odom had some strong proposals to offer, prompted by his experience with fence cutters.

Many citizens and local officials across the state believed fence cutting and violence would cease once the legislature's special session began. Various factions would have their hearing and their problems dealt with during the legislature's meeting. There were even peace treaties of a sort drafted between the cutters and cattlemen in Clay and Brown Counties. Still, there was no peace or halt in the destruction and violence. Fence cutting and violence intensified. County officials, lawyers, persons of influence, lobbyists, and newspaper reporters swarmed into Austin for Governor Ireland's called legislative session. Most major newspaper across the nation had a representative in the state's capital to watch the Texas legislature try to solve the state's barbed wire crisis.[12]

As the crowd arrived in Austin for the special session, fence-cutting activities around Travis County intensified. Near the Williamson-Travis County line, fence cutters destroyed four miles of fence belonging to William Robbins in one night. Robbins owned all of the land in the enclosed pasture, having recently purchased the property from Zimpelman & Company of Austin. Robbins and his son were planning to stock the ranch with purebred cattle. Willis Avery, an elderly Texas veteran, and General Griffith had fence cut the same night. Griffith's fence enclosed only a peach orchard and a small field where he was growing hay. Bud Driskill, a prominent cattleman and Austin citizen with a horse pasture on the outskirts of town, had his fence cut Saturday night while a mass meeting was being held in Austin denouncing fence cutters.[13]

As the special session was to begin, political groups and associations came to Austin to meet and lobby fence-cutting legislation. The Greenback Party was in Austin and made it known that the Democratic Party was in power when the state's land was being recklessly sold off and when fence building began. Except for Alexander Terrell, Austin's senator, little was heard from Democrats other than that they were opposed to the lawlessness of fence cutting. But Senator Terrell claimed he had legislation drafted to solve the state's fence-cutting problems.

The state's small party of Republicans had merged with the Greenback Party in 1882, and the Greenback Party had nominated George W. Jones as their candidate for Texas governor. Jones, a lawyer from Bastrop County, ran against John Ireland and was soundly defeated in the governor's race. George Jones was a real firebrand. One newspaper accused Jones and his party's teachings of causing the fence-cutting problem in Brown, Coleman, and San Saba Counties. Jones and his followers frequently argued that the land, air, and water were gifts of God and were free for use by all men. Jones and the Greenback Party demanded the repeal of the existing laws that authorized land sales, called for a maximum of 160 acres to be sold only to settlers, and opposed the marketing of land to nonresident aliens and corporations. The party strongly opposed a herd law, which would require livestock owners to keep their stock on land they owned or leased. The Greenback Party was considered by many to be the fence cutter party.[14]

The Farmers' Alliance, an organization that had its beginning in Lampasas County and had representatives from several chapters present, demanded fences be removed that enclosed public school lands. They asked that no land to be sold to "aliens," only to settlers. The Farmers' Alliance in one county was said to have an active fence-cutting committee.[15]

The Land League was another farmer's organization with a substantial fence-cutter membership. Their organization never grew or gained much support and probably wasn't meeting in Austin. Their origin was in Brown County, and they held their local meetings at the county's courthouse. The Land League opposed a herd law, wanted no gates on the public roads, wanted public access to streams, and called for severe penalties for those who fenced land they didn't own.[16]

Members of the Real Estate Association of Texas met in Austin, discussed the fence-cutting problems, and railed about the impact fence cutting was having on the economy. The association members drafted and delivered a resolution to the legislature, citing the cost of fence cutting and its destruction of the state's economy. These landsmen called for the protection of properties and demanded everyone have full enjoyment of their land. They deplored the management and status of school lands. They claimed 30 to 40 million acres of the common school, university, asylum, and unorganized school lands earned no revenue for the entities to which they belonged. Citizens of Texas were taxed at the same time to support those institutions, and the Real Estate Association wanted to see this corrected. They called for a law that would make Texas's free grazing lands support the state institutions.[17]

The Texas Livestock Association was a new stockman's group organized the previous year in Austin. At the end of their first meeting, they scheduled their following year's meeting in Austin on the second Tuesday in January of 1884. That date just happened to fall on January 8, the day the governor's special legislative session was to begin. One of the state's leading newspapers blasted the cattlemen, saying they were coming to Austin to bulldoze the lawmakers. Their meeting date was set, however, long before the call for the special session. The stockmen met and discussed the drought, livestock prices, grazing rights, law enforcement, land issues, and fence-cutting problems. Their meeting began with members expressing concern about the public's lack of support on criminal matters and on penalties assessed for theft of livestock and fence cutting. They lamented that in the prosecutions of crimes, jurors seemed always to hand down verdicts with the smallest allowable punishment, whether it be fines or imprisonment.

This new Texas Livestock Association was a geographically diverse group of stockmen coming from different parts of the state, and consequently members had differing views on many of the issues discussed. Several prominent cattlemen presented resolutions that were voted down or referred to a committee. Some members were advocates for leasing school land, but others were opposed. Some members called for free grass and grazing, but others wanted a herd law. A group of cattlemen introduced a resolution calling for support of a herd law, but the resolution was hotly debated, then defeated by a 63 to 48 vote. Members discussed criminal penalties for fence cutting. US Congressman W. H. Crain of DeWitt County, a strong supporter of the South Texas cattle industry, attended the meeting. He offered a resolution proposing comprehensive fence-cutting legislation. Crain's resolution was discussed, debated, and then sent to a committee.

The afternoon of January 10, Governor Ireland came and spoke to the members. In his speech Ireland told the group he knew they were not in Austin to "bulldoze" the legislature, as alleged in the newspaper article. He assured the stockmen they had every right to come and express their views and needs and be heard. In his discussion of fence cutting, Governor Ireland made a special point to emphasize the impotence of his office when support from the public to enforce laws wasn't present. If he were able to gain the moral sentiment and support of the citizens, and if the legislature adopted his ideas, he promised he would put down the state's lawlessness and stop fence cutting. He discussed his recommendations to the legislature. When he got around to denouncing the fence cutters, his remarks were what the stockmen were waiting to hear. The governor denied having advised anyone to use his shotgun to redress a wrong but then said, "If you find someone cutting your fence, and shoot him—well I make no pledges." There was loud applause, the audience picking up instantly the implied promise he would pardon the killer of the fence cutter. Later in the legislature's debates during the called session, Ireland was severely criticized for making such a rash statement.

The governor told the stockmen to look out for each other and speak their minds in public discussions. By standing back they encouraged lawlessness, which had taken heart and advanced. The lawless spirit was being educated to undertake greater lawlessness by the supine ties of the people and local officials. He told the stockmen he did not approve of or support a herd law, but if they owned land and did not wish for other's cattle to graze on it, they must fence it. Wrapping up his presentation, the governor issued a stern warning to the association members. He told the stockmen they must not enclose land they did not own. If they had fenced and enclosed lands that were not their own, they must promptly purchase or lease the property. When the speech ended, there were questions from the audience. Then Governor Ireland departed.

The meeting continued. A letter read from a group of St. Louis cattle companies proposed a National Cattlemen's Association. There was little interest from those present. The last item of the day was the presentation of a resolution concerning the rights of large pasture owners whose ranch enclosed land of small owners. The cattlemen discussed the resolution, sent it to a committee, and the day's meeting of the convention adjourned.[18]

Later that evening a group of cattlemen from South Texas gathered at Simon's Café on Pecan Street (now Sixth Street) for dinner, to discuss cattle and politics, and to celebrate their evening in Austin. Some say this became a boisterous affair. It was reported that during the dinner, the loud and unruly Shanghai Pierce walked down a long dining table in his bare feet to get a bowl of gravy.

Lee Hall, a former Texas Ranger captain, had left the Rangers and now managed the Dull Ranch, which encompassed roughly four hundred thousand acres of land in LaSalle and McMullen Counties. The Dull Ranch was being fenced with barbed wire and was stocked with cattle and sheep. Hall was attending the stockmen's dinner. Being a storyteller of note, with many wild stories to tell, he was holding forth late in the evening to the enjoyment of his stockmen friends. Earlier in the evening, when entering Simon's Cafe, there had been an exchange of bad words between Hall and a friend of Ben Thompson, the former city marshal of Austin. Before midnight a door of the café was pushed open and Thompson entered the dining room with his six-shooter drawn.

As Thompson walked past the seated cattlemen, he smashed glasses and knocked dinnerware from tables with his revolver. Then he pointed his pistol at Lee Hall, who was standing by a high-back chair he used as a rostrum. Immediately there was a rush of cattlemen going out the café's doors. It was reported that Shanghai Pierce left the building by diving through a window and taking the curtains and fixtures with him.

Ranger J. E. Lucy had served under Captain Lee Hall in the Frontier Battalion in the past and now was at the cattleman's dinner as a guest. He witnessed the commotion and saw Thompson pointing his revolver at Hall. Lucy drew his six-shooter, cocked it, and aimed it at Thompson. There was an exchange of words between the two men. From the back of the café rushed William Henry Crain, the former district attorney and now the US congressman from Cuero. He stepped between Lucy and Ben Thompson and asked Thompson for his six-shooter, which Thompson handed to him.

Then he asked Lucy for his six-shooter, and Lucy handed his revolver to Crain. Crain turned and walked out of the café carrying both six-shooters. It was midnight at Simon's Café when the day's activity ended for the South Texas cattlemen attending the convention. It had been a busy day.[19]

The Texas Livestock Association wrapped up its meeting as the week ended, passing several resolutions to deliver to the legislature. They requested the legislature pass laws necessary for the protection of all citizens of Texas. A resolution passed declaring that grass was as much the landowners' property as timber growing on their land, and they asked for the protection of their grass. They urged the legislature to protect the school lands. One of the resolutions adopted said that they did not favor the doctrine of free range yet they deemed it injudicious to pass a herd law at that time. Lastly, a resolution expressed confidence in the wisdom of the legislature. The association declared they would leave the fence-cutting issue in the hands of their legislators, and were satisfied justice would be done. The Stockmen's Convention adjourned. A committee of eleven remained in Austin to watch the legislative proceedings and act as the livestock industry's lobby.

The *Brenham Weekly Banner* monitored the association's meeting and reported that the Stockmen's Association hardly took a position on fence cutting. The *Fort Worth Daily Gazette* had stronger words, commenting, "Resolutions on fence cutting are good enough as far as they go, but a bullet travels faster and goes further." Sentiments not expressed and resolutions which the Texas Livestock Association failed to pass were soon delivered in strongly worded memorials to the legislature by the other cattlemen and sheepmen associations from across the state.[20]

Reviewing the early newspapers, no mention is found of an Austin meeting of fence cutters. Still, members of fence-cutting bands were in Austin lobbying the free-range legislators and anyone that might listen and show sympathy for their cause.

Several days before the legislative session opened, an Austin interview with a fence cutter was published in the Galveston newspaper. The newspaper's reporter managed to find a fence cutter's alleged leader to interview and struck up a conversation. The man gave his name as Theodore F. Newel and implied he was from the Bastrop area below Austin. Newel was probably not his real name. The location is significant, however. Bastrop was the home of George W. Jones, the leader of the Greenback Party. Jones was an advocate for free range and a strong supporter of the fence cutters.[21]

The reporter's conversation with Theodore Newel, identified as the leader of a band of fence cutters, was published December 21, 1883, in the *Galveston Daily News* and follows:

REPORTER: Is it true, Mr. Newel, you are identified with the fence cutting industry?
NEWEL: I am, sir.
REPORTER: Aren't you afraid to say so here at the capital where the Governor lives and has military headquarters?
NEWEL: General King lives here, don't he?
REPORTER: Yes.
NEWEL: Then, I don't care. He is our friend, and the Governor agrees with us. Why I have King's piece, he printed in the news cut out and framed. He says we are the old fashion democracy, and we are, but it ain't a party question. . . .
REPORTER: Why do you destroy other people's property?
NEWEL: I don't do it. No man does it. It's a long story. It is downtrodden humanity doing it. Read General King's story about it. Read what was published in the papers about it. Just look at me. Ten years ago, I was what I am now. I have coffee in my house Sundays and cornbread, dried beef, and a tank of water the rest of the week. Ten years ago, I had as many cows as that cattle king there in front of Malasky's. He ran off the small fellers and the sheepmen. He fenced in the school land and killed off a lot of shepherds on it. Then he bought the land in the name of his kinfolks, paying 30 dollars a section which he borrowed from these Austin Banks. He is worth a million dollars and hires men to take care of his ranch and keep us small fry out in the chaparral or hang us to a mesquite limb if we don't go prompt.
REPORTER: He has more cattle than you, too?
NEWEL: Cattle are property, and he doesn't propose to interfere with them.
REPORTER: Isn't land property, too?
NEWELL: It is public property. Where ever land is sold to private parties, the people go to fence cutting, bushwhacking, landlord killing, or something of the kind. Land public to everybody gives everybody a chance. . . .

REPORTER: But in the name of goodness, can't you get enough land of your own here in Texas for your own stock to feed on?

NEWEL: I exactly can, but I can get air and sunshine for them too without buying it, and I don't propose to buy lands.

REPORTER: But tell me about the cattle kings. Wouldn't you do as he has done if you had it all to do over again and had an equal start again with him and his sort?

NEWEL: No, by God. He has his ranch down the Rio Grande country after we came back from the war. While we were fighting Yankees, he was branding our calves. When we got back, he had a big start. He first ran off the sheepmen and got us little cattlemen to help him. After he got rid of the sheepmen, he commenced on us, little cattlemen. He first built fence and took in his own, other people's land, and the state land. He cut us off from grass and water and told us to go off with our cattle, or we would have to go off without them. We left and have been leaving ever since. I've been pushed way up to Coleman and was fenced off there. But we are going back now. We have been on our pilgrimage and prayed at the shrine of liberty, and we are getting back, freeing the country as we go.

REPORTER: Your party has I see, read the paper, and deliberated on public affairs?

NEWEL: We do deliberate, but not until January.

REPORTER: Now suppose the fence owners had been as impatient as your side and had inaugurated retaliation. Do you think you could have prosecuted your work?

NEWEL: We are too many for them, and that is why they don't resist. Why, in some places, they come into our camps and want us to cut some poor widder's fences. They want to out devil the devil, but we don't propose to extremities until pushed when the time comes and look out for news from the prairies.

REPORTER: Your people are organized?

NEWEL: We have some of the best legal talent in the state in our crowd, and we don't propose to make a fight we can't win.

REPORTER: Tell me about your organization.

NEWEL: There ain't much to tell. We know our men. We know where we can stay at night, and can't be found in the day, where we can get nippers, and what lawyers to consult with. We have maps showing the long fences, and we have a plan of operation. But there is a great deal of independent

>   fence-cutting that we get the credit of. Fences are cut we would have never cut, and we begin to think a great deal of it is done in the farm country lately to influence the Governor and our friends in the legislature.
>
> REPORTER: Why don't you stop that kind of devilment?
>
> NEWEL: We can't stop it any more than the fence owners can stop it. . . .
>
> REPORTER: Doesn't it take money to pay the expenses of the fence-cutting bands?
>
> NEWEL: Unfortunately, we have too much money. I believe the money in it has been the cause of getting men into our camp who cut out of pure devilment. We don't make war on small farmers, and it's the money in it that has brought in these farm fence-cutters, and when real trouble comes, that is the class of men that will go back on us and give us away if the other side puts up more money.
>
> REPORTER: Are you not the chief of the southwest tribe of fence cutters, and is the name Newel or Noel?
>
> NEWEL: Let's take a drink.[22]

The special session convened in Austin on January 8. Both houses of the legislature began preliminary matters of opening the special session. A message from Governor Ireland was read by a clerk in the house and senate listing items in his call for the session. The governor later addressed both the house and senate in a joint session.

As work began in the two chambers, an outpour of statewide sentiment arrived over fence cutting and lawlessness. Senators and representatives were swamped with letters, memorials, and petitions, and with visits from citizens and business leaders representing distressed parts of the state. There were 102 bills introduced in the house and 77 filed in the senate, most related to the fence-cutting problems. Legislation to stop fence cutting took all shapes. One bill would make the county in which fence cutting occurred financially liable for the damages. Another bill would create a much-dreaded statewide herd law, requiring all livestock to be kept on their owner's property. To the free grass men, this meant they would have to keep their stock off public land now grazed for free. There was even a bill introduced making it justifiable homicide to shoot and kill a fence cutter.[23]

As the business of the session started, Representative Owen Brown, who farmed near Cleburne in Johnson County, introduced a resolution that was adopted by the house and became their unofficial guide. A similar version of Brown's resolution is in the *Senate Journal*. In part, the house resolution reads:

> Whereas the destruction of wire fences, the enclosing of public school lands, nonresident land, and the fencing of small landowners by large ones, and the lack of roads, gates, etc., for public convenience, have been for some months fruitful topics of discussion through the press, and our otherwise happy state has been in several localities in a state of commotion bordering on anarchy, and civil war, rendering life, liberty, and prosperity unsafe; and whereas the people are looking with much concern on the action of the present legislature for a solution of the existing troubles, therefore,
>
> Resolve by the House of Representatives, first that it is the duty of each and every member to rise above all sordid or selfish views of the vexing questions, and give his support to such measures as should receive the approbation of every lover of justice, and equal rights.

Brown filed another resolution calling to create a select house committee to receive and consider all bills on "fence cutting troubles." This resolution was discussed. The following day after motions and amendments, a majority house vote created a committee of twenty members appointed by Speaker Charles Gibson to receive bills that proposed remedies for the destruction of fences. Representative A. M. Taylor, a lawyer from Clarksville in Red River County, was appointed to chair the committee. Several days later a subcommittee of seven was appointed to examine the bills sent to the Committee on Fence Cutting and report back a substitute, covering the material for consideration of the full committee. This Special Committee on Fence Cutting spent long hours reading, debating, and drafting legislation for the full house consideration.[24]

Only days before the legislature convened for this called session, there had been a fence-cutting incident in Delta County in Northeast Texas. Few details are found, but a fence was cut on A. G. Hubbard's farm during the night. While the fence cutters or cutter was at work, Hubbard shot and killed a man named Crowder. This incident wasn't the first and wasn't the only report of a fence cutter being killed. Still, it became newsworthy because of the much-publicized legislation the incident provoked.[25]

R. R Hazlewood, a young lawyer and state representative from Cooper, the county seat of Delta County, filed a bill that captured everyone's attention. Hazelwood's bill was numbered H.B. No. 77. The bill was styled

> A bill to amend Article 570, Penal Code, defining justifiable homicide so as to include in the definition, killing to prevent willfully and malicious destruction of property, or when a person is found armed with a deadly weapon in disguise in the nighttime on premises of another, whether the party be killed by a person injured or by someone in his behalf, and when the killing takes place under circumstances justifying a reasonable belief that the party killed then, and there intended to commit one of the offenses above named, the killing to take place before the offense is actually completed, and other provisions.[26]

Hazlewood's house bill appears to have had a companion bill filed over in the senate by J. A. Martin, a senator from Falls County. The *Brenham Weekly Banner* reported that Martin introduced a bill in the senate "making the killing of a fence cutter found at night in the act of offending, justifiable homicide." The Brenham newspaper's brief note ended by saying, "This remedy is heroic, as a dead fence cutter can do no more damage." Martin's bill managed to clear the Senate Judiciary Committee.[27]

This senate bill initially received strong support from Senator Barnett Gibbs of Dallas. Then Gibbs was criticized by the *Dallas Herald*, a hometown newspaper. The paper said Gibbs usually was a cautious person. Still, they questioned how the senator got so far astray as to urge that a person killing someone cutting a fence should be at once acquitted on the plea of justifiable homicide. Quoting the newspaper, "Suppose a neighbor happened to be going for a doctor in post-haste? Or, suppose a case of enmity, what a splendid opportunity. No, no, we are not ready for mob law or Judge Lynch's court."[28]

Early in the legislative session, the bills to make the killing of a fence cutter justifiable homicide appear to have had strong support in both the house and senate. However, as the session progressed, there was opposition in the state's major newspapers, and the papers had power and influence. Senator Barnett Gibbs did an about-face, pulled his support, and testified against Senator Martin's bill. He noted in a passionate speech that "a person whose enemy was near a fence could shoot him down, cut a few wires, drop a pair of wire cutters beside the dead body, then notify the sheriff that he had shot a fence cutter. The murderer would go free." When the legislative session ended, neither the house nor the senate bill became law.[29]

When the special session opened, Senator Alexander W. Terrell, the respected veteran lawmaker from Austin, filed the first two senate bills. His Senate Bill No. 2 had months of preparation and was titled "An act to regulate the grazing of stock, and to prescribe, and provide for enforcing penalties for its violation." The bill was lengthy, comprehensive, and covered the state's fence-cutting and grazing-land problems. The *Galveston Daily News* complimented Terrell's legislation, reporting, "The bill has been examined by jurist of state reputation and met with their warm approval." Spectators filled the Senate chamber on January 21. In a two-and-a-half-hour speech, the Austin senator listed "nine evils of the hour" he said were causing the state's fence-cutting problems. In his lengthy oration, Terrell declared that the state policy of free grass benefited a favored class and encouraged a spirit of communism destructive to property rights. He said his bill would correct all of the evils except the road problems, which would require separate legislation.

Some of the provisions of Terrell's senate bill would require large cattlemen to own or lease ten acres of land for every cow they had grazing on free range. The farmers or small stockmen with no more than twenty-five head of cattle were not affected. They would be exempt from penalties under this provision. Stockmen would be prohibited from grazing livestock on private land and prevented from fencing public-owned land unless they paid an annual lease of four cents an acre. Landowners could not fence and enclose public waters, although they could purchase all of the property surrounding the water.

The Terrell bill would create a Commission on Pasturage, with ten commissioners in charge of various regions of the state. These commissioners were to employ a patrolling force to enforce the new law. The governor would be authorized to declare martial law if necessary to implement provisions of Terrell's proposed legislation, and penalties for violations could run up to $500 with two years in jail. Cutting and destroying a fence carried the same punishment.

As the legislature began its work, the Terrell senate bill was referred to the senate's Committee on Stock Raising. It was reported favorably by a four to three vote, but with amendments. The committee's majority report stated that the bill was a herd law in disguise, but 30 million acres of school land scattered in fifty-four counties were grazed free at no cost to the stock owners, many of whom were from out of state. This matter needed a remedy. The committee's minority report stated they did not want the grass to grow and rot on the unfenced land and benefit no one. They argued that those men who opened the frontier should be permitted to graze the land free and unfenced. Terrell's bill was debated and loaded with amendments. As the end of the special session approached, the senate was divided on the Terrell bill. Late in the legislative session, Senator N. G. Collins of Duval County delivered a report from the senate's Stock Raising Committee and presented a substitute bill. Terrell's bill was set aside. Before the legislature's session ended, however, certain fundamentals parts of Terrell's bill were written into other legislation.[30]

Near the end of this called legislative session, many of the state's citizens gave up on the legislature finding a solution for the fence-cutting problems. The legislators debated many bills coming out of both the house and senate. Many of the measures went to a conference committee for compromise before a final vote for passage. One of the bills that Representative Thomas L. Odom supported came out of the conference committee, went to the house of representatives, and was brought to the floor for a vote. It appears that Representative W. T. Armistead from East Texas attacked a provision of this bill prescribing punishment for fence cutting. Odom rose to speak to Armistead's attack on the bill's punishment. Odom's legislative district was suffering severely. His own large cattle ranch headquartered at Fort Chadbourne had forty miles of fences cut to pieces. Before coming to Austin, he had prepared for a substantial and costly fence-building project. Cutters came in and in one night burned his fresh-cut cedar fence posts and wagonloads of new barbed wire. They hung a fence post in a tree near his home with a note tacked on it threatening his life.

As Odom began to speak opposing the East Texas representative's concerns, his anger exploded, and he poured out his bitter feelings.

Governor Ireland Calls a Special Legislative Session

He chastised his legislative colleagues for having done everything wrong up to that time. Odom said they favored the fence cutters and were trying to crush out the existence of the grandest and greatest enterprise in Texas, the cattle business. Growing louder, he said,

> There are now $10,000,000 in fences destroyed by the nippers and property damages to the amount of $100,000,000 to the state by these ragtag and bobbed tailed ruffians, these hell-hounds of Texas who go around at night time cutting and destroying the property of their neighbors. Odom said he would fight to keep Texas one and inseparable. Still, if justice were not done for all classes, the land, and cattle interests as well as those of the miserable fence cutters, he would be glad to see the state divided (East Texas and the Western Frontier) and would vote for it. He was ashamed to see so many House members rise in their place and defend the midnight marauders who wantonly injured without cause, everything that comes within their reach and against whom attacks, life was not secure. For his part, "If he ever rose to defend such rascals, he hoped that his arms would become paralyzed and that his tongue would cleave to the roof of his mouth."

Newspapers across the state printed parts of Odom's speech with much editorializing. Back home, word of his remarks further inflamed the cutters, and they doubled down on their efforts to ruin Odom's ranching enterprise. His bombastic presentation did have an impact on his colleagues, however. Legislation moved forward with a severe penalty for cutting a fence or burning a pasture.[31]

As the close of the special session came near, compromises were reached on much of the legislation. New laws needed to stop fence cutting and place the state's economic growth back on track passed both the house and senate by a two-thirds vote, went to the governor carrying emergency provisions, and were signed into law. Those new laws went into effect immediately.

One of the leading causes of the fence cutting had been the obstruction of roads by barbed wire fences. There was comprehensive new road legislation passed into law. County commissioners courts received broad new powers and duty to lay out and open public roads where needed. Roads were not to be changed except by shortening distance from their point of beginning to the end of the destination. Commissioners were to act as supervisors of roads for their respective precincts. They would be reimbursed three dollars a day, not to exceed ten days per year, for their inspections and supervision. A process for citizens to petition for new roads was prescribed. A jury of freeholders of the county was to be appointed by the commissioners courts to help the court lay out new roads. A process to compensate landowners for damages on opening new routes was prescribed. Commissioners courts were to appoint a work overseer and workers, in each precinct to maintain the roads. Those workers named were to be assigned road work, as near as possible to their home. Work overseers were to report within ten days to the county attorney and their precinct's justice of the peace the names of appointed workers who failed to work or furnish a substitute worker. Each commissioner was required to make a report under oath on roads in his precinct the first regular term of commissioners court each year. His statement was to describe the condition of each road, give an account of the condition of culverts and bridges, the number of mileposts, and signs defaced or destroyed and report where any new road for his precinct should be opened.

S.B. No. 36 passed and was a progressive piece of legislation titled "An Act to require the commissioner courts to layout and open certain first-class roads." The bill noted that existing conditions of roads in the state made travel difficult and often dangerous and obstructed communication between the different counties and subdivisions of the state. This legislation's purpose was not to open roads closed off by a fence, although it did. It was drafted and passed to create a new network of highways and improve statewide transportation. The bill required counties to lay out and open first-class roads to county seats in neighboring counties. It also called for opening first-class roads into unorganized counties. First-class roads were to be built sixty feet in width and clear of obstructions, and where there were fences, to place gates twelve feet wide. Such roads were not to be laid out across orchards, yard lots, or graveyards, or within one hundred feet of a residence without the consent of the resident.

S.H. Bill No. 11 amended an existing law and established a standard for gates across public roads. Under this act landowners were to keep pasture gates and their approaches in good order. Gates were to be ten feet wide and constructed to avoid any delay for the traveler when opening and closing.

A fastener to hold the gate open while the traveler goes through was required. Also required was a permanent hitching post and stile block on each side and within sixty feet of the gate entrance. A person building a gate across a public road who willfully or negligently failed to comply with the requirements was deemed guilty of a misdemeanor. He could be fined not less than five or more than twenty-five dollars for each offense. Each week of failure constituted a separate offense. Travelers using the gate were responsible for keeping the gates closed. Any person willfully or negligently leaving a gate open was deemed guilty of a misdemeanor, and on conviction was to be fined not less than five or more than twenty-five dollars.

S.B. No. 42 declared it unlawful for any person or persons to build or maintain a line of fence running more than three miles in the same general direction without having a gateway, even though there may have been no road through the pasture. The gate was to be eight feet wide and could not be locked. Large pastures that already had fences constructed had six months to conform to the provisions of this law. Not providing such a gateway was a misdemeanor. On violation and conviction, a person would be fined no less than one hundred nor more than two hundred dollars. Each day of the breach was punishable as a separate offense. Travelers could use these gates, but they were intended for use by stockmen driving livestock across the county and traveled through pastures that were fenced.

H.B. No. 92 was titled "An appropriation to be used by the Governor for the payment of rewards and ferreting out and suppressing crime." The act appropriated $50,000 from money in the treasury not otherwise appropriated and would pay for the employment of detectives. Citizens, local officials, and legislators had been calling for detectives.

S.H.B. Nos. 2, 8, and 9 brought heated debates in both chambers of the legislature over a new penalty for cutting or destroying a fence. Before this special legislative session, cutting a fence was a misdemeanor and punished only as such. The legislature now passed an act that prescribed new and severe punishment for willful cutting or destroying fences. The new statute read,

> Any person who shall wantonly, or with intent to injure the owner, and willfully cut, injure or destroy any fence or part of a fence, shall

be deemed guilty of an offense, and upon conviction therefor shall be punished by confinement in the State Penitentiary for a term not less than one year nor more than five years. A fence within the meaning of this act is any structure of wood, wire, or of both, or any other material, intended to prevent the passage of cattle, horses, mules, asses, sheep, goats, or hogs. Provided, however, that it shall constitute no offense for any person owning, and residing on land enclosed by the fence of another, who refuses permission to such person or persons residing within the enclosure, free egress, and ingress to their said land, for such persons or persons to open a passageway through said enclosure.

In addition to fence cutting, pasture burning was a serious problem and feared by all stockmen. S.B. No. 63 was enacted to stop the dreaded pasture burning from occurring along with fence cutting in parts of the state. The common goal of the cutter was to burn the stockman's grass forage. But there were cases where burning grass, livestock, personal property, and homes was the cutter's intent. This Senate Bill provided that "any person who shall willfully fire any grass within any enclosure, not his own, in this State, with intent to destroy the grass in such pasture, or any part thereof, or any person who shall fires the grass outside of any enclosure with the intent to destroy the grass in such enclosure, by the communication of said fire to the grass within, shall be deemed guilty of a felony, and upon conviction, punished by confinement in the State Penitentiary for a term of not less than two, nor more than five years." Another section of the bill "made it a criminal offense to willfully, and with intent to injure the landowner or his stock, burn grass upon the land, that was not fenced." This section applied to both state-owned and privately owned properties. The penalty of this offense was "a term in the State Penitentiary for not less than one year, nor more than three."

H.B. No. 44 amended the penal code, defining a conspiracy. The penal code was expanded to include other offenses of the grade of a felony (specifically fence cutting and pasture burning), along with murder, robbery, arson, burglary, and rape. This legislation was to punish those leaders of the fence cutters who planned, organized, and carried out fence-cutting activities.

Sub. H.B. Nos. 50 and 84 originated in the house and passed in the senate on January 31, 1884. This bill was cited as "An act to prohibit the unlawful fencing or closing, or keeping enclosed, the lands of another, and of the public schools, university, and asylum lands of the State of Texas, and to prevent the herding, or loose herding or detention of stock upon the lands of the State, the public schools, university, and asylums, and to provide penalties for the violation of this act."

This legislation immediately impacted those who had fenced land they didn't own. Under this new law, any person or corporation was considered guilty if they enclosed or let stand any fence enclosing land of another, or public-owned lands without written consent or a written lease. Those fencing without permission were guilty of a misdemeanor, and on conviction were to be fined no less than fifty cents nor more than one dollar per acre per month for each month enclosed. Violators found guilty could also be imprisoned in the county jail for up to two years. Cases under this act were to be prosecuted as a civil action. One half of the money collected could be paid to the person reporting the unlawfully enclosed land. Individuals and corporations had six months after the act went into effect to conform to the law. The attorney general in person or by proxy could institute proceedings for the state against those unlawfully enclosing the lands. The expenses incurred were to be deducted from fines collected. This section of the act did not apply to those settling on land not owned if their enclosure was two hundred acres or less and their principal pursuit was agriculture. Landowners or lessors with land surrounding the unfenced property of another could build fence on his land's inner boundaries, leaving a sixty feet wide lane to the outer edges of his surrounding property and with two gates at such points the enclosed landowner demanded. The gates were to be kept in good condition for the use of the owner of the enclosed land. Such lane would prevent stock of the enclosed farmer or stockman from grazing on the more extensive landowner's property.

The most surprising, shocking, and significant part of this legislation was that it declared it unlawful for any person, firm, or corporation to herd, or aid in herding, or cause to be herded, loose herded, or detained for grazing by line riders any cattle, horses, mules, asses, sheep, or goats on any vacant public domain, school, university, or asylum land within the state unless the stockman leased the land from the proper authority.

Any person who knowingly violated this section of the act would be guilty of a misdemeanor. Upon conviction, they would be fined one hundred dollars for each section of land (640 acres) or part of a section grazed. This section didn't apply to persons herding stock to deliver to or from the market. And it didn't apply to those moving livestock from one part of the country to another. The days of grazing livestock on the free range had ended; this new law essentially created the pasture or herd law that the free-range men and fence cutters had feared.[32]

The Special Called Session of the Eighteenth Texas Legislature ended February 6, 1884. Bills passed were immediately signed into law by Governor John Ireland. The governor received most of the legislation he had requested at the opening of the special session. The newspapers across the state widely publicized the new laws, and meetings were held in Austin to review the laws with community leaders, lawmen, and the legal community.

The free grass men had been badly trounced when the special session ended, but some refused to admit defeat. They tried to gain control of the Democratic Convention in 1884, but they failed. It wasn't until James S. Hogg, the Democratic reformer, was elected in 1890 that the small man, mostly farmers and free-range men, gained ground with the politics they sought. As difficult as it was for the free grass men and their fence cutter friends to accept their loss in the special legislative session, so it was for some to believe that fence cutting must stop. After assessing the changing times and the new days of farming and ranching at hand, and with a fear of the stiff penalty passed into law for clipping a fence, most men gave up fence cutting. Some didn't, and certain hot spots of fence cutting continued across the state. Some refused to give up fence cutting because of bitter feelings toward the ranchers they clashed with when barbed wire first arrived. Battles continued as in bitter feuds, but now the governor and the state adjutant general brought in the Texas Rangers and employed detectives. Chapters of this book that follow are stories and incidents in which the Texas barbed wire wars were fought under new laws, with more barbs, bullets, and blood.

Chapter 7

Fence Cutters Assassinate Ranger Benjamin Warren in Sweetwater

>Farewell My Wife and Children All. From You a Father Do Call
>—Epitaph on Ranger Benjamin Warren's tombstone

After the special session adjourned and the legislators left Austin, the state's adjutant general, Wilburn H. King, employed the Ferrell Commercial Detective Agency of New Orleans to conduct work on fence-cutting problems in Runnels County. William Carlton, an experienced detective, traveled from his New Orleans headquarters to Austin. On arrival he received credentials and instructions from Adjutant General King, then was sent to Fort Chadbourne and reported to Representative T. L. Odom on March 12.[1]

Detective Carlton arrived in Chadbourne, met Odom, and heard his story. The detective learned that weeks before Representative Odom left for the special legislative session in Austin, a band of fence cutters came on his ranch. They set fire and burned $12,000 worth of fence post, staves, and barbed wire he had purchased to begin fencing seventeen sections of land. Because of his commitment to the state capital and loss of materials, fence building on the large tract of land was suspended. When Odom returned from the legislative session, fence cutters returned to the ranch Saturday, February 23.

They clipped four miles of fences that enclosed his small six-thousand-acre pasture. Representative Odom believed the fence cutters were trying to discourage him from fencing the larger tract of land by cutting the small pasture fence.

In the fall of 1883, A. O. Brown, one of the area's sheepmen, had a large herd of sheep grazing on the representative's land. Odom ordered him to move his sheep off the property. Brown ignored his demand and Odom filed suit against him for trespassing. The lawsuit was delayed, then heard in the Runnels County Justice Court when Odom returned from the special legislative session. Legal action that followed resulted in a mistrial.[2]

Detective Carlton began his investigation by checking on this sheepman who always grazed his sheep on the free range. The detective was quickly convinced the sheepman had not cut the fence. The February 23 fence-cutting incident appeared to have been done by someone else trying to throw suspicion on Brown. The detective believed the fence cutting was carried out by settlers living on Fish Creek up in Nolan County.

As Carlton's investigation progressed, he found a hatchet used by one of the cutters to chop barbed wire off fence posts, which he saved as evidence hoping that someone could be identified as its owner. The detective found footprints with tracks of shoe soles with hobnails. These tracks were along the fence and were measured and recorded. Detective Carlton learned shoes that made these tracks were the type worn by the two Hylton brothers. The Hyltons owned a blacksmith shop up on Fish Creek, and they shod horses there. Notes written on small sheets of paper were found tacked to posts on the fence line with new horseshoe nails. Walking along the fence that had been cut, Carlton found a new and unique .45-caliber rifle cartridge that he called a bottleneck cartridge. Talking to citizens at Fort Chadbourne, the detective learned that Neil Boyett, a resident living on Fish Creek, was the owner of the only firearm of that type in the area.[3]

Colonel Odom watched visitors frequenting Fort Camborne's businesses and told Carlton that a man named George Sutton (a.k.a. George Baker) was a frequent visitor in the Fort Chadbourne community. George Sutton (Baker) lived on Fish Creek, and Odom learned that he moved there from Gonzales. Gonzales County had a reputation for outlawry and crime.

The colonel suspected that Sutton was one of the Fish Creek fence cutters. Odom contacted Sam McMurry, Ranger captain of Company B, stationed in Coleman City, and asked him to find out if there were charges against this George Sutton (Baker) down in Gonzales. The Ranger captain said he would check on Sutton's background.

Carlton assumed Sutton was wanted for a felony offense in Gonzales and came up with a plan. Should Sutton be captured by the Rangers, he should be held, and could probably be convinced to turn state's evidence on the fence cutters to get out of his trouble in Gonzales. The detective also believed money could motivate Sutton to give away the story on fence cutting in testimony. Carlton would follow this plan should Sutton be arrested and taken into custody.[4]

John Aston, a fellow cattleman and Colonel Odom's acquaintance, lived north of Fort Chadbourne near Buffalo Gap in Taylor County. Aston informed the colonel that a man named Ben Warren living among the fence cutters on Fish Creek was reliable and could be trusted to provide useful information on the fence cutters. Unknown to Odom, this man's brother, John Warren, lived with Aston's family and worked for him as a herdsman. John Aston and the Warren brothers had lived in San Saba before they relocated to Nolan County.[5]

Carlton asked Odom to contact Ben Warren and seek his assistance, but the colonel thought it not advisable. He told Carlton to trust no one, not even Sheriff John Formwalt. Odom had had so much trouble recently that he was panic-stricken. He advised Carlton to hold in confidence only his immediate family members. Garland Odom, the colonel's older son, had a conversation with Neil Boyett, one of the suspected fence cutters from Fish Creek, on March 13. Boyett told Garland, "If there is any money in the business, he wanted to make it . . . that he could stand between him and the fence cutters . . . or he could compromise the matter and prevent any more fence cutting."

On learning about this conversation, Carlton asked Garland to meet with Boyett again and find out exactly what he proposed to do on the fence-cutting business but not to make a deal until he, Carlton, could return from a visit with the Rangers in Coleman County. Carlton left for Coleman. Before leaving again he insisted that Colonel Odom contact Warren. He also asked him to locate other persons who could help the detective become acquainted with the fence cutters.

Carlton traveled to Coleman, arriving on March 17, and found Ranger Captain Samuel McMurry in town. McMurry told the detective he had just learned George Sutton (alias George Baker) was wanted for stealing cattle in Gonzales County. Sutton was also wanted on a misdemeanor charge in Sweetwater. McMurry had sent a detachment of Rangers to Fort Chadbourne to find and arrest Sutton. Carlton stayed in Coleman and waited for their return. The next day the detachment of Rangers returned. They had scouted the Fort Chadbourne area but not found Baker. Captain McMurry assured Carlton that his Rangers were still out scouting and would soon arrest Sutton. If he got anything out of him about fence cutting, the captain would let him know. It's not known if Carlton discussed with McMurry his plan to get Sutton to turn state's evidence on fence cutting in exchange for leniency on the Gonzales charges. Carlton asked the captain to have Sutton searched thoroughly to try to find a small pocketbook with missing pages. Notes from such a book were written and tacked to fence posts when the fences were cut, and Carlton had found and saved several of the small notes as evidence. As McMurry assured Detective Carlton, George Sutton was soon arrested by the Rangers and locked in the Coleman City's jail.

Sutton was arrested on March 22, but there was a jailbreak at Coleman, and Sutton made his escape with the other prisoners. The Rangers who arrested Sutton returned to Fort Chadbourne and Fish Creek searching for Sutton, but this time he wasn't found. Carlton, talking with several of the Rangers, learned they knew nothing about searching Sutton for the small notebook Carlton hoped to find with its blank and missing pages.

Word was now out in Fort Chadbourne and among the Fish Creek neighbors that the Rangers had arrested Sutton. Many residents believed the Rangers held him as a witness against the fence cutters, but such was not the case. George Sutton left the country after the Coleman jailbreak. The detective and Rangers missed an opportunity to secure a witness that could have produced testimony against the Fish Creek Gang.[6]

Detective Carlton continued his search for other witnesses. He visited with John McCutcheon, the brother-in-law of Cyrus Odom, Odom's younger son. He learned that back on February 19, McCutheon had been in an angry affront and almost a fist fight with Neil Boyett. The conversation ended with strong words. Boyett told McCutheon, "Yes damn you, we will cut the fence, and God damned you, we will make you help us cut it." The week following this angry confrontation, four miles of fence on Odom's six-thousand-acre pasture had been cut by men of unknown identity.[7]

John Aston, the cattleman at Buffalo Gap, again contacted the Odoms, sending a letter to Garland Odom with information on the fence cutters. Aston advised Garland that Aston's brother-in-law, Andy Pratt, was aware of the fence-cutting incident on February 23. Pratt told Aston that Neil Boyett, Mack Boyett, Jim Yardley, George Sutton, Dow Hylton, and Riley Hylton were the parties that cut Odom's fence. Pratt was scared, not willing to come forward, and was not ready to pursue the matter. Pratt had lived on Fish Creek near the Odom pasture, but he had recently moved to Taylor County near Buffalo Gap out of fear for his life.[8]

Carrying a letter of introduction from Colonel Odom, Carlton traveled to Runnels City. He met with H. A. Thompson, a large landowner and sheepman. Thompson had fenced a tract of land to farm the past fall, and his new field fence was immediately cut to pieces. Thompson hadn't replaced the fence and told the detective that he had no intention of rebuilding under the present circumstances. Unfortunately, the sheepman had no useful information to offer the detective but tendered him any assistance in his power.

Detective Carlton met with G. A. Cooper, who lived on Fish Creek. In his conversation with Cooper, he learned of several more potential witnesses. Cooper told him that Mr. J. M. Goche (Goutcher) and his wife lived in a part of the Hylton's house when Odom's fence was cut. Goche's wife had been out gossiping to people about fence cutting, and the family was forced to move. Carlton visited with Goche, who told the detective that they moved from the Hylton house as "bad friends." Goche said that on the night of February 23, two of the Hyltons had left the house saying they were going cow hunting on the Wagon Tire, the name of the creek and tract of land joining Odom's pasture where the fences were cut. The Hylton boys didn't come home until the next morning. Goche would not say who went with them but told Carlton that he heard Dow Hylton say that "the fences would be cut, and any man who gave it away would be killed." Goche told Carlton that he would say more on the witness stand than he was prepared to say off it. Goche wouldn't acknowledge his wife's gossip about fence cutting being the reason they had moved from the Hylton's house and dissolved their friendship. The detective believed that Mrs. Goche knew a lot about the fence-cutting incident and would make a good witness if sworn and placed on the witness stand.[9]

From the earlier conversation with Cooper, Carlton learned of another potential witness, a Mr. Tandy. This man had observed the fence cutters traveling to the pasture to do their work. Carlton found Tandy and tried to talk to him, but the man was not cooperative. He refused to speak about fence cutting with the detective. Carlton was sure that Tandy knew who cut Odom's fence and was confident that "a grand jury could squeeze it out of him."[10]

On returning from his search for witnesses, Carlton went into Fort Chadbourne to meet with Colonel Odom. On this occasion Carlton had the opportunity to see Neil Boyett, a visitor from Fish Creek, in his animated form. Boyett was talking to the colonel. Carlton overheard him tell Odom, "Look here, old man, I don't believe in one man owning and fencing all the land in the country. Us poor people with cattle are going to have grass for our stock, and I don't care a God damned what it costs."[11]

Cattleman John Aston continued to encourage Odom, his fellow cattleman, to talk with the Warren boy. Benjamin Goodin Warren, or Ben as he was known, was born January 27, 1843, in Bolivar, Tennessee. He came to Texas during the 1840s with his father, Jefferson, and mother, Elizabeth Owen Warren. The Warren family made their home in Travis County. When Ben was thirteen, the Warren family moved to San Saba County, settling on the Colorado River near what is known as Warren's Crossing. Ben was one of ten children in a close-knit family. On becoming a young man, he petitioned San Saba's Masonic Lodge No. 225 and was raised a Master Mason on October 2, 1865. That same year he married Eppie Hubbert and worked in San Saba County as a cowhand.[12]

By 1880 several Warren brothers moved from San Saba with their cattle grazing in Nolan, Runnels, and the Taylor County areas. Ben's brother John Warren lived with John Aston and his family north of Fort Chadbourne in Taylor County. He had hired on as one of Aston's herdsmen. Brother Joseph E. Warren and his wife Tempy were living in the Fish Creek neighborhood in Nolan County. Soon after 1880 Ben Warren moved his wife and children from San Saba to Nolan County with his new home near his brother Joseph on Fish Creek.[13]

With the detective's encouragement and John Aston as the intermediary, Ben Warren showed up at Fort Chadbourne on March 24 to meet Colonel Odom. Their meeting began and the conversation went well—so well that from that meeting a relationship between Ben and the colonel developed, offering hope for Odom's fence-cutting problems. In their discussion Ben Warren told Odom that if the Colonel had contacted him sooner, he could have put him on to the band of cutters the night in February when they cut his fence. He also told Odom that such action was impossible now. George Sutton's arrest had created panic among the cutters, and now they were hiding out. Odom immediately realized he had found a man that knew much about the Fish Creek Gang and was willing to help. Although no record was found for verification, the colonel probably placed Ben Warren on his ranch payroll that same day. Several weeks after this visit with Odom, Ben Warren enlisted as a Ranger in Captain J. T. Gillespie's Company E of the Frontier Battalion. Warren's enlistment was most certainly with State Representative Odom's help. Ben Warren officially became a Texas Ranger private and an undercover operative for Texas, April 18, 1884.[14]

Detective Carlton sent a report to his employer, State Adjutant General King, on March 29, advising that he had a strong case working and believed he could go to the Runnels County District Court and appear before a grand jury during the court's May term. Still, his case would be built on circumstantial evidence. The detective was confident he could get part of the fence cutters indicted using Odom's influence with the judge and the district attorney. But there was a problem. He expressed concern to Adjutant General King that if the fence cutters were arrested and indicted, they would have to go through a preliminary trial, set out evidence, and question the witnesses. There would be no protection for the witnesses, as the nearest Ranger headquarters was sixty miles away at Coleman. Carlton feared the witnesses would be run out of the county by the cutters before their trial began.[15]

As the detective mailed his March 29 report to Adjutant General King in Austin, Ben Warren, working undercover for the state, prepared to testify as a state witness. There is no explanation of why Ben Warren joined the Rangers and agreed to perform this dangerous undercover work. His motivation may have come from cattle-theft and fence-cutting problems experienced back home. San Saba's cattlemen formed a vigilante group to deal with fence cutting and cattle thieves. It is believed this group later evolved into the notorious San Saba Mob. Ben Warren's father and brothers were cattlemen, and Ben was listed in San Saba's 1870 US Census as "raising cattle." He would have certainly had a strong dislike for cattle thieves and fence cutters, having this cattleman background.[16]

An older brother of Ben's, Henry Clay Warren, served as a Ranger. Ben's sister, Vollie Ann, married N. D. McMillin, who had also served as a Ranger. The family had a history of Ranger service, which may have encouraged Ben to sign on as a Ranger for this undercover job.[17]

Elisha Hylton, the Fish Creek blacksmith and patriarch of the community that would later adopt his name, came to Nolan County from San Saba years before, bringing family members with him. Ben might have had bad personal feelings toward some of his Nolan County neighbors dating back to their early days in San Saba.[18]

In February 1884 Ben Warren and his brother Joseph had their names appear on a Nolan County court order requiring road work by residents living along Fish Creek. A new road law passed during the special legislative session that required first-class roads between county seats. New first-class roads were to be cleared a full forty-foot width with trees cut off at the ground. Then the stumps were grubbed or burned to permit unobstructed wagon traffic. With due process and the county commissioners' direction, narrower second- and third-class roads could also be built for use by county residents. Counties were responsible for the construction and maintenance of these roads. They, in turn, called on landowners and residents along the road's route to perform the hard labor of road work.

On February 14, 1884, the Nolan County Commissioners Court appointed and commissioned Cornelius (Neil) W. Boyett, the overseer for District No. 3,

Road Precinct No. 1. This portion of the Sweetwater and Runnels City road traversed the Fish Creek area, then meandered down to Runnels City. The commissioners court further instructed Boyett to gather the Fish Creek residents in the precinct to work on the road. Of those men drafted in the court order and placed under the supervision of Boyett, seven men were fence cutters and members of the Fish Creek Gang. The court order also named Ben Warren and his brother Joseph as laborers for this road work.[19]

Nine days after Boyett was appointed overseer of the road work along Fish Creek, the cutters whacked another stretch of Colonel Odom's fences. Members of the Fish Creek Gang working together on the road had used the work time to plan February 23 as the night to cut Odom's fence. The discussions of the fence cutting were known to the Warren brothers; they were present when the planning took place. After cutting the fence on the Odom Ranch in February, the fence cutters were inactive through March, owing to the arrest and presumed captivity of their friend George Sutton. the cutters struck again on April 9, 1884, cutting a long string of Odom's fences.[20]

Ben Warren was looking out for Odom interests when fences were cut on April 9, although he wasn't mustered into Ranger service until April 18. Court records don't describe Warren's testimony, but he presented his evidence and did a good job. During the May 9, 1884, session of the Runnels County District Court, with Judge Thomas Benton Wheeler presiding, the grand jury heard evidence and testimony from T. L. Odom, Garland Odom, Detective William Carlson, and Ben Warren. Warren presented detailed testimony naming the men who defied civil authorities by cutting Odom's fences and threatening to kill anyone who attempted their arrest. Grand jury members hearing Warren's testimony were jury foreman Alfred E. Hanscomb, Horace A. Thomson, J. W. Hathaway, J. R. Ames, W. N. Copeland, S. R. McCall, J. S. Cotton, N. J. Allen, N. P. Jones, C. D. Patton, A. J. Nichols, and A. J. Stewart.

Following testimony and the presentation of evidence, the Runnels County's grand jury indicted fourteen men, with some receiving multiple indictments. There were a total of twenty-four fence-cutting indictments handed down. Individuals indicted were Dow Hylton, Riley Hylton,

Neil Boyett, Mack Boyett, W. J. Wood, Dave Farley, John Ford, Pete Thompson, George Sutton, Nimrod Franks, Thomas Franks, William Yardley, James Yardley, and Williams Thompson.

Two of the indictments were styled differently from the others for fence cutting. Cause 45 and 46 were styled "State of Texas vs. W. J. Wood and Dave Farley, et al. 'combining and conspiring' together to cut and destroy the fence of another." These two indictments were the first use of the criminal conspiracy charge for fence cutting passed into law during the recent special legislative session. Indictments for other crimes besides fence cutting haven't been found. The *Galveston Daily News*, however, later noted, "Warren was also witnessing against W. J. Wood and others on indictments pending in the District Court of Nolan County for cattle stealing."[21]

Colonel Odom's and Detective Carlton's names were on the indictments as witnesses. Alfred Hanscomb, the grand jury foreman, later testified that Benjamin Warren was the principal witness of the jury's testimony on which indictments were based. Another jury member, Horace Thompson, claimed that Warren's evidence and testimony were directed more toward W. J. Wood and C. W. (Neil) Boyett than the other parties indicted. Upon written complaint, duly sworn to and filed before him, District Judge Thomas Benton Wheeler issued warrants for the arrest of the indicted fence cutters. Odom traveled to Austin to meet with Adjutant General King and Governor Ireland and solicit assistance from Rangers in a roundup.[22]

After the special session of the Texas legislature closed, Adjutant General King had assigned temporary command of the Frontier Battalion to George W. Baylor. Captain Baylor of Ranger Company A was now responsible for deploying the Frontier Battalion's scattered Ranger Force to assist local authorities and support the commercial detectives working on fence-cutting problems. Baylor traveled by rail to Abilene, then rode into Fort Chadbourne on May 4. The fence-cutter roundup began, with a detachment of men from Baylor's Company A, with Rangers from Samuel McMurry's Company B and J. T. Gillespie's Company E. There were twenty-five Rangers starting the search and arrest of the indicted fence cutters and criminals. Two weeks later, in Austin, the *Austin Weekly Statesman* quoted Baylor saying, "eight fence cutters arrested in Runnels County . . . indicted and are safely in jail in Colorado City with good prospects of their conviction." A witness said the Rangers had been a little rough on the fence cutters they arrested before delivering them to the jail in Colorado City. Years after the roundup, Mrs. J. C. Brownfield, an old-timer and one of Elisha Hylton's daughters, said, "Rangers came in and arrested many of the boys. . . . The Rangers mistreated these boys, tying them to wagon wheels."[23]

At the time of the Rangers' arrests, Runnels County didn't have a secure jail. Under this circumstance, District Judge Wheeler ordered the men under indictments to be delivered and jailed in Colorado City until they secured a bond. While in jail at Colorado City, the prisoners were under the watch of Mitchell County Sheriff Dick Ware, a former Texas Ranger. The court issued capiases for those indicted parties still on the loose.[24]

Ben Warren's identity as a Ranger and as the informant testifying before the grand jury was kept secret, unknown outside the court. Indictments on file did not list him as a witness. Once the indictments were handed down, the fence cutters began a frantic search for the informant who had turned evidence. Neil Boyett suspected Warren, and he and Pete Thompson stopped Warren on the road as he traveled home from Sweetwater. They planned to kill him, but Warren spoke to them in such a friendly and different manner than expected that they had second thoughts. Thompson had been indicted but not yet arrested, so they asked Warren to leave the public road and go down into a nearby hollow for a private talk. His readiness to go and deportment as they carried on their discussion convinced the two that they were mistaken in suspecting Ben Warren as the informant.[25]

After escaping this near-death encounter with these two fence cutters he helped indict, Ben moved his wife and children from Fish Creek to Fort Chadbourne, the Odom Ranch headquarters. This move pegged Ben Warren as the informant who had brought in the twenty-four fence-cutting indictments. Now difficult times began for all of the Warren families. Brother John lived up near Buffalo Gap in Taylor County and was away from the heat. Ben's younger brother Joseph Warren was a cattleman who came to Nolan County, recording his brand in the county's brand book in 1881. Joseph lived on Fish Creek with his family. Making matters worse, his brother-in-law was W. J. Wood. Joseph and his family were neighbors of Wood and Elisha Hylton.

Wood and Elisha's sons, Dow and Riley, were now under indictment for multiple fence-cutting offenses.[26]

When the Rangers were in Runnels County arresting fence cutters on May 4, Runnels County Sheriff John Formwalt, Garland Odom, and Captain Baylor went to the home of Elisha Hylton on Fish Creek, searching for Dow and Riley. After their visit Elisha filed a lawsuit in the Nolan County District Court claiming $10,000 actual and $10,000 exemplary damages for wrongful arrest and false imprisonment. Hylton charged that an hour before daybreak on May 5, 1884, Ranger George Baylor, Sheriff John Formwalt, and Garland Odom showed up with armed men under the direction of Representative T. L. Odom. They forced their way into his home, cursed and abused him in the presence of his family, and searched his house. The lawmen arrested Elisha, took him from his home, and held him in confinement for over twelve hours. He said they had no warrant or capias for his arrest at the time, and they acted maliciously in all that was done. Hylton's case came to trial in November of 1884. Judge William Kennedy heard his case in the District Court of Nolan County.

In their defense the lawmen's attorney argued that John Formwalt was sheriff of Runnels County and George Baylor was a captain in the state's Frontier Battalion. On May 5 they were under the order of the governor and the state's adjutant general. Sheriff Formwalt, with Garland Odom's help, was acting under his charges in the execution of the process held by them, directing the arrest of certain parties. No one was acting under the direction or advice of Representative Odom.

They said that there existed in Nolan County at that time fence cutters engaged in lawless acts of destroying fences. As an organization the fence cutters had books and officers, with headquarters in or near the house of Elisha Hylton. Elisha was suspected of being a member of the fence-cutting gang. He was engaged in the manufacture of tools and nippers for the fence cutters who cut the Odom's fences and threatened to kill anyone who attempted to arrest them. Judge Thomas Wheeler of the Twelfth Judicial District had issued warrants to arrest about twenty parties, two of whom were Elisha's sons, Dow and Riley Hylton. One of these sons resided in Elisha's house. Formwalt and Baylor had warrants for the sons but had arrested Elisha Hylton by mistake. Although Elisha had harbored the two sons and counseled and rendered them assistance, the lawmen's attorney advised the court that Hylton was released as soon as they discovered their mistake. At the end of this trial on November 11, 1885, a judgment was rendered against defendants Sheriff John Formwalt, Ranger Captain George Baylor, and Garland Odom for $200 actual damages and $300 exemplary damages. The lawmen appealed the case. Later it was argued before the Texas Supreme Court.[27]

The fence-cutting cases were first brought to trial in Runnels District Court on September 30, 1884, but the state continued the cases. The second court date for the trial of the indicted fence cutters in Runnels County was quickly approaching.[28]

Ben Warren and his family were now living at Odom's Fort Chadbourne headquarters. Several men were heard to express their intent to kill Warren. T. L. Odom, his family, and Warren's family were under the protection of Rangers. The fence cutters were so desperate that in an attempt to discredit Warren's testimony in their upcoming trial, they hatched a plan to file charges against him. If their plan worked and their charge stuck, that could likely discredit his testimony in the fence-cutting trials. The cutter's plan unfolded. Warren was charged in Nolan County with malicious mischief for shooting a two-year-old heifer belonging to the Bunton brothers. Three of the cutters, Riley Hylton, Dow Hylton, and William J. Wood, filed the charges and testified that Warren had shot Bunton's cow and committed the crime.[29]

Following his Nolan County indictment on the cow killing charge, Warren traveled to Sweetwater to find an attorney and secure bond. Arriving in Sweetwater, he was introduced to Royston C. Crane, a young man reading law and just beginning his legal practice under a special license. Crane secured Warren's bond to appear in the court's upcoming term and strongly advised him to leave town and stay away from the Fish Creek neighborhood. He warned Warren that he would be killed before he could testify in the fence-cutting cases. Warren paid Crane with a twenty-dollar gold piece for his services and left Sweetwater as advised.[30]

Fifty years after assisting Ben Warren to secure his bond, Royston C. Crane Sr. reflected on how tough Sweetwater was in those early years.

Crane said Sweetwater had the reputation of being the wildest, toughest, and most lawless town in West Texas. He told a story about the cowboy on a train out of Fort Worth. He said, "A drunken cowboy sat in a westbound train at Fort Worth, and when the conductor came through to take up tickets, he found the cowboy sound asleep. He woke him up and asked him where he was going. The cowboy grunted and said, 'to hell.' The conductor said, 'OK, I will punch your ticket to Sweetwater.'"[31]

The malicious mischief case against Warren was tried in Sweetwater on February 10, 1885, the week before the fence-cutting trial was to continue in Runnels County. The Nolan County trial of Warren convened, but the plaintiffs' testimony against Warren was not persuasive. M. A. Spoonts, the attorney from Abilene who was representing the young Ranger, served him well because Warren had no witness for his defense. There was a hung jury, and a verdict of guilt could not be reached. This was a great relief for Warren, but there would be challenging times the following week when the fence cutters would go to trial in Runnels City.[32]

That night after his trial for killing the cow, Warren was in the office lobby of the Sweetwater Central Hotel with Colonel T. L. Odom. Warren and Odom were carrying on a conversation with a man who had come to Nolan County and engaged in the business of poisoning prairie dogs. A Mr. Dabney and Mr. C. F. Powell of Austin were in the hotel office sitting around the woodstove. W. S. Lester was reclining on a lounge sofa. Colonel Odom was sitting four feet from Warren and leaned forward, punching up the fire in the woodstove. Sitting near the stove, Warren was smoking his pipe and had his hands in his overcoat pockets. At that moment a shot was fired through the glass pane of the office window. It came from the alley that ran past the hotel. The bullet struck Warren in the head, passing below his left eye and exiting below his right ear. The shot barely missed Colonel Odom. Odom later testified he felt the concussion in the air as the bullet passed by his head and struck Warren.

Thinking he was being fired on, Colonel Odom's reaction was to spring through the door entering the hotel dining room. Looking back through the doorway to the office, Odom saw Warren in the chair with blood spurting from his face. He shouted for someone to get a doctor and keep the body from falling from the chair. Seeing a flash in the window he feared was a gun, he ducked back into the dining room, closed the door, and remained in the dark, fearing he would be shot next. Minutes later, Odom again entered the office, where he saw Warren stretched out on the floor and saw Mack Boyett looking down on him. Mack was the older brother of Neil Boyett, both of whom had been indicted for fence cutting by Warren's testimony. Odom then walked out through the Central Hotel's dining room, through the kitchen and backyard, and went to the Palace Hotel nearby, where he secured a room and spent the night.[33]

Early the next morning, Odom went to the Central Hotel and saw Ben Warren's body still stretched out on the office floor. He examined the bullet hole in the windowpane and other surroundings. Outside there was a plank fence about three feet high in the ally on the north side of the Central Hotel, two feet from the wall and window of the office where Warren was shot. The bullet had passed through the glass windowpane about five feet from the ground. Odom carefully examined the ground outside the fence and found a man's tracks. The toe of the right foot showed plainly against the bottom plank of the fence just across from the window. Colonel Odom had handled firearms since he was 10 years old. He was left-handed and always shouldered his rifle and fired from his left shoulder. He was convinced that the assassin's shot was fired from the left shoulder and so testified. This and testimony from other witnesses about a left-handed killer would later lead to a life sentence for one of the men charged with the crime.[34]

Doctor R. E. Moody performed a postmortem examination of Warren's body. Nolan County Sheriff H. G. Bardwell summoned a jury of inquest. Odom attended to the corpse and procured a coffin. One of Warren's brothers took the Ranger's body from Sweetwater to Fort Chadbourne for burial.[35]

The two Boyett brothers, Neil and Mack, and W. J. Wood and Riley Hylton were placed under arrest and held on suspicion. With a week of Justice of the Peace C. W. Steele's hard labor, Cornelius W. Boyett (Neil) and William J. Wood (Bud) were charged by the verdict of the coroner's jury with the murder of Ranger Private Ben Warren. Based on the decision of Justice Steele, rendered on preliminary trial and in the following judgment of District Judge William Kennedy on hearing of the habeas corpus after their indictment, Wood and Boyett were denied bail. Both men were imprisoned in the Sweetwater jail.[36]

In the heat of the day four months later, on July 5, 1885, Nolan County Sheriff H. G. Bardwell went to the Sweetwater jail carrying a bucket of water for the prisoners. On entering the jail, Bardwell was overpowered, and a jailbreak by seven inmates followed. As the escape attempt commenced, someone sounded an alarm. Sweetwater citizens armed with shotguns, Winchesters, and six-shooters rushed to the jail. The newspaper gave special praise to Fellow Decker, reporting he got the drop on the notorious bad man Redmond "Bud" Coleman, who was armed with a Winchester taken from in the jail. W. C. Johnston, the keeper of the Cattle Exchange Saloon, was also commended. He was there and helped stopped the jailbreak. The citizens of the community captured all of the prisoners except William J. Wood. Wood made good his escape on Sheriff Bardwell's horse and headed for home on Fish Creek.[37]

Following the jailbreak, someone in Sweetwater, probably one of Boyett's attorneys, contacted the *Galveston Daily News* and reported the escape attempt. Whoever sent the story to the newspaper claimed that Boyett saved the sheriff's life during the escape attempt. They followed by saying,

> It is the [sic] generally believed that the prisoners Boyett and Wood are not guilty of the murder of Ben Warren and they have the sympathy of a large majority if not all of the city and county, and their counsel, Cowan & Posey, who are said to be the most prominent attorneys of this section of the state, who are defending them, are confident of an acquittal under the evidence of the state and the habeas corpus trial, which is believed to be the full strength of the state's evidence. The case will likely be tried in November next.[38]

In response to the newspaper article, Nolan County Sheriff H. G. Bardwell immediately denied that Boyett saved his life. Correction with the sheriff's written report was sent to the *Galveston Daily News* by the papers Sweetwater correspondent. Bardwell's written and sworn statement was printed July 14, 1885, in the Galveston newspaper.

Fence Cutters Assassinate Ranger Benjamin Warren in Sweetwater

Sweetwater, Tex. July 13, 1885

Sheriff Bardwell's Statement Concerning That Exciting Event. To correct the report of the jail delivery at Sweetwater, as published in your issue of the 9th instant, under date of Sweetwater, July 8, your regular correspondent here, who is in no manner responsible for that report, this morning received from Sheriff Bardwell the following statement. It is written down in his exact language.

On the afternoon of July 5, 1885, I went to the jail to carry the prisoners a bucket of water. The prisoners in jail were W. J. Wood and Neil Boyett, charged with the Murder of Ben G. Warren; Williams and Coleman, sent here from Jones County for safekeeping; Fulton, Smith and Williams, the latter two convicted at the recent term of our District Court to the penitentiary—one for two and the other for four years. I opened the jail door leading into the corridor wide enough to slip in the bucket, none of the prisoners were in the corridor. Williams from Jones County was in the cell next to corridor and grabbed my hand. I pulled away from him, and in doing so, and in the act of closing the corridor, I slipped and fell down, the floor being wet from the saliva ejected through the grating by the prisoners on the inside. Before I could recover from my fall, Williams, Coleman and Boyett had seized me and were holding me down. Boyett and Williams then said, "Bardwell, we do not want to hurt you, but you had better keep quiet." Coleman then ran down stairs to a private room, got a Winchester rifle, ran back, leveled the gun on me, and said, "If you make any noise, I will shoot you." Boyett and Williams were still holding me. One of them said, "Let's lock him up in the jail." Coleman replied, "No, that won't do; I'll carry him before me down stairs." As they carried me downstairs, Boyett and Williams were still holding me, Coleman holding the gun on me. Boyett and Williams, when we got downstairs, partially released me, and I sat down in a chair. Coleman and Williams then ran for the back door and I sprang for the front door. Boyett rushed out after me, and I thought he was trying to catch me. Wood left the jail and ran out the front door, while the others held me, and before I got downstairs. Did not jump out of any jail window but went out the front door. I do not know how he got out of the enclosure around the jail. My horse, upon which he made his escape, was loose in the stable yard, adjoining to and in the rear of the jail enclosure. The Jail enclosure is made of planks placed upright, about fourteen feet high. Boyett did not refuse to go out of the jail so far as I know or have heard. Boyett never interfered to prevent my being hurt except as I have above stated. I did not knock Coleman in the eye; I had no chance to do so. Have never said or believed that if Boyett had not interfered, they would have killed me. I have never said that while Coleman, Boyett, and Williams were holding me that Boyett told Coleman not to hurt me. Boyett did not show any disposition to protect me from being hurt. He endeavored to the last to keep me from letting their attempt to escape from being known. I, at the time, was the only officer in town. Boyett was returned to Fort Worth in obedience to an order from Hon. Wm. Kennedy, judge of the Thirty-second District, commanding me to take him there. I have no order to remove Woods. Woods was recaptured on Fish Creek, about thirty miles from Sweetwater by a posse of officers and citizens under my direction, on the morning of July 8 and is now in jail here. He was out two days and three nights.

Sweetwater's regular newspaper correspondent then reported,

By comparing the statement made by Sheriff Bardwell, and which he will verify on his oath, with that made in your paper on 9th instant, your readers will see the want of accuracy in the latter. In the same report occurs this language: "It is generally believed that the prisoners Boyett and Wood are not guilty of the murder of Ben Warren, and they have the sympathy of a large majority, if not all of the city and county. In justice to the sentiment of our people, this correspondent is compelled to say that the above is not based on any general expression of the public opinion in the city and county. The currently expressed or indicated sentiment is that of acquiescence in the decision of Justice Steel, rendered on preliminary trial, and in the decision of Judge Kennedy on hearing of habeas corpus after the indictment, denying both Wood and Boyett bail. With no desire for anything but the truth, your regular correspondent writes this on behalf of the good people of Nolan County. Let justice be done though the heavens may fall."[39]

Citizens were very concerned over the attempted escape of the dangerous outlaws Bud Coleman and A. J. Williams. Following the attempted jailbreak, George Scarborough, the Jones County sheriff, traveled down to Sweetwater and had the two outlaws chained to the floor of the jail. Two years after this attempted jailbreak, Scarborough killed Williams in a gunfight in Haskell, Texas. Both C. W. Boyett and W. T. Wood were moved from Sweetwater to the Fort Worth jail for safekeeping.[40]

On November 30, 1885, the district court convened in Sweetwater, Texas, and District Judge William Kennedy determined it was impossible to try Boyett and Wood and have a fair trial in Nolan County. Many potential jurors were disqualified because of biases. Others had formed opinions, and a large number were disqualified because of conscientious scruples regarding capital punishment. Judge Kennedy ordered a change of venue. He sent Boyett's case to Abilene in Taylor County, and Wood's case was sent to Mitchell County.[41]

C. W. Boyett was tried before Judge William Kennedy at the Taylor County Courthouse in Abilene, March 23, 1886. The jury found Boyett guilty of murder in the first degree and sentenced him to life in the state's penitentiary. His lawyers immediately appealed his case to the Texas Court of Appeals.[42]

W. J. Woods's case went to trial in Colorado (today Colorado City), Texas, in Mitchell County in January. The *Fort Worth Daily Gazette* reported, "W. J. Woods is on trial today in the district court, charged with the killing of Ben Warren, a state detective at Sweetwater last spring. There are a great number of witnesses in the case, but the evidence is all circumstantial. Today and tomorrow will be consumed in the trial of the case." But there were difficulties impaneling a jury in Mitchell County, and the Woods case was sent to Callahan County to be tried in Baird.[43]

On April 17, 1886, Wood was tried before District Judge Thomas B. Wheeler. Judge Wheeler heard Warren's testimony and was the judge who passed down the fence-cutting indictments in Runnels County during the court's May term of 1884. In the trial in Baird, Wood was found guilty of murder and sentenced to the penitentiary for natural life. He was sent back to the jail in Fort Worth for safekeeping and his case was sent to the Texas Court of Appeals.[44]

When Warren's assassin cases were being made ready for trial, Elisha Hylton's case against Runnels County Sheriff John Formwalt, Ranger Captain George Baylor, and Garland Odom was appealed and argued before the Texas Supreme Court. Hylton admitted he was under an indictment for cattle theft in Nolan County and W. J. Wood, his son-in-law, was under indictment for murder. These indictments did nothing to change the district court finding on Hylton's false arrest. The Texas Supreme Court confirmed that Hylton's case had been fairly presented in the charge. The lower court record disclosed no error. On May 21, 1886, the Texas Supreme Court delivered its opinion affirming the district court ruling against Sheriff John Formwalt, Ranger Captain George Baylor, and Garland Odom.[45]

The following year, in December 1887, the Texas Court of Appeals heard and ruled on the two capital murder cases that Wood and Boyett had appealed. The Wood case tried by Judge Thomas Benton Wheeler was reversed and remanded back to the district court for a new trial. A search of court documents and newspapers has found no record showing Wood was ever retried on the Warren murder charge. In the C. W. Boyett case, the court found no error in the lower court's judgment. It affirmed Judge William Kennedy's district court case that sentenced Boyett to a life term in prison.[46]

Boyett was delivered to the Rusk State Penitentiary in Cherokee County, Texas, arriving on January 27, 1887. The prison clerk entered Boyett's name in the convict register as Prisoner Number 2558. The register entry described Boyett as a 29-year-old cowboy, five feet, eight inches tall, weighing 160 pounds, with brown eyes and sandy hair. He had a scar on his chin and left cheek. In the days in prison that followed, Boyett was not a model prisoner. His name appears in the Rusk State Prison Conduct Ledger dated March 26, 1888, noting that he was receiving punishment for "neglect of work." While Boyett was acclimating to his new environment and prison rules in the Rusk State Penitentiary, his family, friends, and lawyers spent time and money on his behalf. They circulated petitions for his pardon in Nolan, Mitchell, Scurry, Runnels, and Coleman Counties, all of which suffered significant fence-cutting problems. Those petitions—signed by fence cutters, citizens who despised barbed wire and big pastures, and who hated the Rangers—landed on the desk of Governor Lawrence Sullivan Ross. On May 2, 1890, Governor Ross commuted Boyett's life sentence. After serving two and a half years of his life sentence for murder, Boyett was discharged on July 4, 1890, and walked out of the Rusk State Penitentiary a free man. There appears to be some political irony here. Governor Ross was the former sheriff of McLennan County and a former

Texas Ranger. Yet he commuted the life sentence of a fence cutter who assassinated another Ranger, Benjamin G. Warren.[47]

For many years Neil Boyett's father, C. H. Boyett, served as both county commissioner and justice of the peace for Precinct No. 3 in Nolan County. Neil Boyett had been elected constable of Precinct No. 3 in 1884 and was one of the few citizens in Nolan County who legally carried a handgun. When Neil returned from the state's penitentiary, his father, C. H. Boyett, stepped down as the Precinct 3 county commissioner. Boyett replaced his father as commissioner and was elected in the 1890 election and later in 1898 as Nolan County commissioner for Precinct No. 3. Neil Boyett's power in Nolan County politics ended with his death on December 28, 1900.[48]

Hylton, Texas, was established in 1886 and named for Elisha Hylton. Elisha became the community's first postmaster in the same year.[49]

The Runnels County fence-cutter cases built on evidence gathered by Detective William Carlton and evidence and testimony of Ben Warren bounced around for two years. Following the fence-cutter indictments in May of 1884, the first case was tried on September 30. That first case, Cause No. 44 charging Riley Hylton, was dismissed. The state was granted a continuance on the other cases. They were back in court on December 2, and the trials were granted a continuance by consent of both the state and the defendants. The cases were then set for trial in the February term of 1885. Unfortunately, the state's key witness, Ranger Ben Warren, had been assassinated, and the cases were again continued. After this continuance, the first case tried was the *State of Texas vs. Dow Hylton*, Cause 40. It was tried in 1886. This Cause 40 was the state's strongest case. Because of Warren's death and absence, the case was tried on circumstantial evidence in the February term of the Thirty-Second District Court at Runnels City by Judge William Kennedy.[50]

After hearing the case, Judge Kennedy gave the jury three pages of written instructions and emphasized the use of circumstantial evidence, to wit:

> In this case, the evidence is circumstantial, and you are instructed that in order to warrant a conviction of a crime on circumstantial evidence, each fact necessary to the conclusion sought to be established must be

proved by competent evidence, beyond a reasonable doubt, the facts (that is the necessary facts to the conclusion) must be consistent with each other, and with the main fact sought to be proved; and the circumstances, taken together, must be of a conclusive nature, leading on the whole to a satisfactory conclusion and producing in effect a reasonable and moral certainty; that the accused (whether alone or acting with others) and no other person committed the offense charged. The defendant is presumed innocent until his guilt is established by legal evidence, and if, from the legal evidence before you, you have a legal doubt as to the defendant's guilt, you will acquit him.

Dow Hylton's indictment, Cause No. 40 in the Runnels County District Clerks office, has a handwritten note across the front stating, "We the Jury find the defendant not guilty," signed by the jury foreman, J. W. Sanylin. Following Dow Hylton's trial and acquittal, all but three fence cutters had their cases dropped. Later in the year, the state dropped charges against the remaining three men. No records were found indicating further actions against the Fish Creek Fence Cutters.[51]

Benjamin Goodin Warren is buried in the Fort Chadbourne Cemetery near T. L. Odom's family graves. Ben's gravestone displays the Masonic square and compass engraved above his name. Near the base of the monument, there is an inscription that reads, "Farewell my wife and children all, from you a father do call." Eppie Hubbert Warren, Ben's wife, was left with ten children, one of whom was born eight months after Ben's murder. In the 1900 US Census, for Nolan County, Eppie is listed as a stock raiser with two sons and a daughter still living at home.[52]

Chapter 8

Rangers Kill a Fence-Cutting Constable in Brown County

> My order was answered by a shot from a six-shooter fired at us by the fence cutters, then the firing was general.
> —Ranger Captain William Scott

The Eighteenth Special Session of the Texas Legislature had struggled through contentious debates on numerous bills and finished its work. Most of the needed fence-cutting legislation was passed as emergency acts, was signed by the governor, and went into effect immediately. Citizens had asked for detectives believing they were necessary to catch the elusive and secretive fence cutters who destroyed fences during the dark of night. The legislature, feeling the pressure appropriated $50,000 to the governor to employ detectives and pay rewards. The citizens' cry for detectives had been heard and their request granted by the legislature. News of the appropriation spread. When the legislature adjourned and went home, the large Pinkerton National Detective Agency of Chicago and Ferrell's Commercial Detective Agency with headquarters in New Orleans were at the state capital offering their services and soliciting detective work.[1]

After the session adjourned and members went home, incidents of fence cutting still occurred in a few counties. However, the epidemic that flamed across Texas in 1883 and into 1884 ended. Missing were the everyday newspaper stories that had been so prevalent about fences being cut; most newspapers had lost interest.

Still, there were a few hot spots of lawless cutting of fences in the state, where fence cutters refused to give up their malicious activities. With fence cutting now a felony offense, Rangers were sent to those areas, and detectives were employed to gather evidence. Brown County was one of the hot spots where fence cutting continued. The Baugh family became the cutters' primary target; there was a vendetta against the Baughs. Lev and Morg Baugh's fences enclosed much of the land on Pecan Bayou and Jim Ned Creek—land and water that had been accessible to everyone in years past. Further, the brother's aggressive manner of dealing with the fence cutters had created bitter enemies. The role the Baughs played in December 1883, riding with the posse through the farm and ranch country visiting cutters' residences, was still on the fence cutters' minds.[2]

The governor, now with funding, employed the Pinkerton Agency and the Ferrell's Detective Agency to work in several fence-cutting hot spots across the state. These two large agencies with reputations, size, and strong politics appeared to be a good choice. The adjutant general also hired a small number of individuals to perform undercover work as detectives. Those individuals appear to have had questionable skills. An occasional name is found but none showed a measure of success in their work. In a part of South Texas, where fence cutting was still occurring, a detective or a "special serviceman" was working for the Guadalupe and San Antonio River Stock Association. No record of this man's success was found, but he was paid by the state for his undercover work. Several of the state's livestock associations had lobbied the legislature for detectives.[3]

A. E. Kramer from the Ferrell Detective Agency and T. N. Vallin from the Pinkerton Agency were sent to work in Brown County, one of the hot spot and a continuing problem for the governor. The men were sworn in, provided Texas Ranger credentials, and given instructions by Adjutant General Wilburn King. The adjutant general chose Captain

James T. Gillespie and Ranger Company E to headquarter in Brown County and support these two detectives.[4]

The Ferrell's man, Kramer, was first to arrive in Brownwood. In his first correspondence, dated February 19, 1884, and mailed to the adjutant general, Kramer reported he was in Brownwood and spending time with patrons at the bars and gambling halls. Adjutant General King had directed Kramer to contact and place his trust in the Coggin brothers at their Brownwood Bank. In this first letter to the adjutant general, Kramer reported that the bank's men believed that the fence cutters were also bank robbers. Part of his first letter reads

> The difficulty which I consider that I am meeting with is a suspicion that causes me to believe that the good people here want me to work up their bank robbers because therein under the plan state that they are the fence cutters. Whilst I might be mistaken, my sojourning these few days amongst the fence cutters, decides me that that is not the case. My informants are trusted, and men whose native shrewdness, sagacity, and standing will serve me in the future in my operation, hence I must at least appear to give credence to their assertion but what they say prove to be a fact.[5]

Kramer's next report to the adjutant general was written and mailed near the end of February. The detective studied the fence-cutting problem and had a plan. In his letter he outlined the plan, parts of which could not be carried out under Texas law. His assessment of Brown County conditions was on target, however, and prophetic of the struggle the Rangers and district courts would have over the next five years. Kramer was awed by the criminal activity and the lack of law and order in Brownwood. He was the first to express concerns about the credibility of Brown County Sheriff William Nelson Adams. Kramer was awaiting the support of Rangers of Company E, expecting them to arrive in the next several days. His report to Adjutant General King follows:

Brownwood, Brown Co. Texas
Feby 27, 1884
W. H. King
Adjutant General, State of Texas

General:

Last night the temporary court house at this place was burned to the ground the object being to destroy the indictments against four or five horse thieves now in jail, it being anticipated the object was not obtained.

In working up fence cutting brings me in contact with the supposed instigators of the fire, I am positive that I will be able to turn them up with the other criminals at the proper time.

You will likely hear of the other depredations committed here, amongst them fence cutting. The fences now being put up for that purpose, as I am myself operating amongst the leaders and planners (saloon and gambling house) and have two good trusty men among the fence cutters, and will be thoroughly conversant with what is going on and the fact alone of not wishing to frighten my birds as well as to keep my men (the witnesses) in the background concludes me to wait until I am ready to make a general sweep. Besides my "Spies" being sworn members of their organization and it being highly dangerous to them that inform, you will readily understand why I desire to use them only at the last moment, and this raises a question which I wish you would decide at the earliest moment.

Can I cause (when backed by papers affidavit) the arrest's to be made by Rangers (who are due hear on the 1st) and have prisoners with witnesses taken to Austin?

This request is made for the reason that I know positively, that it is almost impossible to have them arrested here (the sheriff is in with the fence cutters through political reason), you cannot get them indicted, and to a dead certainty, you can't get a jury to find them guilty in this county. This is owing to the fact that the lawless element predominates in a large majority, and wiliest some sympathizers through fear of loss of life and property, others do so for pecuniary reasons. (This could be substantiated by evidence.) Further, could I get my prisoners' in Austin "Cell," remove him from the fear and influence of his companions, and by making him go through the "Squeezing" process, I can assure you we would have the majority of the malefactors in Brown County in jail in no time or drive them from their haunts, either case suits the community here (among them are a class who are tired of cutting fences, would like to get out of it). If they were taken to Austin they would give the whole thing away.

Again fence cutting is done at night, the only valuable evidence I can obtain is from the "spies" who will not make affidavit unless they are certain that those whom they are giving away will be convicted (which they know they will not be, if tried here) and from other members (who once in a cell in Austin will become as ductile as down) or by Rangers who will be able to catch them in the act (it being night probably) who will be compelled to turn them over to the sheriff (who is no good) by him turned loose again to fix evidence, juries, etc., and (as a last resort as they have done before) burn down the courthouse to destroy the indictments.

Please excuse presumption in making foregoing suggestions, but I am prompted by the permission extended by you and an experience obtained in Georgia and Alabama [e]tc; among moonshiners, a very similar case, where I found the above works admirably, and with satisfactory results.

Coggins, Ford and Martin, Bankers of this place who were recommended to me by Senator Fleming, and whom I have confidence, with whom I wish you place $50 or $75 dollars to my credit for necessary expenses. I could send monthly statements of expenditures but would rather do quarterly as intimated by you.

"The Ground" I am working on being large, I intend to work one or two Rangers (on their arrival) among the fence cutters but if tractable another operator for Coleman and McCullough would be more than desirable, Brown County requiring all of my attention at the present.

I am General, very respectfully yours,

Your servant, E. Kramer [6]

Rangers were sent to assist the detectives working on the Brown County hotspot of fence cutting. Adjutant General King sent Ranger Company E to Brown County and Company B to Coleman County, west of Brown. A third company, Ranger Company D, was sent to Menard County to work horse and cattle stealing there and in surrounding counties, but they would also serve as a backup if needed for the fence-cutting work. Captain J. T. Gillespie was assigned Brown County, moved Ranger Company E into the county, and establish his headquarters camp.[7]

On arrival one of Captain Gillespie's early actions was the arrest of J. D. Scoggin, the leader of the much talked about Brownwood Fence Cutters Convention. Scoggin's arrest appears to have created quite a commotion. Referring to his arrest in a letter to the adjutant general in Austin, Captain J. T. Gillespie reported, "Two of the boys caught Mr. Scoggin, the one-armed man the other day. Scoggin's wife said she preferred her husband be arrested by Negros before Rangers. As you can see, we are gaining popularity in Brown.

Sure enough, we are, but not with the fence cutting fraternity." On searching records this author found no charges filed on Scoggin.[8]

A. E. Kramer, the Ferrell detective, was now passing on information to Captain Gillespie and Adjutant General King. One night soon after Company E's arrival, one of Kramer's spies named Rucker came into the Ranger camp and met with Gillespie. Rucker told the captain that he was working undercover among the cutters for Kramer and asked to be secretly attached as one of Gillespie's Rangers. The captain saw merit in the request. In a letter to Adjutant General King, Gillespie said, "He will undoubtedly make a success of working with them (the fence cutters), and I respectfully refer the matter of his enlistment to you for your consideration. His enlistment might add zeal to his workings; however, I await your decision to report to him." There was no response from Adjutant General King and no action taken on Rucker's request.[9]

Allen Pinkerton had contacted the governor, soliciting work in Texas. One of his men, Detective T. N. Vallin, sent from Chicago, arrived at the state capital and met with Governor Ireland for his assignment. Vallin's first job was with urgency; he was to work on a recent fence-cutting case in Williamson County. Fences were cut near Taylor, a short day's ride from Austin. The legislature had just returned home, and the Taylor fence-cutting incident was a big news story in the state's capital of Austin. Detective Vallin spent several nights drinking with cowboys in a Taylor saloon and talked with the farmer whose fence had been cut. Vallin concluded this wasn't a malicious act. He reported to Adjutant General King that the only fence cut in Williamson County after the legislature departed Austin was on Mr. Burris's farm on the San Gabriel River. The opinion of farmer Burris and the saloon's patrons in Taylor was that several drunk cowboys cut the fence on the way home after celebrating a night on the town. Vallin found no significant fence-cutting problem in Williamson County. After filing his report, Vallin left Taylor on March 5 for Brownwood, and on arriving located A. E. Kramer, the operative from Ferrell's Detective Agency. After Vallin convinced Kramer of his identity, Kramer briefed the Pinkerton detective of his activities among the cutters. The two detectives now worked as a team.

Vallin mailed a letter to Adjutant General King on March 9, saying, "Kramer has received information from one of his men that about 20 men are going to cut the fence around Baugh's pasture, which is located about nine miles from here. This they intend to do in a few days. It is our intent to have the Rangers there and arrest the whole party."

He continued the letter, expressing concern that Baugh (presumably Lev) had learned of the planned fence-cutting venture that was about to occur. Baugh had his own ideas on dealing with the cutters and intended to take care of the fence-cutting problem himself. Vallin's letter advised the adjutant general: "he wants to take some men that he shall pick and go there which I think is a very bad plan, it being evident someone would be killed, and if any of the fence cutters are killed they can raise 300 men, and there is the kind of men here to agitate them, and there would be a great deal of bloodshed and loss of property. We will do all we possibly can to prevent such a move by Baugh and have the Rangers there instead."[10] Vallin's information about the planned fence cutting did not prove correct; no encounter with fence cutters is found in newspapers or in Captain Gillespie's *monthly return*. The cutters likely suspected there was an informant in their ranks and scrapped the plan.[11]

Three months after their arrival, the Pinkerton and Ferrell Agency detectives abruptly departed Brown County, apparently to save their lives. In June Captain Gillespie notified Quartermaster John Johnson in Austin headquarters that Pinkerton's man, Vallin, returned the horse, saddle, bridle, and slicker Rangers had loaned him, then left the county. In this same letter, Gillespie spoke of the departure of Kramer, the Ferrell Agency's detective. "Kramer has gone, and I think before his departure, several were on to who he was."[12]

In April A. Himmel, another commercial detective, was also working undercover in Brown County. He was carried as a member of Company D but on special duty without pay. Himmel notified the quartermaster in Austin that he had gained the confidence of a member of the fence-cutting gang. The cutter he befriended had told him that the grand jury hadn't come up with indictments. Still, the jury had quite a bit of knowledge on the fence cutting, and the grand jury had the cutters scared. In his note to Austin, Himmel reported, "Being in the confidence of the Jim Ned Gang,

I hear them threaten and sputter about Baugh and his pasture, but that is all bunkum, the fact is they are scared. They have lost the sympathy of the class which gave them the moral support. They know there are traps laid for them, don't know who will sell out, they see the judge and jury ain't a'going to fool with them."[13]

An anonymous report came to Austin from another undercover man saying, "I learned that Bob Parrack, Bill Green, and that crowd were agitating to cutting Baugh's fence. I will do all I possibly can to get with them before they cut it and have Rangers there to make the arrests." Another undercover operative, name unknown, sent a note to the adjutant general concerning a fence-cutting incident in adjoining Comanche County. He reported, "I am convinced that it [the fence cutting] was done by John Burns and his outfit on Gap Creek, as the parties were tracked to that vicinity, which is in Brown County about twelve or fourteen miles from Brownwood."[14]

W. J. Bradly was employed as a detective to work undercover and assigned work in Brown. In June Bradley wrote Quartermaster John O. Johnson in Austin asking for his payment for his previous month's expenses. He asked Johnson to send the payment to Lieutenant Frank Jones of Ranger Company D. In this letter he asked Johnson to advise Adjutant General King that he had arrived in Bluffton (Llano County) and was awaiting further orders. Bradley had conducted clandestine fence-cutting work in Brown County. He was reassigned to gather information presumably on brand blotching and cattle stealing in Menard, Llano, Mason, and McCullough Counties. At the time cattle stealing was rampant in that area. Captain Lamartine Sieker and his Rangers of Company D were working the area and may have requested assistance of a detective to assist under cover.[15]

As commercial detectives left Brown County, Adjutant General King began detaching Rangers from several companies, spooning them into Brown County to perform undercover work. The commercial detectives' expenses had been a draw on the adjutant general's budget and the legislature's appropriation for detectives. King's Rangers received a pittance of what the commercial detectives billed the state. Few records are found identifying those Rangers dispatched to Brown County to perform undercover work. Their piecemeal correspondence and notes in the state archives either have names missing or they used assumed names. Rangers assigned as undercover operatives to Brown appeared to be rookies.[16]

One Ranger from Company D sent to work undercover among the Brown County fence cutters was Private William W. Collier. Collier had been a Ranger barely a year and just paid the balance owed to the state for the Colt revolver issued when he enlisted. Years after his Ranger service, Collier related how Brown County's fence cutters worked in harmony with each other and at times would join together and work in large bands. He described how large groups of men could come in and destroy miles of fence in one night. Collier was honorably discharged and left Ranger service in 1885. For years he didn't acknowledge his service as an undercover operative in Brown County. Forty years later William Collier finally told his story and spoke of his clandestine experience in Brown County. By then he was vice president of the City National Bank in San Antonio.[17]

The undercover man that proved the most effective in breaking up the county's fence cutting happened to be a Brown County farmer. Captain Gillespie wrote Adjutant General King advising that rancher Lev Baugh had a man working in secret with the cutters but didn't identify the person in his letter. Lev's insider had reported Baugh's fences would probably be cut in the next ten or fifteen days, but this expected fence cutting didn't occur. The informant of Baugh's was J. O. Copeland, called Joe by those that knew him. He farmed and was listed on the 1884 Brown County tax roll.[18]

Joe Copeland lived among the Jim Ned fence cutters in northwest Brown County. He joined the Brown County Farmer's Alliance, probably having been introduced to the alliance by some of his fence-cutting neighbors who were active members. Arriving in Brown County, Joe developed a friendship with Lev Baugh, possibly through their church or maybe his Masonic Brotherhood. This friendship soon led Copeland to become an informant and provide the Baugh brothers sensitive information on the fence cutter's activities.[19]

Joab Copeland, known as J. O., or Joe, was born at Hurricane Creek, Tennessee, in 1847. His father, James Copeland, had been a well-to-do Tennessee farmer listed in the 1850 US Census with land valued at $1,500. James Copeland came to Washington County, Texas, bringing his family with him when Joe was 13 years old. The Copelands lived and farmed near the Long Point Community.[20]

When Joe was 17, the Civil War began, and like most Texas farm boys, he joined the Confederate Army. He enlisted as a private February of 1863, in Company F of the 14th Regiment, Texas Infantry. He served for the unit's duration. The 14th Texas Infantry, combined with Walker's Texas Division, often is referred to as Walker's Greyhounds. They were given this name because of their speed in long marches across Arkansas and Louisiana, where they fought the Union troops in numerous bloody engagements.[21]

As the war was ending, Joe Copeland's unit began their return to Texas. They were a ragged bunch, and en route Copeland became too sick to travel. In March 1865 he was left behind by his unit near Racks Pocket in East Texas. His regiment officially surrendered at Galveston in June 1865. After the war Joab took the name "J. O." Copeland and rarely ever used the name Joab. We assumed the troops called him Joe while in the South's service, and the name followed him on returning home to Texas.[22]

By 1870 Joe Copeland was living near Marlin, the county seat of Falls County, Texas. He is found in the Falls County 1870 US Census listed as a farm laborer. James, his father, left Washington County and was on the Falls County tax roll in 1878 and 1879. Joe appears to have spent much of his life in the cotton business. A family tradition passed down says he was a cotton ginner and carpenter by trade in later life.[23]

On February 2, 1870, Joe married his first wife, Nancy J. Bruney, who died during childbirth. He later married Laura Christine Scarborough from Falls County on January 11, 1872. Joe had purchased land and was on the Falls County tax rolls in 1870. While living in Falls County, Joe Copeland became a Master Mason, petitioning the E. M. Wilder Lodge No. 339 at Powers Chapel in Rosebud, Texas. He was initiated on November 15, 1872, passed February 2, 1874, and raised a Master Mason on February 28, 1874. There is no record of Joe's religious affiliation, but he was likely a Methodist. Joseph Sneed, a Methodist circuit rider, organized the congregation later known as Powers Chapel.[24]

Nothing explains why Joe Copeland moved to Brown County, but opening of new fertile farmland selling on the frontier at a low price was likely his reason. The year before Joe arrived, Brown County produced 250,000 bushels of wheat, 5,000 bushels of corn, and 4,000 bales of cotton. When Joe came to Brown County and took up farming, it is assumed that he brought his family with him; we know they were living with him in Brown County later.[25]

When Captain J. T. Gillespie and Ranger Company E arrived in Brown County in February, the Ranger's camp set up by the captain was named Camp Thurmond, located on the land owned by the firm of Thurmond and Houston. Their pasture was one of the first Brown County sites suffering fence cutting. Four miles of their fences had been cut in one night. The Rangers who came with Gillespie were experienced lawmen and served him well in dealing with the fence cutters and other criminals. J. M. Sedberry was his lieutenant, L. F. Cartwright the first sergeant, and the company corporal was W. F. Sheffield.[26]

Adjutant General King shuffled Captain Gillespie's priorities soon after he arrived in Brown County. Company E headquarters was in Brown for a short time before moving to Taylor County. Headquarters moved but Gillespie left three Rangers behind guarding the county jail in Brownwood. Gillespie and Ranger Company E headquarters moved from Camp Thurman in Brown County to Taylor County on July 6, 1884.

Gillespie's new Ranger camp was on Lytle Creek, located west of Abilene, and he named this headquarters Camp Lytle. The camp was located roughly fifty miles from Brown County, and placed Company E Rangers adjacent to Runnels and Nolan Counties. Runnels was another hotbed of fence-cutting activity. Fence cutters in Runnels County were destroying the fences of State Representative Thomas L. Odom, whose ranch headquarters were at old Fort Chadbourne. Ranger Ben Warren, detached from Company E, had worked undercover and secured indictments in the Runnels District Court for fourteen of these cutters. Following the indictments Companies E and B and started the fence-cutter roundup. Rangers from Company E assisted with the arrest of eight of the indicted fence cutters. Gillespie men spent the rest of the year finding and protecting witnesses, attending court, and escorting Odom and Warren back and forth from Fort Chadbourne to the Runnels courtroom. There was concern that fence cutters would assassinate Representative T. L. Odom and Ben Warren, the state's key witnesses.[27]

As Captain Gillespie moved the Ranger headquarters from Brown, there was also a change in the Brown County District Court. The Eighteenth Texas Legislature redrew the state's district court boundaries. The April 10, 1884, issue of the *Austin Weekly Statesmen* contained a note from its Brownwood correspondent saying the county was losing William Blackburn, their district judge. The paper's correspondent lamented, "Blackburn is trying to get cases to trial but finally sent jury home...but grand jury hard at work . . . no arrests yet for fence cutting and no bills yet returned. We are very sorry to be losing our incumbent Judge Blackburn for all regard him as an able and efficient adjudicator . . . no one has filed for his position." The Eighteenth Texas Legislature created new judicial districts and reduced the size of the state's older districts. Brown County was affected and would soon elect a new district judge and district attorney.[28]

As 1884 was ending, Captain Gillespie delivered a convict to the prison for George Scarborough, the new sheriff of Jones County. When he returned to Camp Lytle, Gillespie found a message from Governor Ireland telling him to go immediately to Brown County and investigate cattle killing. The Ranger Captain says in his December monthly return that on arriving in Brown County, "after two days of investigations, the matter was so complicated that it was impossible to take any action." Details of what was found in Brown County are not in the Captain Gillespie's monthly return, but a story passed down says there was a fence enclosing a herd of yearling purebred Hereford Bulls brought to Brown County to upgrade the owner's range cattle. The fence cutters went into the pasture, roped the bulls and cut their tongues out, then released them to starve. Though no record has been found, we do know that Morgan Baugh was an early Brown County Herford breeder. This brutal and costly incident appears to have precipitated the return of Company E to Brown.[29]

When the Ranger company headquarters returned to Brown County, the old judge, W. A. Blackburn, and District Attorney W. H. Browning had a new judicial district with fewer counties. Brown County was not one of them. Following the legislative realignment, Blackburn's new Twenty-Seventh Judicial District encompassed four counties—Bell, Lampasas, Mills, and Burnet—with Burnet being his home. Brown County was now in the Thirty-Fifth Judicial District.[30]

When the district judge and district attorney offices of the newly shaped Thirty-Fifth Judicial District opened for filing, a young lawyer from Coleman County, 28-year-old J. C. Randolph, filed for district judge and was elected. Another Coleman attorney, J. O. Woodard, ran for the district attorney's office and was also elected. Randolph and Woodard took their offices. A new term of district court opened in Brown County, and the newly organized district court's judicial work began.[31]

The Baugh brothers and detectives funneled evidentiary information on fence cutters to the county's district court. On the morning of February 1, 1885, Captain Gillespie returned to his camp from Brownwood carrying capiases to arrest eleven fence cutters. Reaching the Rangers' camp, Gillespie was joined by Lieutenant Sedberry and six Rangers. They rode to the homes of the wanted men and began making arrests. James Lovell, Bob Parrack, Asa Mathews, Squire Eaton, Charles Johnson, and Jeff Johnson were arrested and delivered to a justice court. On February 4 Sergeant Cartwright found and arrested Jake Lewis and delivered him to the justice court. Cartwright and two Rangers searched for Amos Roberts, scouting a ranch on Blanket Creek, and checked several houses, but Amos wasn't found. They returned to their camp empty-handed, with Amos Roberts dodging the law.

As the days passed, Gillespie's Rangers spent their time searching for witnesses, providing witness protection, and delivering witnesses to Brownwood for testimony before the court's grand jury. Rangers spent days sitting in court listening to testimony and providing security, and their efforts paid off. The grand jury completed their work. On March 12, 1885, they indicted Amos Roberts, Jake Lewis, Baz Hooper, Charlie Johnson, Frank Johnson, Ace (Asa) Mathews, John Mathews, James Lovell, and Bob Parrack for fence cutting. Later in the week, the grand jury handed down a second indictment for James Lovell, the constable for Precinct 6. This indictment was for "conspiracy to cut fence."[32]

Company E Rangers had completed their work in Brown County. When March was ending, Gillespie received word of a new assignment. The adjutant general transferred Gillespie and Company E to the Trans Pecos area in West Texas. En route to Toyah in Reeves County, the Rangers stopped and camped near Peg Leg Crossing on the San Saba River and scouted for cattle thieves and brand burners. They then move on to Toyah in Reeves County. The Texas Pacific Railroad had built track through Reeves, and Toyah now had a post office. The small town had become a shipping point for West Texas cattlemen and wild cowboys, and railroad trash became a challenge for the town. Company E Rangers were there a short time before cowhands tried to take the town. In the altercation that followed, the Rangers killed one cowboy and wounded three. Five prisoners were taken, and no Rangers were hurt.[33]

It appeared the fence-cutter roundup in Brown County was a success, bringing better days for the citizens. The Rangers had performed commendably; now it was up to the citizens, the sheriff, and the district court to finish the job. Unfortunately, local law provided little support, and the new district court had problems picking up where the old court left off.

After the indictments, the cases against the fence cutters lingered for a year. The cases didn't appear on the Brown County District Court's docket for trial until March 1886. In the first week of April, Deputy Sheriff Nat Perry shot a man named Joe Griffith, who died in the Brown County jail. The killing may not have been related to fence cutting, but the deputy's ties to the fence cutters weighed on the minds of fence-cutting witnesses. There was no witness protection, the Rangers were absent, and apparently there was no support from the Brown County sheriff. Witnesses were intimidated. Some fled the country, and others simply refused to testify. The new district attorney asked for a continuance on the fence-cutting cases, and the judge granted it. The cases came up again in September 1886. District Attorney J. O. Woodard knew he held a losing hand. With Woodard's request District Judge J. C. Randolph dismissed the fence-cutting cases. Two years of detective and Ranger work were lost. The court's dismissal of the cases caused great concern among Brownwood's businesses and the county's pasture men. Fence cutters were free and on the loose again. They appeared to be untouchable.[34]

It was now apparent to Adjutant General King that the only way to stop fence cutting in Brown County was to capture or kill the fence cutters while they were destroying a fence. When the district judge dismissed the cases, King decided to send Rangers to the county again. His plan was to send Captain William Scott and Company F to Brown County. Scott had enlisted in the Frontier Battalion eleven years earlier, served under four commands, and only recently attained the rank of captain. Back on January 3, 1884, Scott had made a nighttime arrest of three fence cutters on a fence line in Karnes County.[35]

When Adjutant General King made this new assignment, in the late summer of 1886, Scott and Ranger Company F were stationed in East Texas. Their headquarters was south of the town of Hemphill, the county seat of Sabine. Sabine is one of Texas's easternmost counties, with Louisiana the boundary on the east. Captain Scott and his Rangers were enduring a miserably hot summer while rounding up outlaws in the timbers and thickets on Louisiana's border. A piece of Scott's correspondence expressed his feelings and pain to Captain Lamartine Sieker, now the Frontier Battalion's new quartermaster in Austin. In a July letter transmitting vouchers to Sieker, Scott wrote, "I have just gone through fifteen of 'the toughest days of ranging' that you ever saw. I had rather be a pack mule out west than a millionaire in this brush. We have been going out every day, and each man brings back ticks enough to keep him scratching and kussing all night. Yes it's a sure rough country on man and beast. My stock have been fed rotten corn and they will barely make it back to Marshal."[36]

Scott and his Rangers were trying to capture the Conners, a family of outlaws charged with theft, rape, murder, and a jailbreak. The captain's pursuit into Calcasieu Parish of Louisiana ended with the capture of Alfie Conner, one of the notorious Conner family. On bringing Conner in, Scott received orders from the adjutant general directing him to move to Brown County. The captain began wrapping up the company's business in Sabine.[37]

On September 7 he moved his Ranger camp into Hemphill. As they were preparing to leave, Private James Moore captured Ike Gray. Gray had been involved in the Conners' jail break. On the 16th Scott left with the company for what he referred to as western Texas. For his Rangers, leaving the tick and mosquito-infested forest and undergrowth in Sabine County was a blessing. On September 22 Scott arrived at Mineola. He shipped his outfit over the Texas & Pacific Railroad to Baird in Callahan County, the nearest rail terminal to Brownwood. They arrived in the town of Baird on the 24th. Scott rested their horses and mules a few days, then departed Baird, crossing the Callahan County line into Brown County on September 30, 1886. Captain Scott quietly located his new Ranger camp in Brown County, but the camp's location was undisclosed in his September monthly return. Before Scott's assignment to Brown County, careful planning had occurred with the adjutant general working with the Baugh brothers. The Rangers' new camp location was unknown to the public, out of sight in one of Lev Baugh's fenced cattle pastures.[38]

Scott's October monthly return was filed from Brown County but provided no information on his camp's activities or location. Scott's September return noted Sergeant James A. Brooks and Private Henry Putz were attending federal court in Fort Smith, Arkansas. The report also showed other Rangers were absent on detached service without pay. One source says these other men were out with a sickness contracted in Sabine County. William Scott's company was severely understaffed when he arrived and set up camp in Brown County.[39]

On October 15 Scott sent Private James Harry to Vernon, Texas, to pack and ship camp equipage belonging to Company F to "this place." Harry returned to their camp in Brown County on October 22. Under Scott's state property inventory on his monthly return, he listed livestock and equipment, noting that they were now in good condition, except for one mule. The last inventory item on his list was six hundred rounds of .44 and seven hundred rounds of .45 ammunition. Other than Private Harry's Vernon trip, Scott's only comment on activities in his October monthly return reads, "Have made no scouts during the month and daily expecting to be called on to arrest fence cutters near Brownwood." Scott and Adjutant General King had a plan in place, and the Captain was marking time until the next step.

Service records show that on November 1, Scott enlisted William "Bill" Treadwell, a young man who had come to Brown County recently from South Texas. Unknown to Captain Scott, Treadwell was discharged from Ranger Company C down in South Texas by Captain George Schmitt the month before. Bill Treadwell had enjoyed the action-filled life of Rangering, found Captain Scott, and mustered into Company F. Treadwell may have known or heard from Private James Harry; both men had served under George Schmitt in Company C. Both had bad experiences with Captain Schmitt.[40]

Part of Adjutant General King's plan to capture the Brown County fence cutters involved again inserting a Ranger as an undercover man among the cutters. In late summer of 1886, Ira Aten, a young Ranger with Company D in Uvalde County, had received an order with the following assignment from Adjutant General King: "You will proceed to Brownwood for the purpose of investigating lawlessness in that section and will make such report and recommendation as the facts and circumstances warrant. Call on the bank and see Messer's Coggin, Ford, and Martin, or, rather, see Mr. Ford of firm who will indicate parties and places to be seen."[41]

When Adjutant General King detached Ira Aten from Company D, King knew the young Ranger was tough enough to work among the fence cutters. The previous year Aten had tracked down and killed Wesley Collier, a racehorse man wanted for killing Johann Wolfgang Braeutigam, a saloon and horse track owner in Fredericksburg. King also recalled the 23-year-old Ranger worked undercover in Lampasas County. Fences were being destroyed on a ranch, and the sheriff needed help apprehending the fence cutters. As an undercover man, Aten joined the cutters and orchestrated their capture on a fence line. Aten was called again and left Ranger Company D camp in Uvalde, this time on a Brown County assignment. He arrived in Brownwood in September.[42]

Following Adjutant General King's orders, Aten surveyed the situation but avoided contact with Brown County Sheriff William Nelson Adams. Governor Ireland back in Austin didn't trust the sheriff. Arriving in Brownwood, Aten walked into the Coggin brothers' bank housed in their stately building at the corner of Center and Broadway. Following Adjutant General King's instructions, Aten asked to see Mr. Henry Ford. He was introduced to Ford, the former Brown County clerk, who had recently become a partner in the Coggin brothers' bank. There wasn't much about Brown County that the old gentleman didn't know; he was a highly respected citizen and had lived in Brown for many years.[43]

Ford introduced Aten to Sam and Mody Coggin. After a briefing on the current affairs in Brown County, the Coggins arranged a meeting with the Baugh brothers, Morgan and Levin. It's likely their talk started with their concerns about being assassinated. They would have described how their shotguns went out the front door first, and then they followed, and how they always traveled one route and returned another to avoid being ambushed. They described their fence-cutting problem with many details. When Aten gained the Baughs' confidence, they introduced him to Joe Copeland, their informant. Copeland was farming and lived in the northwest part of the county, where most fence cutters lived. Years later Aten declared that "without the assistance of this man Copeland, I would have been powerless to accomplish anything."[44]

As an old man writing about his undercover work in Brown County, Aten said that, following his meetings in Brownwood, he left town, traveled to Coleman, and bought a horse and saddle. Leaving Coleman, he returned to northwestern Brown County, where he appeared as a young man looking for work. He met Robert Parrack with the help of Joe Copeland, the farmer. Joe introduced Aten as his nephew. Aten befriended Bob Parrack and was taken into Parrack's home, working for him and his wife for a short time. While living with the Parracks, Aten saw fence cutters coming, visiting, and leaving Parrack's home. He never spoke, but when opportunities were present, he listened in on their conversations. On one occasion Parrack handed Aten possession of several horses Parrack or another fence cutter had stolen from Mr. J. T. Gilbert. Aten was to deliver the horses to the Belton area and sell them for Parrack. Instead, he delivered and pastured the stolen horses on a ranch in Lampasas County. On another occasion Parrack stole saddles, and Aten, with Copeland's help, gathered evidence to build a prosecution case. Aten rode with Parrack and the fence cutters on several night excursions to Brown County ranches killing and butchering cattle. They distributed the butchered beef among the cutters' families.

During the short time Aten was in contact with Parrack and his fence-cutting friends, he was never taken on a fence-cutting excursion. He gathered no visual evidence of the fence cutters at work. He did gather enough evidence with Copeland's help to get Parrack indicted for horse theft, stealing saddles, and cattle rustling. Ira Aten and Joe Copeland's evidence led to a list of Brown County indictments of Robert Parrack. It's not clear when Aten left Parrack's farm, but he wasn't there in October. Captain Scott knew about Aten's undercover work in Brown County but lost contact with Aten and sent a message by telegraph to Adjutant General King asking for Aten's help. King responded the same day, saying, "Your telegram asking for Aten was received today. As soon as he reaches this city, he will be sent to your point."[45]

Adjutant General King's plan to stop fence cutting in Brown County was clear to Captain Scott; the only way fence cutting could be stopped was to have Rangers witness and arrest the men destroying a fence. King's plan came together on November 8, 1886. Levin Baugh's informant, Joe Copeland, was asked to participate in a nighttime fence-cutting assault on Morgan Baugh's pasture fences. According to one of Brownwood's old-timers, this fence-cutting raid was planned as a big operation. Nineteen men were expected to participate. Copeland would have been one of those in this planned foray. Preparation to intercept, witness, and capture the fence cutters on their assault on Baugh's fence began immediately. Early the morning of November 9, Copeland traveled to Levin Baugh's home. He related the fence-cutters plan and described the location of fence they were going to cut. The cutters planned to destroy one of Levin's brother's pasture fence.[46]

Following Copeland's visit, Levin saddled his horse, rode to the Rangers' camp, and shared the fence-cutter's plans with Scott. Having waited almost two months for this moment, the captain moved quickly. The Rangers saddled up, and Scott and his men rode out, prepared to meet the fence cutters. With Levin leading they made a fast ride to Morgan's pasture where the fence was to be cut. Five Rangers were riding with Scott, and all were enlisted privates. The men were John Rogers, Jim Carmichael, William Treadwell, James H. Moore, and James Harry. They may have all been privates, but all were experienced lawmen.

Scott's sergeant, J. A. Brooks, and Private Henry Putz were under federal indictments for murder following an incident in the Indian Territory; they didn't participate in the stakeout on the fence line. Private Putz was discharged from the Rangers on May 31. Brooks's whereabouts are unknown, but he probably stayed in the Rangers' camp because of his federal murder indictment. Other of Scott's Rangers were still on detached service. When Scott and his Rangers arrived on Morgan Baugh's fence line, Aten and Copeland were waiting for them. Joe Copeland had also notified Morgan. Morg was there and brought several of his own men.[47]

Over the years historians have tried to piece together details of what happened on Morgan Baugh's fence line that cold November night. There are several versions of what occurred. The most accurate and concise account comes directly from Ranger Captain William Scott. Scott's handwritten *Record of Scout* is in the Texas State Archives and gives a clear, brief description of what transpired in Morgan Baugh's pasture the night of November 9, 1886:

> On the morning of the 9th, Mr. Lev Baugh informed me that he had received information to the effect that the wire cutters would cut his fence that night. And on the evening of the 9th with five Rangers and in company of Mr. Baugh [Lev], I left camp near Brownwood for the purpose of arresting fence cutters should I find them cutting fence. About twelve miles from Brownwood and in Morgue [sic] Baugh's pasture, I met Morgue Baugh in company with five or six citizens. At this point, we dismounted, tied our horses and walked five or six hundred yards to a wire fence. Here I met "Detective Aten of the State Troops." After taking in the situation, I placed the Rangers and citizens in the best positions I could find with the view of effecting the arrest of the fence cutters. About eleven o'clock on the night of the 9th, I saw one man leading four horses immediately in front of three men who were cutting and tearing down the wire fence of Mr. Baughs. When they reached a point opposite to myself and men, I started toward them for the purpose of arresting them. When in about twenty steps of the wire cutters, I saw that they had discovered us, and I immediately ordered them to surrender at the same time I told them that we were Rangers. My order was answered by a shot from a six-shooter fired at us by the fence cutters then the firing was general. The fence cutters fired eight or ten shots and the Rangers and citizens about 50 or 60 shots. Mortally wounded two of the fence cutters Amos Roberts and James Lovell, who has since died. Charles Johnson and John Mathews were the other two who made their escape. Mathews is supposed to be badly wounded. We killed one horse during the fight, the property of John Mathews, and also wounded Roberts and Lovell's horses. Jim Lovell died there three hours after the fight and Roberts since I delivered him to the sheriff of

this county. After the fight, I placed guards over the wounded fence cutter and proceeded to scout for Johnson and Mathews who made their escape during the fight, and while on the scout, I arrested Robert Parrock charged with theft of horses. Delivered Roberts and Parrock to the sheriff of this county and returned to camp on the 10th. November 20, I sent Sergt Brooks with three men to scout in the northern portion of this county for John Mathews, and Chas Johnson wanted in this county charged with cutting the fence of another. Failing to find either of them returned to camp the same day. On the 21st, I left camp with four men in company with Mr. Morgue Baugh to scout in the northern portion of the county for Charles Tutwell, and Wood Runnels wanted in the county for fence cutting. Not finding them returned to camp the same day. On the 24th, I left camp with six men and two-horse wagon to scout in the northern portion of this county for Wood Runnels, who is wanted in this county charged with cutting the fence of another. I arrested him on the 25th and delivered him to the sheriff of this county and returned to camp on the same day.[48]

The morning following the night shootout, Joe Copeland and Morgan Baugh brought James Lovell, Amos Roberts, and Robert Parrack into Brownwood in Copeland's wagon. Captain Scott and Ranger Jim Carmichael led the party making the delivery. Aten and the other Rangers didn't go into town. On coming in from the pasture where the gun battle occurred, Joe Copeland and Morgan Baugh were still armed. Copeland was wearing a six-shooter, and Baugh was packing his shotgun or had it in the wagon.

When James Lovell's body and the mortally wounded Amos Roberts and Bob Parrack were taken from the wagon, there was an altercation between the lawmen. In his book *Something About Brown*, T. R. Havins described the incident and recounted what happened. As the Rangers turned the prisoners over to the sheriff, Deputy Sheriff W. A. Butler attempted to arrest Joe Copeland, who was wearing a six-shooter. Seeing Butler with his gun pointed at Copeland, Ranger Jim Carmichael intervened, drawing his revolver and leveling it at Butler. Sheriff Adams drew his pistol and pointed it at Carmichael. Morgan Baugh then entered the fray, and the sheriff was looking into the double barrels of Baugh's ten-gauge shotgun. Captain Scott saw the commotion and yelled for the men to holster their guns. They did. A heated conversation followed. Captain Scott told Sheriff Adams that he had deputized the farmer. As a lawman Copeland could legally carry his six-shooter. Soon after this clash between the sheriff and the Rangers, the Brown County grand jury indicted Joe Copeland for carrying the handgun. Apparently, Sheriff Adams filed the charge. But when the case came up, the judge dismissed the handgun charge. No further detail of the altercation is found to add to what T. R. Havins described.

Feelings were tense when the Rangers delivered the three fence cutters to the sheriff. There were already bad feelings between the Rangers and Brown County's local lawmen. That November morning was one of many times Rangers delivered these men to Sheriff Adams. This trip was different. One of the fence cutters was dead, with another mortally wounded and dying from a gunshot wound. James Lovell was constable of Brown County's Precinct 6. James's sister was married to Asa Mathews, the justice of the peace in northern Brown County. Both Mathews and Lovell had been indicted, charged with fence cutting, and arrested by Captain Gillespie's Rangers in February of the previous year. Amos Roberts received treatment for his gunshot wounds that morning soon after being delivered to the sheriff. A doctor removed a bullet from under his shoulder blade, but Amos died following the surgery. After delivering the three fence cutters, Captain Scott and Carmichael departed Brownwood for the Rangers' camp. Morgan Baugh and Joe Copeland left for their homes. The cutters and their friends now knew that Copeland had broken faith and divulged the wire cutter's plans. Copeland would pay dearly for his actions.[49]

Hearing about the shootout, many men in northern Brown County became nervous; they worried their names were on the grand jury's list. The night of the fence line altercation, a large band of wire cutters had been expected to show up, but only four came. Maybe the other men had grown tired of fence cutting, realized the danger, and feared a trap. The grand jury indicted James Lovell in March for fence cutting and also on a charge of fence-cutting conspiracy. Presumably, Lovell and the other three that came were organizers and leaders of the gang.[50]

On the days following the fence line gun battle, Captain William Scott and his Rangers searched for the other men charged with fence cuttings. On November 20 Sergeant J. A. Brooks and three Rangers scouted northern

Brown County for John Mathews and Charlie Johnson, who were in the shootout but escaped. The Rangers didn't find them. On the 21st Scott and Morgan Baugh, with several Rangers, continued searching in northern Brown County for Charles Tutwell and Wood Runnels. Both were wanted for fence cutting, but neither were found. Brown County's fence cutters were lying low, or may have fled the county. On the 24th Scott and his men found and arrested Wood Runnels and delivered him to Brown County's Sheriff Adams.[51]

In December Scott and his Rangers moved their search from Brown County to the adjoining Callahan County, looking for Charlie and Frank Johnson and John Mathews, whom they thought was wounded in the incident on Baugh's fence line. Sergeant Brooks found and arrested Frank Johnson on December 4 and delivered him to Sheriff Adams in Brownwood. Despite their effort, little progress was made in finding his brother Charlie Johnson and John Mathews in Callahan County, so the Rangers expanded the search into McCullough and Concho Counties. On December 12 Captain Scott mailed a letter to Captain Sieker, the battalion quartermaster in Austin, concerning his equipment. He had two worn-out mules that needed to be replaced, and he needed to replace his old wagon. He closed his letter to Sieker with a holiday note: "will be leaving today to scout Concho for some of my Brown County fence cutters. Will be out 6 or 7 days, and should I find them maybe so something will pop. Unless we make another killing on fence cutters soon, the outlook for a gay Christmas with myself and boys is rather gloomy. Brownwood is a rather light night city for the average Ranger."[52]

In January of 1887, Scott and his men were still working in Brown County. Rangers rode south to investigate fence-cutting reports in Lampasas, San Saba, and McCullough Counties. Early in February Scott was called to Austin to meet with Adjutant General King. McCullough County rancher Richard Sellman contacted the newly elected Texas Governor Lawrence Sullivan Ross. Captain Scott was sent to McCullough County to investigate the Sellman brothers' fence-cutting problems. A few gaps had been cut in their fence; the damage was slight, but the brothers were armed to the teeth. Tom Sellman had been killed by fence cutters with a pocketknife the previous year in the adjoining county of San Saba.[53]

On February 18 Scott was called again to Austin to meet with Governor Ross. Attending this meeting were Adjutant General King and William Weathered, a prominent resident from Sabine County. The meeting was regarding the Conner family, the band of outlaws who were again depredating and terrorizing Sabine County citizens. The governor wanted them captured and prosecuted. Scott left the meeting, traveled to Dallas, and arranged with the Texas Pacific Railroad to transport his Rangers and equipment back to Sabine in East Texas.[54]

The Brown County grand jury met in February. It indicted A. S. (Asa) Mathews, William Green, Charley Tuckness, Frank Johnson, and Shep Byrd on fence-cutting charges. The jury indicted Robert Parrack on fence cutting and three other counts. Scott and his men attended district court in Brownwood from March 1st to the 20th, protecting witnesses and keeping the peace. They then broke camp in Brown County and began the journey back to the part of Texas William Scott and the Rangers despised, the woods and dense thickets of Sabine County. In Sabine Scott and his Rangers would again attempt to arrest the Conners, the backwoods outlaws whom they had pursued the past summer before being sent to Brown County.[55]

Chapter 9

Three Assassination Attempts on the Farmer Who Snitched

> Some of the fence cutters who Copeland played in with and trapped some time ago waylaid Copeland the other day a few miles from his place and fired about six shots after him with Winchesters but didn't hit him. I suppose we will have a racket with them before long as they will surely try to kill Copeland.
> —Ranger Captain George H. Schmitt

The Rangers' shootout with the fence cutters on Morgan Baugh's ranch, followed by the fence-cutter roundup, stopped fence cutting in Brown County. But cattle stealing and occasional fence cuttings were still occurring in neighboring San Saba and Coleman Counties. Adjutant General King continued to have concerns about the fence cutters loose in Brown County and cutters and thieves in the surrounding counties. Brown County and its neighbors still harbored dangerous men dodging the law. King believed Rangers were still needed in Brown County.

With Captain William Scott and his Rangers leaving Brown County and returning to East Texas on an assignment, Adjutant General King replaced Scott's company with Ranger Company C under the command of Captain

George Heinrich Schmitt. Schmitt had come to the United States from Bavaria, Germany, in his earlier years and later settled in Comal County and made New Braunfels his home. He served as a sheriff's deputy, then was elected Comal County sheriff on February 15, 1876. George Schmitt's Ranger career began when his friend John Ireland, of Comal's neighboring Guadalupe County, was elected Texas governor. Schmitt was a determined man, and throughout his years in Texas, he maintained his cultural traits and the conservatism of his German heritage. Schmitt was blunt and openly critical of others, and during his Ranger career, he was critical of other Ranger captains. On occasions Schmitt used his political connections to enhance his position, and he wasn't Adjutant General King's favorite Ranger captain. Regardless of his politics and faults, he had a company of good men.[1]

Schmitt and Company C were stationed in Frio County in March of 1887 when Captain Schmitt received his new assignment. March 13, 1887, Schmitt left Cotulla on a passenger train to Austin with his men following on a freight train with the horses and equipment. After a stopover and several days in Austin, Ranger Company C left the capital city. They rode into the Brownwood on March 20.[2]

When Captain Schmitt and Company C arrived, Captain Scott and several of his Rangers were still in Brown County. The rest of Scott's men and the company's equipment had already left for East Texas. Before departing Brown for Sabine County, Scott made it a point to meet and brief Captain Schmitt on the county's conditions, but it's uncertain how well the briefing was received. There is no record of what transpired at this meeting. The conference between the two captains is only mentioned in a letter from Scott to Captain Sieker. Sieker was now the new battalion quartermaster in Austin. Scott told Sieker, "I have taken great pains to give Capt. Schmitt all the information I could in regard to conditions of affairs in this section, and I think he will render great service here." Apparently the matter of Captain Scott enlisting William Treadwell and James Harry into Company F didn't come up in the meeting. These two Ranger privates both served under Schmitt, and he had dismissed both men. There was no question about Schmitt's feelings on the matter, and certainly there were hard feelings on the two Rangers' parts for their dismissal. When Schmitt finally learned

Three Assassination Attempts on the Farmer Who Snitched

Captain Scott had enlisted two of his former Rangers, Company F was on the way to Sabine County.³

It's not known when Captain Schmitt first met J. O. Copeland, but he wrote to Sieker in Austin the following month, describing an incident that occurred on April 10. Copeland had been attending church and probably had his family with him. Down the road a short distance from the church, eight armed men were seen trying to conceal themselves in the brush and preparing to ambush Copeland on his return home. Impatient, or maybe uncertain of Copeland's whereabouts, two of the men left the brush thicket, went to the church, and peered through a window to see if Copeland was inside. They were seen by those in the church and recognized by Copeland. Copeland quietly left the church, taking a different and safe route home.

Three days later Copeland and Morgan Baugh, on whose ranch the two fence cutters were killed, came to Schmitt's Ranger camp to see Captain Schmitt. J. O. Copeland described his escape at the church for the captain, and Baugh expressed his concerns. They were both targeted for assassination. The two men asked to be enrolled as special Rangers without pay so they could legally carry a six-shooter. Schmitt listened to their story, agreed they were in grave danger, and said he would ask Adjutant General King to authorize their enrolment as special Rangers without pay. No record of Schmitt's request or a response from King has been found. Schmitt took no action to deal with Baugh and Copeland's would-be assassins, and on or about April 15, several men ambushed and tried to kill Copeland.⁴

There was little grazing for Captain Schmitt's stock, and the drought conditions required he buy hay for his horses and mules. Schmitt sent a letter to Quartermaster Sieker concerning a voucher for the feed he had just purchased. In the same message, he told Sieker of the April 15 attempted assassination on Copeland. Schmitt closed this letter to Sieker, saying:

> Some of the fence cutters who Copeland played in with and trapped some time ago, waylaid Copeland the other day a few miles from his place and fired about six shots after him with Winchesters but didn't hit him. I suppose we will have a racket with them before long as they will surely try to kill said Copeland and Baugh. That is a hard bunch of men, and it would do no good to have them arrested for this as they all

ways manage to cover themselves out with their own gang and no one seen this but Copeland, so we will let it go and try to work the matter some other way.[5]

No record has been found of Schmitt taking action to deal with the fence cutters who tried to murder Copeland. His April monthly return showed few arrests by his men who worked difficult fence-cutting problems in Coleman County and cattle stealing and a cow killing case down in San Saba County. Defending his Rangers' few arrests during the month, Schmitt wrote Adjutant General King, "There are not half as much crime committed in this section as reported. Myself and men done all the work that could be done in this and surrounding counties." In May he wrote Quartermaster Sieker saying, "Everything are quiet & peaceable and I believe we are no longer needed in this section, and I could do more work southwest . . . I am prepared to go somewhere else where I can do more work as there will be no work for us here and Rangers are no longer needed here." Schmitt was pushing hard for a transfer to another location, and the transfer finally came. On June 23 George Schmitt and Ranger Company C left Brown County for a new assignment at Helena, which at the time was the county seat of Karnes County. On November 30, 1887, Schmitt's Ranger Company C was disbanded while stationed in Karnes.[6]

The absence of the Rangers in Brown County quickly brought more criminal activity. The fence cutters noted Ranger Company C's departure and tried again to assassinate Copeland. On June 29 men again fired on Copeland, the second attempt to kill the informant who had provided information to the Baughs and Rangers. Details of where or how this assault occurred are missing, but the second attempt to murder Copeland failed, as had their first.[7]

Copeland and his family lived on a farm about eight miles north of Brownwood. During the heat of the summer on the afternoon of July 16, 1887, Copeland and his young son returned home from Brownwood. It is assumed they had gone to town to buy groceries and pick up the mail. They approached the crossing on Salt Creek in Copeland's wagon. Trees and brush growing along the creek concealed two men with rifles, and as the wagon drew close, the two men opened fire on Copeland. This time the farmer's luck had run out. Two bullets found their mark. One of the shots smashed into his right arm at the shoulder and passed into his body. The other bullet tore flesh from the same limb, ranging from the elbow down to the wrist. The bullet that entered the shoulder missed the bone, then passed behind his lungs. Copeland's young son, Bud, was sitting on the wagon seat next to his dad and the bullets fired by the assassins barely missed the boy. At the sound of gunshots, the horse or mule pulling the wagon bolted, carrying Copeland and his son out of range of the shooters. Two men, Pete Shephard and Lewis McClure, found Copeland and his son after the shooting and carried Copeland back to Brownwood for medical care. Copeland's farm wasn't far from Salt Creek, so Shephard and McClure were some of Copeland's poor farmer neighbors. Ranger Captain Scott, in a letter to Austin in February, had described the poor and pitiful families in the fence cutter neighborhood as "having from one to two hipshot cross-eyed bandy shanked sore back good for nothing ponies, and a wife with two to five poor little starved and naked children." Later, when Pete Shephard was attached as a witness in the assault case, he filed papers with the court saying he was financially unable to secure a bond.[8]

During an interview with a correspondent for the *Galveston Daily News* following the shooting, Copeland said he recognized his would-be assassins and told the correspondent he was a witness against one of the men for fence cutting. He said he was also a witness against the other for horse stealing. Based on court records, the fence cutter was Ace Mathews, and the horse thief would have been Robert Parrack. The newspaper correspondent's story on the assassination attempt mentioned that Copeland had been acting as a detective and was a witness against some of Brown County's residents. The newspaper quoted Copeland saying that was the third time these men had shot at him.[9]

While Copeland was recovering from his wounds, Scott and his Rangers were also recovering from gunshot wounds. The past year Captain William Scott and Company F were sent from Brown County to Sabine County on a return assignment to find and arrest the notorious Conner Gang. On March 31, before daylight, about ten miles from Hemphill, Scott led a detachment of his Rangers through bayou bottomland with thick undergrowth and trees.

They were searching for the Conner gang's camp hidden on Lick Branch. The Rangers were ambushed by the outlaws. When the gunfight with the Conners started, Ranger James Moore, the point man, was shot through the heart and died instantly. John Rogers took a shot that glanced his ribs and another that sliced through his left arm, exiting near his elbow. Sergeant Brooks lost the three middle fingers on his left hand. Captain William Scott received a severe wound when the fight began that almost cost him his life. One of the Conners' rifle bullets entered Scott's side and passed through his lungs. Treadwell and Carmichael were firing at any movement in the Conners' camp, and their deadly fire saved the wounded Rangers' lives. Bill Conner was killed, and remaining band members retreated through the thick brush. Scott, Brooks, and Rogers were carried into Hemphill for medical care. Ranger James T. Moore was buried at the site of the shootout.[10]

Sergeant J. A. Brooks, with three fingers missing from his left hand, assumed command of Ranger Company F in April. Private Rogers was recovering from his wounds, and Captain Scott was improving but still in a severe crippled condition. On June 10, 1887, Company F was sent from Hemphill to Weatherford, Texas, responding to a train robbery. The Rangers carried Captain Scott to their new camp, but his only activity was administrative. After a short stay at Weatherford, the Rangers moved to Cisco to suppress election violence in an upcoming election. Because of the Rangers' presence, there was no election violence.

Sergeant Brooks left the Cisco Rangers' camp on July 8, traveling to Fort Smith, Arkansas, with much unease. He was to be tried for murder in federal court for the shooting death of Albert St. John. The shooting occurred a year earlier during an arrest attempt in the Indian Territory. Captain Scott was still recovering from his wound when Brooks left for Arkansas. Private John Rogers assumed command of Ranger Company F.

Rangers J. A. Brooks and Henry Putz and US Indian Police Lieutenant Thomas Knight were tried for murder. They were found guilty of the lesser charge of manslaughter. Brooks notified Captain Scott of the guilty verdict and was discharged from the Rangers on July 31. Private Henry Putz left Company F eight months before the trial began.[11]

Three Assassination Attempts on the Farmer Who Snitched

In August 1887 William Scott, still recovering from his gunshot wound, began taking on work in the field. He left Cisco on August 2, scouting in Brown County for John Mathews, who had escaped during the shootout on the Baugh fence line the previous year. John had a record of fence-cutting indictments and arrests dating back to Captain Gillespie's days in Brown County. He had never gone to trial and had been on the dodge since the fence line shootout. Captain Scott had now learned John Mathews was wanted out of state for murder. Though not recorded in his monthly return, Scott's trip to Brown County was also to learn details about the fence cutter's attempts to assassinate Joe Copeland. The cutters now weren't just seeking revenge. They intended to silence Copeland because he was the state's key witness on the upcoming fence-cutting cases, crimes of theft, and the recent assassination attempts. Time in the penitentiary was a likely outcome if they failed to silence Copeland, the state's key witness.

William Scott's Rangers broke camp on August 7 and left Cisco to establish a new headquarters in Runnels County. En route they stopped and made temporary camp in Brown County, and John Rogers, with seven Rangers, searched for men wanted for the attempted murder of Copeland. Rogers and the other Rangers arrested Bob Parrack, Asa Mathews, Wood Runnels, and William (Bill) Green on August 10; each was charged with assault to murder Joe Copeland. The four men were carried to Brownwood the same day and turned over to Sheriff William Adams. A detachment of three Rangers remained in Brown to search for fugitives from justice, and though not mentioned in Captain Scott's monthly return, most certainly the Rangers were protecting Copeland as he recovered from his gunshot wounds. Rogers and the other Rangers continued on to Ballinger where they met Scott, who selected a campsite for Company F headquarters. The Rangers' new Runnels headquarters facilitated work in Brown and Coleman Counties and permitted the Rangers to work the problem with horse and cattle thieves west around San Angelo and in Tom Green County.

Scott rode to San Angelo on August 19 to meet with stockmen from Tom Green County. He spent several days gathering information on suspected horse and cattle thieves, made notes on ranchers' marks and brands, and recorded their livestock losses. He returned to his Runnels camp on August 24, then left for Brownwood. His monthly return filed for August reports, "left camp for Brownwood for the purpose of attending to business pertaining to the company." He returned to his Runnels camp on the 27th.[12]

Scott's trip to Brown County was for more than evidence gathering. J. O. (Joe) Copeland enlisted in Frontier Battalion Company F on September 1, 1887, and became one of William Scott's Rangers. His enlistment was Scott's witness protection plan; Copeland was still in grave danger of assassination. It's likely that Joe's wife Laura and his children had left his farm and returned to Falls County, Texas, to live with other family members when the farmer enlisted in the Ranger Company.[13]

On September 2 Scott traveled to Austin to meet with Adjutant General King. He left a detachment of Rangers in Brownwood under the command of Private Frank Carmichael to protect witnesses and monitor the district court session now beginning. Copeland, Ranger Ira Aten, the Baughs, and others would appear and testify as witnesses during the court's sessions.[14]

In Austin Scott met with Adjutant General Wilburn King and discussed Copeland's enlistment, the Brown County District Court's proceedings, and the assault to murder charges filed against the fence cutters. Another matter discussed, of great importance to both men, was the ongoing effort to secure a presidential pardon for J. A. Brooks and Henry Putz. Both men were found guilty of manslaughter in the shooting death occurring when they tried to arrest Albert St. John in Indian Territory. Brooks and Putz were now incarcerated in federal prison. Adjutant General King, Governor Lawrence Sullivan Ross, and prominent Texas businessmen were working to secure a presidential pardon for the two Texans. Several days after Scott left the state capital and returned to Runnels County, Sergeant Brooks's imprisonment in Arkansas ended. On September 12, 1887, President Grover Cleveland signed a pardon for Brooks, Putz, and Thomas Knight.

The three lawmen imprisoned in Arkansas were released from federal prison on September 19. Brooks arrived in Texas by rail the following day. When he arrived, he immediately reenlisted in Captain William Scott's Ranger Company F. The September monthly return notes under remarks, "First Sergeant J. A. Brooks gained by enlistment." In this same monthly return, Scott says he placed Brooks in command, availed himself of leave, and departed the state. It appears his health condition was not good, as he was still recovering from the bullet through his lungs six months earlier.[15]

When Scott returned from his leave, he moved Company F headquarters to Tom Green County. On November 11 he established the Ranger camp on the Concho River two miles from San Angelo. Two months earlier Scott had spent several days with stockmen in Tom Green County to "devise methods to break up and apprehend the gang of horse and cattle thieves depredating that section." Scott's sweep would now begin. The captain was back from his leave, Sergeant Brooks was back on duty, and John Rogers had a new understudy, Private J. O. (Joe) Copeland.[16]

Company F began the new year of 1888 in Tom Green County rounding up horse and cattle thieves. Captain Scott's January monthly return reported numerous arrests made during the month. Most of those arrested were horse and cattle thieves, although the first arrest listed for the month was J. H. Hogan, an army deserter brought in by John Rogers. That same day Captain Scott arrested J. Wilson, charged with stealing horses. On January 19 Private Rogers arrested Jim Phillips and Tom Price for stealing horse. Private Copeland had quickly picked up Ranger skills, and on January 20 he arrested Pedro Rialto in Tom Green, who was also charged with stealing horses.

There had been plenty of brand blotting and cattle stealing. The following week Private Frank Carmichael arrested William Massey, who was charged with stealing cattle. Sergeant Brooks traveled south from San Angelo, working a case on stolen cattle. This case took him down into Edwards County. There he arrested Sam Buck, charged with stealing cattle, and also a cowboy, F. Blake, charged with false pretenses. January of the New Year was a good month for Company F, but it was a bad month for horse and cattle thieves in Tom Green County.[17]

As the outlaw roundup in Tom Green ended, fence cutting and theft indictments delivered by the grand jury in Brown County were sent to the Bell County's district court on venue change. In addition to the theft and fence-cutting charges, there were now also three indictments for the attempted murder of Joe Copeland. Attachments for witnesses were being sent out and included attachments for Joe Copeland, the state prosecution's key witness. On March 1, 1888, Copeland was discharged from active duty with Ranger Company F. Although no longer active, he was kept on the state's special Ranger roll, meaning he could still carry his revolver wherever he went and had the same authority as an enlisted Ranger. But he now would receive no pay.

Several weeks after Copeland's departure, Captain Scott wrapped up his Brown County fence cutter work with one last arrest. John Mathews had evaded the law since the shootout that November night on the Baugh Ranch. He was cutting the fence, was wounded in the shooting that followed, but still managed to escape. John was the younger brother of Asa (Ace) Mathews, justice of the peace at Thrifty, Texas. Both brothers at this time were under indictment for fence cutting. Fence cutting, however, was the lesser of John's crimes; he was wanted for a murder committed nine years earlier in Kentucky. On March 15 Scott found John Mathews in Tom Green County and arrested him. Sergeant J. A. Brooks and two Rangers delivered John Mathews to Ballinger. Reaching Ballinger, they turned Mathews over to requisition officer J. M. Walters, who would carry him to Kentucky to stand trial for murder.[18]

Captain William Scott was still suffering from the bullet wound that tore through his lungs during the shootout with the Conner gang in East Texas. He tendered his resignation from the Frontier Battalion, leaving Ranger Company F effective April 30, 1888. Adjutant General Wilburn King acknowledged William Scott's resignation by Special Order No. 126, recognizing him for his bravery, energy, and efficiency as a Ranger since enlistment in 1875. In King's same order, he promoted Sergeant J. A. Brooks to first lieutenant and assigned him command of Company F effective May 1, 1888. Brooks continued his Ranger career along with John Rogers, and both men became Ranger captains. Brooks and Rogers, with John Hughes and Bill McDonald, are known by Ranger historians as the Four Great Captains.[19]

When the assassins had ambushed and wounded Joe Copeland on Salt Creek, Brown County's citizens realized the violent nature and danger of the Jim Ned Gang and the district court worked to shut down the gang. Jury work had started with W. D. R. McConnell as grand jury foreman, then Robert B. Wilson followed as the foreman. Robert Wilson had served as Brown County sheriff when the outlaws burned Brown County's jail and courthouse. G. S. Howard followed Wilson as grand jury foreman, and it was he and his grand jury that delivered indictments for the assassins' three attempts to murder Joe Copeland. The story of the assassins shooting Joe Copeland changed Brown County citizens' sentiments and moved the community into reparative action.

The grand jury, working long hours with their new district attorney J. O. Woodard, handed down a long list of indictments. Their first indictment delivered for fence cutters dated back to the incident where Lev Baugh caught William Green, Shep Byrd, Ace Mathews, and Charles Tuckness cutting his fence and they opened fired on him. The grand jury completed its work, but then there were troubling delays in trying the cases. The cases finally appeared on the Brown County court's docket in the 1887 fall term. Judge J. C. Randolph, the new district judge, declared he was unable to impanel an unbiased jury for the trials in Brown County. In September he sent the entire package of Brown County's indictments to the district court in Bell County. Randolph's orders for change of venues on the indictments read:

> It appearing to the Court that a trial alike fair and impartial to the State and the accused in the above styled and numbered cause pending in the District Court of Brown County Texas cannot be had in said Brown County because of existing combination and influences on the part of influential persons in favor of the accused and against the State of Texas . . . the Court being satisfied of the existence of said combination and influence, on its own motion, it is ordered by the Court that the venue in this cause be changed from Brown County to the County of Bell in the State of Texas said Bell County being a Judicial District adjoining the 35th Judicial District.[20]

Brown County's old judge, William Blackburn, was now the district judge in Bell County. The cases sent over from Brown County were received and recorded in Bell's district court minutes. Changes of venue for criminal cases due to special circumstances is normal practice for the courts. But a transfer of such a large number of varied cases, as sent from Brown County, appears unusual.

The *Brenham Daily Banner*, on October 7, 1887, mentioned that three of Brown County's prisoners indicted and charged with fence cutting were transferred to the Bell County jail following change of venue. The newspaper didn't name the fence cutters. The Bell County District Court's criminal minutes, however, identified them as Ace Mathews, Shep Byrd, and William Green. Brown County historian T. R. Havins says Green had an impressive record. Green was a habitual criminal, having been charged with fence cutting in multiple cases. Havins said Green was a cattle and hog thief who lived on Jim Ned Creek near the community of Thrifty and had been indicted by a Brown County grand jury every year for six successive years. He was tried on each case but convicted on only one. The courts later reversed that one particular case and Green was acquitted.[21]

Brown County's citizens were confident the cases sent to Bell County would be tried before their old judge, W. A. Blackburn, and vigorously prosecuted by District Attorney W. H. Browning. But Blackburn and Browning encountered problems. It became apparent to Browning that the Brown County cases were delivered with faulty indictments and legal deficiencies. Missing documents, lack of evidence, and want of witnesses would make the cases challenging and some would be impossible to prosecute. Bell County District Court records show Blackburn's court met in Belton on January 17, 1888, with Brown County's cases on the docket. On the district attorney motion, the cases were dismissed by Judge Blackburn for "lack of jurisdiction and want of papers" and returned to the district court in Brownwood.[22]

February 8 of the following month, the cases again appeared on the Brown County District Court's docket. Judge Randolph's orders, showing contempt for the Bell County District Court, sent the cases back to Bell County with new orders saying:

> February 8, 1888 this Cause being reached upon a call of the docket and it appearing from an inspection of the record herein that the Cause herein was by an Order of the Court made at the September A.D. 1887 term of this Court, upon the motion of the Judge presiding changed from this Court to the County of Bell and that the Cause has been remanded by the District Court of Bell County to this Court: This Court declines to take cognizance of this Cause until ordered to do so by the Court of Appeals because in the judgment of this Court it has neither the Jurisdiction of this case nor the person of the defendant, it's Jurisdiction having been divested by the order aforesaid made in September 1887. It is therefore ordered that the papers in this Cause together with a

certified copy of this order be returned by the clerk of this Court to the clerk of the District Court of Bell County, and the case be stricken from the docket of this Court.[23]

Brown's cases were picked up again in Bell County, assigned new cause numbers, and listed in the court's criminal minutes dated June 5, 1888. It is not certain that all the cases were returned from Brown County or if proper papers were provided. Still, those returned were placed on the docket to be heard by Bell County's district court.

Most of these cases had trials stretching over long periods of time, with continuances spread over multiple years. Cases returned and tried in the Bell County court had indictments for fence cutting, stealing saddles, stealing horses and cattle, and assault with intent to murder. In addition to his fence-cutting charges, Parrack was the defendant in the other cases tried. Robert Parrack appears to have been one of Jim Ned Gang's leaders and the subject of Rangers Ira Aten and Joe Copeland's evidence gathering during their undercover work.

The fence-cutting cases transferred and placed on the Bell County court's docket had indictments for Robert Parrack, William Green, A. S. Mathews, John Mathews, Shep Byrd, H. H. Reynolds, and Charley Tuckness. Parrock was indicted on four counts. The fence-cutting cases began in Brown with indictments delivered December 1886, then sent to Bell County in 1887. The Bell County court issued capiases, and the cases were continued multiple times through 1887 and 1888. On January 14, 1889, a fence-cutting case against Parrack, Green, Mathews, and Byrd was on the docket and dismissed for "want of evidence sufficient to convict." No record is found showing the case against Reynolds and Tuckness ever went to trial in Bell County.

Cause 3024, the fence-cutting charge filed against Green, Mathews, and Byrd, had alias capias issued. This cause was continued five times between December 8, 1887, and February 3, 1890, before being tried on August 2, 1890. The case was finally dismissed. It's noted here that getting the conviction of a fence cutter in a court of law using circumstantial evidence was virtually impossible.[24]

The Brown County grand jury indicted Parrack on September 14, 1887, for stealing saddles valued at twenty-five dollars each, with jury foreman G. S. Howard presenting the indictment to the court. Witnesses listed on the indictment were Morg Baugh, Thomas W. Jones, R. W. Eddleman, John Burnett, Ranger Ira Aten, and Joe Copeland. The indictment alleged that on or about August 23, 1886, Parrack stole a saddle from Burnett valued at twenty-five dollars, a saddle valued at twenty-five dollars from Jones but belonging to Burnett, and a saddle valued at twenty-five dollars from R. W. Eddleman belonging to John R. Burnett. The indictment also alleged that on August 23 Parrack fraudulently received from an unknown person, then illegally concealed a saddle belonging to Burnett, knowing the saddle was acquired against the peace and dignity of the state. Parrack was delivered to the Bell County sheriff to await trial. On January 5, 1889, the court's attachment was served on Copeland in Coleman County for his appearance and testimony as a witness on January 14, 1889. It is presumed Ranger Aten was also attached to serve as a witness, but his presence at the trial is not noted in court records. Aten appears to have built this case, gathering evidence while working for Parrack. Years after his undercover work in Brown County, Aten corresponded with historian Roy D. Holt. Aten says in one instance, "I failed to appear as a witness. The Court fined me $100 for not appearing but they later remitted the fine." The trial closed in the Bell County District Court on January 17, 1889, with the case being dismissed on the motion of District Attorney Browning saying he "will no further prosecute the case for want of evidence sufficient to convict."[25]

John T. Gilbert farmed about fifteen miles west of Brownwood. In November of 1886, he discovered two of his horses missing. The Brown County's grand jury heard testimony March 3, 1887, alleging Parrack had stolen Gilbert's horses on or about November 1, 1886. Jury foreman Robert B. Wilson delivered the jury's indictment of Parrack for stealing Gilbert's horses. Captain Scott had arrested Parrack on the horse-stealing charge the night of the fence line shootout and delivered him to the Brown County sheriff. The following week Judge Randolph set Parrack's bond at $1,000. After the horse-stealing case was passed back and forth from Brown and Bell

Counties by the two judges, the case came up on the Bell County District Court's docket for trial.

When the Bell County trial began, Judge Blackburn granted the defense a continuance, and attachments were sent for defense witnesses. Frank Lovell, the father of James Lovell, was called as a defense witness to testify that Parrack was at the house of Mrs. Arp (Earp) when the horses were stolen. Parrack's attorney also attached Durham Thomas and Robert Rogers, saying they would testify that "they were acquainted with the general reputation of J. O. Copeland for truth and veracity in the neighborhood in which he lived, and his reputation was bad."

Copeland had vouched for Ira Aten as his relative when Robert Parrack took Aten in and put him to work on his farm. Ranger Aten, the young undercover operative, was trying to build fence-cutting cases while working for Parrack. When John Gilbert's horses were stolen, Parrack sent Aten to find a buyer and sell the two horses. Knowing the horses were stolen, Aten delivered them to a pasture for safekeeping on the ranch of Prock Hullen (Proctor H. Huling) in Lampasas County. An attachment was sent for Huling by the defense, and as the trial progressed, Huling testified that Aten was in possession of the horses and had told him they were his own. Parrack's attorney was building a case that it was Aten who stole the horses. The prosecution called Copeland, Aten, Sam P. McInnis, and L. P. Baugh as the state's witnesses. Following a continuance for Parrack's defense, additional defense witnesses were attached from Mills County. Later, the state continued the case for want of testimony of Copeland and Gilbert, owner of the horses. The two men may have not been served, or there may have been a threat of an assassination attempt.[26]

Aten cited the constant threat of assassination by the fence cutters in a letter to Lamar Sieker, the Battalion Quartermaster in Austin, saying, "Copeland has made enemies, as well as myself that will last him a lifetime. His life is in constant danger from the friends of the parties killed on the fence on November 9." Without question Ranger Aten was a fearless lawman, but Brown County's fence cutters had Aten and Copeland constantly watching for an assassin.[27]

The trial reached its conclusion in February 1890. The jury found Robert Parrack guilty of stealing the horses. After the jury delivered their verdict, Parrack's attorney John Bell filed a motion for a new trial. Judge Blackburn sustained this motion for a new trial. No record was found of why the judge sustained the motion for a retrial, and no record was found showing this case was ever retried. Parrack's attorney beat the horse theft charge.[28]

The Brown County grand jury indicted Robert Parrack for stealing cattle on March 4, 1887. The indictment was served on Parrack by Deputy Sheriff Nat Perry while Parrack was held in the Brown County jail. After the case moved to the Bell County District Court, the court sent an attachment to Brown County for G. W. Cross, Ira Aten, J. O. Copeland, W. M. Baugh, and L. P. Baugh to testify on behalf of the state. Cause 3350 was continued on January 14, 1889, and Parrack's attorney filed an attachment for J. M. Perry Sr., Deputy Sheriff Nat Perry's father. Attachments also were filed for nine other defense witnesses, all in Brown County. As the trial progressed, it was discovered that Henry McGeorge owned the stolen cattle, not G. W. Cross as alleged in the indictment. The district attorney dismissed the case on February 15, 1890, because of insufficient evidence to convict.[29]

After the deadly gun battle between the fence cutters and Rangers on Morgan Baugh's fence line in November of 1886, the cutters had learned Joe Copeland was the informant passing information to the Rangers. Expecting Copeland to testify on a long list of crimes, Parrack and his friends were determined to see that Copeland didn't live to testify in court and tried to kill him on three separate occasions. Robert Parrack was indicted for assault with intent to murder Joe Copeland for an April 15 shooting, again for a shooting on June 29, and for the third shooting occurring on July 16, 1887. On this July assassination attempt, the shooter(s) almost succeeded in their attempt to kill Copeland. Copeland received two near-fatal wounds from rifle bullets.[30]

The prosecution was handicapped when the assault cases went to trial. Joe Copeland was the only person to witness these attempted assassinations. Ranger Captain George Schmitt in April wrote to Lamar Sieker, the battalion's quartermaster in Austin, reporting the cutters' first failed attempt to assassinate Copeland. Schmitt made a point about cutters using alibis in his note, saying, "That is a hard bunch of men and it would do no good to have them arrested for this, as they all ways manage to cover themselves out with their own gang and no one seen this but Copeland." Schmitt's assessment on the use of alibis by the assassins proved true in each of the three assault with intent to murder cases that followed.

Parrack's lawyers called a long list of defense witnesses from Brown, Eastland, Mills, and Coleman Counties for the assault cases. Parrack's primary defense during the trials was alibis that he was elsewhere. His attorney also called on Parrack's friends to impeach the testimony of Copeland by portraying him as untrustworthy and a liar. As the assault trials began, Sheriff William Adams and his deputy Nat Perry were called to testify as defense witnesses.[31]

During the trials Joe Copeland was living and working five miles from Santa Anna in Coleman County, roughly 155 miles from the Bell County District Court. This is borne out by a travel reimbursement forms in the district court's records. This undisclosed site offered protection for Copeland. The Coleman sheriff knew where to find Joe and serve papers sent from the Bell County court.[32]

The cases for assault with intent to murder filed against Parrack were District Attorney Browning's main focus and over an extended period consumed much of the court's time. Robert Parrack had excellent legal representation in the trials. His defense attorneys were John E. Bell and C. H. Jenkins, both prominent lawyers in Brownwood. Jenkins was later an associate justice of Texas's Third Court of Appeals. Attorney John Bell's continuances and witnesses with alibis carried the day for Parrack.[33]

Cause 3351, the case to try the June 29, 1887, attempt to kill Copeland, was placed on the docket in Bell's district court in June of 1888 but continued. After attachments for more witnesses and two more continuances, the case was on the docket for July 18, 1889. It was continued again with Parrack's attorney filing another attachment for witnesses Jno. Weedon and J. H. Prater saying, "The fact expected to be proven by each of said witnesses is that they are acquainted with the general reputation of Joe Copeland for truth and veracity in the neighborhood in which he lived when this prosecution began, and the same is bad."

As the new year began, Cause 3351 was again on the docket for February 13, 1890. John Bell, Parrack's attorney, filed for another continuance, saying his defendant could not safely go to trial because the defendant's witnesses, Henry Bolinger, Ruben Eddleman, Mr. Graves, and Charlie Johnson, residing in Eastland County, were absent. They were not present and did not show up in court, and their testimony was material to Parrack's defense. Attorney John Bell argued they could prove Parrack was forty miles from the scene when the shooting occurred.[34]

This time Judge Blackburn denied Attorney Bell's request for another continuance and gave his charge to the jury as follows:

> In this case, the indictment charges Bob Parrack, the defendant, with the offense of an assault with intent to murder J. O. Copeland in the county of Brown, and State of Texas, on or about the twenty-ninth day of June 1887.
>
> The defendant has pleaded not guilty, and he is presumed to be innocent until his guilt is established by legal evidence, and in case of reasonable doubt as to his guilt he is entitled to be acquitted; and in this case, if you have reasonable doubt to the defendant as charged in the indictment, you will acquit him, and say by the verdict, not guilty.
>
> The use of any unlawful violence upon the person of another with intent to injure him, whatever be the means or degree of violence used, is an assault and battery. Any attempt to commit a battery, or any threatening gesture showing in itself or by words accompanying it, an immediate intention, coupled with an ability to commit a battery, is an assault.
>
> Every person with sound memory and discretion, who shall unlawfully kill any reasonable creature in being within this state, with malice and forethought, either express or implied, shall be deemed guilty of murder. Murder is distinguishable from every other species of homicide by the absence of the circumstances which reduce the offense to negligent homicide or manslaughter, or which excuse or justify the homicide.
>
> Malice and forethought is the voluntary and intentional doing of an unlawful act, with purpose, means and ability to accomplish the reasonable and probable consequences of it, in a manner showing a heart regardless of social duty, and fatally bent on mischief by one of sound memory and discretion, the evidence of which is inferred from acts committed or words spoken.

A deadly weapon is one, which, from the manner in which it is used, is calculated and likely to produce death or serious bodily injury.

If from evidence, you are satisfied beyond a reasonable doubt, that the defendant, with a deadly weapon, or instrument reasonably calculated and likely to produce death or serious bodily injury from the manner in which it was used, and with malice and forethought, did assault the said J. O. Copeland with intent then and there to kill him, then you will find the defendant guilty of an "assault with intent to murder," and say so by your verdict, and assess his punishment at confinement in the penitentiary for a term of not less than two nor more than seven years.

In addition to other defenses set up in this case, is what is known in legal phraseology as an alibi—that is, that if J. O. Copland was assaulted as charged in this indictment that the defendant was at the time of such assault, at another and different place from that at which the assault was made, and therefore was not, and could not have been the person who made the assault—(if any were made).

Now, if the evidence raises in your mind a reasonable doubt to the presence of the defendant at the place where the assault was made—if you believe it was made at all—at the time it is alleged to have been made, then you will find the defendant not guilty.

The jury are the exclusive judges of what facts have been proved in this case, and the credibility of the witness, and the weight to be given their testimony.

W. A. Blackburn
Judge 27th Judicial District[35]

The jury received Blackburn's instructions, met, deliberated, and found Robert Parrack guilty of assault with intent to murder J. O. Copeland. The jury sentenced Robert Parrack to two years in the state penitentiary.

After hearing the jury's verdict, Parrack's attorney John Bell filed a motion to set aside the verdict and requested a new trial saying, "Now comes the defendant and moves the Court to set aside the verdict rendered herein and grant him a new trial for the following cause's to wit: 1st because the court erred in overruling defendants application and in all respects in full compliance with the law and showed on its face that the facts expected to be proved by the absent witnesses constituted a full defense to the accusation against defendant. . . . 2nd Because the verdict of the jury is contrary to the law and the evidence."³⁶ After review of Parrack's attorney's motion, Judge Blackburn responded by granting a new trial.

The case was placed on the docket again in July for a new trial. Attachments were sent from Bell County District Court for defense witnesses residing in Eastland County. F. K. Neal, James Eddleman, R. W. Eddleman, and Henry Bolinger were served. The fifth witness, Charles Johnson, wasn't served. He was under indictments for fence cutting, was in the shootout with Rangers on Baugh's fence line, and had escaped. No one knew Johnson's whereabouts. Both Bolinger and Neal gave bond, while R. W. and James Eddleman were brought to Bell County and delivered to open court.

Cause 3351 was on the Bell County District Court's docket and tried again in August. Bell County's criminal minutes and case papers show that Robert Parrack was tried the second time August 8, 1890. This time he was acquitted; the jury found Parrack not guilty of the assassination attempt.³⁷

Parrack's case for the second assassination attempt on June 29 was numbered as Cause 3352. Over the years, multiple continuances were granted, and long list of defense witnesses were attached by Parrack's attorneys. In February Parrack's attorney filed a request for a continuance because of the absence of testimony of Parrack's wife Mary, of Ellen McGehee, Dr. McGhee, and Bill Earp of Brown County. These witnesses didn't show. Parrack's attorney said Ellen McGhee could show that Parrack was at Mrs. Anderson's house from eight o'clock to nearly noon. Thus, Parrack could not have been at the scene of the shooting four miles away, which occurred at nine or ten o'clock, as claimed. The application for a continuance said the defendant used due diligence to procure the witnesses by attachments issued out of the district court. Parrack's attorney John Bell stated, "The witnesses were not absent by consent of the defendant, and postponement of the trial by application for the continuance was not made for the delay, but that justice may be done." Judge Blackburn approved Parrack's application for the continuance on the second shooting case. After the jury found Parrack not guilty on Cause 3351, the court dropped Cause 3552. No record of further prosecution was found.³⁸

Cause 3354 was placed on the Bell County District Court's docket February 13, 1890, and continued for want of testimony of Asa Mathews and John Halse. After Parrack was found not guilty on Cause 3351 in August 1890, this case was dropped. No records of further prosecution of Cause 3354 were found.[39]

The Brown County grand jury's serious work to shut down the Jim Ned Gang started in 1885 with fence-cutting indictments delivered for Amos Roberts, Jake Lewis, Baz Hooper, Charlie Johnson, Frank Johnson, Jeff Johnson, A. S. Mathews, John Mathews, Bob Parrack, and James Lovell. Two of these men, Amos Roberts and James Lovell, were killed by Rangers in a shootout while again cutting fence in 1886. Five years of criminal court proceedings followed the 1885 indictments and resulted in pain for many people, a great expense for some, and zero convictions for the crimes perpetrated. On a review of the records, the Jim Ned Gang's only penalty for the crimes committed appears to have been delivered by the Rangers in the shootout on the Baugh fence line, where two men died from gunfire.[40]

Fence cutting stopped, however, in Brown County after the indictments went to trial in Bell County. District Judge J. C. Randolph, who was elected to serve the new Thirty-Fifth Judicial District, which included Brown, served only one term of two year and then stepped down. Sheriff William Adams, elected in 1882, served Brown County three terms of two years before stepping down. November of 1888 his deputy, Nat A. Perry, was elected sheriff and served one term. Then on November 4, 1890, three months after the trials ended in Bell County, Brown County citizens elected W. Y. Pearce as their new sheriff.[41]

Robert Parrack suffered hard times following the trials. Parrack owned a small farm in Brown County with a few cattle. Trying to recover from his legal battles, he sold his farm, loaded his wagon, and moved his family to cotton-growing country on the Brazos River. The family picked cotton and earned enough money to travel on to the High Plains in the Texas Panhandle. In the fall of 1899, the family arrived at Emma, the once-thriving county seat of Crosby County. Parrack and his family squatted on two sections of land located near the old Quaker colony at Estacado. Robert Parrack gathered buffalo bones to sustain the family, hauling them to Canyon, Texas, where he sold them. Parrack managed to purchase the land they settled on from the state for one dollar an acre and on credit. Later he sold one section of the land to clear his equity. Parrack farmed his land, producing Sudan grass and milo maize he sold in Lubbock. He raised horses, mules, cattle, and hogs and profited from his livestock sales.

For a brief period in 1910, Parrack and his family lived in Chaves, New Mexico, and then returned to his farm. In 1917 he moved to Lubbock, leasing the farm to tenants. The 1933 Lubbock City Directory lists Robert C. Parrack as an agent for the Colorado Life Insurance Company. He and his wife Mary survived many tough times and raised nine children, the first four born while the family was in Brown County. Robert Cypret Parrack died June 27, 1947, in Lubbock at the age of 93. The family buried him in the City of Lubbock Cemetery.[42]

Little information has been found about Joe Copeland's life during his years following the Bell County trials. When Copeland was sworn in as a Texas Ranger in September of 1887, we assume his family left his Brown County farm and returned to Falls County. Copeland's last testimony in the Bell County trials was in August 1890, and his residence then was near Santa Anna, in Coleman County. After the trials Joe returned to Falls County. Family history passed down says he was in the cotton business, that he was a cotton ginner and skilled carpenter. It's reported he built a boarding house in Temple, Texas, which he and his wife Laura managed. J. O. Copeland died April 16, 1915, in Temple and was buried in the Jena Cemetery in Falls County. His Texas death certificate notes he was a retired farmer. Over the years of their marriage, Joe and his wife Laura had twelve children, but not all lived to adulthood. The 1900 United States Federal Census for Falls County lists Joe and Laura with nine children at home. The oldest daughter Florena was 18, his oldest son James was 16, and they had spent their early life with their father and mother on the farm in Brown County. James was the little boy in the wagon sitting next to his father when the assassin shot Joe that afternoon as they approached Salt Creek.[43]

Chapter 10

Hell Breaks Loose in Coleman, and a Widow Suffers Fence Cutting

> Down with monopolies, they can't exist in Texas and especially in Coleman County; away with your foreign capitalist; the range and soil belong to the heroes of the South; no monopolies and don't tax us to school the [n——]. Give us homes as God intended and not gates to churches and towns and schools and above all give us water for our stock.
>
> —Sign posted in Coleman, Texas

J. C. Jones came to Coleman County in its early years and made it his home. He claimed Clark Mann brought the first barbed wire to the county and used the new wire to fence a section of land on Jim Ned Creek. The old-timer said Mann built his fence using elm poles with barbed wire stretched above the top of the poles. Jones told a story about a man employed by the government to maintain the telegraph line between Coleman, Camp Colorado, and Fort Griffin. The telegraph company's lineman left Coleman and was following the telegraph line when Mann's fence stopped him. He was agitated when he encountered the fence topped with this new barbed wire. The lineman cut his way through the enclosure and then left a gaping window on the opposite side of the pasture where he went out. Mann's fence was Coleman's first fence built using barbed wire; he also suffered the first case of fence cutting in the county. The first significant barbed wire fence in Coleman was constructed in 1879 by cattleman William Henry Day. He enclosed about 7,500 acres of land.[1]

William Day was the son of Jesse and Sarah (Logan) Day and was born May 8, 1833, in Cassville, Georgia. He was one of seven brothers and three sisters. When Day was 14, his family moved to Bastrop, then to San Antonio, and finally to Hays County, settling near the community of Mountain City, about twelve miles from San Marcos, Texas. Williams's father, Jesse Day, was one of Texas's early cattlemen and made one of the first cattle drives to the Midwest in 1856. Day worked for his father, caring for wagons and teams and freighting to the gulf ports and back to Austin. When old enough to work for himself, he saved money freighting and enrolled in Cumberland University in Lebanon, Tennessee. With the money he saved and his father's help, he graduated with a civil engineering degree. Returning home from Tennessee, William found Central Texas farms suffering from a drought with little use for work animals. He gathered a herd of mules and horses, driving them to Louisiana. There was a need for draft animals in Louisiana, and it was a seller's market. Buying and selling horses and mules proved to be profitable, and Bill continued the trade until 1860.[2]

In April of 1860, William, his brother Dock, and his father Jesse started a herd of cattle on a drive to the Kansas City market. When they reached the Brazos River at Waco on April 22, they found the river flooding. Knowing the flooding river would delay them for many days, they decided to swim the herd across. This decision was a tragic mistake. Jesse, the boy's father, jumped his horse off into the flooded river and the current took both him and his horse underwater. William and Dock tried to save their father, but he drowned in the Brazos River. The brothers recovered and returned their father's body to Belton, where they buried him. Later his body was reinterred in Austin. On returning and driving their herd onward to Kansas City, the brothers encountered a group of armed farmers who refused to let them cross their land. From past experiences the Kansas farmers feared the dreaded tick fever carried by the Texas cattle. The brothers make a detour and finally delivered and sold their cattle in St. Louis. William invested the proceeds of the cattle sale in horses and mules and again drove them to Louisiana. He returned home in January, and in February 1961 Texans voted to secede from the Union.

As the war began, the Day brothers and Jesse L. Driskill, William Moon, and Ezekiel Nance of Hays County delivered beef to the Confederacy's Army's Commissary Department. William Day later joined Captain William Pitts, whose company was a unit of the 1st Regiment, Texas Mounted Riflemen, operating from Camp Colorado in Coleman County. William Day enlisted July 1, 1861, serving his unit as a teamster. A year later he mustered out of service on July 1, 1862, at Fredericksburg, Texas. On leaving the Confederate service, Day purchased a herd of cattle, driving them to Alexandria, Louisiana, and selling them to the Confederacy. Until the war ended, he made a business of buying cattle and delivering them under contract to accessible Confederate army depots. When the war ended, Day was in Mason, Texas, with all of his assets in worthless Confederate currency. He took a job with a livestock commission company in New Orleans.

He soon came back to Texas, setting up a sawmill for a short career in the lumber business. In late 1868 William entered into a partnership with his brother-in-law Jesse Lincoln Driskill who married William Day's sister Nancy Elizabeth. Jesse later came to prominence as a cattleman in South Texas, Kansas, and the Dakota Territory. During his later prosperous years, Driskill purchased an entire city block on Congress Avenue in Austin and built the Driskill Hotel on the tract. The hotel became the center for politics, business, and Texas society.[3]

William Day and Jesse Driskill secured a letter of credit from Spencer Ford's general merchandise store in Bryan, Texas, in February 1869 to buy cattle and outfit a drive north. They delivered 1,400 head of cattle to Abilene, Kansas, for a good profit. The following year there was a bad market with a glut of Texan cattle. Day left the cattle business for several years and profited by locating and selling land. In 1874 he built a beef slaughter plant in Denison, Texas, bought cattle for himself, slaughtered them, and shipped beef carcasses to the eastern market in refrigerated railroad cars. Day had a reputation as a sharp businessman and shrewd operator and was sought for his skills in the cattle business. The St. Louis livestock commission firm of Hunter, Evans & Newman persuaded Day to take over their entire Texas business. Their expansive operation took him to all parts of Texas, and he extended his network of cattlemen and businesspeople. With Day's success he gained the title of colonel, which he wore for the rest of his life.[4]

As he was now known, Colonel William Day envisioned a time in the years ahead when Texas cattlemen would need to change their operation from raising and grazing cattle on the free range to pasturing them and upgrading their herds. Upgrading a herd would require buying, owning, and fencing land. Day began to venture into land investments. He observed and was impressed with the excellent grasslands in Coleman County while stationed at Camp Colorado during his duty in the Confederate service. When Day learned that Brazoria and Fort Bend Counties were putting their school land in Coleman County on the market, he went to the respective county courts. He purchased twenty-two thousand acres of their school land, paying fifty cents an acre for the real estate, with twenty-five cents per acre paid in cash. The balance was paid out over time. This school land purchase made William Day one of the earliest and largest landowners in Coleman County. Bill McCauley, a stonemason and son-in-law of the early Coleman settler Rich Coffey, built a two-room rock house on the Grape Creek tract. Day bought the tract with the rock house and made this his ranch headquarters. After closing his purchase, he bought cattle in to graze his grassland in Coleman.

In 1877 William delivered several large herds of cattle to Dodge City, Kansas, and sold them in June. After selling the cattle, he traveled to Brownsville, Missouri, to visit Miss Tommye Mabel Doss, who was spending the summer there. Mabel Doss was a strong-willed music teacher he had met in Denison; he had frequently visited her. During this visit with Mabel in Missouri, William proposed marriage.

On returning to Texas from his Missouri visit, Day purchased another 7,500 acres of land, adding it to his school land purchase and the Grape Creek tract. After making another cattle drive to Kansas, William traveled to Missouri, visited with Mabel, and succeeded in winning her hand. Miss Tommye Mabel Doss and Colonel William H. Day were married in the First Presbyterian Church in Sherman, Texas, on January 26, 1879. They left Sherman and traveled to Austin, where Mabel stayed with Colonel

Day's mother. It wasn't until September that Mabel made her first trip to the Coleman County ranch. In letters mailed from Coleman, she praised the beauty of the land, the wildlife, and the good-hearted but uneducated people. She said many of the settlers lived in dugouts.[5]

During the spring of 1879, Colonel Day started construction of a four-strand barbed wire fence around the 7,500-acre tract of land. He purchased the barbed wire and cedar post in Austin, freighting the materials to the ranch in Coleman County. When the fence materials arrived in Coleman, a crew of about twenty men worked continuously digging post holes, setting and tamping fence posts, then stretching and stapling the barbed wire. Day's pasture was named the Red Wire Pasture for the barbed wire painted red at the factory. Although the most commonly used barbed wire for fencing in Texas over the years was Glidden wire, Day's Red Wire Pasture was not fenced with Glidden wire. The wire was a heavy nine-gauge, single-line wire wrapped with four-point twisted barbs. This strong wire with a thick diameter often was referred to as buffalo wire. It was manufactured by the Ohio Steel Barb Fence Company of Cleveland, Ohio. William Day's red wire fence was the first fence of distinction built in Coleman County, taking almost a year to construct. Mabel's letters spoke of traveling horseback with her husband and watching him give instructions to twenty or so men building the fence. Day's fence builders finished building the Red Wire Pasture in November of 1879. As soon as the men had built the Red Wire Pasture, they started building fence to enclose the Grape Creek headquarters pasture.[6]

Winter approached and Mabel and William returned to Austin, spent several months in town, and then returned to the ranch in late February 1880. Day and his brother-in-law Jesse Driskill borrowed $10,000 from the Armour Brothers Banking Company in Kansas City. They purchased cattle, making up the herds for that year's drive to Kansas. The stock was delivered, the note paid off, and William and Mabel left Texas for a vacation to Colorado. While they were in Colorado, William Day's cattle buyer S. R. Goodrum contracted with a group of Concho County cattlemen to deliver ten thousand head of cattle to Day's ranch in Coleman County by August of 1881. Because of an act of nature and Texas's unusual weather, this purchase of cattle from the Concho would prove to be a financial disaster.

When Day returned from Colorado, he drove a herd of yearlings and two-year-old cattle to Camp Supply in New Mexico. Colonel Day and his wife's brother, William Doss, delivered the cattle to Camp Supply on November 23 in miserably cold weather. Ten inches of snow was on the ground. Colonel Day returned to Austin from this cattle drive in time to be present for the birth of his daughter Willie Mabel on December 18 and celebrated Christmas with his family.

The winter of 1880–1881 was severe, with ice and snow. Mabel's brother reported that the Coleman ranch fence building was very slow and that cattle were poor, in bad shape, and some were dying. Ridge Goodman (Goodrum), Day's agent and cattle buyer, wrote from Paint Rock, Texas, saying he was checking on yearlings and two-year-olds that could be put together for the spring roundup. He found the weather had caused cattle on the open range to drift south and delayed getting a herd together for several months. In February William Day, short on cash and now overextended, traveled to Kansas to find financing for his next drive. Day had spent every dollar available buying land. He had lawyers in Coleman and land agents in Austin looking for more land as it came on the market. W. T. Simms had Day's power of attorney for land purchases and had earlier helped acquire thousands of acres for the colonel at fifty cents to one dollar an acre.[7]

Spring arrived and in April, Colonel Day and his cowhands rounded up cattle and were branding and marking calves in the open country near the Grape Creek Ranch headquarters. After a hard day's work, William had no problem going to sleep, but he awoke in the middle of the night hearing cattle stirring on the bedding ground. Hurriedly dressing, he rushed to the yard gate where he kept a horse saddled for emergencies. Mounting the horse, Day loped through the darkness to the bedding ground to help the cowhand on night duty. As he rushed toward the herd, his horse stumbled and fell, possibly stepping in a prairie dog hole or maybe slipping on a rock ledge. The saddle horn and swell of the saddle with the horse's weight falling on Day crushed his abdomen and pelvis, causing severe stomach injuries. He was in pain from his injury for several weeks; the Coleman doctor could not help him. Day sent for Dr. James Johnson, his physician in Denison. When Dr. Johnson arrived, he found the injury had caused gangrene; there was no treatment available to save William Day's life. Before his death the colonel spent painful hours with his wife Mabel, trying to communicate details of his business and advise her on the best course of action when she would have to take over the ranch and cattle operation. William Henry Day died on June 14, 1881, leaving cattle, a large ranch with 77,550 acres of fenced land, some of which was unpaid for, and an estate indebtedness of $177,500 for Mabel to manage.[8]

Mabel had a long list of issues to deal with following the colonel's death and burial. Colonel William Day's cattle buyer and attorney-in-fact, S. R. Goodrum, had entered into a contract on November 29, 1880, with a group of Concho County cattlemen. Goodrum had purchased several large herds of cattle grazing out on the free range. Their contract called for delivery of ten thousand head of cattle to Day's ranch in Coleman County, on or before August 1, 1881, for $9.50 per head. John Doss, Mabel's brother who worked on the ranch, reported the cattlemen delivered thirteen or fourteen hundred cattle before the bad weather came.[9]

William Day had died between the date of the contract and the delivery date of the cattle. One of the Concho County cattlemen who owned part of the contracted cattle also died. The winter before the cattle contract's delivery date was severe. There was extreme cold, the snow froze, and north winds caused cattle on the free range to drift far south out of their normal grazing country to unfamiliar territory. Many of the drifting animals died; those surviving were in poor condition. After executing the contract, the sellers delivered cattle to the Day's ranch at various times. Some cattle brought to the ranch were rejected because of their poor condition. There was no provision in the contract that stipulated animals could be rejected because of their poor condition. Their rejection caused bewilderment and anger among the Concho cattlemen. The men had delivered only 5,061 head of cattle accepted by the buyer when the final date for delivery arrived on August 1.

Colonel Day's former business partner Jesse L. Driskill was the estate executor. A dispute arose between Driskill and the cattlemen over rejecting the cattle. The cattlemen maintained they had complied with their contract using diligence in the gathering and delivery. William Day's estate refused to pay a remaining balance of $18,079.50 on the cattle delivered. They claimed damages for the alleged breach of contract. They claimed that the cattlemen had failed to use proper and reasonable care, diligence, and energy in gathering the cattle. The contract called for the delivery of ten thousand head more or less, emphasizing "due diligence in collecting and delivering the cattle in designated marks and brands."

Mabel Day was an independent, strong-willed woman, and Jesse Driskill was a knowledgeable and experienced cattleman. Unfortunately, before the filing of a lawsuit by the parties from Concho County, there were issues between Driskill and Mabel. Driskill resigned as the executor of the estate, and Mabel Day became the executrix. The Concho cattlemen sued, and Mabel stepped in, pursuing the case with tenacity. Concho cattlemen R. Y. Cross, William Mullins, Charles Mullins, and Julia Barron (heir of Isaac Mullins, deceased) filed suit in Travis County against the estate of William H. Day (deceased). The cattlemen sought to establish a claim of $18,079.50 with 10 percent interest and a lien on cattle in the Day herd with the Concho cattlemen brands. The case was tried in Travis County and began on December 26, 1881. The jury returned a verdict on November 10, 1882, finding in favor of the Concho County cattlemen. Mabel Day appealed the case to the Texas Supreme Court. The court heard the case and then affirmed the lower court's ruling on June 8, 1883.[10]

As the case went through the courts, Mabel's financial problems multiplied. She had to find money to cover indebtedness on cattle and land her husband purchased before his death. Before marrying William Day, Mabel had been schooled at the Female Academy of Hocker College in Lexington, Kentucky. Her old professor, J. M. Hocker, had left the business of educating young women and went into the horse business. Being in Kentucky's horse country, this was probably a profitable business move for its founder. Mabel contacted Hocker for help, and her plea received a favorable response. Hocker and William Tarr, a prominent Kentucky distiller, traveled to Coleman and surveyed the Day Ranch and Mabel's cattle. Despite the drought and dry conditions, they were favorably impressed with what they saw.

On returning to Kentucky, Tarr discussed a business proposition with his associate, Ephraim Sayre, the president of the First National Bank of Lexington, and George White, another distiller. They wired Mabel to come to Lexington to conclude negotiations of a package. The deal, in simplest terms, was to organize the Day Ranch Company with a capitalization of $200,000 and give Mrs. Day $75,000 to settle the claims against her cattle, provided she deliver a title on the animals clear of all obligations. Problems and delays occurred when settling the claims, but Mabel succeeded, and the parties created the Day Ranch Company.[11]

Before Mabel was able to find temporary relief from indebtedness, another big problem moved out front. Fence cutting in Coleman began. Mabel wrote J. M. Booth, a close friend and secretary of the Texas House of Representatives on September 28, 1883, saying fence cutters had destroyed five miles of her fences. "The south side fence is cut all to pieces. That fence costs $240 per mile to build, and cattle from outside are already taking possession. There are not enough hands for keeping cattle out, and I cannot get them. She complained that Governor Ireland appeared to be supporting the fence cutters in a letter in the newspapers addressed to the public. Booth wrote her back, advising that she had misinterpreted Governor Ireland's position. He would probably be calling a special session of the legislature to solve the fence-cutting problem.[12]

Word now had spread across Coleman County that Mabel Day had formed a $200,000 cattle corporation with a group of Kentucky businessmen. The story upset Coleman's citizens, and the reaction was volatile and immediate. The fence cutters focused their wire cutting on the Day Ranch and posted a sign on the streets of Coleman reading, "Down with monopolies, they can't exist in Texas and especially in Coleman County; away with your foreign capitalist; the range and soil belong to the heroes of the South; no monopolies and don't tax us to school the [n——]. Give us homes as God intended and not gates to churches and towns and schools, and above all, give us water for our stock."[13]

Mabel quickly responded to the unrest caused by her financial deal with the Kentucky businessmen. In a panic she responded to the sign displayed in Coleman by writing a letter to the community newspaper, the *Coleman Voice*.

> Dear Sir,
>
> Having heard from several that Governor Ireland encouraged fence cutting by a recent letter, I felt anxious to read that letter, which I had the pleasure of doing, and find to my satisfaction that our governor does not encourage any such outlawry, but aims to denounce certain sensational letters that are being sent from Texas to other states.
>
> It is true that he shows in some instances where the wire cutters have had plausible excuses, as was the case in North Texas where foreign capitalist had enclosed large bodies of land which they had not bought or leased, and to which others had as much right as they; but this does not argue that Governor Ireland approves of fence cutting as has been indulged in this county. Here we own the land enclosed. I can speak at least for myself. Within my pasture, there are only two tracts of land owned by other parties, Messer. Gann and Cleveland, and I have these gentlemen to say whether I have cut off any of their legal rights or privileges.
>
> For my part, I think the men who destroyed five miles of my fence last week could have with as much justice burnt my house. I do not want to be understood as complaining of law enforcement. I cannot expect lawful protection until I can designate the guilty parties. This cannot be done as they prefer the dead hours of the night for the accomplishment of the dark deeds. It is my pleasure to show that none of the plausible excuses which Governor Ireland presents are applicable in the case of my pasture. Those men, who found it to their interest to cut my fence, cannot quite their guilty conscience with any of these excuses.
>
> 1. Although my fence is a nuisance, according to Governor Ireland, it was not the business of those men to remove it but of the civil authorities to cause me to do so.
> 2. As before mentioned, I have bought or leased all lands within my enclosure except those previously mentioned. Hence no one has any right to grasses or water but by my consent.
> 3. I have not, to my knowledge, annoyed either of the parties who own land in my pastures, but they enjoy their full privilege and are on amicable terms with me.
> 4. I have gates on all main roads through my pasture; and have not complained of parties tying down the wire so they can pass over any portion of my fence—only request such parties to untie the wires so that stock could not pass out or until my fence rider could

get around to repair it. I have not even complained of certain gaps, which have proved quite a nuisance to me.

Here I request to add that I intend as soon as possible to put in gates for the convenience of those who have recently requested them.

It is true that I have recently sold a half interest in my cattle to gentlemen who do not live in the State of Texas. I regard their engaging in this business as a great accommodation to me as a benefit to them, and don't begrudge them the money I believe and hope they will make here in the next five years. It was my intention two weeks ago on my return to my ranch to immediately prepare me a permanent home in this country; but, since I have seen my property destroyed without cause, I defer my action in this matter.

I would like to address a question to the stockmen of this section. Is there no recourse for us in this matter? Should you, as business and law abiding men, adopt any plan to protect your property? I would beg to be considered as one among you.

Yours Respectfully,
Mrs. Mabel Day[14]

The *Fort Worth Daily Gazette* expressed a gentlemanly view on Mabel's fence-cutting problem, saying, "The Coleman County fence cutters might have had gallantry enough to have let Mrs. Days wire fence alone. She may be rich, but she is a woman, and that ought to go a long way with true men." Of course, the fence cutters didn't share the paper's view, and Mabel being a woman certainly didn't stop their frequent attacks on her fences.[15]

Mabel thought Coleman County Sheriff Ben Pittman appeared sympathetic to the fence cutters. Still, Pittman had plenty of other criminal activity keeping him busy, specifically cattle and horse thieves. Sheriff Pittman and his deputies worked with the sheriffs of San Saba, McCullough, and Concho Counties, gathering cattle with blotted brands and searching for cattle thieves. There was a concerted effort by sheriffs from the four adjoining counties to break up the band of thieves. Cattle rustling and fear of the outlaws prevailed in Coleman and McCullough, with some cattlemen afraid to go into herds and cut out their own stock. They needed a sheriff's help. Sheriffs from the four adjoining counties made slow progress. Ranger Company D scouted these counties for cattle thieves and brand blotting. Several years later Captain

William Scott and Ranger Company F, working out of San Angelo, cleaned up remnants of the thieves.[16]

Adjutant General King talked with Sheriff Pittman about Coleman's fence-cutting problem. Pittman explained to King that fence cutters worked at night, and capture was nearly impossible. He said he needed no assistance outside of his subordinates and from willing citizens. Pittman assured Adjutant General King that he was more than ready to serve anyone for wantonly cutting fences if a citizen would step forward and swear out a complaint against the cutter. But if a fence cutter were captured, there would be difficulty getting an indictment in Coleman, and further, fence cutting was only a misdemeanor. Sheriff Pitman had higher priorities.

Of those Coleman citizens concerned about fence cutting, Colonel J. E. McCord, head of the local law and order league, pushed the matter. He asked Johnny Jones, another citizen member, to go and find the parties cutting the fence. Jones replied, "I love to live too well to do that."[17]

Mabel's Day Ranch Company suffered severe fence cutting, but so did all of Coleman's large landowners. Another favorite target of the cutters was George W. Mahoney. This easterner was a businessman and investor who came to Texas from New York. Mahoney purchased several thousand acres of land southwest of the Santa Anna Mountains, and his barbed wire closed off portions of Home and Loss Creeks. During the droughty summer, his fenced tract of land had the only surface water in the area. This newcomer from New York and his Santana Livestock and Land Company was the talk of the town. His ranch had improvements unheard of in Coleman County. He built a large house for his family and him, a barn three hundred feet long, homes for his hired hands, underground cisterns for water storage, and an elaborate arrangement of pens and corrals for working his livestock. When he finished construction, he brought in cattle and sheep to stock his new ranch. Mahoney apparently had total disregard for neighbors from whom he fenced off grass and water on which their livelihood depended. When fence cutting began in Coleman County, his problems were as serious as Mabel's. His fences were cut, the wire spliced, then cut again. One night a coffin was left in his front yard to emphasize the cutters' serious intentions. A note was left in the coffin saying, "This will be your if you keep fencing."

The irate Irishman responded by placing the casket in the horse corral and made it into a water trough. George Mahoney survived Coleman's fence-cutting war, but his ranch was one of the first large ranches cut up into small tracts and sold to farmers when the barbed wire war came to an end.[18]

R. H. Overall had been a free-range man. He came to Coleman County in 1876 and settled on Home Creek west of Mahoney's ranch. On arriving, he partnered with the Beck brothers and ran cattle and also sheep. Later he managed to purchase several thousand acres of prime grassland and fenced his property. Overall was a respected citizen, and he had good relations with his neighbors. In 1883 his fences also suffered the wrath of the fence cutters. After a section of a pasture fence was destroyed, he announced to the public that he would remove his fence and spool his wire within ten days. Within twenty-four hours after his announcement, a band of fence cutters went to his ranch and cut his remaining fence to shreds. One newspaper labeled the cutting of Overall's fence pure devilry, and the paper's editor recommended "legislation with a little hemp in it." Overall survived Coleman's fence-cutting days but at great expense. He kept his neighbors' respect and continued ranching in Coleman until his death.[19]

Another recent arrival was Horace R. Starkweather. He was raised in Lucas County, Ohio, and educated as a bookkeeper and accountant. He came to Texas in 1877 and four years after his arrival located in Coleman. With financial support from his brother, Horace purchased forty thousand acres of land in southern Coleman County east of the Day Ranch. His ranch was close in size to the Day Ranch. At great expense he built forty miles of barbed wire fence on his land. Although Starkweather stocked the ranch with cattle, he invested heavily in sheep. Sheep and wool had become a profitable venture. Republican tariffs had increased the wool price, and farmers and even some Texas cattlemen ventured into the sheep business. Owning land and fencing was now essential for the sheepmen. At the urging of cattlemen, several years earlier in 1881 the Texas legislature passed legislation making it unlawful to graze sheep on another's land without permission. This law was now forcing sheepmen to purchase property and build fences. Starkweather traveled south to the border country and purchased eight thousand head of ewes and top-grade rams from Santo and Carlos Benavides, prominent

Laredo sheepmen. His shepherds drove the sheep from Laredo to his recently fenced Coleman County Ranch.[20]

During the dry summer of 1883, fence cutters began cutting Starkweather's barbed wire fences. His ranch hands spliced fence wire where possible and rebuilt his fences. Rock from his pastures was gathered and stacked under the lower fence wire to secure the enclosure and keep his sheep inside. Starkweather now badly needed new financing to maintain his investment in Coleman County. He decided to obtain funding from one of the large banks in Chicago. Traveling to the big city, Starkweather met with the bankers and incorporated his ranch to secure needed funds. His financing package with one of the banks was nearly completed. Then the next morning, he purchased a newspaper from a street vendor and opened it. An article stood out in bold print. The headline read, "Hell Breaks Loose in Texas, Wire Cutters Cut 500 Miles of Fence in Coleman County." The paper headlined and then described for its Chicago audience the barbed wire war raging in Coleman County and across Texas.

Starkweather's effort in arranging bank financing collapsed; the Coleman County stockman boarded a train for the long ride home. By the end of the year, thirty miles of Horace Starkweather's fences had been cut. Then the outlaws burned his sheep sheds and shepherd's houses. They also burned two thousand of his fresh cut and carefully stacked cedar fence post. The cutters despised Starkweather's sheep as much as his barbed wire fences. When he was trying to replace sections of his fences, the cutters herded sheep infested with scabies into his pastures, mixing them with his herd. The infestation of scabies caused him and his shepherds to have to dip eight thousand head of sheep during the cold winter. This resulted in the loss of many of his flock.[21]

The financial impact of the fence-cutting troubles broke Starkweather, forcing him to sell most of his ranch land. But he stayed in Coleman County. Its citizens appreciated this upright gentleman and in time, he became president of Coleman's Farmers State Bank. In later years the elderly gentleman said that cattle were selling for thirty dollars per head when fence cutting started in Texas. The next year they were five dollars, and practically all free grass cattlemen were broke. About $90 million were loaned to Texas cattlemen. Then, fence cutting broke out, and their loans were called in by the eastern bankers from whom they borrowed.[22]

Like others across the state, Coleman County landowners and pasture men sought help with their fence-cutting troubles from Governor Ireland and the Rangers. There were too few Rangers to help, and Adjutant General Wilburn King questioned the state's legal authority to intervene. Mabel Day lobbied and applied pressure at the state capital with help from her close friend J. M. Booth, secretary of the Texas House of Representatives. Booth advised the governor of Mabel's problem and communicated there would be an armed conflict with bloodshed between Coleman's pasture men and the fence cutters. At the time of the discussion, Adjutant General King was not at the state capital in Austin. He had traveled to North Texas and was meeting with officials in Clay, Wise, and Denton Counties on fence cutting and related incidents of the most violent nature. There was a shootout on a fence line in Clay County between fence cutters and ranch hands; a fence cutter had been killed and another wounded. While meeting with officials in North Texas, King received a telegram from Governor Ireland, directing him to take Rangers and go to Coleman to prevent another outbreak of violence and bloodshed.

Adjutant General King left North Texas, rushing to Coleman ahead of Captain Samuel McMurry and his Company B Rangers. When King reached Coleman, the district court was in session and farmers and ranchers had come to town. As King mingled with citizens, he heard stories and found excitement about the rapid fencing of large land tracts and fence cutting that followed. But the adjutant general soon determined there was no foundation for armed conflict or a violent outbreak in Coleman. King talked to citizens on the streets representing both sides of the fence-cutting issue. The district court was in session during the day, so he called a meeting at night to allow all parties to speak. There were speeches and testimony from pasture men and their earnest advocates and also the fence-cutting faction and their supporters. Unfortunately, Mabel Day was in Austin when King arrived in Coleman and didn't attend and testify at his meeting. Her brother William Doss, who managed the Day Ranch, wasn't there either.

Adjutant General King returned to his headquarters in Austin with a clear understanding of the problems in Coleman County, and he discussed them in his 1883 adjutant general's report. The citizens he talked to satisfied him that there was no danger of a violent armed battle between the factions in Coleman. Though feuds might arise, they would be confined to the persons immediately involved. King observed that most of Coleman's citizens supported fence cutting and pasture burning because of their intense, deep, and open hostility to large pastures and fencing. The *Galveston Daily News*, reporting on King's Coleman trip, said Adjutant General King wasn't happy with what he learned about the pasture men: "Adjutant General King found 60 percent of the people are opposed to large pastures and are in sympathy with the fence cutters. He indicated, as a sample of their grievances, two pastures were occupied with a frontage of eighty miles on the Colorado River to the exclusion to the rest of the world."[23]

Reporting to the governor, King shared both sides of the issue. On behalf of the pasture men, he said that the pasture owner's legal rights had been violently and ruthlessly trampled underfoot with no hope of redress or reimbursement for their loss. There was immeasurable damage to these landowners, county businesses, the Texas state's school fund, and the state at home and abroad by the depreciating of land and livestock caused directly by this lawlessness.

King also cited grievances and showed sympathy for the small man, the farmer, and free-range men who supported the fence cutters. Their objection was to the vast tracts of land owned and fenced by individuals and corporations who they believed inhibited the progress of settlement and lasting prosperity. King noted the citizens' view that the present land system produced two extremes in social and political life, a small number of rich and a large number of poor people. The citizens' most obvious complaint was barbed wire fences in Coleman County stretching in every direction and often enclosing land not belonging to the fence owners. There were fences across public roads and fences enclosing streams and flowing springs once used by all citizens over the years. Travel was restricted or entirely prevented so that the citizens couldn't reach the county's schools, mills, and churches in many parts without great difficulty. Getting into Coleman to carry on private businesses required considerable effort. Cattle on the range were often seriously injured and died from screwworms growing in barbed wire cuts. In the dry season, cattle, sheep, and horses owned by small operators died for want of water, abundant but fenced in and exclusively controlled by owners of the large pastures. Adjutant General King shared his findings from his Coleman trip with the governor and published his conclusions in the 1883 annual adjutant general report. The annual report was provided to the legislature when they came to Austin for the special session to address fence-cutting problems.[24]

Trickham, one of the oldest communities in Coleman County, was located a short ride from the Day Ranch on Mukewater Creek. The town had been a stop-off for cowhands trailing cattle north in earlier years and had a post office, hotel, several shops, and a saloon. There was a shootout in Trickham on the evening of September 17. For months there had been simmering anger between Tom Hayes, a cattleman, and Abraham Pendleton, a cowhand. Pendleton worked for William Day at one time but now was the bartender at Trickham's saloon. Hayes walked into the bar, ordered a drink, and after downing the shot of bourbon, drew his six-shooter, pointed it at Pendleton, and fired. Unfortunately for Hayes his bullet missed the bartender. Expecting trouble, Pendleton had his revolver ready and returned fired, hitting Hayes in the head. His second shot hit Hayes in the right breast as he fell. When the Galveston newspaper picked up this story, Hayes was still alive but in serious condition. Eventually, his wounds proved fatal. The Galveston newspaper's correspondent in Coleman in his report said, "Pendleton left the saloon and hadn't been heard from." The correspondent then wrapped up his story saying, "We had a good and general rain here last Sunday, which put the creeks to running and new life in the fine Mesquite Grass." Coleman was suffering a drought, and to the farmer and ranchers, the rain was as important as a shooting.[25]

Soon after the shooting, Mabel learned Abe Pendleton was hiding out at one of her cow camps. Her brother, William Doss, rode out to the camp and brought Pendleton in to meet with his sister. After hearing his story, they talked. Mabel offered to pay Pendleton's bond and hire him a lawyer, providing he would work for her as a fence rider. Mabel believed Abe was good with a gun and would serve her well riding her fence lines. Pendleton was worried about criminal prosecution for shooting and killing Hayes. Desperate for help he accepted her job offer. All else had failed, and Mabel was ready to hire a gunman to protect her property. Rangers from Company B were in Coleman when Adjutant General King was there but soon left, and fence cutting started again across Coleman County.

Soon after hiring on to work on the Day Ranch, Abe Pendleton, Mabel's fence rider, rode up on a band of fence cutters hard at work. The men had blackened their faces to hide their identity, and there were sixty or seventy scattered along the fence clipping barbed wire. Abe was overpowered and forced at the point of a Winchester to help the men finish their job cutting Mabel's fence. Details on what action may have followed are missing. On hearing of the incident, Mabel's close friend and attorney J. M. Booth insisted that she have Pendleton immediately file charges against any men he recognized and have Sheriff Pittman arrest them. No record of a complaint filed has been found. Pendleton appears to have valued his life more than loyalty to his employer and disappeared.[26]

Fence cutting on the Day Ranch and other Coleman ranches continued. Mid-November of 1883 Mabel learned that fence cutters cut the barbed wire between the post in what she called her new pasture and a six-mile section of wire cut out of the old pasture. On November 19 Mabel composed and sent a letter to the *Coleman Voice*. She pleaded that the cutters oblige her by not cutting more of the fence around the old pasture until the legislature met and passed laws settling differences between the free grass men and the pasture men. Pleading her case as a woman, Mabel said it would not be possible to manage her cattle as they drifted south in the winter. She informed the citizens of Coleman her husband's death had left her heavily in debt, and she had to sell half of her cattle to cover that debt. The out-of-state businessmen didn't buy her land, only leased it for five years. She said that she and her little child still owned the ranch's acreage and would live there and run the operation.[27]

The Texas legislature convened on January 8, 1884, for the special legislative session called by Governor John Ireland. After a contentious session, the legislature passed multiple bills creating new laws dealing with the state lands, roads, fencing, and fence cutting. They made fence cutting a felony with mandatory time in prison. The new 1884 laws on fence cutting went into effect immediately after passage with the governor's signature. Fence cutting slowed, then finally became an occasional and sporadic occurrence in Coleman. The Day Ranch fences had been destroyed when fence cutting finally stopped. Mabel began rebuilding her fences and, in time, completed the job at the cost of $29,000. Adding to those expenses was money she owed the state of Texas for land purchases. Her indebtedness was now over $66,000.[28]

After fence cutting stopped and Mabel's financial situation stabilized, her brother, William Doss assumed most of the cattle and ranch management activity. Mabel was spending time traveling and visiting old friends. Much of her time was in Fort Worth. The town's Pickwick Hotel listings of arrivals printed in the *Fort Worth Daily Gazette* show her as a frequent visitor in the city. During Mabel's barbed wire battles and politicking efforts at the state capital, a relationship developed between Mabel and Col. J. M. Booth, secretary for the House of Representatives. The April 26 issue of the *Daily Gazette* noted, "Mrs. Mabel Day and her brother Capt. Dows [Doss] of Austin are in our city for a few days, the guest of Col. J. J. Long. We need hardly add that our Col. Booth is at home now, and when we say he may be a lucky dog and soon have his Day, we hear many a hearty amen." Another announcement in the paper later in the fall noted, "Mrs. Mabel Day of Coleman, one of the wealthiest ladies in the state, was in the city last night."[29]

As Mabel made visits to Fort Worth, so did Joseph Lea, a New Mexico rancher and businessman. In his past Joseph C. Lea served the South during the Civil War; he was one of Quantrill's Confederate guerrillas. After the war Lea he received a pardon from the president and went to New Mexico in 1877 with a few cattle and sheep. Despite Lea's experiences and background of violence during the Civil War, he was never again known to wear a gun. Captain Lea, as he was known, purchased large tracts of New Mexico land with water and formed a corporation under the name Lea Cattle Company. His major investors were Horace B. Thurber of the United States Steamboat Lines and John and Charles Arbuckle of the Arbuckle Coffee Company.

In 1885 Mabel met Joseph Lea while he was in Texas buying cattle for his New Mexico ranch. Lea was a widower, having lost two wives, and Mabel was a widow. Joseph Lea and Mabel both owned large ranch spreads, Lea's in New Mexico and Mabel's in Texas. With both having many responsibilities, there was a four-year courtship before they married. They were joined in marriage on April 29, 1889, in Mabel's rock ranch house on the Day Ranch. Following the wedding, Mabel turned over all ranch operations to her brother, William. She, her new husband, her daughter Willie Mabel Day, and two Black servants, Mattie and George, loaded up their belongings and traveled to their new home in Roswell, New Mexico. Mabel's new family now included Joseph's two children, his son Wildy and daughter Ella.

Over the years that followed, Joseph and Mabel had many accomplishments to their credit. Two contributions that stand out were growing and developing the town of Roswell and the founding of the New Mexico Military Institute. Captain Joseph Lea, known as the Father of Roswell, died February 4, 1904, and Mabel passed away two years later, on April 4, 1906. For twenty years after losing her first husband and surviving the fence-cutting war in Coleman County, Mabel managed to stay ahead of her indebtedness and retained the Day Ranch ownership. Before her death, Mabel began breaking up and selling her ranch in small tracts to farmers. Still, she left a sizable parcel of ranch property to her daughter and grandson at her death.[30]

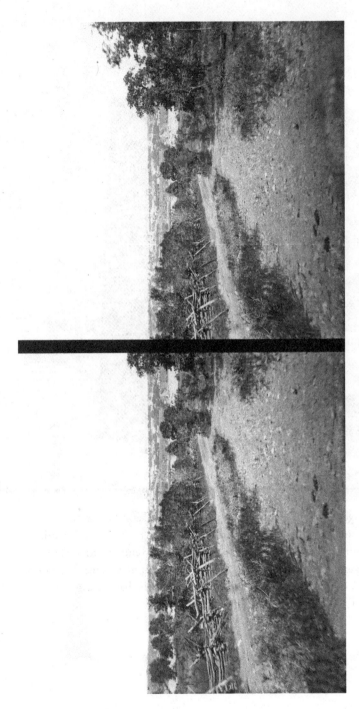

This stake-and-rider fence is dated 1860. Austin and the old Texas State Capitol are in the distant background; this fence would have been in use when John Grinninger was murdered in 1862. Stake-and-rider fences made from cedar rails, such as the one in this photograph, were in common used in early Austin and Travis County before commercial barbed wire arrived. Courtesy of Austin History Center, Austin Public Library, Jones Glass Plate Negative Collection, J141.

The Grinninger Historical Marker was erected by the Texas Historical Commission in Austin on the site where John Grinninger, an old iron worker, built Texas's first barbed wire fence. His barbed wire invention was used to protect his commercial garden and orchard. This invention was the first barbed wire in Texas, in use in 1857, eleven years before the first barbed wire was patented in the United States. Author's photograph.

Henry Bradley Sanborn was employed as Joseph Glidden's salesperson and brought Glidden's barbed wire to Texas in 1875. Eight years later the *Galveston Daily News* reported Sanborn's wire sales from his Houston headquarters for 1883 were $1 million. Photo from B. B. Paddock's *A Twentieth Century History and Biographical Record of North and West Texas*, vol. 1 (Chicago: Lewis Publishing, 1902).

These early fence staples were forged and used on the King Ranch in South Texas. The King Ranch's first wire fence was built using three strands of smooth nine-gauge iron wire and fastened to posts with staples such as these. Progress followed, and in 1880 Richard King had fenced a total of 253,000 acres with the new sharp-pointed barbed wire. Author's photograph.

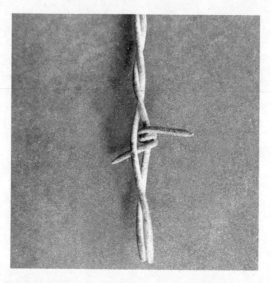

Joseph Glidden filed his first barbed wire patent application on October 27, 1873, for his sticky, pointed barbed wire, made by hand and used on his farm. He was issued his patent on November 24, 1874. Author's photograph.

Jacob Haish filed the patent application for his S Barb wire on June 17, 1874. He then filed interference papers against Joseph Glidden, whose application was filed in October of 1873. Haish's famous S Barb patent was issued August 31, 1875. Author's photograph.

Joseph Glidden's barbed wire came to Texas in 1875 and is displayed on the right. It was the first barbed wire to come to the state, but soon other wires were available to stockmen and farmers. Over the years Glidden wire proved the most practical and successful of all the barbed wires sold in Texas. Author's photograph.

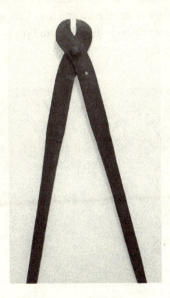

This unique wire cutting tool is on display with other wire cutting and fence building tools in the Devil's Rope Barbed Wire Museum at McClean, Texas. The wire cutter appears to be the popular fence cutting tools made and sold by a blacksmith in San Saba, Texas. Its long handles permitted a man to clip wire without getting off his horse. There were reports that fence cutters came to San Saba from across Texas to buy this tool. Courtesy of the Devil's Rope Museum in McLean, Texas.

Remnants of fence made of cedar post or rails are found on the old Davis Ranch, which was established in 1857 in Blanco County. The first fence on the ranch was built with six miles of rock and over four miles of cedar post. It's estimated there were over twenty-five thousand posts used in the original fence. Author's photograph.

Rock fences built with native stone were usually crafted by farmers to retain or prevent entry of livestock. They were built to protect crops growing in fields, but there were exceptions. Sections of this rock fence are still standing in one of the pastures of the large Davis Ranch in Blanco County. Author's photograph.

In 1875 Henry Bradley Sanborn left his job as a horse trader in Illinois and traveled to Texas, selling the nation's first manufactured barbed wire. Years later he and Joseph Glidden invested in land and cattle in Potter and Randal Counties and fenced the 250,000-acre Frying Pan Ranch. Always an owner, admirer, and breeder of fine horses, Sanborn is shown here in his later years with a pair of his well-groomed harness horses. Courtesy of the Panhandle-Plains Historical Museum, Canyon, Texas.

Abel H. "Shanghai" Pierce was a prominent South Texas cattleman who made his opinions known with his loud, bellowing voice. He was an opponent of barbed wire when it first came to Texas but soon built fence with barbed wire. In the 1890s Pierce commissioned sculptor Frank Teich to create a large statue of himself out of gray marble, and today it marks his grave in the Hawley Cemetery in Matagorda County. Author's photograph.

William Plemons grew up in North Carolina and came to Texas in 1865. Admitted to the bar in 1876, he established his law practice at Henrietta, the county seat of Clay County, and gained fame as a criminal defense lawyer.
In 1876 he represented pasturemen at a meeting with fence cutters at the Post Oak community in Jack County and negotiated a peace treaty. Courtesy of the Clay County 1890 Jail Museum–Historical Center, Henrietta, Texas.

Thomas Lawson Odom was a prominent Texas cattleman and state legislator ranching at Fort Chadbourne, Texas. He had forty miles of fence cut, and the fence cutters burned wagonloads of cedar fence posts and spools of barbed wire he had freighted to his ranch. Courtesy of Fort Chadbourne Foundation, Coke County, Texas.

This fence cutters' note was written with a pencil and tacked to a fence post riddled with bullets. The post and warning note were then hung in a tree near the home of State Representative Thomas L. Odom at Fort Chadbourne.
This note was later part of prosecution's evidence in one of the fence cutter trials in Runnels County. Author's photograph.

Garland Good Odom was Thomas Odom's oldest son. Garland entered the cattle business by buying cattle in South Texas, shaping them into herds, and driving them to Kansas. He entered a partnership with his father in 1876, and when the Odom & Luckett Ranch Company was formed in 1879, Garland became the general manager. Courtesy of the Fort Chadbourne Foundation, Coke County, Texas.

John Ireland practiced law in Seguin, Texas, enlisted in the Confederate Army as a private, and rose to the rank of lieutenant colonel. Later he served in the Texas House of Representatives and Senate, then was elected governor in 1882 and reelected in 1884. As governor, his administration struggled with the Texas fence cutting wars, state's land issues, and, in his second term, labor strikes by the Knights of Labor. Courtesy of the Texas State Library and Archives Commission, Austin.

Wilburn H. King (*third officer from the left, standing and wearing his Texas Volunteer Guard dress uniform*) was an officer during the Civil War. King came home and served two terms in the Texas legislature, and then served as Texas's adjutant general from 1881 to 1891. His military background and political knowledge helped him manage the poorly funded Frontier Battalion of Texas Rangers. Stephen H. Daren Collection, 1999/190-38-1, courtesy of the Texas State Library and Archives Commission, Austin.

Benjamin Goodin Warren enlisted as a Texas Ranger and preformed undercover work among fence cutters in Runnels County. His testimony soon produced twenty-four criminal indictments of fourteen men. The week before their trial, Ben Warren, the state's key witness, was assassinated by fence cutters in the Sweetwater Central Hotel's lobby. Warren died from a rifle shot fired through a hotel window. Courtesy of Fort Chadbourne Foundation, Coke County, Texas.

John McEwan Formwalt came to Runnels County in 1874 and was elected Runnels County's first sheriff in 1880, serving until November 3, 1896. This six-foot, four-inch-tall lawman was one tough hombre and showed an unsparing hand for outlaws and fence cutters. Courtesy of the West Texas Collection, Angelo State University, San Angelo, Texas.

Following a jury of inquest, Nolan County Sheriff H. G. Bardwell placed two of the fence cutters under arrest for the assassination of Ranger Benjamin Warren. A jail break occurred the following summer when Sheriff Bardwell was overcome by jail prisoners and the assassins. One of the assassins escaped but was captured three days later. Photo Courtesy of Pioneer City County Museum, Sweetwater, Texas.

A large group of concerned citizens met in Brownwood with free-grass men and fence cutters on November 17, 1883, to find a temporary solution and stop fence cutting until after the called legislative session. The meeting failed to stop fence cutting; a threatening message was delivered to the presumed fence cutters. On December 10 thirty-six armed fence cutters rode into Brownwood ready for a fight with armed citizens. A shooting was averted. The second meeting in Brownwood is remembered as the Fence Cutters Convention. Courtesy of Brownwood Public Library, Brownwood, Texas.

The Coggin brothers and W. C. Parks, their early cattle business partner, built this two-story rock building in Brownwood. The building housed the Coggin brothers' mercantile, hardware, and early bank business and was known for its opera house located on the upper floor. The opera house served as a culture attraction and temporary courtroom and was a fortress in a standoff with fence cutters. Courtesy of Brownwood Public Library, Brownwood, Texas.

Here is an inside view of the Coggin, Ford, and Martin Bank in Brownwood. *Standing, left to right*, Ed Smith, Henry Ford, G. W. Smith, Samuel R. Coggin, and Frank Crumb. The brothers' financial manager and the community's banker, Samuel Coggin, stands in front of the bank teller's cage. Courtesy of Brownwood Public Library, Brownwood, Texas.

Samuel R. Coggin was the younger brother and the entrepreneur who managed and grew the brothers' finance, mercantile, and commodity enterprise. Brother Moses J. (Mody) Coggin managed their livestock, land, and farming operations. Although rarely noted, the Coggin brothers' cattle business was in the same league with G. W. Slaughter, Charles Goodnight, and John Chisum. Courtesy of Brownwood Public Library, Brownwood, Texas.

Levin P. Baugh came to Brown County with his family in the 1850s. He was an Indian fighter and prominent rancher and was in scrapes with the fence cutters. Lev, as he was known, was one of the early pasturemen to suffer fence cutting in Brown and one of the last to do battle with the fence cutters. Courtesy of Brownwood Public Library, Brownwood, Texas.

Brown County Sheriff William Nelson Adams didn't work with the Rangers and wasn't trusted by Governor John Ireland, but he had a strong constituency in Brown and neighboring counties. He was elected Brown County Sheriff on November 7, 1882, and reelected November 4, 1884, and again on November 2, 1886. In later years he was elected Texas state senator for Brown and seven neighboring counties. Courtesy of Texas State Preservation Board, Austin.

Captain James T. Gillespie and Company E were the first Rangers sent to Brown County and were support for detectives trying to build fence cutting cases. Later, Ranger Company E was transferred to Toyah in West Texas, then disbanded in 1887 because of decreased appropriations. After leaving the Rangers, James T. Gillespie was elected and served as the first sheriff of Brewster County. Courtesy of Archives of the Big Bend, Bryan Wildenthal Memorial Library, Sul Ross State University, Alpine, Texas.

> Chicago July 8/84
>
> Capt. Jno. O. Johnson
> 1st Bat. Rangers Austin Texas
>
> Dear Sir,
>
> Yours of 5th received with enclosure of ch for $668.50, in payment of my bill. I note what you say in regard to the difference of $100.00, which is not placed to your credit. This matter is all right. The operative on his return had $100.00 which he could not account for, and when he was sent out again the matter was left in such a way that we could straighten it when we got word from you. Therefore this is all right.
>
> Respect. Yours
> W. A. Pinkerton

Pinkerton Detective Agency's correspondence in the Texas state library shows Allen Pinkerton writing Quartermaster John O. Johnson concerning reimbursement for his detective's work in Brown County. The Pinkerton agent had left the state in a hurry with expense money unaccounted for. Using commercial detectives in Brown County to secure fence cutter indictments was expensive and proved to be a failure. Courtesy of the Texas State Library and Archives Commission, Austin.

William Collier claimed he was 17 in 1883 when he enlisted in Ranger Company D and served under Captain Lamar P. Sieker. He had just paid the balance owed on his six-shooter issued by the state when he was detached and assigned undercover work in Brown County. In his later life Collier was vice president of the City National Bank in San Antonio. Courtesy of Western History Collections, University of Oklahoma Libraries, Norman, Rose #1507.

Ranger Ira Aten, a clean-cut young man, enlisted in Ranger Company D at the age of 20. In his early years as a Ranger, he was assigned as an undercover operative working on fence cutting cases. He had successes in Lampasas and Brown Counties. Aten's work was exemplary, but he detested every minute of the fence cutting detective work. He preferred more action and during his career found it in several deadly gunfights. Photo courtesy of Local History and Genealogy Branch, Brownwood Public Library, Brownwood, Texas.

The Rangers standing worked on the fence cutting problem in Brown County. *Left to right*, Frank Carmichael, John Rogers, Captain William Scott, J. A. Brooks, T. S. Crowder, and James B. Harry. The Brown County veterans missing are William Treadwell and James Moore. Moore was killed soon after leaving Brownwood in a shootout in Sabine County, and William Treadwell had resigned. Seated (*left to right*) are Rangers J. E. Randall, William C. Bridwell, Curren L. Rogers, Allen Newton, and a Ranger of uncertain identity. Courtesy of Western History Collection, University of Oklahoma Libraries, Norman, Rose #1411.

Captain George Schmitt is standing on the far right. Schmitt and Ranger Company C were in Fort Worth on April 4, 1886, on temporary duty suppressing violence caused by striking railroad workers, the Knights of Labor. The following year Schmitt and Company C were transferred from South Texas to Brown County to prevent new fence cutting and search for cattle rustlers. Courtesy of Western History Collections, University of Oklahoma Libraries, Norman, Rose #1412.

William Henry Day purchased a large block of school land in Coleman County and in 1879 fenced 7,500 acres with barbed wire painted red at the factory. The tract was known as Day's Red Wire Pasture. William Day died in an accident in 1881, leaving his wife Mable with over 77,000 acres of fenced land, cattle, and huge debts as fence cutting began in Coleman County. Courtesy of Ralph Terry, Coleman County historian.

The photograph of Mable Day Lea with her new family was made years after her suffering of fence cutting in Coleman County had ended. Mable remarried and moved to Roswell, New Mexico. *Left to right*, Mabel's second husband, Captain Joseph C. Lea, Ella Lea, Willie Day, Wildy Lea, and Mable Day Lea. Courtesy of Historical Society for Southeast New Mexico Archives, Roswell, Chief Archivist Janice Dunnahoo.

Green Lake on the Greer Ranch in Edwards County is a small, isolated body of water once used by free-range men watering livestock. As state lands were sold and barbed wire arrived in Texas, Green Lake was fenced and soon became the site of a deadly gun battle between fence cutters and Texas Rangers. Author's photograph.

Joseph W. Greer watched the Rangers' gun battle with fence cutters at Green Lake in Edwards County. A fence cutter was killed, and Ranger W. W. Baker received a severe wound. Joseph saddled his horse and rode all night to Junction City, returning with Dr. J. W. Burt to care for the wounded Ranger. Courtesy of Judy Greer McCoy.

Oscar Dudley Baker, known as "O. D.," enlisted in Ranger Company D in 1882 and was in the deadly shootout with fence cutters at Green Lake in 1884. Baker later became a printer in Uvalde, then assumed a newspaper editor's job in Milam County. In 1920 he was elected as a state representative, serving in the Thirty-Seventh and Thirty-Eighth Sessions of the Texas Legislature. Courtesy of Western History Collections, University of Oklahoma Libraries, Norman, Rose #1430.

Corporal Phillip C. Baird of Ranger Company D was dispatched from Camp Leona in Uvalde with three Rangers to investigate a fence cutting problem in Edwards County. Soon after arrival at the Greer brothers' ranch at Green Lake, the Rangers were in a deadly gun battle with fence cutters. Leaving the Rangers soon afterward, Baird was employed as a sheriff's deputy and then in 1888 elected Mason County sheriff. He served a total of twelve years. Courtesy of Mason County Historical Commission, Mason, Texas.

These crumbled remains of the old rock fence at Green Lake still stand. Fence cutters came to Green Lake and cut a barbed wire fence that joined this rock fence. When the fence cutters discovered the Rangers and were called on to surrender, they fired on the Rangers and used the rock fence as a fortress in the deadly gun battle. Author's photograph.

William Joseph Greer arrived in Edwards County in 1882 with horses, a wagon, and 385 head of sheep. He and his brother fenced their homestead on a small body of water known as Green Lake. Joseph survived fence cutting, droughts, and other hard times and in the years that followed served as president of the First State Bank in Rocksprings. Courtesy of Judy Greer McCoy.

It was in the Medina County Courthouse in Castroville that Sheriff Fritz Thumm shot and killed his third man, the young lawyer John W. Hildebrand. The old courthouse in Castroville was abandoned years later when Hondo was voted Medina's new county seat. This photograph of the Castroville Courthouse was taken by Mrs. Alexis Ihnken Boehme before it was destroyed and is dated circa 1920. Courtesy of Bradford Boehme.

John Lytle and other South Texas stockmen were a force behind the scenes that helped bring an end to fence cutting in Medina and Frio Counties. Lytle began his cattle business in Frio County and moved his headquarters to Medina County in 1879. In 1904 he was elected and served as secretary and general manager of the Cattle Raisers Association of Texas. Photo from B. B. Paddock's *Twentieth Century History*, vol. 1.

Cooper Wright came to Texas from Virginia, settled at Buffalo Springs, and was there for a short time before he was in a shootout with fence cutters. He moved to Henrietta and was elected sheriff of Clay County on November 2, 1880. One of his most heartbreaking experiences was investigating the killing of the three young brothers who tried to stop construction of a barbed wire fence on land they believed they owned. Courtesy of Clay County 1890 Jail Museum–Historical Center, Henrietta, Texas.

Menard County Sheriff Richard R. "Dick" Russell began his lawman career as a Ranger in Company D under Captain Dan Roberts. He was honorably discharged after two years of service and in 1886 was elected sheriff of Menard County. Sheriff Russell gathered evidence and built the case that sent a Menard fence cutter to prison. Courtesy of Western History Collections, University of Oklahoma Libraries, Norman, Rose #1640.

Albert W. Moursund Sr., an immigrant from Norway, was the district judge for the Thirty-Third Judicial District Court in 1887. He sent a Menard County fence cutter to prison. This was one of the very few cases where a fence cutter was sentenced to prison. Moursund had been a state representative in Texas's Eighteenth Legislature's Special Session in 1884 that made fence cutting a felony offense. Courtesy of Gillespie County, Texas.

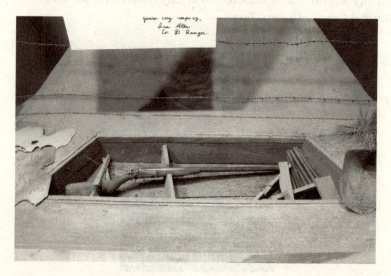

A replica of Ira Aten's Dynamite Boom on display in the Texas Ranger Hall of Fame and Museum. Failing to penetrate the Navarro County's fence cutter gang after months of undercover work, Ira Aten built what he called his dynamite boom. The device was an old shotgun stuffed with dynamite to be buried along the fence line and set to trip when fence wires were cut. Courtesy of Texas Ranger Hall of Fame and Museum, Waco, Texas.

Of the Rangers working on fence cutting, Ira Aten is probably the most often remembered. Aten conducted successful undercover assignments among fence cutters, then washed out in Navarro County. But Aten's law and order experiences cover much more than fence cutting. He returned from Navarro to Ranger Company D with significant wins, served as a sheriff in two different counties, and spent a decade as a manager on the large XIT Ranch. Courtesy of Western History Collections, University of Oklahoma Libraries, Norman, Rose #1453.

Lamartine Pemberton Sieker, known as Lamar or Lam, was a Civil War veteran and is wearing his Texas Volunteer Guard dress uniform. Sieker conducted business in a structured military manner while serving as captain of Ranger Company D and during the years he served as quartermaster of the Ranger's Frontier Battalion. He was a fearless leader, an excellent administrator, and a gentleman. Courtesy of Western History Collections, University of Oklahoma Libraries, Norman, Rose #1433.

Rangers standing (*left to right*) are Captains John A. Brooks, John H. Rogers, and George A. Wheatley. Wheatley was a captain and Frontier Battalion quartermaster from 1893 to 1895. Seated (*left to right*) are Captain Lamar P. Sieker, Lieutenant John B. Armstrong, and Captain William J. McDonald. Captains Brooks, Rogers, and Sieker played important parts in bringing Texas barbed wire wars to an end. This photograph was made circa 1893. Courtesy of Libraries Special Collections, University of Texas at San Antonio.

Chapter 11

Ranger Wounded, Cutter Killed at Green Lake, Edwards County

> The Rangers on the hill called to us not to touch him. I said, "We just want to look at him." I raised up the blanket, and if I live to be a hundred years, I'll never forget what I saw. It was July, and the flies were bad. He had about ten days' growth of red beard and I wish I had never looked.
> —Tom Dragoo as a boy. He was at Green Lake after the shooting.

Following the Civil War, the livestock industry was the primary source of income and a salvation for many Confederate veterans returning home to Texas. The cattle population roaming the free range in Texas multiplied and grew during the Civil War. Returning home from the war, men began moving cattle up the Shawnee and Chisholm Trails to the railheads in Kansas and selling cattle for good prices. History glorifies the cowboy and Texas longhorns. Certainly, the cattle industry was a critical part of the state's recovery, but so was the Texas sheep industry. The state's sheep business was slower to grow, however, and herders were necessary. Sheep required protection and care while grazing out on the free range. Although delayed by a lack of herders following the Civil War, the sheep industry did prosper. There were an estimated 1.272 million sheep in Texas by 1870, and in 1884 Texas led the nation in sheep production with an estimate of 8 million sheep on the range. By 1882 some of the sheepmen on the Edwards Plateau also raised Angora goats. One of these men was William Leslie Black of Fort McKavett, an entrepreneur and founding member of the New York Cotton Exchange. Black became interested in sheep and wool and purchased thirty thousand acres on the San Saba River's headwaters around old Fort McKavett to begin his sheep business. Black later bought more land reaching in all directions from his Fort McKavett headquarters.[1]

In 1882 the John J. Marsh and P. H. Wentworth Partnership from Boston, Massachusetts, bought the old Fort Terrett property and made it their headquarters. Wentworth moved from Boston to the Edwards Plateau to manage their sheep ranch and over time amassed about 100,000 acres of land in Crockett, Sutton, Edwards, and Kimble Counties. The ranch was stocked with native and Spanish Merino sheep. Mexican sheepherders were employed to care for the herds on the open range.[2]

Throughout these counties and across the Edwards Plateau, cattlemen both large and small grazed their stock on the open range. And as in other parts of the state, cattlemen here also had a strong dislike for sheepmen and their sheep. Very few fences were built in these counties; most of the range was left open for free grazing. But as fences were built, these counties had fence-cutting problems. In correspondence to the adjutant general in Austin, Ranger Captain Lamartine Sieker referred to the fence cutters in Edwards County as the North and South Llano Fence Cutters Association. Sieker claimed the big cowmen directed their operations. Large landowners and sheepmen such as Black, with fifty thousand sheep on his unfenced range, and his neighbors, Wentworth, refused to build fences for fear of problems with the cattlemen and fence cutters.[3]

By the fall of 1883, damages from fence cutting statewide were huge, with disastrous impact on the state's economy. Governor John Ireland, whose own fences had been cut, had called the Texas legislature to Austin for a special session and charged them with finding a solution to the fence-cutting problems. The session convened January 8, 1884, and worked into February, passing legislation to remedy the problems. The lawmakers made fence cutting a felony punishable with mandatory prison time, fences across public roads were required to have gates, and other new laws were passed to address the problems.

William Joseph Greer and his older brother Green Berry Greer were farmers at Rockwell, Missouri, but in 1878 Green Berry relocated to Mason, Texas. William Joseph soon joined him. In 1882 both brothers left Mason and came to Edwards County, with Joseph bringing horses, a wagon, and 385 head of sheep. Like most other ranchers, he grazed his stock on the free range. His first sheep camp was located where the town of Rocksprings stands today. He and his brother soon moved and settled at Green Lake, a small body of water located twenty or so miles northeast of Rocksprings.[4]

After homesteading on Green Lake, the Greer brothers purchased barbed wire, cut cedar posts, and fenced their property, enclosing the small lake. It wasn't long before they began having trouble with cattlemen who had livestock grazing the free range. There was bitterness toward the Greers for bringing sheep to the area and outright anger for fencing in this natural watering hole. While the brothers were shearing sheep in picket pens under a shading cedar arbor, they were fired on by a shooter from the top of a distant cliff. Fortunately for the Greers, the cliff was far enough away that the shots had no effect.[5]

The Greer brothers' new barbed wire fence at Green Lake was cut on October 4, 1883. With some prodding from Rangers, a cowhand turned state's evidence, and authorities discovered the guilty parties. Corporal Lindsey and two Rangers from Company D made a scout from Fort Terrett to the Green Lake area. They arrested J. D. Creech, E. Beech (Creech), and Henry Wood, delivering them to the justice court and charging them with fence cutting. The leaders of the fence-cutters' band sent men to settle for the fence the three men had destroyed and paid the Greer brothers $125. One of the Greers then signed an agreement not to prosecute the case in court. A justice of the peace on the South Llano took evidence, but the court records were later stolen and destroyed.[6]

After the Texas legislature met and made fence cutting a felony, the adjutant general unleashed the Texas Rangers to assist sheriffs in the hot spots where fence cutting continued. Green Lake was one of those places. In July 1884 the Greers' fence was cut a second time. Edwards County

Sheriff Ira L. Wheat contacted Lamar Sieker, captain of Ranger Company D, and asked for help. Sieker dispatched Corporal Philip C. Baird and three Rangers from Camp Leona in Uvalde County to investigate the problem in Edwards County.[7]

The Rangers rode from the Nueces River Country to the upper South Llano Range, avoiding roads and traveling at night to avoid being seen. They arrived at Green Lake at midnight on July 28. Their horses were hidden in a cedar break two miles from the Greer home by a Greer employee. The Rangers pitched a hidden camp inside the rotted-out remains of an old cabin overlooking Green Lake. Corporal Baird learned from the Greers that fence cutters had established a cow camp 250 yards from the lower east end of the lake on the Greers' land without their consent. The Greer brothers had protested the camp.[8]

Baird instructed the brothers to splice and rebuild the cut fence. Work began early the next morning. At 9:00 a.m. on July 29, John Landigan, an employee of the Greers, was working on the fence when four men—Mark Hemphill, John Brunson, Henry Burton, and a man known only as Mason—approached. They were driving about 150 head of cattle and wanted to water them on Green Lake. Landigan refused, telling them the Greers had told him to close the fence and let no one in. One of the four men, Hemphill, drew his pistol and warned Landigan he would kill him if he didn't get out of their way and let the stock come in. Landigan believed him; without protest he left his job of rebuilding the fence.

Ranger Corporal Baird and his men were concealed about one hundred yards from where this occurred, and Baird said it was quite an effort to hold his boys down. He later wrote, "They were raring to go and anxious to open the ball ... in my judgment, the time was not ripe for such action, but the plum was ripening fast, and when the opportune time came to be plucked, business would pick up and get much warmer than it was on this already hot day. Hemphill and the men drove the cattle in and watered them at Green Lake."[9]

After Hemphill and his men left, the Greer employee rebuilt the fence, and everything was quiet. Later in the afternoon, John Brunson delivered a note written by Hemphill to the Greers. He said if they didn't build a gap in the fence, he would build one for them. The Greers refused and sent word to

Hemphill for him not to make one either; they wanted no trouble with him. When Hemphill received the Greers' response, he made good on his word. Hemphill and Mason saddled up, rode to the lake, and cut the fence at a point where the wire and a rock fence's skeleton joined. Henry Burton and John Brunson rounded up the horses and drove them through to the water. The four Rangers witnessed this activity.[10]

While the fence cutters were under the lake's bank and out of view, Corporal Baird moved his Rangers into position. He split them up, intending to flank Hemphill and his men if they sought to use the old rock fence for cover in a fight. Baird took a position on the north side of the lake across from the rock fence, and Rangers O. D. Baker, W. A. Mitchell, and W. W. Baker made a run for a position on the south side. On discovering the Rangers, the fence cutters quickly dismounted and took cover behind the rock fence as Baird had expected. The Rangers walked toward the fence. When they were within 150 yards, the fence cutters placed their rifles in shooting position and shouted, "Come and take us in, you damned sons-of-bitches." The Rangers continued to advance, calling to the fence cutters to surrender. On the fourth call to surrender, Hemphill shouted back to the Rangers, "Go to hell, you son-of-a-bitch." Shots followed his reply with Hemphill firing the first shot. A shootout followed, and Baird said, "We answered them shot for shot when we could get a shot at their heads over the rock fence. As expected, the rock wall served them as a complete fortification and with portholes to train their guns on me."[11]

Green Berry Greer witnessed this gun battle from nearby and gave the following account in a letter he wrote to Governor Ireland on July 30. Greer said,

> Baird's other Rangers attempted to flank the cutters. In the process, W. W. Baker was shot with a painful wound on the left side soon after the fight began and was rendered very weak from loss of blood. O. D. Baker and W. A. Mitchell crossed the stone wall and came on the enemy's flank. The fence cutters squatted behind some Mesquite bush and pounded a galling fire on the two rangers who, in advancing were unprotected. For a moment, it seemed the Rangers were going to get the worst of the deal. O. D. Baker, unfortunately, by mistake placed cartridges of a different caliber in his Winchester Rifle. He sprang

behind a Live Oak Tree that stood nearby and soon extracted the cartridges from the magazine. Mitchell got behind one of the stone fences, and the boys began to make it warm for the cutters. Mason stepped from behind his bush and raised his gun to shoot Mitchell. Baker's gun cracked, and Mason staggered with a bullet in his breast. Quick as lightning Mitchell planted another one in his bosom. Mason moved back behind the bush and, in doing so, exposed himself to Baird's fire. Soon the smoke boiled from that gentleman's gun and down went Mason with a bullet in the brain. The other fence cutters immediately mounted their horses, set spurs, and quickly disappeared from the scene.[12]

In an interview in 1947, Tom Dragoo said Henry Burton, a 17-year-old boy, was one of four fence cutters and held the horses until the other men mounted and fled the scene.[13]

Baird ran around the lake's west side and found Ranger W. W. Baker with a severe wound on his left side. The Greers nearby witnessed the shooting and carried Baker to the ranch house for care.[14]

Baird then walked toward Mason's dead body. He spotted one of the cutters he identified as John Brunson, returning to the dead man to get his firearms and ammunition. Baird said he fired several shots, striking the ground near Brunson's feet and raising a fog of dust. "At this juncture, the man who was six feet three to four inches tall went straight up in the air and was making a desperate effort to run long before he got back to earth" and ran to his horse. The Rangers proceeded to the dead body and recovered Mason's Winchester rifle, pistol, and belt of cartridges, adding to the Rangers' much-depleted ammunition supply. In his letter to the governor reporting the incident, Green Greer said he thought about 150 shots were exchanged. Tom Dragoo, a kid, came to the ranch after the shooting and said he picked up .22 cartridge hulls from rounds fired during the fight. John Brunson, or maybe the Burton boy, was firing a .22 rimfire firearm.[15]

The evening after the shootout, J. D. Gaines and Jack Turner showed up at the Greers' ranch reporting they had seen the fence cutters six miles up the draw at Gaines's ranch headquarters. The fleeing men stopped long enough to get a drink of water. They told Gaines they were retreating for the North Llano River to recruit their forces and intended to return and clean up on the Rangers.

As night approached, Turner went on guard duty. The Rangers made a fortification out of large cedar fence posts, anticipating the return of the fence cutters with their friends from the North Llano Country. Green Berry Greer and his wife Julia were taking care of Ranger W. W. Baker, who had been shot in the side. They gathered up all the buckets and tin oil cans they could find, wrapped them with wet salt sacks, wet rags, and such, then filled them with water and hung them in the open air to cool the water. One of the buckets with a nail hole was suspended over Baker and dripped cold water on his wound throughout the night to keep down the inflammation.[16]

Before night approached, Joseph Greer tied his two sheepdogs at the edge of a clearing to act as night watchmen, then saddled his horse and started a long ride to Junction City, about thirty-five miles away. He would find the doctor to attend the wounded Ranger and get more ammunition. Joseph returned the next morning with Doctor James W. Burt, who practiced medicine in Kimble and adjoining counties. Mrs. Julia Greer had stayed up all night in the dark taking care of the wounded man. After probing and dressing the wound, Dr. Burt commended the Greers on their excellent care of Ranger Baker.[17]

Corporal Baird managed to have a telegram sent from Mason, Texas, to Ranger Captain Sieker in Uvalde. The telegraph read, "Send men to Green Lake Edwards County. Had fight with fence cutters. Baker wounded bring wagon to move him. My wagons at Wrights please bring it. One cutter killed." On receiving the telegram, Captain Sieker mailed it along with a brief note to Adjutant General King in Austin saying, "Received the enclosed dispatch from Corporal Baird, which speaks for itself . . . haven't received report but will send as soon as received. I have sent wagon and ten days supplies."[18]

Joseph Greer had found the doctor while in Junction City but had been unable to find a coroner to perform an inquest on the dead fence cutter. An Edwards County official had been summoned but didn't show. The July day following the shootout was scorching hot. The outlaw's body was in bad condition and lying in the sun where he had been shot. His body was covered with a saddle blanket, waiting for a coroner.[19]

Word of the shootout spread fast, and ranchers came to the Greer Ranch to render aid. Lemuel Henderson, M. M. Bradford, E. A. Dragoo, J. D. Gaines,

Jack Turner, Frank and Fred Haggerman, Frank Harris, and others were at the ranch on July 30. Two kids, Tom Dragoo and Lee Smadler, had ridden over to Green Lake from a neighboring ranch to check out the excitement. In an interview conducted late in his life, Tom Dragoo said, "This fellow Mason was lying on the ground, covered with a saddle blanket. The Rangers on the hill called to us not to touch him. . . . I said, 'We just want to look at him.' I raised up the blanket, and if I live to be a hundred years, I'll never forget what I saw. It was July, and the flies were bad. He had about ten days' growth of red beard and I wish I had never looked."[20]

No official arrived to perform an inquest, so at 2:30 p.m., the ranchers buried Mason at Green Lake next to the grave of William Tillery. Ironically, Tillery was killed in an affray with William (Bill) Turner at Green Lake thirteen months before. Tillery had shot Bill Turner but didn't kill him, and poor shooting cost him his life. Jack Turner, the rancher who stood guard with the Rangers the previous evening, helped bury Mason. It was Jack Turner's son Bill who had killed William Tillery the past year.

The Rangers turned the dead fence cutter's possessions over to Edwards County Sheriff Ira L. Wheat. His possessions consisted of a few dollars' worth of money, a watch, a pocketknife, his spurs, rifle, and scabbard, and a six-shooter. Following published newspaper accounts about the incident, two men claiming to be brothers-in-law of Mason's showed up, identified his possessions, and took them back to Coryell County.[21]

It was later determined the outlaw that the Rangers killed was John Bailey, who had been using the alias of John Mason. He was a relative of the two brothers Dee and James Bailey who had killed US Deputy Marshal Mastin Reynolds Greene in Comanche County in May 1877. In 1883 the two brothers had been arrested and were jailed in Comanche. They were taken out of jail and lynched by citizens from Comanche and Coryell Counties.[22]

John Bailey had once lived on Cow Creek in Coryell County, and William Tillery, the man killed by Bill Turner, was from the same neighborhood. Little is known about Tillery, but John Bailey (alias John Mason) was an associate of the Dublin brothers, who had lived on the South Llano River. Old man Jim Dublin and his sons Dick, Dell, and Role came to Kimble from Coryell County in 1874. Several years before the shootout at Green Lake,

Rangers broke up Dublin's outlaw gang. Role and Dell were sent to federal prison. Ranger James Gillett killed Dick Dublin on the South Llano River roughly fifteen miles from Green Lake.[23]

After the gun battle at Green Lake, the Rangers began to search the surrounding country for the fence cutters who escaped. In a letter to the adjutant general dated August 21, Captain Sieker reported scouts by the Rangers found the area quiet. He expressed a reluctance to post a squad there, saying he had few men in camp, and several of their horses had scalded backs. With the hot weather, their horses were unfit for duty.[24]

Ranger O. D. Baker was still scouting, and Sieker transmitted part of a note he received from Baker to Adjutant General King.

> Joe Burton, father of the young fence cutter Henry Burton, has returned from Mexico and word is that he intends to go to Mexico as soon as he can gather his cattle. Burton is at Dodson's now and hasn't shown up at the lake yet. His hands have moved some of the things from the cow camp where the fence cutters were staying. G.B. Greer is going to Mason tomorrow and wants me to go with him very badly. He is afraid he will be assassinated on the way. I have not decided to go yet. If Burton and Dodson leave, it would be useless to station a squad here, but if they stay, there will be trouble in the future. I'll try to see Burton and give him a good talking to at the first opportunity.[25]

The Greer brothers had plenty to worry about and sought continued protection by the Rangers. On August 26 G. B. Greer wrote Captain Lamartine Sieker saying,

> Water is about dried up and cattle are drifting down, anticipate more trouble soon. I have been advised by several persons to leave the country as Mason and Hemphill's friends hold me responsible for the death of Mason. Captain Roberts advises me to stay and ask for protection. I would leave until matters settle, but I am unable to do so. All I have in the world is here, and I can't move. It's sheep shearing time, so if I was to leave, it would almost ruin me. Burton's hands came by today and say he intends to stay, and I am confident he intends further mischief. I am confident that Hemphill is on the North Llano where his wife lives, Dr. Coleman's ranch is there, he's there with his friends and they intend to fight. He swears he will never be taken, and should you round

him up, think it would be well to have plenty of men. I am very thankful for the interest manifested in my behalf and the kindness shown me and hope you will continue to assist me until the trouble is over.[26]

On the same date, August 26, 1884, Green Greer and his brother Joseph wrote Adjutant General W. H. King in Austin, asking to be commissioned as Texas Rangers. The letter to King written by the two brothers reads:

Dear Sir,

Owing to the conditions of affairs caused by the killing of Mason the fence-cutter, we are held personally responsible for his death by his friends, which places us in a dangerous situation, and our lives are in danger as they are liable to attack us at any moment. We wish to join the service and be carried on the rolls without pay, which will allow us the privilege of being armed. We will stand some chance for our lives, besides we are acquainted with everyone in this country and can be of good service to the company by keeping them informed of what's going on and can assist when called on. My desire is to abide by the law but the nearest peace officer is forty miles distance and when the Rangers are withdrawn, will leave us entirely in their power, they violate the law with impunity in regard to carrying pistols. These are my reasons for making the above request.

Respectfully, G. B. Greer, W. J. Greer
Post Office, Junction City Kimble County[27]

On September 6 Ranger Lieutenant Frank Jones, stationed in Llano County, received a letter from Adjutant General King, sending him to Edwards County to investigate the state of affairs. He was probably also asked to check on the Greer brothers' reputation and recommend their request to become Rangers. Jones traveled to Edwards County and pitched camp near Greer's ranch, finding this was the only place above the South Llano, where there was grass for grazing.[28]

In correspondence dated September 13, Lieutenant Jones reported to Adjutant General King saying, "Old man Burton says he has sixty-thousand dollars to spend in the prosecution of the Rangers who participated in the fight here, but I don't believe he has the audacity to even have them indicted.

Mason, the man who was killed, was undoubtedly a fugitive from justice and Hemphill is wanted in Taylor County for theft."[29]

Lieutenant Jones had carried his investigation into Kimble County, inquiring about the Greer brothers in Junction City. Jones reported in a letter to Adjutant General King that he checked their character and standing. He learned "they were honest and reliable men. I think they are prudent and would not act without proper discretion, and I therefore recommend that they be sworn in as Rangers and carried on the rolls without pay." The Greer brothers soon received a letter from Sieker advising they would be carried as Special Rangers without pay but with the right to bear arms. Sieker sent blank oath forms to the Greers, instructed them to take their oath before the county clerk, and have the documents certified. After the oath and paperwork were complete, the forms were delivered to Lieutenant Frank Jones.[30]

Jones received another letter from the adjutant general on September 23 asking him to scout the Fort McKavett area, probably searching for Hemphill and his friends. Jones found no leads to the fence cutters' whereabouts but reported that without a sheriff at Fort McKavett, "It's a common occurrence for men to "shoot up" this place. He also noted that "the people in the Green Lake section are very bitter against the Rangers and say that they had no right to come into the country in the night. They say that if Hemphill had known the Rangers were in the country, he would not have cut Greer's fence."[31]

Lieutenant Jones had written to Adjutant General King in September saying Joe Burton was boasting he had $60,000 to spend on the prosecution of the Rangers, participating in the Green Lake Fight. Jones didn't believe Joe Burton would follow through on this statement, but he was wrong. On September 30 Captain Lamar Sieker sent his monthly return to the adjutant general and in his transmittal letter said, "Lieutenant Jones is now in Bullhead. He is attending the justice court where Corporal Baird and squad are being tried for intent to murder young Burton."[32]

The Burtons were cattlemen, with their history going back to the Texas cattle industry's early days. Over the years the Burtons had probably known John Ireland, who was now the governor. When young Henry Burton fled the Green Lake shootout, he went to John Burton's ranch in Kimble County for protection. John Burton wrote a letter to his cousin, D. Elisha Burton in Kyle, Texas, telling his side of the Green Lake story. Cousin Elisha then sent the letter to Governor Ireland, asking for an investigation of the Rangers in the Green Lake incident. Elisha said he and Captain Fergus Kyle would be coming to Austin to see the governor. Fergus Kyle was politically connected and knew his way around Austin and state politics. He was a Confederate veteran, having served with Terry's Texas Rangers, and wore his gray uniform throughout his life. Kyle served in the Texas House of Representatives as one of the few Democrats during Reconstruction and later served as the senate's sergeant-of-arms. The town of Kyle, Texas, where Elisha Burton lived, was named in honor of Fergus Kyle. Despite Elisha's threat, no record is found of politics at the state capital entering or influencing the Green Lake affair.[33]

Within a few days of the Green Lake shootout, Corporal P. C. Baird arrested John Brunson and turned him over to Edwards County Sheriff Ira Wheat. Brunson appeared before an Edwards County justice of the peace and was charged with fence cutting and assault with intent to kill. He was required to give bond of $500 for the fence-cutting offense and $1,000 for assault with intent to kill.[34]

John Brunson's father, James Brunson, was listed as a stock raiser in the 1880 Edwards County US Census. Based on census records, son John would have been about 20 or 21 years old at the time of the Green Lake incident. He was described by Corporal Baird as "a bad actor and general rustler over the country, and dreaded by all who chanced to know or come in contact with him."

At some point in the 1880s following the shootout, the Brunson family moved from Edwards County to the Tonto Basin in Gila County, Arizona, and appeared in the 1890 Census. Their move may have occurred because grazing cattle on the free range ended, and the severe drought lasted through 1887. The move to Arizona may have happened because of the legal issues resulting from the Green Lake shootout, or possibly for all of these reasons. John Brunson lived in Arizona for many years. Late in his life he suffered a stroke, and in failing health he returned to Texas to live with his sister. He died and was buried near Kerrville, Texas.[35]

Following the Green Lake gun battle, Mark Hemphill disappeared for close to a year. Originally from Albany, Texas, he was shown in the 1880 US Census to have a wife and two daughters in Shackelford County. He may have returned to his old home after the shooting. The Greers thought he was in the Fort McKavett area with his wife, but the Rangers couldn't find him there. In a 1947 interview, Tom Dragoo said Hemphill hid out in a cave in the Kickapoo section of Edwards County. He said a friend, Jesse Thurman, fed him until he came in and surrendered. There is a large cave on the Johnny Whitworth Ranch, and Whitworth claimed it had been an outlaw hideout in the 1880s. Dragoo had visited with Hemphill in 1925 at Batesville and said they discussed the Green Lake fight from every angle. Apparently, Mark Hemphill never left Edwards County.[36]

About a year after the shootout with Rangers at Green Lake, Mark Hemphill surrendered to Ranger Searce Baylor, who took him to Uvalde. Arriving in Uvalde, he turned the fence cutter over to his brother, Henry W. Baylor, serving his first term as the sheriff of Uvalde County. Hemphill may have known the Baylor boys, or maybe their father, John R. Baylor, who ranched in Uvalde County, and trusted them to treat him fairly.[37]

Rangers arrested all three fence cutters who survived the shootout at Green Lake, and several were indicted. But no record has been found of any one of the three men being tried for fence cutting or assault with intent to kill. The two Rangers with the last name Baker who were in the shootout at Green Lake were not related. After the shootout, Ranger W. W. Baker recovered rapidly from his gunshot wound and was back on duty in twenty days. O. D. Baker later left the Ranger service, bought a ranch near Orange, Texas, and raised purebred cattle. He became a newspaperman and was elected and served in the Thirty-Seventh and Thirty-Eighth Texas Legislatures. By 1927 W. W. Baker had died, and W. A. Mitchell was a resident of San Antonio.[38]

Corporal Phillip C. Baird left the Ranger service in November of 1884 and took the job as chief deputy for Mason County Sheriff John Calvin Butler. Baird married Kittie Margret Holden, a young lady from Llano, Texas. In 1888 Baird ran for Mason County sheriff against his old boss and won. Swapping roles, Butler hired on as Baird's chief deputy, and the two men continued to work together as a team. In 1889 the two lawmen were in a shootout on the streets of Mason and killed two brothers, John and Jesse Simmons. Baird later gave up his sheriff's job, became a stockman, and was president of the Mason State Bank. Baird again ran for Mason County sheriff and was elected on November 12, 1912, serving three consecutive terms before stepping down. In January 1920, the Fourteenth US Census showed Phillip C. Baird as a stock farmer living with his wife Kittie in neighboring Menard County.[39]

After the gun battle at Green Lake, the two Greer brothers were carried on the muster roll of Texas Ranger Company D as Special Rangers without pay. In the years that followed, Green Berry and his family moved back to Missouri, later returned to San Angelo, Texas, and then moved again and ranched near Carrizozo, New Mexico. Green Berry Greer died in New Mexico in 1925.

Joseph, his brother, continued the ranch operation at Green Lake, stocking sheep, goats, and cattle, and raised large mules for pulling freight wagons. He served as bailiff for the county court when Leakey was the Edwards County seat and carried a 44-40 revolver, probably acquired when he was enlisted as a Special Ranger. In the following years, Joseph served as president of the Edwards County Wool and Mohair Company and was one of the organizers and presidents of the First State Bank of Rocksprings. Joseph Greer passed away on February 23, 1933. After his death, his wife, Mrs. Ida Jane Armstrong Greer, continued to live on the ranch and was elected to serve in Joseph's place as president of the First State Bank. The Greers' Edwards County ranching operation, which starting as a preempted tract of land, eventually grew to approximately 26,900 acres. Today William Joseph Greer's ranch at Green Lake is still owned and operated by his descendants.[40]

Chapter 12

Lawmen Stop Medina's Fence Cutting but Suffer Revenge

> The Blue Devils of the West, as they call themselves, have cut every pasture fence in Medina except two and are now destroying fences around the farms. Even the old fashion rail fences are being burned. The people of Medina County would be fully justified in swinging the Blue Devils to a limb.
> —*Fort Worth Daily Gazette*, December 29, 1883

Public opposition to barbed wire fences and the public's sympathy for the fence cutter was common in most of Texas's barbed wire wars, especially in the early stages. Many of the Medina County folks, like the citizens in other parts of Texas, opposed barbed wire fences and despised corporations, the syndicates, and the moneyed cattlemen buying large tracts of land and building fences. Change was difficult for folks. In some parts of the state, opposition to barbed wire fences carried over to local lawmen and elected officials. Some sheriffs gave little or no attention to the landowner's problem when someone cut his fence. The crime was only a misdemeanor, and catching a fence cutter was a lot of work. And if the sheriff did a good job, his actions could cost him his constituency. Medina County officials were an exception. Medina County was one of Texas's early hot spots in the fence-cutting wars, but Medina's lawmen and the district attorney took seriously the job of ending fence cutting in this county. Despite opposition and mixed public opinions, they made arrests and prosecuted the law to the fullest. And they stopped fence cutting. Afterward they would pay dearly for their success.

Medina County is on the west side of Bexar County and north of Frio County. In 1842 Henri Castro, a Frenchman, negotiated an impresario contract with the Republic of Texas. With the help of Ludwig Huth, a German wine merchant, Castro arranged to bring Germans and French farmers from the Alsace region of France to Texas. When the farmers reached Texas, Castro, with Charles DeMontel and Ranger Jack Hays's help, located the farmers on a sharp bend of the Medina River covered with countless large pecan trees. In this beautiful setting, Castroville was founded and patterned after villages in the Old Country. In the 1850s a visitor described the community as being very "un-Texan." Houses often had an upper room and a steep thatched roof, and their interiors appeared to be European. The buildings were spread over acreage rather than along parallel lines on the streets.[1]

The Texas legislature created Medina County from the Bexar District on February 12, 1848. The county was organized the same year, with Castroville becoming Medina's county seat. Years later, in 1892, Hondo would become the county seat. When the Civil War began, Medina was one of the Texas counties voting against secession. Many members of immigrant families loyal to the Union fled to Mexico. Following the war, however, most returned, and more immigrants began arriving from Germany. The majority of Medina County residents were German and French.[2]

In the 1870s the cattle industry flourished. Medina and neighboring Frio County's populations and land values increased. Ten years later Medina County still had open tracts of grassland grazed by cattle, and small farmers were moving in. Most settlers farmed, but many also benefited from their livestock's free grazing on the open range. Frio County, which bordered Medina County, was prime cattle country, but in 1880 the county also reported 46,961 sheep. Here too, as in Medina County, farming began a rapid growth with people moving in from San Antonio. In 1881 and 1882, the Galveston, Harrisburg, and San Antonio Railway, followed by the International and Great Northern Railroad, crossed Medina County. Railroads and the new barbed wire brought rapid and significant change to Medina, Frio, and counties to their south. Indian raids ended with the last Frio County raid in 1877, but now Mexican bandits were sweeping in, stealing cattle, and driving them to Mexico. Anglo cattle and horse thieves were also a problem, operating out of the brush country in LaSalle, McMullen, and Atascosa Counties. Cattle stealing in Medina and Frio and counties south kept the sheriffs and Rangers busy.[3]

From its earliest days, Medina County had capable and dedicated law enforcement. Although difficult transitions took place as the Civil War began and lasted through Reconstruction, the sheriff's office appeared to have been occupied by competent men, usually with German surnames.[4]

On returning from the Civil War, cattlemen suffered from the Indian problems but still prospered. One of those men who did well was John T. Lytle. He enlisted in Company H, 32nd Texas Cavalry, and on returning from the war worked for his uncle William Lytle, a prominent Bexar County cattleman. He went into the cattle business for himself and in a matter of years made his mark in trailing and marketing cattle from Texas to Kansas, Colorado, Montana, and Dakota. John Lytle established his headquarters in Castroville in 1873 and in 1879 purchased and fenced ranch land in Medina County. John Lytle directed investments in livestock totaling $9 million over fifteen years and was an activist for law and order. The International and Great Northern Railroad crossed nearby; the station was named Lytle. Other less well-known but prominent cattlemen were running stock in Medina, Frio, and LaSalle Counties. They also purchased and fenced land. Of note are Thomas McDaniels, George J. Wilson, J. R. Skates, Joseph Carie, B. L. Crouch, James and Stephen Speed, E. R. Lane, and the Dull brothers with Lee Hall.[5]

Lee Hall built his reputation as a Texas Ranger captain. He decided to leave the Frontier Battalion in May of 1880 to marry and begin a new life as a stockman. He was hired as the manager and agent for the Dull Ranch, sometimes referred to as the Hall Ranch or the Dull and Hall outfit. The Dull brothers of Harrisburg, Pennsylvania, owned the ranch and it grew to near four hundred thousand acres. On taking on management of the Dull brothers' ranching business, one of Lee Hall's first projects was to fence the ranch. Fence building began, and thousands of reels of barbed wire were loaded into wagons in Cotulla. Teams of mules struggled to pull the wagons over sandy roads to the ranch. As ranch hands built fences, the Dull Ranch soon began suffering fence-cutting problems. Some of Hall's cowhands were former Rangers who served with him when he was a Ranger captain. They left the Rangers service and came to work on the ranch. They were good cowboys, but they were also the Dull Ranch's protection against cattle thieves and fence cutters.

John Lytle, Lee Hall, and the other prominent stockmen often worked behind the scenes as a force for law and order in the war on fence cutting and cattle stealing in Medina, Frio, and LaSalle Counties. Though their names were not often seen, they were behind the curtain in the battle with Medina's fence cutters.

Ferdinand Niggli, or Ferd, as local folks knew him, was a respected citizen, cattleman, and lawman in Medina County. Ferdinand Niggli's father (also named Ferdinand) and his mother came to Texas when the Castro Company arrived and established Castroville. The 1860 United States Census shows his mother as being from Germany and his father from Switzerland. Ferdinand was their first child and was born in Texas in 1849.

Ferdinand grew up in Medina County working as a cowhand. He knew the livestock business well and was a landowner on some of the land his father accumulated in Medina's early years. On becoming a young man, Ferdinand took a job in San Antonio as a blacksmith, employed at John Coleman's blacksmith shop on San Pedro Street. He returned to Castroville, where he practiced his blacksmith trade until he was appointed a sheriff's deputy for Sheriff Valentin Vollmar. On February 15, 1876, Ferdinand Niggli, son of one of Castroville's founding family, was elected sheriff of Medina County. He served a second term beginning November 5, 1878, and a third term starting November 2, 1880. Hal Gosling, an attorney and former owner of the community newspaper, the *Castroville Quill*, was appointed United States marshal for the Western District of Texas in May 1882. The following month Gosling appointed Ferdinand Niggli as a deputy United States marshal. Niggli captured a smuggler named Brooks four months after assuming his new job and that resulted in a shootout. When he tried to place handcuffs on the smuggler, Brooks broke free, grabbed another man's gun, and tried to shoot the marshal. That was a mistake; Niggli fired first, and his shot was fatal.[6]

Although operating out of the marshal's office in San Antonio and working the territory south to the Rio Grande, Niggli continued to manage his ranching operation, spending a portion of time in Medina County. When he resigned his job as Medina sheriff, Joe Ney, an upright and popular citizen, was appointed to replace Niggli. Ney served until the next election. On November 7, 1882, the Medina County residents elected William B. Foster for the new term. Little background information is found on Sheriff Foster, but during his time in office, fence cutting started, and then all hell broke loose in Medina County. It was also during this period that Niggli's battle against the fence cutters became personal. The ranch fences of Deputy US Marshal Niggli were cut on two occasions.[7]

The date barbed wire came to Medina and Frio Counties is not recorded. Barbed wire probably arrived when Henry Sanborn made his first trip to San Antonio in 1875 and established Norton & Dentz Hardware Store as a Glidden wire dealer for the area. Following his San Antonio visit, Sanborn left the city and traveled the ranch country south in his buggy selling Glidden barbed wire. He probably sold wire in Medina and Frio Counties as he made his trip to the South Texas ranches.

Some of the state's first fence cutting occurred in Frio and Medina Counties. Before most newspapers began picking up on fence cutting across the rest of the state, an item in an 1882 issue of the *Castroville Quill* appeared. "We learned that some unknown parties last Sunday night went to the pasture belonging to Jos. Laman and destroyed over two miles of pasture fence." While Deputy Sheriff Hagaman of Frio County was at a meeting in Fort Worth, he told authorities, "Frio is where fence cutting took its start."[8]

The *San Marcos Free Press* named the instigator of this first fence cutting, a man who is a Texas hero. The following statement appeared in Hays County's newspaper:

Big Foot Wallace, the old Indian fighter, is said to be the man who first started fence cutting. It is a well-known fact that the first fence was cut in

Frio County and belonged to the Hawkeye Cattle Company. Canon and other Frio County ranchmen were the next to suffer. Big Foot is said to be the man who worked up the people to do the cutting. He is said to have taken a great interest in the cutting done in Medina County. Wallace is now a very old man, but he has considerable vitality left. He claims that the men who whipped the Indians out of the country and reclaimed it ought to have the first choice of range.[9]

Large tracts of land in Medina and Frio Counties were fenced in 1883 and were suffering fence cutting. Noted was the Dull Ranch in McMullen, LaSalle, and Frio, managed by Lee Hall. Another was the Page Pasture Company, owned by the Page Wire Manufacturing Company. They came to Medina County from Jacksonville, Michigan, and fenced their land with a galvanized wire having long, sharp, vicious barbs tough on livestock. Another ranch, the Hawkeye Land and Cattle Company from Muscatine, Iowa, owned land in Medina and Frio Counties. They bought most of their land from the state but purchased an adjoining tract from Louis Schorp. They began fencing the property, and their new fences were cut. Soon Louis's brother, Joseph Schorp, was arrested and became one of the first men charged with destroying fence in Medina.

The Hickey Pasture Company, a South Texas breeder of Shorthorn cattle, purchased rangeland in Medina County near Devine and fenced their pastures. They immediately suffered fence cutting. They reported twenty miles of the fence was cut in a week. A letter from the Devine community concerning the Hickey Pasture Company was published in the *Galveston Daily News* saying, "Never before has such bitter feeling existed against a pasture company. No man can cast reflections upon the members of the company individually, as they are real gentlemen, but the pasture encloses convenient water for such dry season as is now prevailing. This causes people of small means to unite in a regular organization to resist."[10]

Fence cutting started earlier in Frio County, spilled into Medina, and spread across the entire county by the fall of 1883. Fences were cut near Devine in November. George Karm was arrested and charged with the fence cuttings. He was given an examining trial and released.[11]

Soon after Karm's arrest, the *Galveston Daily News* reported a fence cutter was shot with a Winchester while cutting the fence on a Mr. James's ranch south of Devine in Frio County. The paper said the man shot was the son of a good citizen. Trouble was expected, and pasture men joined together in San Antonio to voice their support for any rancher who killed a fence cutter. Several men left San Antonio for Frio County in anticipation of a fight following the shooting. As the men were leaving, a group of thirty-five citizens opposing fence cutting formed a coalition. Several hundred more citizens were expected to join by the end of the week. This group's purpose was to provide money and other support in prosecuting fence cutters and protecting private property.[12]

A mass meeting of community leaders, politicians, farmers, and ranchers was held in San Antonio's Krisch Hall on December 14. The meeting was called to draft resolutions and memorialize the legislature for laws to stop damages by the fence cutters. Hal Gosling, a former Castroville newspaperman, now US marshal for the Western District of Texas, called the meeting to order.[13]

Judge T. J. Devine was elected chairman of the group. Major J. H. Kampmann, Judge Jacob Waelder, M. Halff, Major Frank Grice, and Dr. H. P. Howard were chosen as vice presidents. W. J. Story, a San Antonio alderman, asked Judge Waelder to address the group concerning the purpose of the meeting and remedies proposed. The judge responded that fence cutting was rampant across Texas. It was the duty of every citizen to protest against the depredation of the fence cutter and try to catch and punish him. The judge said he spoke as a state and county citizen; he wasn't a stockman. His fence was around his residence. Fence cutting, however, occurred two and a half miles from the main plaza of San Antonio. It was not known what was to prevent the cutter from entering the city and destroying property within its limits. The judge said there were many misguided men among a group referred to as the Javelinas. The judge desired no violence, no agrarianism, and no communism. As a law-abiding citizen, he felt satisfied the legislature would pass a law to meet the emergency, and citizens would see it strictly enforced.

A committee was appointed to draft resolutions for the legislature. The chair named Judge Dibble, Mr. Brownson, Captain Story, Sol Halff, and Dr. Amos Graves as committeemen. On a request from the floor, the chair added Judge Waelder. Judge Devine called on US Marshal Hal Gosling to speak while the committee was out. Gosling received applause and began by saying he saw men in the audience "who had suffered the fence cutters' deviltry. These men toiled all their lives carefully and laboriously. They pioneered the march of civilization here, yet spoliations of the midnight cutter had left them bereft of a lifetime toil and economy."

After Gosling's stirring speech, State Senator W. S. Thompson of Bexar County spoke, saying he believed the fence cutters were the persons who mavericked and branded other people's cattle and horses for years and stole them in bunches. "This class filled our penitentiaries and occupies the attention of the courts." Senator Thompson assured the audience he would carry with him to Austin the sentiments of this meeting and work without tiring to make fence cutting a felony.

After several other individuals spoke, the Committee on Resolutions returned to the hall, and Judge Dibble read the committee's resolutions to the audience.

> Whereas, It is a fact so well known to the citizens of this State and the whole country as to become a black page in its otherwise resplendent history that there are now in many counties of the State many men calling themselves "Javelinas" and "Blue Devils of the West," and similar names, who have banded together in unlawful combinations for willfully, maliciously and unlawfully cutting down and destroying the fences surrounding the property of landowners, large and small, and destroying other property in other ways; and
>
> Whereas, In carrying out the vandalism which seems to constitute the principles of the parties engaged in such destruction of the property of others who are law-abiding and valuable citizens, said parties so banded together, have been for the last several months willfully and maliciously destroying fences of great value, and that too, when no lands were enclosed thereby except those owned in fee simple by proprietors of the fences and possessors of the lands; and
>
> Whereas. This spirit of lawlessness, vandalism, and agrarianism has already deterred nearly all good citizens from further investing in

or becoming owners of land over which the law extends insufficient protection to render them useful and valuable to the proprietors thereof, the effects of which is to depreciate the value of our school lands and all other within State until loss has already been felt amounting to millions of dollars in the aggregate and of hundreds of thousands of dollars to the education fund, which has been so zealously guarded to enlighten and make good citizens of our children; and,

Whereas the Legislature of Texas has been called to meet on the second Tuesday of next month to consider, among other matters, the best means of correcting this evil so pernicious and damaging to every material interest of the State, the viscous effects of which are becoming apparent and are being felt in the business of every good citizen, be he rich or poor, no matter what his occupation or calling in life may be; therefore be it,

Resolved, That it is the unanimous sense of this meeting: 1. That the question of the expediency of roads to or from county seats, churches, etc., has nothing to do with this question, there being now upon the statutes of the State sufficient and ample power to establish and maintain roads of whatever class desired wherever the needs of the people require them, and that need seems manifest to the County Commissioners of any county, and it is our opinion that in any case where there are not sufficient and suitable roads for the needs of the public, the same should be provided by the county courts. 2. That the only penalty now imposed for the crime being the penalty for malicious mischief, which, in its extreme, cannot exceed $100 fine, and in addition thereto imprisonment in the county jail not exceeding one year, it is wholly wanting in severity to deter the continuance and nightly repetition of the crime; therefore, it is our opinion that the crime should be made a felony with a penalty not less than two years and not exceeding five years imprisonment in the penitentiary, and also a fine of not less than $200 nor more than $500, one-half of which fine to go to the informant. 3. That the Executive of the State be empowered to call into and keep in the service such State constabulary or police force as he may deem necessary for the purpose of enforcing the law as the legislature may pass, and that an appropriation be made to enable the governor to carry into effect this part of the law. 4. That a copy of this preamble and of these resolutions be furnished to each of the papers of this city, and that a copy of the same be sent to the Senator of this district and each of the members of the legislature of this district by the secretary of this meeting.[14]

Following the resolution's reading, several men stood and spoke words in favor of the resolution and made promises of a vigorous nature regarding the fence cutter's treatment should he fall in their hands. Then before the resolution was adopted, a gentleman named John Copeland arose, took the floor, and surprised the group, making a passionate talk against the resolution. He warned the audience to beware of such expressions as "flooding the state with blood." He said, "There are two sides to the question."

By then Copeland was receiving a few hisses. But undismayed, he kept his thread of thought. He told the audience, "Men who are branded as traitors today are worshiped as patriots tomorrow." He cited the men struggling for natural rights under King John and George III. "You may have legal rights, but if behind these, the natural rights are thwarted, time will not be slow in crowning supremacy of the latter." The use of water was one of these, and the men who drove their cattle to distant markets or pastured on their own land in the vicinity of the lordly rancho were entitled to this gift of God.

When Copeland finished his remarks, there was a deep silence. Then Charles Seabaugh broke the tension in the air and brought much laughter from the audience. Seabaugh rose to his feet, saying he had long desired to see a live fence cutter. Now his wish had been granted, for in this gentleman (Copeland), he beheld one.

The meeting wrapped up with the resolution adopted. There was a vote of thanks to the officers of the large gathering. San Antonio's newspaper reporting the meeting but made no mention of attendance by the prominent southwest Texas cattlemen suffering from fence cutting. It's a good bet they were an unmentioned sponsor of this much-publicized event.[15]

Soon after the San Antonio meeting was held, a fence cutter, allegedly one of the Javelinas of Medina, was interviewed by a Galveston newspaper reporter. The gentleman made clear the fence cutter's position and expressed the free grass men's resolve to have an open, free range. The fence cutter's interview was published in newspapers across the state and even appeared in the *Chicago Tribune*. From the *Fort Worth Daily Gazette*, the interview reads:

CUTTER: We are like minnows in a pool of hungry trout. Some big stockmen buy all the land around on all sides. His cattle graze on our land and ours on his. When he makes his roundups, our cattle are driven off to some distant point on his large ranch. Our calves are separated from their

	mothers, and in the confusion, are branded with his brand and are driven off with his cattle.
REPORTER:	But if the land were not enclosed, wouldn't this same thing happen?
CUTTER:	No, not to the same extent it does now. When the range was free, everybody's cattle ran at large, and no one thought of rounding up and driving off every cow in sight.
REPORTER:	Don't you think if a man owns land, he has a right to fence it if he wants to?
CUTTER:	No sir, no man has a right to fence you up or enclose the grass and water. He didn't plant the grass or have anything to do with making it grow. Neither did he create the springs and rivers. God made them free, and before these land-sharks and cattle kings put fences around them, they were free. The grass is just as good and will fatten his cattle just as fast without a fence around it as within.
REPORTER:	But what is the use of owning land if you can't do as you please with it?
CUTTER:	You can do as you please with it. If you want to cultivate it, put up your fence, plow up your land, and plant it. We won't bother you. What you work for and plant is yours, but grass is free, and no man has a right to claim what does not belong to him.
REPORTER:	Haven't the pasture men offered to do almost anything you ask?
CUTTER:	Yes, they offer us everything; but what we want and are going to have is free-range. We are determined to have our rights, and if it causes bloodshed, we can't help it. We must and will have free range. There are not enough men in the regular army of the United States to guard the lines of wire pasture fence in Texas.[16]

Several days later the *Galveston Daily News* reported the Blue Devils of the West were cutting fence again and had begun burning pastures. Pasture burning struck fear in all stockmen. When fences were cut, their stock was loose on the range, and they lost the capital investment made when they built the fence. But when cutters burned a man's pasture, fences were destroyed, livestock—be it cattle, horses, or sheep—were set loose or burned to death, and all forage for grazing destroyed. That same week fences were destroyed on Marshal Niggli's Medina ranch. The Dallas newspaper reporting this incident said

Niggli was on the warpath. "Niggli says he does not propose to wait on the legislature to redress his wrongs but will do it himself."[17]

As the Dallas newspaper noted Niggli's fence problem, an article in the *Fort Worth Daily Gazette* reported, "The Blue Devils of the West as they call themselves have cut every pasture fence in Medina except two and are now destroying fences around the farms. Even the old fashion rail fences are being burned. The people of Medina County would be fully justified in swinging the Blue Devils to a limb. The men who justified fence cutting at the outset can now see their terrible mistake."[18]

As December closed out the year of 1883, the barbed wire war in Medina County was underway and would be fought to the bitter end. Capable men represented the law-and-order interest. Ferdinand Niggli served three terms as Medina County sheriff before joining the US marshal service. In addition to his law enforcement responsibilities, he owned land and livestock in Medina County and suffered a financial loss from fence cutting. Niggli's partner in the fence-cutting battle was Medina's new sheriff, William B. Foster, and Willis R. Wallace, the district attorney for the Thirty-Eighth Judicial District. Wallace would push his legal authority to the limits trying for fence-cutter indictments and then prosecutions. Edmund DeMontel, an attorney and son of Charles DeMontel, one of Castroville's founders, would support Wallace. Justice of the Peace J. M. Smith and Medina Sheriff's Deputy George Brown would be participants in Medina's fence-cutter roundups. Brown would later run a hard-fought election campaign for Medina County sheriff when William Foster stepped down. Texas Ranger Lieutenant Joseph Shely would be able to provide limited help; he and his Rangers were busy working on cattle stealing and fence-cutting problems in Gonzales and DeWitt Counties.[19]

As 1883 was ending, the lawmen arrested a small number of fence cutters. The arrests caused the rest of the cutters to draw into a clandestine organization or brotherhood made up of two separate bands. One of the bands, made up of Germans, had Emil Bader as their captain. Bader's fence cutters were known as the Blue Devils, Blue Devils of the West, or often just called the Germans. The second band of cutters, the Javelinas or the Americans, was led by W. D. Burnett, their captain. Bob Morris served as a courier for both squads. A spy named Pete Ketchum kept the organization advised of what their adversaries in Castroville were doing. The two bands of cutters shared a watchword or countersign. Their sentinel used it while the main group was cutting fences at night. The watchword was *D'Hanis-on-the-Seco*. When a man joined this clandestine organization, he was thoroughly checked and required to take an oath, which he signed. The oath read: "I solemnly swear that I will stick to this crowd, through thick and thin, and help each other out in trouble, so help me God."[20]

As the fence-cutting war heated up, the lawmen were handicapped. The lawmen needed help from someone inside the gangs to gain essential information about the clandestine cutters and their operations. The lawmen learned limited amounts of information by squeezing several men captured earlier. Still, undercover work would be necessary to end the fence cutting.

Probably on the recommendation of Ranger Joseph Shely, Medina's sheriff brought in private detective Robert S. Davis to work undercover and gather information and evidence on the fence cutters. Lieutenant Shely worked with the detective in January of 1883 when Davis was working undercover for cattlemen on stolen cattle cases. Detective Robert Davis's undercover work on fence cutting in Medina began in January 1884 under the supervision of Sheriff William Foster. Davis received papers enlisting him as one of Sheriff Foster's deputies. However, it appears the law-and-order group of prominent cattlemen were to pick up the cost for his undercover work.[21]

Preparatory to being inserted into the fence cutter's organization, Robert Davis first had to overcome suspicions and prove himself worthy of joining the secretive fence cutters' ranks. To accomplish this Davis took on the identity of an outlaw. He was booked and built his credentials as an inmate in the squalor of the Medina County jail. Following his stay in jail, he was released under bond, jumped bail, and fled, becoming a fugitive from justice. He was then taken in by the fence cutters and spent roughly a month among them. Davis gathered information about the gang's inner workings, their organization's structure, who the members were, and where they lived.

As Davis began his detective work, District Attorney Willis Wallace began a countywide investigation with help from Marshal Niggli, Sheriff Foster, and his deputies. Large numbers of rural people with varying degrees of knowledge about Medina's fence cutting received a summons to appear in Castroville's court. They were placed under oath and questioned on what they knew about the fence cutting and pasture burning. District Attorney Wallace aggressively sought facts and truth from their testimonies. Persons not responding to this summons were attached by the court and brought in by the lawmen.

At the end of fourteen days of questioning, 135 persons had been examined, and the district attorney's inquiry was still in progress. Based on testimony during the fourteen days, there were eight arrests made. Those offenders were brought in and placed under a $500 bond. Peter Rhein, Jacob Mangold Jr., Louis Numant, Joseph Bohl, George Karni, Stephen Biediger, and Joseph Schorp were all farmers. Joseph Jungmann was a sheepman, and Joseph Bohl was one of Castroville's aldermen. Jungmann was released on a $500 bond, but because of perjury, he was arrested again and placed under an additional $1,000 bond. This arrest was the second time around for Joseph Schorp. He was arrested, charged, and released for fence cutting in the summer of 1883. The newspapers reported these men were raised in the county and were considered good German citizens.[22]

In addition to identifying fence cutters, the district attorney's investigation discovered forty miles of fence cut or burned and more pastures burned. Damage estimates were at a quarter of a million dollars. The investigation found not one acre of the land fenced belonged to the state, the railroad, or the school domain. In one instance a man cut half a mile of fence and shortened his route to Castroville by five miles. In his mind, his snipping of the barbed wire had a reasonable justification. As the investigation progressed and more arrests made, there were threats to Sheriff Foster's life.[23]

On February 25 Sheriff Foster and Marshal Niggli brought ten more fence cutters into Castroville. This group appeared to be from the American group, the Javelinas. Taken into custody were Jacob Biry, Sam Jones, Bob Morris, Sam Ellison, John Ellison, Martin Tomerlin, Joe Millhartz, August Millhartz, Henry Bonflie, and an older man, W. D. Burnett. Burnett was about 60 years old and later identified as the captain of the American squad of fence cutters. Evidence against these men was said to be conclusive. Several days earlier Brown Litburu and his brother were captured; they turn state's evidence to lighten their charge.[24]

By late February, after twenty-eight days of work among the fence cutters, Medina's detective Robert Davis had gathered a wealth of information and evidence, but his luck ran out. As the undercover man, he spent roughly a month inside the clandestine organization before the fence cutters discovered they had brought a detective into their ranks. Their immediate response was to kill him. Angry and with revenge in mind, they planned to burn the detective alive in the dry bed of Hondo Creek. Davis learned of their intentions and fled to Castroville. Reaching the town, Davis told Sheriff Foster of their plan, left a report and list of names with the sheriff, then left Castroville for San Antonio. When Davis told Foster the cutters discovered he was a detective and planned to burn him alive, the sheriff didn't believe him. But Foster checked on Davis's story and found, as the detective had stated, wood piled in the dry bed of Hondo Creek, all in preparation for the burning.[25]

Based on the alleged plan for a violent murder, and with the names provided by Davis, Sheriff Foster and Niggli gathered a posse from Castroville. As they rode through the ranch country in the night, they added several ranchers to the posse. The lawmen began their sweep in the brush country between Hondo and Castroville. Fence cutters were rounded up in small groups, then held in a central location as others were arrested and brought in. Riding at a fast gait and covering a large area, the posse arrested most of the men named in Detective Davis's report. With the roundup complete, a strange procession over the old road from Hondo to Castroville commenced. Every fence cutter was mounted, with his horse's bridle rains tied to the horse's tail ahead of him. A guard from the posse traveled in the lead, men on the right and left side of the group and men behind, like a cattle drive. Riding out of brush country onto the old road, this strange single-file procession of fence cutters and lawmen made a slow approach to Castroville.[26]

Sheriff Foster, US Marshal Niggli, and the deputies rode into Castroville on February 27, with thirteen fence cutters riding horses with tails tied together. Men placed in jail were Julius Hartung, Louis Hartung, Joseph Webber, Olise Dully, Rufe Rathbone, August Hutzler, August Bader, Sam Nail, Joseph Wernette, and Emil Bader. The *Austin Weekly Statesman* described Emil Bader as the "most potent, grave and reverend seigneur and big boss of the gang." There were warrants out now for other men who would be arrested and brought in the following days. Austin's newspaper reported there were a total of thirty-five fence cutters now in Castroville's jail, ten more than announced in an earlier dispatch to the governor. The newspaper speculated the Medina County dragnet could now bring in rewards totaling $7,000 under the governor's recent proclamation offering rewards for fence cutters. The jail was now full. More room would have to be found.[27]

The newspapers reported the men just delivered were full of pluck, looked their fate squarely in the face, but didn't recognize the consequence of their crimes. They were not wealthy, but they believed they could raise funds for a vigorous defense. The enormous bonds required were beyond their means, but they took the matter coolly and were willing to talk to the reporters. Leaders of the two gangs, American and German, were both men of standing, had families but little wealth, and looked like simple working citizens, which they were before their fence cutting began. Pete Ketchum, the fence cutter's spy, came into the town the night following the roundup, looked around, and was soon arrested. Niggli held a warrant for him and said he appreciated his obliging disposition of coming in and making his appearance. The town of Castroville soon filled with friends of those jailed, and the law-and-order stockmen also came to town. Residents feared big trouble. The town's officials sent a request for Lieutenant Joseph Shely and his Rangers to come and assist.[28]

With the roundup of fence cutters nearing completion, the war was not over. The legal phase would now begin. The accused employed capable lawyers for their defense. The state also retained counsel of acknowledged ability to assist District Attorney Willis Wallace in prosecuting the cases. Edmund DeMontel, R. M. Vance, and several other capable lawyers were brought in to help with prosecution. Soon with pressure now exerted by the accused cutters and their friends, sureties for Sheriff Foster withdrew his bond. The sheriff telegraphed his predicament to supporters in San Antonio. A new bond was made for the sheriff within forty minutes in a strong show for law and order. His new sureties represented twenty times more taxable value than his original bondsmen. One newspaper reported Medina's law and order group "had grappled with the county's Blue Devils and completely shattered their organization."[29]

Detective Robert S. Davis reached the safety of San Antonio. He was now talking to the newspapers, bragging about his role in Medina County's fence-cutter roundup. In an interview Davis told a reporter for the *San Antonio Express* that he had risked his precious scalp to ferret out the houses of fence cutters in Medina County. Davis said he didn't see fences cut but gained the confidence of the men engaged in it and was told all of their secrets and plans. The fence cutters believed he sympathized with them in their work. Davis named Emil Bader as captain of the German squad and W. D. Burnett as captain of the American squad. The detective said two or three of the cutters proposed to turn evidence to clear their skirts. The Litburu brothers were among those. Davis told the reporter he was going back to Castroville. He claimed he joined the Rangers and said the cutters had threatened to murder him; but he could shoot as fast as they could and wasn't scared. Davis did join the Rangers, mustering in and serving as a private in Company F of the Frontier Battalion. But if he went back to Medina, his trip may have been as a witness during the court proceedings, and he would have been under heavy guard.[30]

Medina's fence-cutter war was burning hot, and help from Rangers was needed. Lieutenant Joseph Shely's Ranger Company F were seeing plenty of action with fence cutters and cattle stealing south and east of Medina County. When Medina County's fence cutters were being rounded up and jailed, Lieutenant Shely redeployed the Company F Rangers. One detachment of Rangers moved from Yorktown to the corners of Karnes, Wilson, and Gonzales Counties. Another detachment was pulled from San Diego and moved to Pearsall in Frio County to be closer to Medina. Castroville's lawmen were in dire need of help, so Rangers from LaSalle County were dispatched to Castroville to guard the jail, keep order, and protect witnesses.

To the relief of Medina's lawmen and citizens, the Rangers arrived as the last cutters were delivered to Castroville's jail. Witnesses were now being terrorized and threatened with death if they remained in the county. The only witness protection Shely could offer was to encourage witnesses to camp near his Ranger detachment's Castroville base. On a visit by a newspaper man, Lieutenant Shely said he believed convictions in the large number of cases on hand would depend on the first three cases tried. He predicted the cases would be tried as a misdemeanor. If the first parties were found guilty, then the rest would likely plead guilty.[31]

As fence cutters were arrested and brought into town, the jail was overcrowded. The town was full of outsiders; tensions were high. A local newspaper, the *Medina County News*, was upset with bad publicity heaped on their community. Over the past months, the paper said little or nothing about the fence cutting in Medina but now had much to say about other newspapers with critical stories reflecting negatively on their county. The local paper printed a column saying:

> For the past two weeks, there has appeared in the columns of outside newspapers, many sensational telegrams and other notices about State of affairs in Medina County, which are very injurious to her reputation as a good, law-abiding county, and are as false as they are injurious. There is not a county in State where the love of order and good government is greater than here, all these newspaper reports about the people being up in arms against the authorities, and there being imminent danger of the sheriff being overpowered and the prisoners liberated to the contrary notwithstanding, it is unjust that she should be slandered in the way she has been by these reports. Nobody in Medina County ever thought of resisting the authorities, and we think these bogus sensationalists would do better to let us alone and mind their own Knitting.[32]

On April 14 the Medina District Court opened with a grand jury and the petit jury impaneled. District Judge Thomas M. Paschal gave a strong charge to the juries. As the court session began, all interest focused on the fence-cutting cases. The chief in this war on fence cutting was Deputy US Marshal Ferdinand Niggli. District Attorney Willis Wallace was prosecuting, confident of getting indictments, and claimed to have two hundred cases of this class. The *San Antonio Light* reported Castroville was crowded with lawyers, many coming from San Antonio looking for clients. Some lawyers were employed, and the newspapers described others as being of the "Barkis is willin'" order. Following their report on Castroville's legal activities, the *San Antonio Light* closed with a short statement of much significance, giving a glimpse into Medina County's future politics. The paper reported,

"Candidates are beginning to crop up largely for the next election. It is said that the fence cutter's ticket will be placed in the field."[33]

When the fence-cutting cases were presented to the grand jury in the Castroville District Court, an out-of-state newspaper, the *Omaha Daily Bee* in Nebraska, published a clip with the heading "Texas Cowboy Outlawry." The *Daily Bee* reported sixty indictments had been returned in Medina County for fence cutting. The district attorney believed he would be able to get twenty more indictments for cutting, burning fences, perjury, and conspiracy to kill the sheriff. A few days later, another report with detail came from San Antonio. District Attorney Wallace was in the city and announced fifty-three men were indicted for fence cutting in Medina County with about a hundred charges against them. There were forty-one charges for burning pastures and pasture fences. As expected, finding an impartial jury to try the men in Medina County was impossible, so the judge transferred the cases to San Antonio on a change of venue for the trial. There was much agonizing by the cutters and their friends. They feared the outcome of a trial in San Antonio. Wallace reported that the defendants' counsel offered a plea of guilty for misdemeanor cases if the felony cases were dismissed but said he hadn't accepted their offer. After the grand jury's indictments, the fence cutter's bail bonds were raised to $1,300, and many fence cutters in jail were unable to secure bond. This increase in bail caused more anger among cutters, their families, and their friends. District Attorney Wallace's report ended by saying that two faithful bulldogs who assisted with guarding the Castroville jail for many years were poisoned the night before.[34]

When preparing for the fence cutter trials began in April, District Attorney Wallace was arrested in San Antonio and charged with carrying a pistol. The charge was heard in the recorder's court by San Antonio Mayor French. Wallace was asked if he had the authority to carry the pistol and complied with the city's ordinance. District Attorney Wallace responded, saying he reached the city at nine o'clock that evening, was on his way to his hotel, and was not familiar with the city's ordinances. Testimony by Medina's Sheriff William Foster explained Wallace was prosecuting a large group of fence cutters in San Antonio and aroused such vindictive spirit his life was seriously endangered. Mayor James French accepted Foster's explanation and dismissed the charge against Wallace.[35]

District Attorney Wallace was again back in San Antonio in June, preparing for the trials. On this occasion Wallace was with Marshal Niggli and Ranger Captain Joseph Shely (Shely had been promoted to captain). About ten o'clock in the evening, they were in the White Elephant Bar on Main Plaza and there was an altercation between Constable Fred Bader and District Attorney Wallace. There was excitement and a crowd gathered in front of the bar. Several police officers arrived. Captain Shely was unavailable or unwilling to comment on what occurred. But a reporter interviewed Billy Simms, manager of the vaudeville theater nearby. Simms was reputed to have plotted the killing of Ben Thompson and King Fisher in his theater in March. Billy Simms had a story for the newspaper saying Constable Bader grabbed Wallace and said, "Here, none of that."

This episode in the White Elephant Saloon raises questions, and answers haven't been found. Was Constable Fred Bader a relative of August Bader or Emil Bader, the German gang leader about to be tried in San Antonio? Constable Fred Bader worked on a San Antonio counterfeiter's case with US Marshal Niggli the year before. These men in the bar were acquainted.

It's noted that Niggli was a friend of King Fisher. When Niggli was Medina County sheriff, Fisher was in the Castroville jail awaiting trial in San Antonio for his desperado day's murder indictments. While in Niggli's jail, a friendship of sorts developed. The court eventually cleared Fisher of his misdeeds, and he was the acting sheriff for Uvalde County when he and Thompson and were assassinated in the vaudeville theater. At the time Fisher was dealing with fence-cutting problems in Uvalde, and that issue placed him working with Marshal Niggli on their adjoining counties' fence-cutting problems. Billy Simms was paranoid; he lived fearing Fisher's friends would kill him. Did Simms's fear prompt his *San Antonio Light* story, telling of this encounter with the lawmen?[36]

In January 1884 the Eighteenth Texas Legislature met in their special session, passed bills expected to solve the state's fence-cutting problems, then adjourned. Governor John Ireland signed the fence-cutting bill into law on February 6 and the pasture-burning bill into law on February 7.

Because of the date these bills were enacted into law, the cases against Medina's fence cutters appear to have been misdemeanors rather than felony charges. Little information is found on Medina's fence-cutter trials held in San Antonio. The trials were anticlimactic and received little or no coverage from the newspapers. Willis Wallace, who worked so hard on the Medina investigations and secured indictments, apparently had no choice but to let the cutters plead guilty to misdemeanor charges. The only report found on the trial in San Antonio comes from a short note printed in the November 8 *Runnels County Record*. The newspaper reported, "When Prosecuting Attorney Wallace of Medina arose the other day in court and announced State ready for the trial of the celebrated fence-cutting cases, twenty-six defendants appeared, and all pleaded guilty. The court assessed a small fine on each, and this settled it."[37]

Just days after the trial, District Attorney Wallace, who aggressively prosecuted the fence cutters, was found dead in his room at the Southern Hotel in San Antonio. Wallace passed away in his sleep the night of November 11 from a heart attack. His brother-in-law, US Marshal Hal Gosling, said Wallace's constitution was impaired from the arduous nature of his duties as district attorney on the frontier. He suffered attacks of suffocation from the congestion of the heart and lungs. The law-and-order folks from Medina County lost a courageous fighter and one of their strongest advocates.[38]

The capture, trial, and prosecution of the fence cutters ended fence cutting in Medina, but the war would continue. The arrests, jail time, and expense of counsel for the defense, coupled with stringent new state laws, took away the desire to destroy fences. With legal costs and humiliation, bitterness followed with a desire for revenge in the absence of fence cutting. On November 4, 1884, the fence cutters and their families and friends went to their polling place, voted, and elected Medina officials sympathetic to their cause. A slate of fence cutters and sympathizers took office. Christopher Friederich Thumm was elected Medina's new sheriff.

Christopher Friederich Thumm, called Fritz by those who knew him, immigrated to Texas from Baden, a country of the German confederation. He married a lady in Mason, Texas, named Caroline Dannheim, and they had children. The family was listed in Mason County's 1880 US Census, with

Fritz being 28 years old, and his occupation was farming. In 1878 there was trouble at a house on Upper Willow Creek about ten miles northeast of the town of Mason. It was reported that Fritz Thumm had been on intimate terms with his sister-in-law, and she had been spreading slanderous information about Thumm's wife. Fritz and his wife went to the sister-in-law's house to discuss the matter. As they rode up to the house, the angry sister-in-law came to the door with her rifle and fired at them without effect. Theodore Wahlburg, a hired man, grabbed the Winchester, levered another shell in the chamber, and threatened to shoot Thumm. That was a mistake. Thumm drew his revolver, jumped out of the wagon, and shot and killed Theodore Wahlburg. Sheriff Jesse W. Leslie, the Mason County sheriff, arrested Friederich Thumm and placed him in jail. Thumm went to trial defended by Holmes and Todd, two prominent Mason attorneys, and was acquitted.[39]

In 1882 Friederich Thumm moved his family to another community with a large German population, this time in Medina County. He soon became a member of good standing in the German community at Castroville. Fence cutting started in Medina soon after his arrival. Thumm appears to have joined a German element of fence cutters, the Blue Devils. He may have been indicted as a fence cutter at some point, but his name didn't appear on any records reviewed. Testimony by a witness in a court proceeding several years later, however, indicated he may have been indicted.[40]

As forecast in the April 14, 1884, issue of the *San Antonio Light*, the fence cutters did bring forward a fence-cutter's ticket at election time. They ran Fritz Thumm as their candidate for Medina County sheriff. There were three other candidates for sheriff: Joe Finger, Joe Lehman, and George W. Brown. Sheriff William Foster didn't seek reelection, but his deputy, George Brown, stepped in and was the candidate supported by Marshal Ferdinand Niggli and Medina County's law-and-order group. Deputy Brown had played a significant role in the fence-cutter roundup.

When ballots were counted following the November 4 election, Christopher Frederick Thumm was elected the new sheriff of Medina County. After the election citizens learned that Thumm was not an American citizen. He had filed an intention to become a citizen ten years earlier, and had enjoyed the privileges of citizenship, but had not received his naturalization papers. The newspaper reported that a defeated candidate contested Frederick Thumm's election before the court but without success.[41]

The years that followed brought more angst and torment for the law-and-order group in Medina County. In May of 1885, Robert Davis filed a lawsuit in Bexar County against Marshal Niggli and the Medina and Frio County cattlemen. Davis was brought in as a detective to work undercover among the fence cutters. As the plaintiff he was suing for a sum of $10,000 for his detective work. Defendants named in the lawsuit were Ferdinand Niggli, John Lytle, Thomas McDaniels, George J. Wilson, J. R. Skates, Joseph Carie, B. L. Crouch, James Speed, Stephen Speed, E. R. Lane, and Lee Hall. His suit claimed these men owed him pay for his detective work among the fence cutters. This lawsuit gives a glimpse of who the main parties were in Medina and Frio Counties' law and order group during this barbed wire war.[42]

Davis's lawsuit, however, may have been the lesser of Marshal Niggli's problems. A verbal battle raged between Niggli and Medina County's new sheriff, Fritz Thumm. The consensus in Medina was that Thumm was in full accord with the fence cutters. Niggli made this an issue in the sheriff's race when he supported Deputy Sheriff George Brown. Sheriff Thumm wrote a scathing and abusive letter to a German newspaper in Boerne over in Kendall County in the days that followed. His letter was published for the public to read. In response, Marshal Niggli followed in like manner with more bitterness in a letter to the *Medina County News* in Castroville. It, too, was published. Following these vitriolic letters, Niggli filed an affidavit in the US court charging Thumm with selling beer without a license. Sheriff Thumm was convicted of the offense. Several other events occurred that added fuel to the fire, brought these two men together eye-to-eye, and assured a reckoning.[43]

In Castroville's early years, families of St. Louis Parish gathered in Biediger's River Bottom nearby to celebrate the feast day of their patron saint, St. Louis IX of France. In the years following, the St. Louis Day celebration grew in size and importance in Castroville and is still celebrated today. On August 25, 1885, US Marshal Niggli was in Castroville to participate in the St. Louis Day Celebration. Ranger Joseph Shely noted that his friend Ferd "began drinking pretty freely."

That evening Niggli went into Charles Wernette's saloon across the street from the courthouse. Something happened or was said that bothered him. He reacted by drawing his revolver and firing off two rounds, the first going into the frame holding the bar's mirror. His second shot went through the mirror. In a matter of minutes, Sheriff Thumm entered the saloon. Thumm later told the *San Antonio Daily Express* that when he came into the bar, Niggli was sitting on the counter with his elbows on his knees and his pistol pointed at him. Thumm said he courteously ask Niggli to put up the gun. Niggli responded, "Get out, you god damned fence-cutting son of a bitch." Charles Wernette, the saloon owner's story, appeared in the *San Antonio Light*. Wernette was standing behind the bar when Thumm came in. Niggli told Thumm, "You can have me in the morning, but you can't have me now and I want you to go home." Then shouting and yelling commenced. Thumm was behind an iron post, dodging to keep Niggli from hitting him with his pistol. Thumm shouted to Niggli, "I don't want you; I don't want you."

According to Wernette, Niggli's revolver was pointed at Thumm. It was never fired, and the US marshal proceeded to march Sheriff Thumm from the saloon into the street. Thumm later described how Niggli shoved the cocked revolver in his back and walked him to his house. After taking Thumm home, Niggli returned to Wernette's Saloon, went to the bar, and took a drink. Then he walked outside, found a chair, and sat with friends, talking about how he took Thumm home.

Niggli was leaning back in his chair, feet braced against the wall and facing the building instead of the street. By then it was getting dark as two men approached from the direction of the courthouse. When they were close, Wernette, the bartender, recognized the two men as Sheriff Thumm and Anton Beetz. The bartender tried to warn Niggli. The marshal didn't hear Wernette, so the bartender tapped Eugene Bohl on the shoulder, noting their approach, then stepped back three or four steps.

Bohl, on recognizing Thumm, cried out, "Look out, Ferd, there comes Thumm again."

Niggli dropped his feet to the ground and turned halfway around with his left side instead of his back to his foe. As Niggli turned around, Thumm raised his revolver, which he had held behind him cocked. With both hands he leveled the piece at Niggli and fired. The bullet struck Niggli on the left shoulder, glanced off, went through his left jaw, and passed through his neck between his windpipe and throat. Niggli fell on his back, unconscious. Sheriff Thumm and his deputy, Anton Beetz, holstered their revolvers and left.[44]

Marshal Niggli was unconscious but still alive; his friends carried him to the courthouse. A telephonic dispatch was sent to Joseph Meny, a close friend of the Niggli family in San Antonio, asking him to convey the news to Niggli's wife and mother and send a San Antonio physician immediately. When the message arrived in San Antonio, Ranger Joe Shely, Dr. Amos Graves, and Frank Meny left for Castroville.

The morning following the shooting, the wounded marshal was made as comfortable as possible and brought to San Antonio. On arrival, he regained consciousness and reported feeling very easy. Captain Shely shared his knowledge of the unfortunate event with a reporter from the *San Antonio Light*. The newspaper published details of the altercation.

At four o'clock that same morning, Thumm was arrested by City Marshal Peter Hoog, delivered to Deputy Sheriff Louis Arh, and placed in the Castroville jail. The following day Anton Beetz was arrested. Both men were arraigned on attempted murder charges, received a preliminary examination, and released on bond. Late Sunday, August 30, Niggli's condition took a turn for the worse with a high fever. The next morning, August 31, word of Niggli's death spread through San Antonio and across the state.[45]

On the word of Niggli's death, Deputy US Marshal Fred Loring filed a complaint in San Antonio, Bexar County, charging Fritz Thumm and Anton Beetz with murder. Loring gave warrants to Bexar County Sheriff Deputies Nat Lewis and Ed Stephens for servicing. The following day Beetz was arrested, jailed, and held on murder charges. Thumm wasn't found. Several days afterward Castroville's City Marshal Peter Hoog and a San Antonio constable located Thumm in the little town of Quihi but were unable to arrest him. Thumm was protected by a crowd of about thirty friends and refused to surrender. On September 15 he turned himself in. A hearing was held in Quihi, and Thumm was released on a $1,500 bond. Following his arrest the Bexar County grand jury refused to return a true bill and returned the case to Medina County. Beetz, Thumm's deputy, was released and returned to Castroville.[46]

On October 5 there was an altercation in a Castroville business. Sheriff Thumm attacked Joe Jungman, a Castroville resident, severely beating him to the floor. Frank Seekatz, a former deputy of Ferd Niggli, fearing Thumm would kill the man, picked up a chair and broke it over the sheriff's back. Thumm, being a large man weighing over two hundred pounds, shook off the blow. Pulling his revolver, the sheriff proceeded to pistol-whip Seekatz, probably with the same revolver that killed Ferdinand Niggli two months before.

The severe pistol-whipping of Seekatz was probably an act of vengeance. Seekatz was a sheriff's deputy under Niggli and likely a supporter of George Brown in the last sheriff race. He may also have participated in the fence-cutter roundup. Joe Jungman and Frank Seekatz both suffered a brutal beating by Thumm. Seekatz filed an aggravated assault charge against Sheriff Thumm in the Medina District Court. Thumm was indicted on the charge on October 10, and a capias was issued for his arrest. It was served by Constable D. S. Robinson, and Thumm was placed under a $300 bond. No record of the outcome of this case is found.[47]

Days later the October term of the Medina County District Court convened, with Judge Thomas M. Paschal presiding. A grand jury was impaneled, sworn, and heard Thumm's and Beetz's cases. After hearing the evidence, the jury refused to indict either of the men for murder. The jury issued the following report on Thumm's case.

> The grand jury have carefully examined and considered the evidence in the matter of F. Thumm charged and under bond to await the action of the grand jury for the homicide of F. Niggli on August 25, 1885, and do not believe that facts are such to justify the indictment of the said, Thumm. We, therefore, speaking through our foreman, recommend that the said Thumm be discharged from further attendance of the court, and his sureties be released from further obligation under the terms of the bond.
>
> James E. Merriman, Grand Jury Foreman[48]

Lawmen Stop Medina's Fence Cutting but Suffer Revenge

Seeing that no indictment was delivered in Medina County, the Bexar County grand jury reconsidered the Thumm case on December 23, 1885. This time they indicted Sheriff Thumm for murder. Thumm was brought to San Antonio a week later and after arraignment was released on a $10,000 bond. The following year of 1886, while still under the murder indictment in San Antonio, Thumm again ran for sheriff of Medina County. Little is known about the campaign for his reelection, but his fence-cutting associates supported him. The county's large German population probably felt that Bexar County was meddling in Medina County's business when they indicted the sheriff for an incident in Medina County. While he was still under the murder indictment, Medina County residents again elected Fritz Thumm their Medina County sheriff. During the spring of the following year, on March 21, 1887, Sheriff Fritz Thumm was tried in San Antonio for the murder of Ferdinand Niggli. His attorneys argued his case was self-defense. The Bexar County jury, hearing testimony and legal arguments, found Thumm not guilty.[49]

Years earlier, when District Attorney Willis Wallace was securing the fence cutters' indictments, a young lawyer named John William Hildebrand arrived in Medina County. The exact date that John Hildebrand arrived in Castroville is uncertain. His law practice appeared to have been land law. Still, there is some indication that Hildebrand may have been one of the attorneys brought to Castroville to help Wallace with the fence-cutter prosecutions. One historian, Gary Fitterer, indicated that John Hildebrand may have assisted Fritz Thumm with his sheriff's campaign. Although his early role in Castroville is unclear, it is clear that he soon became one of Sheriff Thumm's antagonists.[50]

After Hildebrand moved to Castroville, there was an incident involving Thumm. The sheriff wrote a note of insulting character to a female relative of Hildebrand. It's not known who this relative was. According to a newspaper account, young Hildebrand announced around town that Thumm was a scoundrel and a coward. He searched for Thumm several days with a double-barrel shotgun loaded with buckshot. The matter settled with Hildebrand relocating to San Antonio. In San Antonio he practiced law and did real estate title work with Cocke, Franklin & Hildebrand.[51]

On June 22, 1887, John Hildebrand traveled to the Castroville Courthouse, arriving about ten o'clock to try the case of *Volmar vs. Ihnken*, representing Volmar. While Hildebrand talked with his client upstairs in the courtroom, Sheriff Thumm was in his private office near the judge's bench. Thumm, a large man, left the office, walked past Hildebrand, wheeled, and faced him, but he spoke not a word. Thumm then walked back to his office. Hildebrand finished his discussion with his client, did some preliminary work in consultation with the other party's lawyer, and received a continuance for the case. Finishing his business in the courtroom, Hildebrand went downstairs to the county clerk's office.

When he entered, Joseph Kemp was alone, sitting at his desk in the corner of the clerk's office. Joseph, an older man who served as county and district clerk of Medina County for many years, left the position in 1884. His son, August Kemp was elected the new county and district clerk. Following the election of his son, Joseph Kemp assumed the deputy clerk position. With his years of county service, Joseph Kemp was well known, respected, and held in high regard by citizens throughout Medina County. Coming into the clerk's office, Hildebrand spoke to Mr. Kemp and asked about some records. Kemp answered, telling him they were in the vault where they were usually kept. Hildebrand went into the vault, came out with a large book of deed records, and took a desk farthest from the hallway door. He seated himself at the desk and proceeded to examine the deed records bound in a large book.

About ten minutes after Hildebrand was seated, Sheriff Thumm entered the clerk's office through the hallway door, looked at Kemp without speaking, and approached Hildebrand from behind. He then struck Hildebrand several times in the head with his fist. Hildebrand raised an arm to ward off the blows and partially fell between his chair and a window. Thumm grabbed a large quart bottle half full of mucilage from the windowsill and struck Hildebrand over the head with it. On the second blow, the bottle shattered, and Thumm continued to hit the lawyer with the broken bottle until he could no longer hold it. Hildebrand, still conscious, covered with blood and mucilage, managed to get to his feet. In a stooped position with blood streaming as he went, he staggered to the clerk's office door and out into the courthouse hallway. Joseph Kemp was still sitting at his desk watching but could no longer see Hildebrand when he left the clerk's office and staggered down the hall toward the courthouse porch. Thumm followed Hildebrand closely until he reached the door to the hallway, but he stopped. His feet and body were inside the clerk's office, with his left hand on the inside door facing of the clerk's office. He leaned forward, with his head out the door, watching Hildebrand stumble down the hall. Thumm's body was protected by the stone wall of the clerk's office. Kemp heard a shot from the courthouse porch's direction and saw Thumm draw his pistol with his right hand and fire down the hall. Thumm then left the clerk's office and walked down the hallway to the porch.

Celeste Pingenot, the Medina County Treasurer, closed his office for the morning at about eleven o'clock and went to the courthouse porch, where he had a brief business conversation with several men. As the discussion ended, he heard sounds like falling chairs coming from the county clerk's office. Pingenot went across the courthouse porch to the east window of the clerk's office and, looking in, saw the sheriff strike Hildebrand with the mucilage bottle. Having no desire to be summoned as a witness should this incident result in a criminal proceeding, Pingenot attempted to get away unobserved. As he recrossed the courthouse porch, he ran into Lindy and Hornung, the two men with whom he had the conversation. When Pingenot got fifteen or so steps from the porch, he turned and saw Hildebrand come staggering out the hall door, step onto the porch, turn with his pistol in both hands, and fire one shot into the hall of the courthouse. Two others followed that shot, the report of which blended. A shot had been fired from the hallway a fraction of time before Hildebrand fired his second shot. Pingenot saw Hildebrand begin to fall and rushed from the scene, crossing the street and going into a saloon.[52]

Hildebrand fell, pierced through the brain by a .45-caliber bullet, the ball entering between the eyes. Thumm escaped without a scratch but was arrested and awaited preliminary examination on the following day.

Three months after being tried and acquitted for the murder of Ferdinand Niggli, Thumm killed his third man, John William Hildebrand, in the Castroville Courthouse while court was in session. Joseph Kemp sat at his desk and observed this entire ruckus, except he did not see Hildebrand fire at the sheriff with his revolver. Consequently, Kemp was the primary witness for the state in the court proceedings that followed. L. G. Denman, who was in the courthouse at the time of the incident and who knew Fritz Thumm, described the sheriff as a strong man weighing about 225 pounds. John Hildebrand's father described his son as a weak child from the first, who never became a strong, robust man. He was five feet, eleven inches high and weighed 135 to 140 pounds. John had a crippled left arm with the elbow cap knocked off in a fight in 1883. He could use the left arm to push but not to pull.

Medina's County's attorney, W. N. Park, was a witness for Thumm's defense. Parks claimed that after the incident, Joseph Kemp told him that Fritz Thumm came into the clerk's office and spoke to Hildebrand before he struck him. According to Park's testimony, Thumm asked Hildebrand, "Are you hunting up some more indictments against me?" Joseph Kemp denied he told Parks any such story. However, Parks's statement lends credibility to the theory that Fritz Thumm was one of the fence cutters in 1883. Hildebrand may have assisted District Attorney Wallace in building a case against him and his fence-cutting friends in 1884.[53]

After the fence-cutter roundup and their prosecution four years earlier, fence cutting stopped in Medina County. Three weeks before Hildebrand arrived in Castroville to try the *Gerhart Ihnken vs. John Volmer* case, fence cutters struck again and cut a mile and a half of pasture fence belonging to George Thuken. Mr. Thuken's pasture was almost within sight of Castroville, and this fence-cutting incident caused plenty of excitement. An Austin newspaper claimed there was no cause for this outrageous act of cutting the Thuken fence other than pure maliciousness. Did Hildebrand's return and presence in Castroville cause concern in Thumm's mind about new fence-cutting indictments?[54]

The jury of inquest over Hildebrand's body concluded its work on June 24, finding death was caused by a pistol fired from within the Castroville Courthouse on June 22, 1887, at 11:30 a.m. The inquest provided few details, noting that testimony before the inquest jury was meager. They said the grand jury would meet the following Monday and investigate the affair thoroughly. Though not mentioned in the inquest, the bullet entered Hildebrand's forehead near the hairline, penetrating the brain. There were two contusions on the head, one caused by a blunt instrument and the other caused by a sharp instrument. Neither of these wounds caused Hildebrand's death but were said to have dazed him for a short time.[55]

The *Austin Weekly Statesman* reported that on June 28, 1887, the Medina County grand jury brought an indictment against Sheriff Fritz Thumm, charging him with murder in the first degree and placing him in the custody of Constable Galbraith. A motion for a habeas corpus hearing was made before Judge Thomas Paschal, and Thumm expected a change of venue for the trial. The Austin newspaper added, "While the killing of so estimable a young man as Hildebrand has created no excitement and threats of vengeance, there is yet a very decided public opinion here that the killing was no less than a murder most foul."[56]

The habeas corpus hearing that Thumm demanded went on three days before Judge Paschal in the Castroville Courthouse. The hearing ended July 2, with the sheriff being remanded to jail without bail. With all testimony brought out in the hearing, the prosecution was confident of a final conviction. Of course, this raised considerable concern among Thumm's friends because they had not expected that he would be locked up without bond. An appeal of the verdict on his bail was filed with the Texas Court of Appeals.[57]

Several days later Sheriff Thumm was moved from Castroville to the San Antonio jail for safekeeping with five officers escorting him. Thumm didn't suffer the humiliation of leg irons and handcuffs like others who committed murder and was quite cheerful when he reached the San Antonio jail. However, his cheer vanished when the jailer put him in the secure cage prepared for such prisoners. The sheriff insisted that he be treated with more respectful consideration. Thumm remained in jail in San Antonio until taken to Boerne, the county seat of Kendall County, where his trial took place.[58]

It's not clear at what point the sheriff's counsel for the defense was employed, but Thumm and his friends were aware of the strong public sentiment and recognized he had a serious problem. The best legal counsel available was sought to defend Sheriff Thumm; William M. (Buck) Walton of Austin was employed for the defense. Walton was known statewide for his acclaim in murder cases. Murder defense was his specialty.

When Ben Thompson killed Jack Harris in the vaudeville theater in San Antonio in 1882, Buck Walton was on Thompson's defense team. They beat the San Antonio prosecution.

Thumm's appeal from the judgment denying him bail was heard by the Texas Court of Appeals on October 20, 1887. The district court's judgment was affirmed without a written opinion. A few days later, Thumm was tried for murder in the district court of Kendall County at Boerne. Buck Walton of Walton, Hill & Walton presented Thumm's defense. The strong evidence of the assault on Hildebrand and the shooting was difficult to defend. The arguments Walton chose to use in this trial appear to have been similar to those used to defend Thumm in the Niggli trial. Walton argued Thumm's killing of young Hildebrand was self-defense. The judge gave the jury its charge. After deliberation the jury returned a verdict of second-degree murder. It sentenced Sheriff Fritz Thumm to twenty-five years in the state penitentiary. The case was passed up to the Texas Court of Appeals and heard in January 1888. Attorney Walton's appeal claimed the lower court erred in refusing to instruct the jury on the law of self-defense and manslaughter.[59]

After a review of the case, the court of appeals said in part,

> If any necessity arose for him to kill the deceased to protect himself from injury, that necessity was produced by his own willful and malicious act. It is manifest to our minds, from the evidence that the assault was made by Thumm in the first instance with deadly intent, and a heart fatally bent on mischief, with the purpose and formal design that such assault should result in the death of the man he hated. There is no room, it seems to us, for the impartial mind to reach any other conclusion from the evidence as to the intent of the defendant. We cannot construe the facts so as to make them fairly raise the issue of imperfect self-defense. We are clearly of opinion, therefore, that the court did not err, but acted properly in omitting and refusing to charge the jury upon the law of self-defense.[60]

The opinion was delivered by Judge Samuel A. Wilson and concurred on by Judges James M. Hunt and John P. White on January 28, 1888.

In a matter of days, Christopher Thumm was removed as sheriff of Medina County and delivered to the Huntsville State Prison. He served fifteen years of his twenty-five-year sentence in prison, then was pardoned and released in 1903. He lived until 1918.[61]

During the heat of Medina's fence-cutting war, Sheriff William Burl Foster served only one term as sheriff, retiring in November 1884, then moved on. In May 1887 there was a brief note in the *Dallas Times Herald* stating Sheriff Foster had been arrested in San Antonio on charges of perjury, but there were no other details.[62]

Joseph Ney was a respected Medina County citizen. When Niggli resigned as sheriff after accepting the deputy US marshal appointment, Ney was appointed sheriff and served out the balance of Niggli's term. When Thumm was delivered to prison, the Medina County commissioners again appointed Joseph Ney to serve out the rest of Thumm's term as sheriff. On November 6, 1888, Medina citizens elected Joseph W. Lemon sheriff. In 1890 Joseph Ney decided to run for office and was elected sheriff. He was reelected in 1892, 1894, 1896, and 1898, serving until November 6, 1900. He ran for office again and was elected in 1902, reelected in 1904, 1906, and 1908, and served until November 8, 1910. He was an extremely popular sheriff and served Medina County for nineteen years, four months, and nine days.[63]

Reviewing Medina County's history over the years following Sheriff Fritz Thumm's delivery to the Huntsville prison, Thumm's departure from Medina County marked the end of the county's fence-cutting war. Although the fence-cutting war took its toll on Medina's blood and money, their farm and ranch country stayed fenced and productive. Medina County and its communities recovered and prospered.

Chapter 13

Tragedy and Death on a Clay County Fence Line

> Henrietta, Tex., July 8. One of the most horrible tragedies that ever took place in this or any other community occurred five miles northwest of town yesterday . . . three brothers had been shot . . . two were dead and the other badly wounded.
> —*Iola (KS) Register*, July 16, 1886

As the fence-cutting wars slowed and were coming to an end in Texas, farm and ranch land in the Red River Country continued as an attractive investment for agriculture interests from the Midwestern states. Good grassland for cattle, good soils for farming, and new railroads continued to lure small farmers and investors to Clay County. Clay County appears to have been especially attractive to moneyed individuals from Missouri. The Red River Land and Cattle Company, made up of Missouri investors, was organized in Texas in 1880, then purchased and leased sections of Clay County land. They fenced the acreage and encountered fence-cutting problems, but their problems crested when their cowhands killed a fence cutter. Now another group of investors from Missouri saw opportunities and profit in the North Texas land and cattle industry. This group filed a charter in Austin, Texas, on April 4, 1883, creating the Clay County Land & Cattle Company. Henrietta in Clay County was their base of operation, and the value of their stock was $250,000. The incorporators were S. F. Scott, N. B. Childs, B. F. Whipple, J. M. Hopkins, John R. Foster, W. H. Conover, George E. Wittich, M. A. Crouse, A. E. Butcher, and N. Butcher.[1]

Nathaniel Butcher, or Nat as he was known, and Alice E. Butcher, his wife, had lived and farmed near Walnut Grove, Missouri. Nat and his wife packed their belongings and moved to Clay County once the Clay County Land & Cattle Company was chartered in 1883. The other investors continued to live in Missouri. Nat now lived and ranched near the Riverland community. Their neighbors were the Harrises, also from Missouri. Miss Maggie Harris and Alice were friends and rode out to watch Nat and his cowhands count the first 2,500 head of cattle they gathered. Nat Butcher was the company's foreman, responsible for managing the cattle, ranch land, and fencing operations. The company recorded their brand in Clay County as JOC.

Two of the first Clay County cowhands hiring on with the Clay County Land & Cattle Company were Sterling Dawson and Joseph W. Douthitt, or Joe as he was known. The Douthitt brothers and Sterling Dawson came to Clay County from Collins County. Ambrose Douthitt, the boy's father, a Confederate veteran, had enlisted in Collins County in 1862 and served in the 16th Texas Cavalry with Fitzhugh's Regiment. He died in 1865 as the war ended, and his family, the widowed mother Nancy Smith Douthitt and the children, were living in Collins County. Ambrose's children were sister Smithy and three brothers, Lee Morris (Dink), James Taylor (Tack), and Joseph White (Joe). After Ambrose's death Nancy gathered her children, moved to Tarrant County near Grapevine, and later moved the family to Clay County.[2]

In 1874 brothers Tack and Joe were hunting buffalo west of Clay County, near the head of the Big Wichita. They bought supplies for their hunts in Henrietta and hauled their buffalo hides to the rail in Sherman and Fort Worth. Tack, the older brother, was head of the buffalo hunter's outfit, made up of his brother Joe, Bill Lytle, Frank and Jim Sands, and a man named Barnes. Bill Lytle later married Tack's sister, Smithy.[3]

A large block of land north of Henrietta had been granted to Angelina County schools by the state. In the years that followed, this school land was sold to cattlemen and tracts were homesteaded and sold to immigrant farmers. Jackson M. Haley, a farmer from Tennessee, acquired one of the school land tracts. Jack Haley and his wife Nancy R. Haley had arrived in Clay County several years before 1880.[4]

James M. Smith and his wife Nancy J. Smith moved to Clay County, probably from Illinois, bringing three sons and a daughter during this same period. The 1880 US Census enumerated the oldest son, Lewis C. Smith, 23, James A. (Jim) was 19, and Elmer 18. The Smith daughter, Clara, was 13 years old. Their father, James M. Smith, bought and farmed the tract of land that joined Haley's tract.[5]

Dates and many details are missing, but about 1880 two significant events occurred. James M. Smith, the boy's father, died, and the three sons took over the family farming operation. Soon after the boy's father died, Jackson Haley, the Smith's neighbor, was having difficulty making payments on his tract of Angelina County school land. Lewis, the oldest Smith boy, purchased Haley's farm joining the Smith's farm with a contract for deed. Then Jack Haley died, and there was a default on his land payments. Jack Haley's wife, Nancy, gave Lewis Smith a quitclaim deed on the Haley property after her husband's death and moved back to Tennessee. After Jack Haley's death and his default, Angelina County repossessed the land tract. They then sold the farm to the Clay County Land & Cattle Company.[6]

Many other farm families had settled on the Angelina school land north of Henrietta, with the preference of buying their tracts. As farmers suffered the severe drought, some missed payments. Angelina County declared a forfeiture of their land for nonpayment of their annual installments. As Angelina County took possession of the farms, they sold the tracts of land to the Clay County Land & Cattle Company. The farmers argued the forfeitures were unjust and claimed the right to hold the land they had settled. One of the disputed land cases was tried in court in Henrietta as a trespass to try title case, *Clay County Land & Cattle Company vs. J. P. Earl*. The Clay County jury favored Earl, the farmer, and the company appealed the case.[7]

Soon there was a bitter dispute over the Haley tract of land. Based on their purchasing transactions, both Lewis Smith and Nat Butcher, foreman for the Clay County Land & Cattle Company, believed they owned the Haley Farm. Each held documents they thought showed ownership. They discussed the ownership issue but reached no agreement; nothing was settled. Butcher's solution to the problem was to take the matter to court, but the Smiths refused to go to court to resolve the landownership dispute. The Smith brothers' refusal may have been due to lack of money to hire legal counsel.

The continuing drought of the 1880s caused serious problems for the Clay County farmers. The two older Smith boys, Lewis and James (known as Jim), left home and traveled to West Texas to find employment. When the brothers returned in the summer of 1886, Clay County Land & Cattle Company's cowboys had set up camp on the unfenced range near Haley's old crumbling log cabin. Their camp was about a quarter of a mile from the Smith home. In years past Butcher's cowhands would borrowed the key to the old Haley cabin from Mrs. Smith and used the log building when working cattle. Now there was a new corral on the disputed land being used by Butcher's ranch hands. Coming back home, Lewis Smith discovered the camp and corral near the old Haley house. Causing more concern, Lewis learned that the Clay County Land & Cattle Company was about to start building a new barbed wire fence that would enclose the Haley tract. Nat Butcher had reviewed the matter with his directors and decided to fence this tract they purchased from Angelina County. Fencing the land would force a legal settlement of the ownership issue.[8]

Two of the Douthitt brothers, Joseph and Tack, had worked for the Clay County Land & Cattle Company from the time it was chartered and were two of the company's first cowhands. Nat Butcher now employed Tack, the older brother, to build fence enclosing the Haley Tract. Tack's fence-building crew had established their camp near the old Haley cabin, and they would begin the string of fence located near the Smith family's headquarters. This fence would separate the disputed property.

As the fence building was about to begin, Nat Butcher came to the property surveying and staking the fence line boundary near the Smith's farm. Butcher was near Smith's house when Lewis saw and called to him, asking what he was going to do about his land claim. Butcher said, "Lewis, I thought we settled this long ago, that you didn't want to go to the law and gave it up."

Lewis responded by saying he had not given it up; he had paid money for the land and wanted the property or wanted to be paid for it. Butcher responded, telling Lewis the Land & Cattle Company had bought the land from Angelina County with improvements, but he didn't want the improvements. Lewis asks Butcher if he would buy the land, which he considered was his. Butcher said the land belonged to the company, and being their foreman, he wanted no trouble. If the land belonged to the Smiths, that was alright, but if the property was the company's, he wanted possession of it. Butcher said he would write and consult the company. Both men said they wanted what was right in the eyes of the law and parted.[9]

In 1886 fence building was one of the few sources of income for farmers starved out by the drought, or for a cowboy whose skills were no longer needed because wire fences closed off the free range. Fence building tools and posthole digging equipment in use today didn't exist in the 1880s. Drills, compressors, and even dynamite to break layers of rock in the postholes came into use in later years. Posthole bars were the tool of the early fence builder. This length of an iron bar used by the men to dig the holes had a sharp tempered blade forged on one end that would dull after a day of chipping rock. As the posthole bars dulled, they had to be carried to a blacksmith and sharpened.

Fence building started by laying out a line on the property's boundary, then measuring and staking where each posthole would be dug. Holes were dug chipping in dirt and rock using the posthole bar. Then the soil and rock chips were scooped out of the hole with a tin can. The fence builder set a post in his posthole, and rock and dirt were pitched in around its base and tamped solid. Digging postholes and setting posts was the backbreaking labor of the fence builders' job. Stringing, stretching, and fastening the barbed wire to the post came last.

Tack Douthitt had an agreement with Nat Butcher to build the cattle company's fence around the Haley tract. When he started the job, he probably didn't know there was a dispute over the Haley tract and the resistance he would encounter. Eli Delk hired on as one of Tack Douthitt's fence-building crew and moved to the fence builders' camp near the old Haley cabin. Delk would dig postholes, but his main job was loading and freighting in the fence post cut on the cattle company's land on the Little Wichita River. Douthitt also hired Frank Collins, an Italian, as part of his fence-building crew. His background is a bit cloudy.

Collins had recently come to Clay County from the Indian Territory. He said he had lived "off and on in the Indian Territory for about twelve years." Later he testified in court that his real name wasn't Frank Collins. He said he just used that name when in Texas. A young man named Andy Ryan was also hired on as part of Douthitt's crew. Nat Butcher, the cattle company's foreman, sent J. L. McCloud and two cowhands, Dock Thompson and Sterling Dawson, to clear brush for the new fence line. New fence construction began in the searing heat of July 1886, a short distance from the Smith family home.[10]

The Smith boys were well known in Henrietta and the neighborhood; they had many friends. They were well thought of by their neighbors and held in high regard in the community. They belonged to the Old School Presbyterian Church, and two of the boys had at one time engaged in teaching. Friends said they had quiet dispositions and lived exemplary lives. Although living wholesome lives and with many attributes, the brothers used poor judgment in one of their decisions. Rather than pursue legal action in court to solve the landownership issue, they chose to stop the Clay County Land & Cattle Company from building the barbed wire fence by force.[11]

On the morning of July 6, Frank Collins went to work digging postholes and setting fence posts for the new fence line. Lewis Smith, the older brother, came to where Collins was working and began filling up postholes. He pulled up a fence post not yet firmly tamped and set on the ground. There was an exchange of words and Collins went to where Douthitt was working and told his boss what just occurred. Douthitt told Collin, "Go back and dig some more holes; Smith won't stop us."

Collins walked back to the fence line and went to work digging postholes. Lewis soon returned to where Collins worked. Again words were exchanged, and Lewis told Collins, "Any man who comes here to build this fence is going to have to fight."

Collins retreated to where Douthitt was working and told him what Lewis said. Douthitt returned with Collins, met the Smith boy, and a volatile conversation about the fence building followed. Douthitt asked Lewis if it was his intention to stop the fence building and how did he plan to stop him and his crew. Lewis responded that he was going to try him every way he could. If nothing else would do, he was going to stop him by arms. Lewis added, "If anyone builds this fence, it will be over my dead body."

Douthitt replied, "If an officer were to come and tell me to quit building the fence, I would quit, but I have a hundred dollars in this fence, and I'm not going to give it up unless they beat me out of it."

Following this encounter, Tack and Collins returned to camp, and Tack Douthitt shut down his fence-building crew's work for the day.

Later, Frank Collins testified that he brought a rifle with him when he came to Texas from the Indian Territory. He thought he might need a gun down in Texas and purchased the Winchester from a man in the Indian Territory. The rifle was with him in the fence builders' camp. Several nights before the encounter with Lewis, the younger Smith brother, Elmer, came by the camp. While talking with Collins, Elmer expressed an interest in the gun, and Collins offered to sell it to him. But when Elmer learned that it was a rifle, he lost interest and told Collins he preferred a shotgun. Following the fence line encounter with Lewis, Tack Douthitt bought the Winchester from Collins, paying him ten dollars, and agreed to pay a ten-dollar balance later. It's clear Douthitt expected trouble after Lewis's threat and probably by now had learned of the property and fence dispute from Nat Butcher.[12]

Two or three weeks before Lewis threatened the fence builders, the brothers borrowed a single barrel shotgun from Lee Williams. Then several days before the fence line confrontation, William Weddington, an old Clay County frontiersman, loaned Lewis Smith his shotgun to take hunting. While visiting with Weddington, Lewis confided in the old gentleman that he was having trouble with Nat Butcher over the Haley tract of land. Butcher was fencing it. Weddington didn't see a relation between Lewis's problem with Butcher and the shotgun that the Smith boy asked to borrow.

The next day, Lewis and his brother Jim visited W. J. Williams, one of their neighbors, and borrowed another double-barrel shotgun. The Smith brothers were ready for their next confrontation with the fence builders. They now were armed with three breach-loading ten-gauge shotguns.[13]

Early on the morning of July 7, Elmer, the younger Smith brother, rode by the fence builders' camp. Sterling Dawson saw him and loudly shouted to him, saying fence building would resume, and the Smith brothers were to not come within three hundred yards of the men while they were working. Elmer returned home and told his brothers about the fence builders' warning. The brothers talked about the warning and concern about Tack Douthitt, but Jim said there was no danger in Douthitt; he was only blowing. The boys' mother later said that Tack Douthitt thought they were cowards because her sons had good morals and didn't use bad language. The three brothers definitely weren't cowards.

Soon after Dawson had called out the warning to Elmer Smith, two cowhands, Emmitt Curry and Dock Thompson's younger brother Charles, rode into the fence builders' camp. They were working on a road nearby and stopped by to see Dock and maybe share an early cup of coffee.[14]

J. L. McCloud was first to leave camp to work on the fence that morning. When he was leaving, Douthitt, Dawson, Dock Thompson, and Andy Ryan were near the old Haley cabin talking. McCloud noticed three Winchester rifles leaning up against the south side of the building. McCloud went on to the fence line and began work. He worked only a short time and, looking up, saw the Smith boys in the distance coming toward him in a wagon. The men in the camp saw the wagon too, and Douthitt shouted, "I see the boys coming. Let's go out there."

Andy Ryan was talking to Dock Thompson, and seeing the Smith brothers coming, told Dock, "Don't go out there."

Dock didn't answer. From the conversations heard earlier that morning, Ryan said he "expected a ruckus." Ryan went to get his horse and planned to leave the fence builders' camp.

McCloud was working about fifty yards from the camp. When he looked back, he saw Douthitt, Dawson, and Dock Thompson walking to where he was working, each carrying a Winchester rifle. The Smith boys drove the horses and wagon up to the posthole that McCloud was digging. Sterling Dawson walked up close to McCloud. Lewis jumped out of the wagon with a shovel in his hand, and Dawson said, "You are going to fill them up, are you?" Lewis said, "I am."

When Lewis had filled the posthole, one of his brothers told him to pick up the post. Dawson put his foot on the post and told Lewis, "Put it down."

As he spoke, Dawson had his rifle in his right hand, pointed down. Lewis made no reply to Dawson's order to put the post down. By then Tack Douthitt was about twelve steps southeast of the wagon, with a rifle in his hand. McCloud was about three feet from a rear wheel of the wagon when Jim Smith raised his shotgun.

Douthitt shouted, "Damn you; put it down."

McCloud glanced around to see what Dawson and Lewis Smith were doing. As he did, guns began firing. Sterling Dawson was behind him, and McCloud heard a shot that he thought came from behind. Lewis Smith ran toward the back of the wagon. McCloud saw him just as he fell and hit the ground on his face. McCloud later testified he thought that the shot from behind him killed Lewis.

Frank Collins watched the gunfight from a distance and saw both Jim Smith and Douthitt pointing guns at each other. Both guns fired, but Collins wasn't sure which fired first. Jim Smith jumped from the wagon, ran around near the horses' heads, and fired again toward Douthitt, then Jim fell. Collins also thought he saw Elmer Smith and Dawson with their guns pointed at each other.

Emmitt Curry and Charles Thompson had expected trouble and got back on their horses as the Smith brothers' wagon pulled up. When the shooting commenced, they were watching from horseback, about fifty yards out from the shootout. Curry said he heard Tack Douthitt say "shoot," and the firing began. Curry's horse was spooked by the shooting and started spinning around, but Curry saw Lewis run and clutch at the back of the wagon, then fall. Charles Thompson saw the shootout and said he saw Jim Smith "throw his gun down on Douthitt, and Douthitt threw his gun down on Jim, and the shooting began."

He said, "Jim and Elmer Smith got out of the wagon on the same side, and Elmer had his gun and was fixing to shoot."

Curry said, "The shooting lasted about the time it takes to count to twenty, and when it was over, the three Smith brothers were laying on the ground."

In a matter of seconds, Emmitt Curry and Charles Thompson saw more than they wanted to see of this incident and rode off, leaving the scene of the shootout.[15]

The shooting scared the horses hitched to the wagon; they bolted and ran for the Smiths' barn and pens about a quarter of a mile away. The Smith boys' mother heard the gunshots and ran from the house toward the fence builders' camp. Running toward the shooting, she met and stopped the horses pulling the wagon, crawled up on the wagon seat, and drove rapidly to the shooting scene. On arriving, she found Jim and Elmer lying dead a short distance from Lewis. One of the shotguns was lying across Jim's arm, and another near Elmer. Lewis was still alive and beckoned his mother to come to him. He told her that Douthitt killed Jim and Elmer, and that he was shot in the back and spine and thought he would die. Clair, the brothers' sister, ran from the house through the pasture to the shooting scene. She managed to have a few words with Lewis, her older brother, before he died. Lewis told Clair that Sterling Dawson had shot him. He continued to breathe for a while longer, but Clair never heard him say another word.

Seeing the men who witnessed the shooting standing off in the distance, Mrs. Smith went and asked them to please come and help her put her boys in the wagon. Collins finally went with her to the bodies and helped her load her sons in the wagon. Collins said, "Lewis was still alive but didn't say anything."

The mother climbed up on the wagon seat and took her boys home. Years after the shooting, Mrs. W. C. McMurry, an elderly resident of Clay County who knew the Smith family, told an interviewer the mother prepared the boys for burial with her own hands.[16]

Douthitt, Dawson, and Dock Thompson saddled their horses, rode into Henrietta, and turned themselves over to Sheriff Cooper Wright. Sheriff Wright checked their rifles and determined that Dock Thompson's rifle had not been fired. Deputy Sheriff Will Bratton examined it and found Douthitt and Dawson's guns had been fired but agreed with the sheriff's conclusion that Thompson's rifle hadn't been fired.[17]

A coroner's inquest was held later that day, with Doctor J. H. Ferris examining the three Smith brothers' bodies. Lewis was shot in the center of the back. The bullet ranged straight in, striking the sixth dorsal vertebrae. He said there were no other wounds, but that would have produced death. Jim Smith was shot in three places. One wound was four inches from the right nipple, another bullet wound was three inches above the right wrist joint, and the third bullet caused a flesh wound on the left elbow. The bullet causing the wound near Jim's right nipple had penetrated the heart, causing death. Elmer's wound was below the left nipple, with the bullet ranging back and lodging under the skin by the left shoulder blade. That wound was fatal. The bullet passed through the heart. Dr. Ferris said all of the injuries appeared to be caused by large-caliber slugs, probably .44 or .45 caliber.

Arriving at the Smith place for the inquest, Sheriff Wright had found a shotgun still in the wagon and two left in the stable. He examined the shotguns and removed four empty hulls from the two double-barrel guns. Looking through their barrels, Wright determined those two guns were fired that morning. He examined the single barrel shotgun and removed a loaded round marked "B" for buckshot. He looked down the gun barrel and said this gun had not been fired since it was last cleaned. After the inquest the shotguns were taken into Henrietta and kept in A.V. Winter's drugstore. Attorney R. R. Hazelwood, of the law firm employed to represent the defendants, came to the drugstore to view the weapons. Soon a flood of curious citizens were going to the drugstore to see the shotguns.[18]

On the day of the shooting, July 7, the *Fort Worth Daily Gazette* received a dispatch from a correspondent in Henrietta reporting, "The Smith boys have a host of friends. They were among the best citizens of our county. Their deaths are much lamented, and their remains will be interred at this place tomorrow morning at 10 o'clock." The three brothers were laid to rest in one large grave in the Hope Cemetery.

Several days later, the incident made the news throughout the Midwest. On the 8th, the Iola, Kansas, paper, the *Iola Register*, published the story from Henrietta. Henrietta's report was titled "One of the most horrible tragedies that ever took place in this or any other community occurred five miles northwest of town yesterday."[19]

On the morning of July 9, the preliminary hearing of cases against Dock Thompson, Sterling Dawson, and Tack Douthitt began in Henrietta's district courtroom. The cases were heard before the Honorable P. M. Stine, county judge, and the defendants were charged separately, with the murder of each of the Smith brothers, making three cases against each of the defendants.

County attorney E. B. Munday, L. C. Barrett, and Vincent Stine represented the state. The law firm of Plemons, Hazelwood, and Templeton represented the defendants. The triple murder case's preliminary hearing closed on July 13, 1886, with bail refused for Tack Douthitt and Sterling Dawson. For $3,000 in each case, Dock was admitted to bail on the charge of killing the three brothers; his bond totaled $9,000.

Two months later, on Wednesday, September 15, 1886, the grand jury returned nine true bills for murder, three each against Tack Douthitt, Sterling Dawson, and Dock Thompson for killing the three Smith brothers. On September 16, 1886, an application for a writ of habeas corpus was granted both Sterling Dawson and Tack Douthitt by District Judge B. F. Williams.[20]

District Judge P. M. Stine tried Dock Thompson on three separate charges. On April 7, 1887, the Clay County jury found Thompson not guilty of the murder of Louis Smith. The cases against Thompson for the death of Elmer Smith and James Smith were dismissed on September 22, 1887, by the county attorney for insufficient evidence. There was a lack of testimony by witnesses J. L. McCloud, Clara Smith, and Nancy Smith.[21]

Benjamin "Dock" Thompson was in Clay County in 1880 based on US Census Records. In 1883 he was working for the Clay County Land & Cattle Company. After the shootout Thompson left Clay County, and in 1900 he lived and farmed near the town of Bangs in Brown County. B. F. "Dock" Thompson died in Bangs, Texas, on April 29, 1939.[22]

On March 21, 1887, the defense filed applications for change of venues for Dawson and Douthitt, and on April 4, 1887, a change of venue to Wise County was endorsed. On April 5 Dawson and Douthitt each made bond for $1,500 to appear in the Wise County District Court in Decatur, Texas. Attorneys J. A. Templeton and L. C. Sparkman were in Decatur on August 26, 1887, representing Dawson and Douthitt in district court. The court set the trial for September 15, 1887. In September the court granted a continuance until the February term of 1888.[23]

The murder case spilled into 1888, and the Wise County District Court's February term opened in Decatur. On February 11 the *Wise County Messenger* reported, "The present term of the district court is moving along very smoothly, and the general public seems to take very little interest in it." A few days later, the paper reported, "There being no cases at the present ready for jury trial for district court, the petit jury for the week were dismissed on Monday." The paper speculated that the district court would probably close the following week.[24]

Late into February, the first sign of activity related to the Douthitt-Dawson murder cases appeared. There was a note in the *Wise County Messenger* reporting that Sheriff William Mann had left for Indian Territory the previous Thursday to find an important witness for the district court. Sheriff Mann was searching for Collins and McCloud. Following the sheriff's departure, the next notice of activity appeared in the March 3, 1888, issue of the *Wise County Messenger*. It was but a short statement. The Decatur newspaper reported, "The Clay County murder cases in our district court on change of venue were dismissed on account of the absence of prosecuting witnesses." Murder charges were dropped with no publicity and hardly noticed by the public. Tack Douthitt and Sterling Dawson were free men.[25]

Census records and a Texas death certificate show Sterling Dawson was born on October 4, 1856, in Collins County. He had been a friend of the Douthitt boys and followed them to Clay County. After working for the Clay County Land & Cattle Company and the Smith brothers' shootout, Dawson moved to the Indian Territory, now Oklahoma. He had two children who were born while he was in the territory. In later years the 1910 US Census listed Sterling Dawson as a ranch boss in Crosby County. His Texas death certificate showed he retired as a farmer in Potter County and died on January 4, 1932. Dawson's grave is in Amarillo, Texas.[26]

In 1887 Tack Douthitt married Dorothy "Dollie" Hart, a young lady only 15 years old. When the court dismissed the murder charges in 1888, Tack and Dollie left Texas and moved to the Indian Territory. Tack built a sizeable business in cattle, operating in the Indian Territory and North Texas. In 1891 he and a partner from Henrietta were selling choice heavyweight steers at high prices at the National Stock Yard in St. Louis, Missouri.

Later, Tack participated in the opening of the Cherokee Outlet in what's now Oklahoma. In the land run on September 16, 1893, known as the Cherokee Strip Land Run, Tack managed to stake a prime claim on the Enid townsite's edge. In years that followed, the tract of land claimed by Tack made him and his wife Dollie wealthy. They became prominent citizens of Enid, built a mansion for their home as the town grew around their farm, and sold their land as town lots. Tack was an organizer of the Garfield County Fair Association and was instrumental in building its famous horse racing track.[27]

Tack's prosperity and luck finally came to an end on April 26, 1904. His wife, Dollie, shot him. The Enid newspaper reported, "Tack Douthitt was shot three times by his wife at the Douthitt home on Sunday evening. It was said that jealousy caused the shooting. The infuriated woman shot her husband three times in the lungs, arm, and thigh." Tack lived through the summer but didn't recover. He died from the bullet wounds on November 3, 1904. Before he died, Tack prepared a sworn statement, exonerating his wife from the shooting charges.[28]

Chapter 14

Menard Fence Cutter Sent to the Penitentiary

Nephew: "If they put me on the witness stand, I will tell the truth if the heavens fall. I would not perjure my soul to save my best friend."... Uncle: "If you swear against me, it will be your last; I will kill you as sure as powder burns."
—Elisha Goodin's threat to his nephew at Menard fence-cutter trial

As the 1880s began, Menard County's citizens suffered frequent crimes by outlaws that returned after Major John B. Jones Ranger's 1877 outlaw roundup in neighboring Kimble County. Horse and cattle were stolen, stagecoaches and the mail were robbed. The old-timers claimed there was pure devilry coming from the riffraff from around old Fort McKavett and down in Kimble County. The one crime that was hard to find in Menard County, however, was fence cutting. Fence cutting, a statewide problem, wasn't a problem in Menard. The county had very few fences and no one was building barbed wire fences in Menard County.[1]

Menard, like neighboring Mason, Llano, and Gillespie Counties, had an early German population, and they had rock fences. Many of the German were skilled in stone or rock work and built fences and pens with stacked rock. The large W. P. Lockhart Company Ranch and the vast Premier Ranch east of Menard in Mason County were fenced with rock. Most of the stacked rock fences on the Premier Ranch were built by German workmen from San Antonio. After use of barbed wire spread across the state, the wire fence was less expensive than the labor cost for building a rock fence. Barbed wire costing eighteen cents a pound, was used almost exclusively.[2]

Compared to the rest of Texas, barbed wire arrived late in Menard County. During the fence-cutting wars of 1883–84, Menard and those counties on its south and west side were open range and the cattlemen were free grazing men. The land buyers coming into this area from out of the state respected the cattlemen's free-range domain and feared the fence cutters and outlaws. One of those land buyers was Colonel William Leslie Black, a Confederate veteran who had been captured twice by the Union forces and spent time in Fort Alcatraz. After the war he was a founding member of the New York Cotton Exchange. Quite an entrepreneur, he visited Menard County in 1875. When the US Army abandoned Fort McKavett in 1882, Black moved his family near the old fort at the San Saba River's headwaters. There he built a house and established his ranch headquarters. The colonel began purchasing land and acquired about eighty sections over time. Some of his land was purchased for as little as ten cents an acre. He stocked this property with native sheep, then shipped in carloads of purebred rams. Black also brought in angora goats and pioneered the goat and mohair business in Menard and on the Edwards Plateau. Several years later when the price of mohair fell, the colonel established the Range Canning Company. This was a meat canning operation on the ranch that processed and canned goat meat. His canned goat meat was labeled Roasted Mutton and Chili-Con-Carne. The canned goat meat sold poorly in the United States, but Black found a market for his goat meat in Europe.

John J. Marsh and P. H. Wentworth, two men with wealth, came to Texas from Boston, Massachusetts, in 1882. They established their ranch headquartered at what had been old Fort Terrett in Sutton County, near the southwest corner of Menard. Wentworth managed the ranch, and John Marsh was the financier who spent very little of his time in Texas. Wentworth stocked their newly purchased land with native sheep, then brought in Spanish Merino sheep. Soon he had over fifty thousand sheep grazing on his range.

Wentworth amassed about one hundred thousand acres of land and had over two hundred Mexican sheepherders employed.

In the early 1880s, the area's two largest sheepmen, Black and Wentworth, were afraid to build wire fencing. They knew this would antagonize the cattlemen, and they feared they or their fence cutters would cut the fences and destroy their sheep-raising business. Both Colonel Black and Wentworth had herders managing their sheep on their open range and apparently had little conflict with cattlemen. In later years, however, Black and Wentworth both fenced with barbed wire. By the year 1891, Wentworth had built about ninety miles of pasture fence on his land and sheep country.

Menard had a population of German immigrants during the 1870 and 1880s; John Wilhelm, a German sheepman, came to Menard County in 1882. He brought sheep with him and profited from his livestock operation through the severe drought of the 1880s. When Wilhelm died in 1890, the old gentleman had fenced over twenty sections of rangeland.[3]

Eventually Colonel Black built his first pasture fence with barbed wire he purchased in Brown County. The colonel was always watching for a good deal and, thinking he found one, bought rolled up coils of barbed wire that had already been in use. Because of fence cutting and violence in Brown County, a threatened and scared rancher changed his mind about fencing. He took down his barbed wire, rolled it up, and wanted out of the wire fence business. Black bought this wire for a pittance. His employees loaded the wire, freighted it to Menard County, and several years later used this wire to build his first fenced pasture. His grandson said the wire from Brown County was definitely not a bargain; it was extremely brittle and constantly breaking. Black had a man spending most of his time riding the fence lines and splicing broken wire. When building barbed wire fences finally became a serious effort in Menard County, stockmen were using Glidden wire and several varieties of Scutt's wire. Another wire popular with sheepmen was a twisted ribbon wire called Allis' Buck Thorn. Many Menard and Kimble County sheepmen preferred Buckthorn because its small barbs or points were not severe and didn't tear or hang in sheep's fleece.[4]

By the mid- and late 1880s, many changes occurred in Texas. The state's population increased, cheap state land sold off, new railroad tracks were built, and barbed wire fences closed what was once open, free range. By 1886 1887 towns across Central Texas became more urban, and many were trying to solve sanitation and nuisance problems. Hogs roamed the streets of towns, rooting under outhouses, destroying gardens, and wallowing in flower beds. They were an absolute nuisance. For years in Texas, hog owners, like the cattlemen, placed their recorded earmark on their hogs. Their pigs ran free to forage, as did their free-range cattle. Like brands, earmarks were their record of ownership filed in their county courthouse.[5]

A new state law was passed authorized a local option by petition and a vote to prohibit hogs from running at large. Towns' citizens now began signing and bringing petitions to their commissioners, calling for what were referred to as hog elections. The election's purpose was to prohibit by law stockmen running their swine loose and free in the communities.

In Ballinger, the county seat of Runnels, voters passed a hog law in April of 1887. Menard's neighbors in Mason County were having hog problems, and Mason citizens circulated a petition. They gathered fifty-one signatures and delivered the petition to their commissioners. The commissioners called a hog election, and Mason's good citizens thought they would soon have a hog law and keep the pigs out of town. There was a heated campaign, but Mason's citizens voted down the proposed hog law. Several years later the citizens tried again in several precincts, but each time the hog law's vote failed.[6]

As Mason was having its hog problem, so was Menardville, the county seat of Menard County. The free-ranging hogs were a nuisance in the town, and Menardville's citizens decided to petition for a hog election. Like Mason and many other counties, Menard's farmers and ranchers raised hogs that ran lose on the range and in the river bottoms. Some of their pigs would come into town. A referendum on the hog law was called and a heated campaign followed. One of the most vocal opponents of the proposed law was a citizen named Elisha Goodin, a hog raiser and local mail carrier.

Elisha and several other hog men campaigned hard to defeat the hog law, but their efforts failed. Menardville good citizens cast their votes and declared by a majority that free ranging of hogs in Menardville would stop. No longer would pigs roam the streets, root up the citizen's gardens and privies, and bed down on the town square. The election and the new hog law enraged Elisha Goodin, who had always run his hogs on the free range. Becoming violently upset, he announced to the community that "any man, whether officer or citizen, who impounded one of his hogs would pay dearly. He would take his Winchester and release his property."[7]

A doctor named Eber Green Dorr graduated from the Medical College of Ohio and move to Texas. Eber Dorr's early days in the Texas were in Austin, where he and his brother Hadley, a pharmacist, opened a business and medical practice. Their Texas Surgical Institute was located on the corner of Congress and Cedar Street (now known as Fourth Street). Dr. Dorr, a widower, relocated to Burnet County several years later. In 1881 he married Flora Murchison, a member of a prominent Menard County family. The couple moved to Menardville, and Dr. Dorr opened his office and pharmacy on Main Street. In addition to providing medical services to the county, the doctor's pharmacy manufactured and sold *Dorr's Kidney Drops*, advertised in the newspapers "For all Kidney and Bladder Troubles. Relieves Pain in the Bladder, Removes Gravel. Recommended for Weak and Lame Back. For Both Men and Women."

The Menardville doctor was also a veterinarian of a sort; he sold Dorr's Screw Worm Killer. He advertised his screwworm medicine as "The Best Oldest Worm Medicine on the Market. Remember it keeps off the Flies, It Does the Work Instantly." Details on Dorr's medication sales aren't found, but his screwworm medication for livestock was undoubtedly popular and a best seller. Screwworm flies and their larva were a serious problem for the Menard County stockmen. Once infected, animals died if not treated for a screwworm infestation.[8]

Several years later Dr. Dorr fenced a sizable tract of ranch land above Menardville. He happened to be a neighbor of Elisha Goodin, who continued to run his hogs on the open range. Dr. Dorr built a new barbed wire fence, and apparently his fence wasn't hog tight. In a short time, Goodin's hogs were in one of the doctor's fields, destroying his crop. The doctor penned the destructive hogs, and Elisha Goodin, true to his words, took his Winchester rifle, went to the doctor's ranch, and released his pigs. While he was there, he also made it a point to heap abuse on the doctor and threatened to kill him.

Dr. Dorr believed his life was in danger. He met with Menard County Sheriff Richard R. (Dick) Russell, a former Texas Ranger, and Russell arrested Goodin. The doctor filed charges against the hog man in J. P. court.[9]

While this case against Goodin was pending, someone cut three miles of Dr. Dorr's new pasture fence in multiple places. Sheriff Russell conducted a thorough investigation and, based on evidence gathered, charged Elisha Goodin with maliciously cutting the doctor's fence. Unique footprints up and down the fence line were part of circumstantial evidence collected by the sheriff. The prints of a large man's shoes had a unique hobnail, initial, or device. Russell traced the shoes' purchase to a local dry good store. The store's owner told the sheriff he sold a large pair of these shoes to Elisha Goodin.

Tracks along the fence line also showed footprints from a small shoe with a worn-off heel. The shoe presumably belonged to Elisha's nephew Nathaniel; the nephew was lame. The boy worked for Elisha, helping operate a mail line out from Menardville. An unnamed source claimed Nathaniel had shared the fence-cutting story with boyhood friends, and a concerned parent notified Sheriff Russell. The sheriff prepared his case and presented his circumstantial evidence to a grand jury. Elisha was indicted and charged with "wantonly, and willfully, and with intent to injure the owner, cutting, and destroying a part of a fence not his own."[10]

Elisha Goodin's fence-cutting trial was the most newsworthy event to occur in Menardville in quite some time. Ranch families came to town to watch the trial and camped under the pecan trees in the river bottom of the San Saba River the night before this big event. It was common knowledge the Texas legislature had made fence cutting a penitentiary offense. But the big question in everyone's minds was, would a jury in Menardville send a man to prison for cutting another man's fence? Menard County still had tracts of unfenced rangeland. Citizens took note that only the wealthy landowners were financially able to build these new barbed wire fences. The town gamblers were giving heavy odds and betting on an acquittal of Goodin.[11]

The November term of Menard County District Court began on November 9, 1887, with District Judge A. W. Moursund presiding. Judge Moursund emigrated from Norway in 1869, located in Texas, and acquired his license to practice law. During his career he served as a county judge, district attorney, and member of the Texas House of Representatives. Moursund was in the legislature during the Eighteenth Special Legislative Session that made fence cutting a felony. Now he was the district judge for the Thirty-Third Judicial District of Texas and traveled from Fredericksburg to Menardville to hear *State of Texas vs. E. Goodin.*[12]

Goodin hired a capable attorney and was confident that he would beat the charge and would not be convicted. That changed just before the trial. On the morning of the trial, word leaked out that "someone was going to turn State's evidence." Goodin took his nephew aside in the courthouse and asked him if he was about to testify against him in the trial. The boy responded, "Uncle, if they put me on the witness stand, I will tell the truth if the heavens fall, I would not perjure my soul to save my best friend. I cannot and will not swear a lie. You lead me into this trouble, and if you suffer, you cannot justly fix the blame on me. I shall tell the truth." The infuriated Goodin responded, "If you swear against me, it will be your last; I will kill you as sure as powder burns."[13]

Judge Morrison was noted for take unusual actions to make a point in his trials. Following a grand jury's review of a case in San Saba, he instructed that the jury's report be published in the local newspaper. The *San Saba News* published the jury's report, which contained some racy matters of rare interest. Morrison was especially popular with the public for his harsh tactics against criminals.

Several days before the fence-cutting trial began, Judge Moursund took one of his unusual actions. He requested the Menardville school principal bring his students from their classrooms to the courthouse for a lesson on "the majesty of the law, and the duties of American citizenship." In response, the school principal brought a large group of students to the courthouse the morning of the trial. They were ushered into Morrison's courtroom and seated to observe the proceedings. This visit to the courthouse was the boys' and girls' first experience in a court of justice. It was probably some of the best schooling they ever received. The accused was a neighbor; his children were their playmates and classmates.[14]

The trial opened on the morning of November 9, 1887. The state, represented by District Attorney G. W. Walters, and defendant Goodin, represented by his attorney, announced they were ready for the trial. Goodin pleaded in open court not guilty of the charges in the fence-cutting indictment. The jury was empaneled and sworn, with Mr. Abner Harris, a Menardville stone mason, serving as jury foreman. The state presented its evidence and testimony. The attorneys argued the case and then made their closing presentations. Judge Moursund read his charge to the jury before they retired in the care of the proper officers to consider the verdict. Late in the afternoon, they returned with their verdict. Their verdict was read by District Clerk Thomas A. Gay: "We the jury find the defendant guilty as charged in the indictment, and assess his punishment as three years in the State Penitentiary."[15]

Judge Moursund responded, "It is therefore considered and adjudged by the Court, that the defendant, E. Goodin is guilty of the offense of wantonly, and willfully, and with intent to injure the owner, cutting, injuring, and destroying a part of the fence, not his own as found by the jury, that he be punished as determined by the jury by confinement in the State Penitentiary for three years, and that the State of Texas house, and care for said defendant Elisha Goodin."[16]

Several days later, the official court action was read into the record. The defense appealed the case, and the judgment was suspended until acted upon by the state court of appeals. The appeal was acted on promptly, and the verdict of the Thirty-Third District Court in *State of Texas vs. E. Goodin* was affirmed.[17]

Menardville, from the day of the trial forward, enforced their hog law. Like the rest of the state, Menard County's open rangeland was soon fenced with barbed wire. Goodin was delivered to the penitentiary and served out his sentence. Warren Hunter, a teacher at Fort McKavett at the time, said that Elisha, on release from prison, returned to Menardville and searched for the nephew who testified against him. The nephew, of course, had fled Menard County for safer territory. Elisha loaded up his belongings, and he and his family left Menardville for California.[18]

Dr. Eber Dorr lived in Menardville for several years after the trial, then moved his family to Burnet. Later he returned to Austin and again established his medical practice. Eber Green Dorr died November 2, 1926, in Austin and is buried in the Oakwood Cemetery.[19]

When the special session made fence cutting and pasture burning a felony, there were fence-cutting trials that followed. Some of the prosecutions were successful in getting convictions, but most were not. The jurists' intense pursuit of justice, such as that of Judge A. W. Moursund, and time in prison for defendants found guilty significantly impacted the state's fence-cutting problem. Prison sentences for two men in Hamilton County, northeast of Menard, followed Goodin's three-year sentence. These two fence cutters, with names Post and Price, were tried, found guilty, and sent to prison the following year. Cases such as these had a real impact and changed men's desire to cut wire fences. Penitentiary time, coupled with several deadly encounters from Texas Rangers working hard cases, stopped the fence-cutting epidemic that Texas was experiencing.[20]

Chapter 15

Ranger Has a Dynamite Solution for Navarro County

> I exploded the bombs, and they were heard for miles around, the word was passed that there were bombs planted on all the fences, and these people were ready to believe it. That settled fence cutting activities in Navarro County. I was never again ordered to catch any more fence cutters after my bomb experiment, and that pleased me mightily.
>
> —Ira Aten, Texas Ranger

Navarro County is in North-Central Texas and bordered by Henderson, Freestone, Limestone, Hill, and Ellis Counties. Its northeast boundary is the Trinity River. The county was named after José Antonio Navarro, a friend of Stephen F. Austin and one of three Mexican signers of the Texas Declaration of Independence. Navarro was a strong supporter of annexation of Texas to the United States.

During the Civil War, sixty percent of Navarro County's white males were in the Confederate service. The Navarro Rifles were the first military company organized, and they fought with Hood's Texas Brigade in Virginia. After the Civil War and the period of Reconstruction in Texas, Republican governor Edmund Davis was voted out of office by the election of Democratic

Governor Richard Coke. With support from the new governor, the Texas legislature passed "An Act to provide for the protection of the frontier against the invasion of hostile Indians, or other marauding or thieving parties" on April 10, 1874. In this statute the legislature created the Frontier Battalion. For the first time in the state's history, the Rangers were institutionalized as a permanent force rather than the periodic, short-term ranging companies of the past. The words "Texas Ranger" were not used in this legislation or the new law. The title came from newspapers and the citizens of the state.

Governor Coke appointed John B. Jones, a Confederate veteran, former state legislator, and Navarro County businessman, as commander of the new Frontier Battalion. Then, following the election of Governor Oran M. Roberts in 1879, Jones was appointed the state adjutant general. As the state's adjutant general, Jones continued his direct command of the Frontier Battalion, making field inspections and ranging tours with his Rangers. In 1881, at the age of 46, John B. Jones suffered an early death. The Rangers' leader was gone, but his father, Colonel Henry Jones, was still living and maintained a prominent place in Navarro County's politics and activities.[1]

Farming was Navarro County's primary source of income after the Civil War, with cotton, corn, tobacco, and sweet potatoes the main crops. When barbed wire came to Navarro, there were 2,793 farms in the county in 1880, and the cattle and hog business was rapidly growing. Many of the farmers gave up the picket or rail fence and began using the new barbed wire to keep livestock out of their fields and crops. Cattlemen with money were buying land on the Navarro prairies and building barbed wire fences to protect their grass from the free-ranging livestock. Still, many cattlemen with small herds and some with large holdings refused to buy land. Why buy land and pay property taxes when you can buy more cows? These men held out for free grazing on the open range and would fight to the bitter end to keep the range open.[2]

Buying land and fencing property became controversial. In September of 1883, word came from Corsicana that a rail fence belonging to A. B. Love was destroyed; thirteen thousand rails were burned. More destruction near Corsicana followed in October. Colonel Henry Jones told the editor of the *Corsicana Observer* that his neighbor Fred Grimes had his fences cut.

The cutters left a note saying that Grimes's barbed wire fences would be cut again if it were rebuilt. Fred's father had received his land as a bounty grant from the state a generation ago for service in the Texas Army. The newspaper commented, "There may have been grounds for such action in the west, but now, such unlawful precedent was being established by vengeful and cowardly persons seizing the chance to destroy their neighbor's property often through pure spite."[3]

As the new year of 1884 began, fences were cut along the Navarro County line and in Hill County, east of Hubbard City. The *Hubbard City Times* reported that W. R. Moore had a pasture of 1,600 acres with fences cut. Two weeks before, signs had been nailed on his fence posts, telling him to take the fence down. He enclosed no roads, so he ignored the warnings. Soon another of his pastures with 1,500 acres was cut, and fence cutting spilled onto Navarro's big pastures.[4]

The Eighteenth Texas Legislature was called into the special session by Governor John Ireland and met in January of 1884 to work on the state's fence-cutting problems. The short session produced new laws, and the attention grabber was the statutes that made fence cutting and pasture burning a felony with mandatory penitentiary time. The free-range advocates had been beaten badly in the special session by the pasture men. Still, some men refused to admit defeat. A letter from a fence cutter in Navarro's neighboring Hill County appeared in the *Galveston Daily News* immediately after the special legislative session warning of a turbulent future for the area.

> The extra session has gone from Austin and has done no material good toward the poor. But the wealthy has a better showing still than the poor. Large pastures are yet permitted to be fenced, which is what this whole trouble came up over. Open range we want, open range we must have for large pastures ruin the poor. One man can keep stock up on the commons as well as another, and that is equal rights to all, and when land is thrown open except for what a man cultivates then we will stop clipping their damn wire and not before, and the man who reports a wire cutter had better keep himself clost or he will lose his scalp or the officer who puts himself to extra trouble to arrest a nipper. Give us liberty or give us death. What is ours we must have. There has been, but little wire cut in Hill County yet, but the nippers are ready, and large

pastures are being fenced around us, and hell will be to pay here soon. Shooting is a game two can play at, so in that respect nippers and fencer are equal and no other. If John Ireland trots himself out for governor he can't get our vote. We want a man who is for all men alike and not a man of the monopoly stripe. Our homes have been taken and given to the railroad men and they are permitted to come through and rob us by excessive freight, while their lands are exempt from taxation, but the wool hat boys had to foot the bill and pay the expense of the government. Done by order of the fence-cutters with a request that the News publish the same so that good men in office will not endanger their lives by trying to arrest or inform on one of our little squad.[5]

Following the governor's special called session and passage of new laws, local lawmen were making serious efforts to ferret out, arrest, and prosecute fence cutters. Grand juries overcame intimidation that occurred in the past and began indicting the cutters. Fence cutting slowed, becoming only an occasional occurrence in Navarro and North Texas counties. Governor Ireland finished his second term in office, focusing on land lease and land sales issues.

During the Civil War, Lawrence Sullivan Ross served the Confederacy and had risen to brigadier general. After the war, he was back in Texas farming near Waco. Ross began his political career when he was elected sheriff of McLennan County. He served as a delegate at the Texas Constitutional Convention, served as a state senator, and was elected governor when John Ireland finished his second term. Ross served as Texas governor from 1887 to 1891. During his time in office, he would deal with sporadic fence-cutting problems and land issues carried over from John Ireland's administration.[6]

As Sullivan Ross became governor, some free-range men decided the battle for free range should continue. Fence-cutting incidents flared up in 1887 north of the governor's McLennan County home, reaching all the way into Tarrant County. The Fort Worth newspaper reported that in March, Arch Earl's fence north of Navarro in Tarrant County was cut. The following month Earl's fences were cut again. The newspaper lamented:

The knights of the nippers seem not to have altogether disappeared from the land, as Mr. Arch Earl, a substantial farmer living near

Birdville, can testify. His pasture fence has been repeatedly cut of late by unknown parties. Last Thursday night, the miscreants cut it in more than a score of places. Their act was not only lawless but mean to a degree, since the fence enclosed but a small piece of land and does no inconvenience to anyone. From the nature of the case, fence cutting is a species of crime, the perpetrators of which are extremely hard to detect, unfortunately for the victims of their malice and the welfare of society.[7]

In April Governor Ross received a letter complaining of fence cutting near Whitney, a community in Hill County adjoining Navarro and the governor's home county, McLennan.

Dear Sir,

There is a spirit of lawlessness now existing in this part of our county that must be prevented. To wit: fence cutting. Between the 15th and 20th of the month, there have been cut, wire fences belonging to the following parties: Gatewood's pasture fence on the Nolan River near the Johnson County line, A. Walker's pasture near Fort Graham, J.M. Holt's farm fence, at or near Fort Graham, B.F. Faulkner's farm fence near Fort Graham and G.F. Sensing's sixty-five acre farm fence near Fort Graham was cut between every post. Mr. Sensing is a very poor man. He bought his land on credit last fall, and mortgaged his only work horse and milk cow to buy wire to fence the same, and had twenty-five to thirty acres planted in cotton, and on the night of April 20, the cowardly scoundrels cut his wire.[8]

Local law officers were busy. On June 16 Weatherford's newspaper, *The Sun*, reported "Joe Gayle's case charged with fence cutting is being argued this morning." A fence cutter had been indicted and was now being tried.

The next day, June 17, the *Fort Worth Daily Gazette* reported, "The jury in the case of the state against Joe Guyle, charged with fence cutting rendered a verdict of guilty, and assessed the punishment at one year in the penitentiary." Joe Guyle was on the way to the penitentiary. However, in the same issue of the newspaper, fence cutting was reported near Cleburne in Johnson County: "Mr. J. W. Terrell is reported to have said that fence cutters had recently destroyed about a half-mile of pasture fence for him.

Mr. J. W. Terrell is a prominent citizen living ten miles west of the city. The fence cutting was done at night, and no clue has yet been discovered as to who are the guilty parties."[9]

In July, a report came in from Bosque County, west of Navarro: "Charles Albert, an elderly farmer of good standing had his fence destroyed. The same party of cutters also laid low the fence of Colonel Thomas Griffin. W. H. Kingsbury three miles north of Albert also had his fence cut." The paper commented, "This country got its full share of these cowardly and rascally depredations several years ago, and it's safe to conjecture that if the wretches who committed these acts are ever discovered, they will be harshly and hurriedly dealt with."[10]

Local officials were committed to stop fence cutting, but it was extremely difficult to gather adequate evidence for conviction. Nothing short of capturing a cutter in the act of destroying a fence was sufficient. Northwest of Navarro in Van Zandt County, a large pasture owner, Dr. S. R. Russell, had his fences cut to pieces. His neighbors A. P. Sullivan and George Province's fences were also cut. Three Baker boys and a man named Mabray were arrested, indicted, and prosecuted. Their capture was one of those instances where the prosecution failed to make its case, presumably for want of hard evidence. The cutters were tried under the new state law, found not guilty, and released.[11]

In November of 1887, fence cutting broke out in Navarro County. Again, fences across the entire county were going down. Local officials were unable to stop the destruction. On the Navarro Prairie edge, R. A. Davis built a four-strand barbed wire fence around a thousand-acre pasture. Within two days it was cut in 3,500 places. The cutters systematically performed their work by removing two out of every three panels around the entire pasture. After his fences were cut, Davis received threats and a warning not to rebuild the fence. If he did the fence would be cut again, his pasture burned, and his water tanks emptied.

Lawlessness now overpowered the local law in Navarro. Prominent citizens who were Governor Ross's friends and supporters petitioned the governor for help. Those leading the call for the state's assistance were the former state legislator Colonel Henry Jones, the father of the

Frontier Battalion's late John B. Jones, Samuel R. Frost, the district judge for the Thirteenth Judicial District, and Navarro's Sheriff Hezekiah P. West, known as Ki West.[12]

With fence-cutting problems burning hot in Governor Ross's home territory, the situation demanded his attention. The Rangers should have been working these North-Central Texas fence-cutting cases earlier; however, Adjutant General Wilburn King and Rangers of the Frontier Battalion had their own problems.

The Frontier Battalion was created back in 1874 to protect the state against raiding Indians and thieves coming out of Mexico. Six Ranger companies were authorized, and the legislature initially appropriated $300,000 to fund the Frontier Battalion and county militias. Indians were finally pushed out of the state, and the Rangers focused on criminal activities, serving as the state's internal police force. Settlements had moved farther west, and legislators from the state's more populated areas were reluctant to continue funding Rangers to police a dwindling frontier.

When the Texas legislature convened in Austin for their twentieth session, they reduced the Frontier Battalion's already meager appropriation of $60,000 to $30,000. A reduction of men alone would not sustain the operation with this cut in funding. Ranger Company A was disbanded, followed by Company E's disbandment. Several months into the new fiscal year, Adjutant General King determined that it was impossible to continue his current operation with the state's appropriation. He sent Quartermaster Lamar Sieker to the field to disband Company C. Captain Sieker mustered the men out of Ranger Company C and sold their state-owned property. When Navarro County called for help with their fence-cutting problems, the Frontier Battalion had just been reduced by three companies, with fewer Rangers enlisted in each of the remaining companies.[13]

Governor Ross and Adjutant General King had to make a tough call on handling the destructive fence-cutting problems in Navarro and the adjoining counties. King decided to work with the local officials and plant a Ranger in Navarro County as an undercover operative if the governor agreed. Adjutant General King had used Rangers for clandestine work on fence cutting, with some success, during John Ireland's administration.

On May 12 Ranger Private John R. Hughes of Company D, headquartered in Uvalde County, received the assignment from Austin and departed for Navarro County as the state's undercover man. When he arrived, his first contact was with District Judge Samuel R. Frost. Working with Judge Frost and several other officials considered to be confidants, Hughes plotted undercover work to apprehend the cutters. He befriended a suspected fence cutter, expecting to gather names and learn fence-cutting plans in the Richland area down south of Corsicana. On May 26 Hughes penned a note from the Richland community to Quartermaster Lamar P. Sieker, his Austin supervisor. "I am now staying with a man who is suspicioned of cutting wire and have almost gained his confidence. He talks freely to me about stealing cattle. He and I stole a stake rope a few days ago and expect to kill a beef as soon as we eat up what we had on hand when I came. Then if he knows who the wire cutters are, I think he will tell me."[14]

Unfortunately, with a month of undercover work complete, John Hughes's plan of action came to an abrupt halt. Ranger Hughes gathered his belongings and traveled to Waco, where on June 13, he wrote Captain Sieker. "I was getting along very well with the fence cutters until someone made a confidant of the wrong man and gave the whole thing away. . . . They are the best-organized band that I ever worked after. They keep spies out all the time. The big pasture men live in town, and the people in the country are almost all in sympathy with the wire cutters."[15]

There had been recent problems among Navarro County's officials, specifically between Sheriff Hezekiah P. (Ki) West, Judge Beckham, and the county commissioners. Sheriff West had been fined $100 and sentenced to three days in jail for failing to sell the Chase Trading Company's attached stock, as Judge Beckham directed. Then, not long afterward, Sheriff West and his crew put down a carpet in the courthouse and turned over a large stove. The new carpet caught fire, and the courthouse was doomed to ashes before help arrived and extinguished the blaze. Now it appeared that the sheriff, a farmer and dairyman by trade whose lawman career was blessed with problems, had spilled the beans on Ranger Hughes's undercover work.[16]

John Hughes aborted his assignment and returned to the Ranger camp at Leona Springs in Uvalde County. His identity had leaked out to the fence cutters, and Hughes had to make a hasty retreat to save his hide. Fence cutting in Navarro County continued.

Two years earlier Rangers had broken up a band of fence cutters in Brown County with the undercover help of Ira Aten. Aten's good work hadn't gone unnoticed; he was now the First Sergeant of Ranger Company D. After Hughes's failed attempt to gather evidence in Navarro, Adjutant General King decided to send in another man to infiltrate the band of cutters operating in Navarro. Ranger Aten was chosen as the adjutant general's new undercover operative.

Ira Aten was called to Austin in July of 1888 for special detached duty. Frank Jones, his captain in Uvalde, was short of men and certainly wasn't happy to lose his sergeant. Aten arrived in Austin and met with Adjutant General King. After a briefing and receiving names of some of Navarro's fence cutters, he was sent to meet with Governor Ross. Aten later reported in his biography, "It was the first time I had ever seen the governor, as he had been elected to office the last election. His bald head and a friendly smile made him look like a good old farmer, and I liked him. He gave me instructions to go to Navarro County to arrest the fence cutters, leaving the method of doing so up to me. Stop the fence cutting at all costs were the only order he gave me."[17]

During his meeting with Governor Ross, Aten requested another Ranger as a backup for the Navarro undercover operation. Aten shared with the governor his experiences working undercover, alone in Brown County. The work would be dangerous and could turn deadly at any moment. The governor granted Aten's request. Jim King, also from Company D, was detached to work as his backup.[18]

Rangers Aten and Jim King began their mission on July 25, 1888, traveling by train to Waco. On arriving they bought a small mule, a one-eyed horse, and an old wagon. From Waco they traveled north, stopping in Mexia. There they read a newspaper report that said fence cutters were captured by Navarro County Sheriff Hezekiah West. Surprised at this news, the Rangers drove to Mexia's outskirts, unhitched the wagon in the brush, and made a temporary camp. King stayed with the wagon and Aten caught a train to Corsicana, where he met Judge Samuel Frost. The judge briefed Aten on what had occurred. Judge Frost was a large landowner and owned a ranch southeast of Corsicana near Eureka. Two men had turned state's evidence. Sheriff Hezekiah West learned from the two prisoners that the fence cutters would soon cut Judge Frost's fence. Sheriff West hid his deputies on the fence line at night and captured the cutters after the fence cutting began. In filling in details for Aten, Frost insisted, "Those men Sheriff West arrested were only petty cutters." The judge claimed the hard case fence cutters operated out of Richland, below Corsicana in the south-central part of Navarro. Those Richland cutters were still cutting Navarro County's fences. The judge wanted the Rangers to work on the continuing problem. Gathering information from the judge, Aten returned to Mexia.[19]

When the trial of the fence cutters captured by Sheriff Hezekiah West came, District Judge Frost disqualified himself and stepped down. His was the fence these men were cutting when captured. Lawyers of the Navarro County Bar chose Honorable G. H. Groce of Waxahachie as the special judge to hear the cases. There was difficulty selecting jurors, but finally a jury was seated and the trial commenced. Humphries, one of the men captured, was convicted and received a two-year prison sentence. On learning of the conviction, the Richland fence cutters were outraged and sent word they would come to Corsicana and release Humphries and his two partners. The pasture men from Navarro held an indignation meeting at the county's courthouse, daring the fence cutters to come to town and try to take the prisoners. Later the cutters held their own indignation meetings at the little community of Angus, six miles south of Corsicana, protesting the prosecution of their friends and the conviction of Humphries.[20]

When Aten began his Ranger career in 1883 with Company D, Captain Lamar Sieker was his first boss. Now Captain Sieker was the Frontier Battalion's quartermaster, managing the battalion's operations from Austin. Sieker again became Aten's contact and supervisor. Aten penned a letter to Sieker from Corsicana on August 21, 1888, reporting what he had learned and his mission's status. He expressed concern that the county sheriff's arrest of fence cutters in eastern Navarro County might cause those they were planning to catch to stop their malicious work. Aten ended the letter to his old boss and friend by venting his feelings. In this first communication with Sieker, he expressed his disgust for undercover work.

> We will do our best, although it may be a failure, nobody knows. However, I will ask it a special favor of the Adjutant Generals office never to ask me to work after fence cutters again under any and all circumstances, for it is the most disagreeable work in the world, and I think I have already done my share of it for the State Texas and her people. I don't see that I get any credit at the Adjutant General Office for such work, although I am satisfied they do the very best they can under the existing circumstances of the small appropriation made by the legislature. I would rather be in camp and only get $30 per month than get $500 per month and have to work after fence cutters. If it was any other detective business besides fence cutting where I would not have to be guilty of the same crime as themselves, I would like it. However, being I have consented to try these villains, I will ask for plenty of time, so don't get out of patience with me if we don't do anything right away.[21]

Ranger Aten had his say, put aside his dislikes temporarily, and began his new assignment. Arriving back at Mexia, Aten and King hitched the mule and one-eyed horse to their wagon. They traveled north through Wortham on toward Richland, where their undercover operation was to begin. They were disguised and presented themselves as two "out-of-work hoboes."[22]

On August 31 Aten wrote Captain Sieker in Austin, advising that he and King had traveled through Wortham and onward to Richland. But they put out a misleading story saying they were going to Kauffman County. A mile from Richland, they encountered what appeared to be a difficulty, but the whole incident was a ruse. Aten said,

> Our wagon tyre run off about a mile on the other side of Richland and in a little rough place our wagon wheel broke down. I had a hard time pounding off the tyre and then had to break the wheel with an ax. Another wagon and the man helped us move our wagon out of the road and sympathize with us very much due to it looking so reasonable to break down. I came on back to Richland on the mule and made a pitiful talk, and all seemed to sympathize with us in our break down. I went back to where I left Jim King and the wagon and fell in

with a noted fence cutter, and he told me where he thought we could get work making hay. We camped at our wagon that night, and the next morning drug it back to Richland on a pole and a large crowd of fence cutters all seen us, and I don't think any of them suspicioned us being detectives.

Aten and King set up their camp in a clump of big trees on the edge of Richland, and the fence cutters would drift by, checking them out. The adjutant general had provided Aten with names of some of the alleged cutters. When one came by camp and visited, the Rangers would identify him quickly. The two Rangers made friends and soon discovered the fence cutters would talk freely about fence cutting, as it seemed they didn't care who was around and listening. When night came, King would bring out his fiddle and play for the fence-cutters' dances. Aten described Ranger Jim King as a fiddling fool. He said he and King were having a great time at those dances but not catching any fence cutters. The Rangers fit in well with their new friends. Aten believed the cutters thought he and King were cutters too.

Having made their camp, the two Rangers set about finding jobs. King found work in the cotton gin baling cotton. Aten followed the lead of a new fence-cutting friend and tried to hire on with a hay harvesting crew but found they had filled all their jobs. He finally hired on picking cotton for the cotton gin owner's son, an alleged fence cutter. Later the two Rangers worked building a rock furnace around the cotton gin's boiler. That was a mighty unpleasant job. Busting, carrying, and setting large rocks all day was rough, hard work, and King and Aten weren't happy. After finishing the cotton gin's rock work, they took on any odd jobs they could find.

The fence cutters hung out at the cotton gin, and the Rangers were getting to know them quite well. Aten now realized it would take a very long time to gain their confidence. He heard several cutters say that only a fool would take in an outsider to help cut fences. These men were a tight-knit group and made clear they didn't need help. Aten described the cutters as mostly cowboys. He said some were small cowmen, owning as few as fifteen head, and some as many as two hundred heads of cattle along with a few cow ponies. Most owned small tracts of land, and several had a small field in cultivation. Aten said the fence cutters hated the farmers, or grangers as they call them. The grangers owned and fenced pastures, as did the prominent stockmen with extensive landholdings. T. C. Frost and old Buck Berry were exceptions. They were the only two big landowners who didn't fence. Anyone that had a fenced pasture was despised and suffered at the hands of the cutters. Aten claimed these men were a hard lot and thieves as well as fence cutters.[23]

Writing a letter to Captain Sieker in Austin, Aten reported on the fence cutters:

> They threaten to take up arms and go into Corsicana and take the fence cutters out of jail. That is all talk, they won't go. They had another indignation meeting over at Angus night before last. Most of the men that are holding these meetings are villains of the deepest dye and death would be too good for them. Now for the good citizens, what do they deserve? I will simply state a great many good citizens that don't own one-half as much as the parties that have been the instigators of all this fence cutting have had their fences cut from around their little horse pasture and from around their cultivated land where corn and cotton was planted. There is not a pasture of no kind up on the west side of the Houston & Texas Central Railway in this section where these wild and wooly wire cutters operate. Some have been cut time and again until the owners have no means to put up the wire anymore . . . all pastures are down, and this is called the free-range country. Many have took down their wire and rolled it up to save it from being cut. The fence cutters themselves have told me that while a man was putting up his fence one day in a hollow, a crowd of wire cutters was cutting it back behind him in another hollow back over the hill. They delight in telling all such things, and most of it is true . . . I have dropped on another plan to catch the villains much sooner, I think than working in with them. That is this, to have two or three of these good citizens put up their fence and I with one of the pasture men watch the fence every night with a double-barreled shotgun and if they cut the fence arrest them if possible and if we can't do that then take them the best way we can.[24]

Aten now lost all patience with his assignment, and in late August he got carried away writing a letter to his old boss in Austin. He told Sieker,

> These are my last fence cutters whether I catch them or not. I don't want to make a failure in this, but when I see that nothing can be done

rest assured I will report such to the Adjutant Generals Office for I had rather be in Hell than here. We have had to tell ten thousand lies already, and I know we won't get away without telling a million. Here after it will take $500 to get me to go out and see how many lies I can tell or be placed in a position so that I will have to tell them to keep from being murdered.[25]

Soon after this letter to Sieker, one of Navarro County's officials confided in the wrong person, saying Governor Ross had detectives in the county. Word got out, and the wire cutters stopped cutting fences. Suspicion appears to have fallen on the two out-of-work hobos. On September 17 Aten wrote another letter to Captain Sieker.

King and myself have given up our cotton contracts and went to work (or pretend to work) for the Love ranche about two miles west of Richland.... The Love ranche is run by two good men and they know who we are etc.... They only had about three miles of fence, and when the villains cut they cut down the three miles and it is still down. They will put it up whenever I say so but I don't deem it a wise idea for them to put it up yet, owing to us just going to work for them, and already suspicion lays upon us. Why the rascals would smell a rat, they would never cut the fence.[26]

Aten's plans soon changed. The ranchers rebuilt the ranch fences where four pastures cornered, with new lanes for driving cattle from pasture to pasture. Here Aten and King staked out the fence lines, hiding in the brush and sitting through the long nights waiting and listening for fence cutters to come in and clip the wires. Aten wrote to Sieker in Austin:

We have a double-barrel shotgun apiece, and if the villains cut the fence we are guarding, and they don't surrender when we call, somebody will most likely go away with their hands on their belly.... We have an excellent place to watch. It's at what is known as the Cross lanes where four pastures come together.... We can hear them cutting on either of the eight strings of fence from a half to 3/4 of a mile.... If such a thing is possible, I want to take the villains without killing them but I think a little more of my life than theirs, and I will stand a trial for murder before I will stand up and be shot down like a fool. I expect some of these days to stand up before a fire and shake off my six-shooter and Winchester, kick them in and watch them burn and go up to the Panhandle and settle down upon a little farm, go to nesting, be a better boy, and read my bible more. When I'm called upon by an officer to assist him in making an arrest, I will go out to the barn and get a pitchfork or the hoe and follow in behind the officer like old grangers do. So I don't want to kill these rascals and have any more deadly enemies on my trail than I already got.[27]

The pasture's four new lanes of fence were never cut. The cutters knew there were detectives in Navarro County and weren't willing to risk an encounter with Rangers. Aten and King were worn down from this long, unsuccessful assignment. Aten was looking for either a way out or to change the direction of his mission. The cutters wouldn't cut the fence he and King were watching at night, so Aten hatched a new plan, a dynamite bomb idea he began to mention in letters sent to Captain Sieker in Austin. His next letter introduced his plan he refers to as his "dinamite boom" (dynamite bomb).

Should I fail to get these rascals by watching the fence I am going to try my dinamite boom racket. I can't explain it to you by writing but don't you forget but what can be done if a man can get the dinamite in the right shape. I wish you would look up the law, captain to see if a man has a right or not to put dinamite along on his own fence and on his own land for its protection. It seems like a man ought to have the right whether the law gives it to him or not. Don't get frightened, for I haven't invested any money in dinamite yet, but have invested some money in about 15 cartridges each one loaded with buckshot and they will be better than dinamite booms if the rascals will only go to work as they have done heretofore.

I don't want to lay on a fence two or three years just to catch a few villains while dinamite booms could always be there for them whenever they took a notion to cut. But I haven't got the dinamite and don't know how I could get it unless I go to Chicago and join the anarchist and get them to fix it for me.

Well I'll quit writing none-sense. I know you will have a big laugh over my idea about the dinamite booms. This is a lengthy letter for me to write up to headquarters but having nothing to do this eve but sit down by the spring and think, I have written my thoughts.

Yours Very Re'ply, Ira Aten[28]

Although not found in Ranger correspondence, Aten says in his memoirs that he and King had made enough money picking cotton to fix their wagon wheel. The blacksmith repaired the wheel and they drove to Corsicana and sold the outfit for what they could get, then Jim King boarded the train returning to the Ranger's camp in Uvalde County. Aten said he traveled to Dallas and bought dynamite and caps.[29]

The following month Aten wrote his old friend at battalion headquarters advising that he had purchased dynamite and would execute his planned boom.

October 8, 1888

Capt. L. P. Sieker Quartermaster

I have only one more chance with any hopes of stopping fence cutting in this section, and that is with my dynamite boom as I call it. I have had the law examined, and it don't say anything about a man having the right to protect his property by the use of dynamite or by the use of a shotgun either. So I have come to the conclusion if it was not against the law to guard a fence with a shotgun to protect the property, it would certainly not be against the law to use dynamite for the same purpose. Therefore I have invested some money in dynamite and will, in a few days set my dynamite booms upon the few fences that have been put up recently.

Should the gov. or the Genl. disapprove of this, all you have to do is to notify me to that effect etc. They sent me here to stop fence cutting any way I could and to use my judgment how to do it. And that is what I am doing and if they will let me alone the balance of the month I will have my booms set and when the fence is cut why they will hear of it in Austin.

I cannot explain the workings of my boom thoroughly but can give you an idea of how it works. It is simply taking an old shotgun or musket put some powder in it as if for shooting, then sliding down a dynamite cap on the powder & then the dynamite on top of the cap until you think you have enough. Put cap on the gun ready for shooting, fasten wire to trigger & then to the bottom of a post that is not in the ground, place gun in a box made for the special purpose and place the box just under the ground and cover it up so it can't be seen. Of course cock the gun when you put it in the box and a fellow will have to handle it carefully. So you see by this post being very crooked and not in the ground and only supported by the wire and when wires are cut or torn down the post will fall and the end will fly up and give the wire at the bottom end of the post a jerk sufficient to shoot the gun off. The powder explodes the dynamite cap & and the cap explodes the dynamite and then small pieces of that gun will be found all over Navarro Co. Well, if it don't kill the parties that cut the fence, it will scare them so bad they will never cut another fence. Thinking it was a mere scratch shot they never got killed. When one of my booms once explodes, all fence cutters will hear of it most likely and then all a pasture man has got to say to secure the safety of his fence against these midnight depredations is: "I have dynamite booms along my fence." We have quit guarding the fence and now I am going to put on my dynamite boom and see what success I can have in that way.

Keep your ears pricked, you may hear my dynamite boom clear down there. I will use the greatest precaution and see that no innocent man gets hurt from them. They are dangerous in setting them unless a man is awful careful. However if I blow up, you will know I was doing a good cause. Not necessary to write more.

Yours Very Respt' ly
Ira Aten
"Co. D Rangers"[30]

Before Adjutant General King sent the two Rangers to Navarro County, dynamite played a deadly role in a northeastern United States incident. Chicago was an industrial center with tens of thousands of immigrants, mostly German, Bohemian, and Irish. Many worked nine- to fourteen-hour shifts for a pauper's wage, going to their job six days a week. By May of 1886, a general strike was called nationwide. In Chicago thirty to forty thousand workers went on strike, with citizens participating in the striking worker's demonstrations. A local anarchist group printed and distributed flyers calling for a protest at Haymarket Square, a busy commercial center. The rally and protest began peacefully the evening of May 4 with a crowd estimated at between six hundred and three thousand people gathered. Chicago's police arrived, marching in formation and demanding the crowd disperse. Someone tossed a bomb into the ranks of the policemen. The bomb, a brittle metal casting filled with dynamite, had a burning fuse. The fuse sputtered, then the exploding dynamite bomb scattered shrapnel among the police, killing one officer immediately and wounding six others. Police began firing on the demonstrators, some indiscriminately, and wounded many of their officers.

Sixty officers were known injured, and four were killed. It was difficult to determine how many demonstrators were injured because they were afraid to seek medical care. The *Chicago Herald* claimed that when the melee ended, about fifty dead or wounded citizens were lying in the street.[31]

Aten's early letters to his old friend Lamar Sieker had not been shared with Adjutant General King, or with the governor. But when Aten's last letter reached Austin, it immediately went up the chain of command. It hit a nerve at the state capital, prompting quick action. The Haymarket incident was fresh on everyone's mind, especially the state leadership. Governor Ross would have no Haymarket incident in Texas. There would be no dynamite bombs exploding and killing people in Navarro County. Ranger Aten's proposal to use dynamite brought him immediate orders to cease the operation and come to Austin. Aten sent another letter to Captain Sieker.

> Now I have your order to show them that I am forbidden to set the booms & they will not expect me to do it. You say I have failed. It is true. I have not cut fence with any of the villains & I don't want to as I would be harassed in the court for years, but the failure part was not because we did not try to work in with them but simply because the Adj. Department had ask some-thing of me which is an impossibility to do, hence I invented my boom racket to keep from making a failure. Of course I am forbidden from having anything to do with the dynamite boom directly & the order will be strictly obeyed.[32]

In his memoirs published in *Hunter's Frontier Times* many years after his dynamite boom plan was scrapped, Aten provided some more details about the end of his Navarro project. He had traveled to Dallas, purchasing about fifty pounds of dynamite and two dozen dynamite caps. Then he returned to Navarro County by train with dynamite in his luggage and the blasting caps in his vest pockets, not knowing he was violating federal law. Aten claimed he placed bombs on fences that had been cut several times before he boarded the train to Austin to meet the adjutant general. Adjutant General King frowned on his job and sent Aten to meet with the governor. On reporting to Governor Ross, Aten said,

> While I was telling him of my experiences and the finishing touches of my job, that bald head of his got redder and redder, and when I finished my story, it was on fire. I thought he was going to have me

court-martialed and then shoot me. I was to go back and take up the bombs. Instead, I exploded the bombs, and they were heard for miles around. The word was passed that there were bombs planted on all the fences, and these people were ready to believe it. That settled fence cutting activities in Navarro County. I was never again ordered to catch any more fence cutters after my bomb experiment, and that pleased me mightily.[33]

Tradition in stories handed down say Aten's boom racket put fear in the heart of fence cutters and stopped fence cutting in Navarro County. That's possible, but his stories may be stretching the truth a bit.

Aten's story wasn't the first story about dynamite bombs placed on fences as a deterrent to fence cutting. One account appeared in the *Fort Worth Daily Gazette* in December of 1886, about two years before Aten's Navarro County assignment. Seven months after the Chicago Haymarket Bomb incident, the *Daily Gazette* printed a story on the front page titled "Death to the Fence Cutters, A wonderful Invention by a Shrewd Yankee which will prove a Blessing to Texas." The story was published as a letter to the paper's editor, describing an interview with Mr. F. K. Wrenn, a New York chemist visiting Texas. The interviewer wrote the letter and signed his name K. Lamity, which indicated the letter was probably a spoof. Regardless, to some individuals the idea in the story probably sounded like an ingenious way to stop fence cutting. One of those, reading the letter to the Fort Worth newspaper and making a mental note of using dynamite as a fence-cutting solution, was probably Ira Aten.

This letter claimed a New Yorker chemist had come to Texas selling a dynamite bomb he invented and now manufactured. He called it the Angel Maker. The interview with the chemist supposedly occurred during a train ride from San Antonio to Temple. Mr. Wrenn had been trying to sell his device to the pasture men, who suffered from fence cutting. The interviewer's letter began with a description of the continuing fence-cutting problems in Texas. The story even mentioned Ira Aten by name, noting his undercover work in Brown County: "Recently the state rangers have made it lively, and one of their members, Ira Aten, has done more detective work in this line than any other man in Texas. But notwithstanding some of the rascals have been caught and quite a number shot and killed, the dirty work still continues, and it at last has been the active brain of a New York Yankee that has solved the *problem*."[34] Ranger Aten may have read the story in the Fort Worth newspaper about F. K. Wrenn's Angel Maker Bomb and decided to improvise his own.

After their undercover assignment in Navarro County, King and Aten returned to Company D at Camp Leona in Uvalde County and from there went their separate ways. Ranger Jim King would again do dangerous undercover work for the state down in South Texas. He tried to make a case against cattle thieves in Zavala County on the Rio Grande, but his efforts failed. His undercover work had to have been stressful. On September 4, 1889, he was discharged from Ranger service for drunkenness. In February of the following year, he was assassinated near Loma Vista in Zavala County. Three men— Fox Adams, George Rumfield, and William Speer—were charged with King's murder, but the district attorney couldn't get a conviction.[35]

Aten returned to Company D and continued his Ranger career. He was soon working on a complicated murder case with his old friend John Hughes. Three women and a boy were taken from San Saba, brutally murdered on the Rio Grande, and their bodies thrown in the river. Aten and Hughes built a case with circumstantial evidence, and Richard "Dick" Duncan was indicted, convicted, and hung. This was an unusual case for those early days; it was prosecuted and won on circumstantial evidence.

The adjutant general then sent Aten to Fort Bend County, where he was cast into a deadly feud between two factions known as the Jaybirds and Wood Peckers. Following a shooting war and a visit to Fort Bend by Governor Ross, Aten was appointed sheriff of Fort Bend County. Later, he traveled to Castro County, purchased a tract of land in the Texas Panhandle, and took up farming. He married and again was appointed as sheriff, this time of Castro County. Soon he was employed as manager of the Escarbada Division of the vast XIT Ranch, staying with the ranch for ten years. In 1905 he moved his family to Imperial County, California, where he established the Calipatria Ranch. From his new California home, Aten served on the Imperial Irrigation District board and had a role in assuring the construction of the Boulder Dam. Aten became a civic leader, bank director, and philanthropist. To his last day he was a strong advocate for law and order.[36]

Epilogue

Joseph Glidden, a DeKalb, Illinois, farmer, patented and manufactured a fence wire in 1874 with sharp prickly barbs. Soon the Glidden barbed wire was brought to Texas and sold to cattlemen by Henry Sanborn. The November 19, 1875, issue of the *San Antonio Daily News* took note of the wire's arrival and commented, "This Glidden barbed fence is exactly the thing our hardy frontiersman has been sighing for." Glidden's wire was the first barbed wire to be sold in Texas, and soon it was used throughout the state. Henry Sanborn sold $1 million worth of Glidden barbed wire out of his Houston warehouse in 1883. It was also in 1883 that fence cutting and the barbed wire war erupted in Texas. Glidden's vicious wire with sharp points began a new chapter in the history of fences, cattle ranching, and farming in Texas.[1]

Strong cattle prices, cheap Texas land, and barbed wire's ease of use as a low-cost fence material presented unique opportunities for investors. Eastern investors with big money arrived in Texas buying large tracts of land and cattle, and so did foreigners. The British, seeing the big profits, came to invest, and Texas cattlemen with a vision of the future began buying large tracts. But many Texas stockmen who couldn't imagine what the future held argued, Why spend money on land and pay taxes when I can buy more cattle and graze them free? Those who refused to buy land and whose livestock grazed free on the open, public domain soon discovered that the new fences were removing their access to grass and water. Anger and bitterness over barbed wire fences with the loss of free grazing and obstruction of travel soon brought fence cutting.

By 1883 fence cutting was occurring throughout the state, with the worst problems along a line of frontier counties running from Clay in the Red River Country down into South Texas. Early hotspots were Clay, Brown, and Medina Counties. As problems with the fences grew, a criminal element joined the revolt against barbed wire. Not only did they destroy fence, but soon they were also burning properties, killings livestock, and making death threats. Deaths followed but they were usually the fence cutters. On reviewing all sources, the number of deaths over fences and fence cutting appear be comparable to deaths in several of the bloody Texas feuds of the 1860s and 1870s. Fence cutters were killed, but lawmen also died as fence cutting peaked. The destruction, protests, violent encounters, and killings described in this book are but a few of the incidents that occurred.

Beyond trying to count the lives lost, it is equally difficult to find an accurate accounting of the financial and economic cost of fence cutting in Texas.

The *Fort Worth Daily Gazette* reported property values decreased by $30 million, and the *Galveston Daily News* said actual fence-cutting damages were $20 million. The Galveston paper claimed loss of fences in Brown County alone was $1 million. During a debate in the 1884 called legislative session, Representative T. L. Odom told the house members there was $10 million worth of fences destroyed and a $100 million economic loss to Texas. That's quite a sum of money converted into today's dollars.[2]

Fence cutting probably began soon after barbed wire arrived in Texas, but it was first cited as a problem in the state's large newspapers in 1879. In 1881 John H. Belcher fenced twenty-seven thousand acres in Montague County and had his fences cut in 1882. Fence cutting peaked in 1883 and 1884. Clay County and its neighbor Montague experienced violence in 1883, with Clay claiming the first fence cutter killing covered by the major newspapers across the state. Fence cutting was now statewide, but the violence in Clay County, violence in Brown County, and rampant fence cutting in Medina and Runnels Counties pushed Governor John Ireland into calling the Texas legislature into special session to find a solution and stop the destruction.

Governor John Ireland, Adjutant General Wilburn H. King, the Texas legislature, and Texas Rangers all share credit for bringing an end to the barbed wire war. After new laws were passed and the legislative session adjourned, most of the state's fence cutting ended, and the state's newspapers lost interest. Still, after the special session there were several counties where fence cutting persisted and cutters continued their destruction. At this point the Rangers stepped in. The death of several fence cutters during violent clashes with Texas Rangers made an impression on those still thinking about cutting fence. The state's barbed wire war was actually short if we consider only the violent part occurring in 1883, 1884, and 1885.

Big landowners showed little compassion for the free-range stockmen, small farmers, or homesteaders. But the small landowners and the free-range men living on the frontier were an essential part of the rural community's businesses. Over 84 percent of Texas's population was rural in the 1880s, and the majority of this population resented the big landowners and their fenced pastures. It's important to note these citizens were the sheriff's constituents, and this created big problems for state officials in Austin and for the Rangers when they tried to end the barbed wire war.

Besides the pasture men, the Rangers had very few friends during the barbed wire war. At times Rangers were in conflicts with the counties' sheriffs. Such was the case in Brown County. The governor and the Rangers received no support from Brown County Sheriff William N. Adams. Adams was popular with the citizens in Brown County, and he wanted no help from Governor Ireland or his Rangers. His popularity is reflected in the elections. Adams was first elected in 1882 and served three terms as Brown County sheriff. He retired, then was elected and served two terms as the state senator for Brown County. Rangers working fence-cutting problems were enforcing the state laws and performed commendably under difficult circumstances.[3]

The district courts provided little assistance during the barbed wire war. Initially fence cutting was only a misdemeanor, but the legislature made it a criminal offence with severe penalties in 1884. District attorneys and judges had difficulties as it was nearly impossible to get an indictment in the district courts unless a witness actually observed fences being cut. It was even tougher getting a fence cutter convicted of the crime. Witnesses were threatened. When the defense lawyers succeeded in getting continuances in a trial, witnesses and evidence quickly disappeared. Cases with continuances would drag on and over time would be dropped from the court's docket. Very few fence cutters were found guilty and spent time in prison.

There were Rangers from the early years of rangering who harbored bitter feelings about the state's land policies and barbed wire fences, which closed the free range. Their sympathy was for the free-range men. Big Foot Wallace (William A. Wallace), the folk hero and an old Ranger, argued that the use of the state's land and grass should be for the men who fought the Indians and opened the frontier for settlement. Big Foot had strong feelings about the free range and fences and made his feelings known. As the barbed wire war peaked, the January 10, 1884, issue of the *San Marcos Free Press* accused Wallace of being an instigator of fence cutting.

Ranger Captain Dan Roberts, the retired and aged Indian fighter, lamented the plight of the frontiersmen in his book, *Rangers and Sovereignty*. Writing about the fence cutters, Roberts poured out sympathy for the free-range men. He said, "Many men on the frontier who thought they were helping to conserve a public interest in the public domain of Texas, began to see that capital had shut out small interests. . . . Nearly all frontiersmen were poor in the purse. . . . Texas was liberal to capital, but all her people didn't share her liberality in a measure that they had earned . . . frontiersmen resented being fenced out on the range and revolted in a manner that made them criminals. . . . They got epitaphs piled high on them, as law breakers and undesirable citizens and had to subside as felons. . . . The poor fellow that made the land available only got a little mock turtle soup."[4]

As we examine the cause of Texas's barbed wire war, we could cover it broadly, saying it was the result of the state's abundant cheap land, cheap wire for fencing material, and a highly profitable livestock industry. Land was sold cheap by the state of Texas, with the land and its grass and water a bargain for stock raisers. Cattle grazing and fattened on good native grasses were profitable, selling for high prices, and livestock and grass could be protected by fences built with the new barbed wire. The barbed wire fences could be built for half the cost of lumber or native materials. Inside this broad coverage, specific issues prompted fence cutting. Looking closer for causes we find the issues that follow.

Soon after barbed wire arrived in Texas, this wire with sharp points was criticized for injury to livestock. Cattle cut by barbed wire often were infested with screwworms and died. When a man's cow or horse ran into or became entangled in a barbed wire fence, it was injured or crippled, and many were never again fit for use. There was an attempt to outlaw barbed wire fences soon after barbed wire arrived in Texas. The states legislature considered the issue but only required that boards called blinders be hung on the top wire of the fences for livestock to see.

Fences were built across roads and closed trails that settlers used to travel to business centers, courthouses, churches, and water sources. Mail routes were obstructed. Barbed wire's closing of roads and trails that had existed over the years was sure to bring fence cutting. Obstruction of travel quickly became a big issue.

The Texas legislature passed the Fifty Cent Act in 1879 and the state began selling the state's land for fifty cents an acre. The stated purpose was to pay public debt and fund a permanent school fund. But large purchases and rampant land speculation followed. This cheap sale of state land brought the rapid purchase and fencing of large tracts by well-to-do Texas cattlemen and out-of-state investors.

The majority of the state's citizens were strongly opposed to eastern bankers, corporations, European syndicates, and wealthy Texas cattlemen buying and fencing large blocks of the public domain. There was a hatred of corporatism, as the public called it. A rural newspaper, the *Marlin Ball*, noted, "The wire fence cutting troubles are only one of the many evils growing out of the fallacious and dangerous policy of the state in selling off its domain in such large tracts, creating principalities, Paschalis and baronets among a few capitalists and arousing a spirit of agrarianism among the poorer class."[5]

When the big pastures were fenced, cowboy labor used by large cattle operations was reduced, leaving men without jobs. Fencing land kept cattle from drifting south out of their home range during winter storms. The big spring roundups that had the joint participation of many cattle operations soon stopped. And fenced pastures eased raising, gathering, and working cattle all to the benefit of the owner. Fewer hired hands were needed. Unemployed cowboys soon were searching for employment. Some became fence builders, some found other jobs, and some of those harboring bitterness became fence cutters.

Cattle thieves and an outlaw element became part of the fence-cutting movement. Skinning for hides, blotching brands, and stealing cattle that drifted many miles south from their home range in cold winter months was stopped by pasture fences. And the stealth of rustlers entering and stealing

Epilogue

cattle in fenced pastures was difficult compared to stealing cattle off the open range.

Fence cutting was only a misdemeanor offense when the cutting started. In the beginning some men of influence expressed favor or ignored the problem, and many citizens winked at the crime of fence cutting. Then damages and criminal violence became a statewide crisis. The magnitude of damages changed opinions, and there was a public cry for help from the state governments.

There were often conflicts between the cattlemen and homesteader or small farmer who moved onto the open, free range and resided on the frontier. Over the years cattlemen claimed range rights on large areas but had no legal standing or ownership. Once barbed wire arrived and land tracts were sold, it was the homesteaders and small operators who were surrounded by large tracts of purchased land and fenced in. Being surrounded by barbed wire fences, they often became fence cutters.

The great Texas cattle drives to the northern markets were obstructed, then stopped by barbed wire fences. Texas cattle drives were forced to moved west from the Chisholm Trail and follow the Western Trail to avoid fences. But soon barbed wire ended drives up the Western Trail, and the cattlemen were at the mercy of the railroads.

Cattlemen and sheepmen had problems driving livestock purchased or sold from one ranch to another distant ranch, or to a railyard for shipping when ranch land was fenced. Barbed wire fences obstructed movement of livestock across ranches. The special legislative session solved this problem by passing a law requiring unlocked gates every three miles on a fence line. These three-mile gates were for driving livestock across country to another ranch and retrieving cattle that had broken through a fence.

English and Scottish investors were purchasers of large land tracts that were soon fenced. Texans resented these Europeans, their culture, and their large land purchases. The British landowners and their managers were an aristocratic and privileged class, and their dress and customs showed it. Their aloofness, demeanor, and dress—with hunting caps, velvet jackets, corduroy pants, and patent leather boots—amazed the cowhands. The cowboys they employed quickly discovered the Brits didn't understand the Texas cattle business and were difficult to work for.

The Greenback Party, known by many as the fence cutters party, had a large following in Texas during the barbed wire war. The Greenbacks were strong advocates for free range and for the free-range men. They bitterly opposed corporations and large land sales and came to the defense of the fence cutters. They said fence cutting was a war between capital and labor and likened selling of large Texas land tracts to the communistic movement in England, socialism in Germany, and communism in France. George W. Jones was their leader. He recently had been defeated by John Ireland in the states governor's race.

The newspapers, especially the large papers, gave regular statewide coverage to the fence-cutting incidents across the state. Fence cutting was the newspapers' sensational topic of the day, with damages and secrecy stoking the interest of their readers. The newspapers' coverage also appears to have stoked the efforts by the fence cutters.

Taxes were an issue of the time. Large out-of-state cattle corporations and European investors owning large land and cattle operation avoided taxes; large Texas cattlemen often were underassessed on their property. Farms and small cattle outfits rendered their property, paid their taxes, and struggled. Frequent were the claims of inequity in taxing.

Cattlemen and investors buying large tracts of land often fenced and enclosed state land or railroad land, which they neither owned nor leased. An investor would buy a large tract of state land made up of multiple surveyed 640-acre blocks, then build fence around the entire tract purchased. In the process he also enclosed the adjacent checkerboarded 640-acre blocks of railroad land that had previously been available for free grazing. Rarely was it possible to buy the adjacent sections of land his fence now surrounded. This became a scorching issue when discovered and was publicized and editorialized in the newspapers across the state.

The state's land issues, which were a significant contributing factor to the barbed wire war, continued even after new laws were passed and the fence-cutting war ended. In 1887 there were 3.5 million acres of public land still unlawfully fenced, and open state lands were grazed without leases or the state's consent. More laws were passed that increased penalties for the unlawful use of public land, but problems continued into the early 1900s.[6]

As Texas's barbed wire war was ending, the big land and cattle operations' growth and profits reached their peak. Barbed wire, which brought these big operations into existence, now helped bring their demise. Cattle prices were down, and ranch lands were overstocked and overgrazed. The year 1885 brought a severe winter. A hundred miles of barbed wire drift fence in the Texas Panhandle stopped thousands of cattle drifting south in the snow and ice of a blizzard. Reaching the drift fence, cattle stopped, piled up, froze, and died. Another disastrous winter followed in 1886–1887, and cattle die-off occurred in other parts of Texas. Cattle surviving the harsh winter were in poor condition and unfit for slaughter; most were not marketable. Barbed wire stopped the northern cattle drives, so cattlemen and the big investors now were at the mercy of the bankers and the railroads. In 1888 the nation's leading livestock journals finally brought down the curtain on large pastures and their barbed wire fences. The big ranches were soon being subdivided, with land sold

Epilogue

off in smaller tracts to new purchasers, many of whom were farmers. As the barbed wire war ended, Eclipse Windmills were arriving in Texas and provided ground water to these smaller tracts of land, where no water was available in the past. In the early 1900s the new net wire, or wolf-proof wire, as it was known, came into existence and became popular. It was used along with barbed wire on Texas sheep and goat ranches.

As ranching practices in Texas changed, barbed wire found a new use on a global scale. It became an instrument of war and imprisonment. During the 1899–1902 Boers War in South Africa, barbed wire was used for construction of prison compounds. Then World War I arrived and barbed wire became a strategic military weapon used as barricades and as a weapon of entanglement. Corpses of soldiers hanging in barbed wire entanglements became a memory of horror for many of the men who survived the war. As the Great Wars were fought, barbed wire was used in prison compounds. Nazy Germany's barbed wire enclosures found at Auschwitz and Buchenwald's death camps left horrible memories of barbed wire impoundments. In America, the industry that John Gates and Isaac Elwood built and brought to prominence played a big role in the defense of democracy. The American Steel & Wire Division of the United States Steel Corporation supplied America and its allies front line defenses with great quantities of entanglement wire.[7]

Today the great benefactor of barbed wire that fenced the state is Texas agriculture. Farming and ranching has grown and exceeds all the frontiersmen could have imagined. Longhorn cattle are gone (some are raised as a hobby), and quality beef and dairy cattle are found across the state. In 2021 the Texas state comptroller of public accounts reported nearly $25 billion in cash receipts for Texas agriculture. Cattle represented the state's top agriculture commodity, generating 40.4 percent of the cash receipts. The US Department of Agriculture reported Texas had 247,000 farms and ranches, more than double that of the next two states.[8]

There are over 450 patents of barbed wires recorded today, but on review, there are over 2,000 varieties and designs of barbed wire that have been found by barbed wire collectors. Of the many patents and all the wires manufactured, Glidden's barbed wire, manufactured in 1874 and brought to Texas, proved the most practical and successful of the wires sold. Most barbed wire on ranches today are versions of the Glidden wire. Wire fence and the barbed wire war that followed dramatically changed the Texas landscape and farming and ranching. Barbed wire is still used on farms and ranches across Texas today, and yes, there are still fence-cutting incidents across the state.[9]

Acknowledgments

Collecting material and writing a book of history is not the work of one person. Such a book requires the contribution of many individuals. Doing justice to those who provided support and made contributions becomes a daunting task when the research extends over a long period. Such is the case here. My collecting of barbed wire history began during my college years with encouragement from William H. Pool, PhD, who taught history at Southwest Texas State College (Texas State University today). Dr. Pool was a personal friend of mine. I have collected interviews, barbed wire stories, and records ever since then, and recalling and properly acknowledging all who contributed along the way has become a daunting task. Where to begin?

For the recent years I owe a big thanks to two well-known Western historians and prolific authors who have helped me. Bob Alexander, friend and Western writer, promoted my barbed wire interests, lining up speaking engagements and encouraging me to write this book. When I slowed down, Bob was there to give me a push. Chuck Parsons, a researcher, writer, and editor of Western histories, heard one of my presentations on fence cutting and referred me to a national journal where the paper was published. Both men were there when I had questions or needed help.

Thanks go to Rick Miller of Harker Heights, Texas. Rick is a former lawman and attorney and is now retired as county attorney for Bell County. He is an authority on Texas outlaws and lawmen and has authored a collection of well-researched books about men who made Wild West history. Rick was there when I needed help finding and deciphering legal documents relating to several fence cutting incidents and an assassination attempt.

Max Brown of Ringgold, Texas, a member of the Montague County Historical Commission, provided valuable information on North Texas ranching and cattle history. Max introduced me to Lucille Glasgow of Petrolia, Texas, at a Clay County Historical Society meeting in Henrietta, Texas. Mrs. Glasgow was an encyclopedia of Clay County history and keeper of historic documents at the old Clay County Jail Museum.

Traveling across Texas, I've spent hours in county and district clerk's offices poring through old records. Clay County District Clerk Dan Slagle and assistant Gail Jarvis went beyond the call of duty pulling records and later spent time on the phone answering my questions and guiding me to needed information. Dan's ancestors were some of the early arrivals in North Texas; he knew the country and its history well.

Frederica Wyatt of Junction, Texas, was the keeper and primary reservoir of Kimble County's history for many years and was knowledgeable of local histories in the surrounding area. For many years she served as secretary of the Edwards Plateau Historical Association, which includes twenty-one Central Texas counties. Her guidance, contacts, and assistance in gaining access to historical sites in the Texas Hill Country were invaluable.

In my early search for barbed wire war history, Tai D. Kreidler, PhD, at Texas Tech University provided invaluable help. Tai took time from his busy week guiding me through the university's Southwest Collection / Special Collection Library's materials. Monte L. Monroe, PhD, was the archivist for the Southwest Collection / Special Collections Library and was there with Tai to see all my needs were met.

Roy T. Holt was born in 1897, growing up in Coleman County, the heart of Texas fence cutting territory. Years before I began work on my book, Roy Holt earned his master's degree at the University of Texas studying under Drs. Eugene Barker and Walter Prescott Webb. His fellow students included J. Evetts Haley and William C. Holden. Roy made his career in public education. Over the years he served as a history teacher, principal, and school superintendent. He loved Texas history and spent countless hours interviewing and corresponding with old-timers still living who had witnessed the barbed wire wars. Roy was a grassroots historian, publishing in magazines and journals. Today his papers are preserved in Texas Tech University's Southwest Collection at Lubbock. I have drawn heavily on Roy Holt's research; I owe him a thank you and regret that I never had an opportunity to meet the gentleman.

Garland Richards grew up and resides on the old Fort Chadbourne Ranch, owned by his great-great-grandfather T. L. Odom. Garland and Lana, his wife, have a passion for family history and have placed the old historic fort and Odom Ranch headquarters in the Fort Chadbourne Foundation. Today this family's privately funded museum is a tremendous source of West Texas history. Garland and Ann Pate, the museum's archivist, were important sources of information for this book.

Bradford Boehme is a member of the Medina County Historical Commission and a descendant of early Castroville settlers. Bradford provided help finding material on the fence cutting incidents and law enforcement in Medina County and provided old court papers documenting early incidents.

Roy B. Young, friend and retired editor of the *Wild West History Association Journal*, edited and published one of my first barbed wire articles and offered suggestions that stayed with me over the years.

Suzanne Campbell has retired as head of Special Collections and Programs at the Porter Henderson Library at Angelo State University. She provided valuable support. On Suzanne's retirement, Shannon Strum continues the support for researchers and writers as did her predecessor.

Donaly E. Brice, now retired from the Texas State Library and Archives Commission, guided me to material buried in the state archive's records and

Acknowledgments

answered questions. The staff of the State Library were always there assisting my search, pulling records, and making copies of documents.

A thank you goes to Michael Oldham and Delbert Trew at the Devil's Rope Museum in McLean, Texas. This historical museum of barbed wires and fencing tools is a treasure and an educational experience for visitors. It is also headquarters and a meeting site for Texas barbed wire collectors.

Byron A. Johnson, director, and Christina Stopka, assistant director of operations at the Texas Ranger Hall of Fame and Museum in Waco, were there to help when I called.

In compiling the research for this book, many individuals were consulted. Those providing special materials used in this book follow: Frederica Wyatt Burt, interview by the author, May 2008, Junction, Texas; Frank J. Douthitt, telephone interview, December 1, 2014; Harry Douglas Jobes, Junction, Texas, author's paternal grandfather; Roger Q. (Jake) Landers, interview by the author, May 4, 2019, Menard, Texas; Nannie Nichols, interview by author, June 1963, Fredericksburg, Texas; Ann Pate, historian, Fort Chadbourne Foundation, September 30, 2011, and March 7, 2013, at Fort Chadbourne, Bronte, Texas; Garland Richards, descendant of T. L. Odom and owner of Fort Chadbourne Ranch, September 30, 2011, March 7, 2013, and July 24, 2021, at the Fort Chadbourne Museum, Bronte, Texas; Neuman Smith, October 5, 1995, EPHA meeting, Menard, Texas; Edmunds Travis, interviewed February 1967, Austin, Texas; Robert Lee (Johnny) Whitworth, interviewed in 1958 at Rocksprings, Texas; John Miller Winslow, October 6, 2001, (EPHA meeting, London, Texas, and December 2001 at Menard, Texas.

Other individuals contributing in various ways follow: Janell Appleby, Mason County Historical Commission, Mason, Texas; Dennis and Nell Ann McBroom, Trails and Tales Museum, Nocona, Texas; Judge Tommie Sappington, Montague, Texas; Ruth Cooper, Runnels County Historical Commission, Winters, Texas; Edmunds Travis, Austin, Texas; Jan Robinson, Jack County clerk, Jacksboro, Texas; Frank J. Douthitt, attorney, Henrietta, Texas; Robert J. Duncan, Dallas, Texas; Betty Turner, co-curator, Pioneer City County Museum, Sweetwater, Texas; Jane Hoerster, Mason, Texas; Fran Hoerster, Mason, Texas; James Hays, MD, Early, Texas; Carole Goble, Burnet, Texas; Donald M. Yena, San Antonio, Texas; Robert Feuge, PhD, Scottsdale, Arizona; Pat Malone, Peru, Illinois; Doug Duke, Leander, Texas; Bill and Denise Etherton, San Antonio, Texas; Candice Ducoin, Georgetown, Texas; Paul Noack, Austin, Texas; Ginger Andrew, Junction, Texas; Gene Hall Miller, Llano, Texas; Judith Anne Greer McCoy, San Saba, Texas; Sherry Duncan, DVM, Menard, Texas; Jake Landers, PhD, Menard, Texas; J. D. Evans, Henrietta, Texas; Bob Chamblee, McKinney, Texas; Dale Duggan, Ballinger, Texas; Harold L. Hagemeier, Amarillo, Texas; Tammy Burleson, Runnels County District Clerk, Ballinger, Texas; Linda Cook, Ballinger, Texas; Janice McKenzie,

Decatur, Texas; Warren Striker, archivist, Panhandle Plains History Museum, Canyon, Texas; Lynn S. Blankenship, San Saba County Historical Museum Foundation, San Saba, Texas; Judge John M. Winslow, Menard, Texas; Jan Davis, district clerk, Fredericksburg, Texas; Shelia Norman, Bell County District Clerk; Nannie Duderstadt Nichols, Fredericksburg, Texas; David Williams, San Saba, Texas; Danese Murray, librarian, Menard, Texas; Clay Riley, Brownwood Public Library, Genealogy Branch, Brownwood, Texas; Bill and Denise Etherton, San Antonio, Texas; Jackie Reese, Western Histories Collections Librarian, University of Oklahoma, Norman, Oklahoma; Molly Hults, collections manager, Austin Public Library's History Center, Austin, Texas; Ernest Woodard, Pecos County Historical Commission, Fort Stockton, Texas; Ann Daggett, Annie Riggs Memorial Museum, Fort Stockton, Texas; Clifford R. Caldwell, historian and author, Kerrville, Texas; Ron DeLord, historian and author, Georgetown, Texas; Marti Dryk, PhD, Austin, Texas; Millie Riley Williams, Burnet, Texas; Harold J. Weiss Jr., PhD, historian and author, Leander, Texas; Janice Dunnahoo, chief archivist, Historical Society of Southeast New Mexico, Roswell, New Mexico; Lynnette Cen, Texas State Historical Commission, Austin, Texas; Lona Keetch, Dallas, Texas; Brian Keith Anderson, Hillsboro, Tennessee; Ralph Terry, Coleman County historian and author; Chester and Denise Sams, Hemphill, Texas; Kurt House, historian, San Antonio, Texas; Will Moursund, attorney, Round Mountain, Texas; Daniel Jones, Gillespie County judge, Fredericksburg, Texas; and Pansy Benidict, Fredericksburg, Texas. For those whose names I have overlooked, I offer my sincere apology.

Ronald Chrisman, director of the University of North Texas Press, has guided my manuscript through the publication process with knowledge, skill, and patience. He produced a well-designed book with a component of Texas history I am proud to see published. Amy Maddox, managing editor at the press, edited the manuscript and was great to work with. Thank you, Ron and Amy. Dave Johnson—friend, Western historian, and author—was there to prepare the book's index.

Brian and Samuel, my two sons, were there to help. Brian on occasions chauffeured me across Texas, searching for stories and helping with research. Over the years Sam kept my PCs, which often crashed, up and working. He always arrived to "fix it" when I called for help.

Setting me on course to appreciate Texas history were my mother and father, Blanche and Noble Jobes. Their families were early Texas arrivals. They, like their ancestors, raised their family ranching. They suffered through droughts, government destruction of the wool and mohair market, and erratic cattle prices.

Last but most important, a big thank you for Cheryl Smith Jobes, my loving wife, for her support and forbearance. She was patient and understanding, read my work, and encouraged me to finish the book.

Appendix 1

Governor John Ireland's Message to the Eighteenth Legislature Special Session at the City of Austin, Texas, January 8, 1884

The special session of the Eighteenth Texas Legislature called by Governor John Ireland convened in Austin, Texas, on January 8, 1884. There were issues besides fence cutting in the governor's call, but the governor's main charge was "To Consider, and Provide a Remedy for Wanton Destruction of Fences." That portion of his message to the Senate and House of Representatives follows.[1]

The first subject to which to invite your attention is the fence cutting troubles. There may have been, and doubtless were, causes of complaint, in some instances, against the action of large pasture men; but they amount to nothing but excuses. On the other hand pasture men found excuses for acts neither justified or excused by law. Indeed, they were simply excuses on either side. As for justification, there were none.

If the law-abiding people had acted promptly, at the beginning of these troubles, the law would have proven ample. But the mistaken policy of standing back prevailed. As the good people stood back, the lawless advanced, until the small penalty affixed to the offence of fence cutting is inadequate to stop the evil. If the law had been put in motion the entire able-bodied force of the State would have been invoked, if necessary, to execute it.

There is not, and has not been, necessary means placed at the disposition of the Executive to meet extraordinary emergencies. He cannot employ detectives; for he neither has the lawful authority nor money to pay such a force. He cannot call into active military service a single man, except in the case of rebellion, insurrection or invasion; and even in such emergencies he has not, at his disposal, the money to feed, move, or equip a military force. If he should declare fence cutters as outlaws, as has been suggested by a learned district judge, the country would still be in ignorance as to who were the outlaws. Besides, such proclamation would not make any man an outlaw, and would violate Sec. 20, Art. 1, of the Constitution.

Rewards have been offered in all cases, of course bearing some proportion to the punishment affixed by law to the offense.

There are no effective laws in republican governments without moral forces behind them. It is an erroneous idea that the man whose fence has not been cut has no interest in the contest between the neighbor, whose fence has been cut, and the person who cut it. There is not and cannot be a violation of the law, and individual rights, without affecting each and every individual and the whole body politic. It is only a question of time when the lawless disease will affect the whole. A man who can educate himself to the idea that it is not wrong to cut and destroy the fence of another, will soon reach the point in his vicious schooling that will make him believe the corn crib, the barn, the factory, the dwelling, the bank, the law office, printing office, and in fact, all the material wealth of the country to which he is inimical must also go. There is not a single grievance, real or supposed, for which there is not a peaceful remedy. If a man encloses public lands without paying for them, they can and should be punished under the law. If men enclose public highways, the law provides penalties therefor. If a small farmer or ranchman has been enclosed by another, the law affords ample relief. If large territories are enclosed, and the public inconvenienced thereby, the commissioners' court can open roads. If the laws in any event are not ample, the people must seek relief at the hands of the legislature.

When we become a member of society, we expressly agree to yield some of our natural rights for the good of all, and there is nothing that can justify us in departing from the peaceful methods to secure relief except it be eminent and pressing danger to us, or those dependent upon us, that will not admit of delay.

If a public highway was enclosed, any citizen could remove the obstruction; and in such case, he need not seek cover of night to do it. If on tomorrow morning we go to the avenue of this city and find a long line of fence crossing it, anyone is justified in tearing it down to the extreme edges of the street; but when he goes one foot beyond the highway, he himself becomes a trespasser and may be punished for the act.

If it was against good policy to allow an individual, or a number of individuals to enclose large bodies of land in one enclosure, it was an act of the people's representatives.

The doctrine that land and water are free, and individuals cannot acquire separate and exclusive rights thereto, cannot prevail here until society is disrupted. Constitutions and laws must perish and the whole structure of our civil government ruthlessly swept away, and in its stead, chaos will rule and ruin becomes universal.

You, gentlemen of the two houses, come fresh from the people, some of you from the very midst of the disturbances, and must be better prepared to deal with the subject than I can possibly be, but I make the following suggestions and recommendations.

I recommend the absolute repeal of the law permitting persons to enclose school lands of any sort.

I recommend the enactment of a law making it highly penal for anyone to enclose any public land without a contract from the state, by which he may lawful to do so.

I recommend a law making it a highly penal offence for any person to knowingly enclose or surround the residence or land of another, without expressed authority of such person or owner.

I recommend a liberal system of highways wherever the public good demands it, requiring full and complete payment to the land owner for all damages.

I recommend a law making it a felony, punishment by confinement in the penitentiary for a number of years, for any person to willfully or wantonly destroy or injure the fence or other property of another.

I recommend the repeal of the limitation laws in cases named above for past and future offenses.

I recommend a law making it a highly penal offense for anyone to drive their stock onto any lands, private or public, for the purpose of grazing without the expressed authority from the proper source to do so; or to herd stock on any public or private land without expressed authority from the proper source to do so.

I recommend the repeal of limitation laws so far as they would bar recovery in a civil suit for damages for the destruction of fencing.

I recommend a law giving land owners a lien on stock that may trespass on lands, without the knowledge or consent of the owner and against the will of the land owner, for all damages done by said stock, and the value of grass and property destroyed by them.

The present emergency points out, very clearly, the weakness of our form of government, under the present constitution. While the present Executive doesn't covet extraordinary powers, the suggestion is made with the view of bringing the subject before the people of Texas.

It is a singular system that charges the Executive with causing the laws to be faithfully executed, and, yet does not give him the power of a justice of peace, or county attorney, except in cases of insurrection, rebellion or invasion; and even then, he has not been provided with the means to meet these extraordinary emergencies.

While I have exerted every power and agency placed at my disposal to protect society and punish evil doers, and shall continue to do so, I will not trample underfoot the Constitution that I have sworn to support. But the lawless conduct must be checked and punished, and I trust that your experience and wisdom will suggest and formulate remedies equal to the demand.

Appeals are often made for the appointment of officers in remote parts of the state. No particular officer is designated, or authority pointed out or such appointments; but it is undoubtedly true that in the large counties of the west, some unorganized, there are persons and settlements that rarely see an officer and are not thrown in contact with the administration of law; and as a means of enforcing the laws, and in justice to these people, I recommend the creation of such courts and officers in those parts of the State, as in your judgment may be deemed necessary.

Some question may arise as to your power in this respect. I think that the clause, "and in such other courts as may be established by law," found in Sect. 1, Art. 5 of the Constitution ample authority. I recommend this as one of the repressive means in the fence troubles. Doubtless other remedies will suggest themselves to the members of the two houses. Whatever may be done, however, will prove inadequate, unless the law-abiding element in the disturbed districts will unite in self-defense, not by resorting to violence, but in the moral force that will compel the local officials to do their duty. Looking to this end, I recommend a heavy penalty be attached to the failure or neglect of any sheriff, deputy sheriff, or constable who shall fail or refuse to go at once, when notified of a violation of law, to the scene of the trouble and to do all in his power to assess certain the guilty party and arrest them. The same penalty should be attached to the failure of any justice of peace or county attorney who folds his arms when informed of a violation of law.

If the lawless element that are now destroying fences and other property do not cease their depredation, it may be necessary to try them for their misdeeds in other jurisdictions, and I recommend a provision by which they may be prosecution in any locality, when the state may choose to do so.

There are no classes, no industries or material interests in our State that have not suffered by the hands of the lawless element here referred to. Every energy of this government, under the Constitution, should be invoked to restore order and punish crime; and I have great confidence that your wisdom and prudence will bring into life remedies that will prove adequate. I wish to express the fact that I have more anxiety to see the laws enforced and life and property protected than I have about the success of any measure herein suggested, and I will gladly yield to other measures that may offer more fruit.

Appendix 2

Governor John Ireland's Message to Members of the House and Senate at the Conclusion of the Special Called Session of the Eighteenth Texas Legislature

EXECUTIVE OFFICE
Austin, Texas, February 6, 1884

Gentlemen of the Senate and House of Representatives:

No more grave or weighty responsibility ever rested upon the law making department of any government than did upon you when you came here on the eighth of January. All over the land there are men who have fully and readily told you, and the country, what you should do, and if each one had been the sole arbiter of the matter, he would doubtless have arranged matters at once, and possibly satisfactory to himself. It is, however, more difficult for one hundred and thirty-six men, each charged and expected to exercise to a reasonable degree his own free judgment, and no man is fit to represent a people who does not do so. This being the case, no just minded man will blame anyone for going to reasonable lengths to engraft his own ideas upon the laws that he is called upon to assist in making. Reasonable limits in this direction being reached, it becomes each to yield something. You have proven in your final action that you appreciate the idea. While the measures you have adopted are not in all things what I desired, I shall omit no opportunity they offer to use them for the interest of the people of Texas, and if I can have the active support of the local officials throughout the State and the earnest sympathy and support of the people, I have great confidence that the law will be enforced and property protected. For your earnest efforts for the people I thank each and every member of the two houses, and trust that all may be well with you on your return home.

JOHN IRELAND
Governor of Texas

Endnotes

Notes for the Preface

1. Washburn & Moen Manufacturing Company, *The Fence Problem in the United States as Related to General Husbandry and Sheep Raising* (Worcester, MA, 1882), 8.
2. Harold L. Hagemeier, *Barbed Wire Identification Encyclopedia*, 5th ed. (Kearney, NE: Morris Publishing, 2010), xiv.
3. Boone C. McClure, "History of the Manufacture of Barbed Wire," *Panhandle Plains Historical Review*, no. 31 (1958): 5–9. Over the years that followed, Glidden's wire proved to be the most popular and was the bestselling of the many types of barbed wire marketed.
4. Thomas Lloyd Miller, *The Public Lands of Texas, 1519–1970* (Norman: University of Oklahoma Press, 1972), 48–57, 62, 300; Texas Legislature, House Journal, Sixteenth Legislature, called session, 1879. On July 14, 1879, the Fifty-Cent Act was passed and set aside public land in fifty-four Texas counties to be sold for fifty cents an acre.
5. James Cox, *Historical and Biographical Record of the Cattle Industry and Cattlemen of Texas and Adjacent Territory* (St. Louis: Woodward & Tiernan Printing, 1895), 500–503; Washburn & Moen, *Fence Problem*, 8; *Galveston Daily News*, September 1, 1883.
6. Will S. James, *27 Years a Maverick, or Life on a Texas Range* (1893; repr., Austin: Steck Vaughn, 1968), 107.
7. "Fence Cutting in Coleman County," no date, Roy Davis Holt Papers, 1870–1987, and undated, Southwest Collection / Special Collections Library, Texas Tech University, Lubbock (hereafter cited as Holt Papers).
8. *Fort Worth Daily Gazette*, January 29, 1884; H. P. Starkweather to Roy D. Holt, October 4, 1928, Holt Papers.

Notes for Chapter 1

1. Mary Starr Barkley, *History of Travis County and Austin, 1839–1899* (Austin: Steck, 1962), 34–35, 37, 73; Ron C. Tyler, ed., *The New Handbook of Texas*, 6 vols. (Austin: Texas State Historical Association, 1996), 6:258–59. As a state senator, Alexander W. Terrell was an opponent of large corporations. He saw their power as threatening independent labor. When the statewide barbed wire wars erupted, Terrell introduced comprehensive legislation in the Texas Legislatures Eighteenth Special Session dealing with barbed wire, large cattlemen, and foreign investors.

2. Edmunds Travis, interviewed by author, Austin, February 22, 1967 (hereafter cited as Edmunds Travis interview). Grinninger's name in various documents is spelled seven different ways. Historian Walter Prescott Webb spelled the ironworker's name *Grenninger* and said the old immigrant was Swedish. Frank Brown, an early historian and Travis County Clerk who knew the man, spelled the name *Grinninger* and said he was German.
3. Henry D. McCallum and Frances T. McCallum, *The Wire That Fenced the West* (Norman: University of Oklahoma Press, 1965), 47–48; R. P. Smythe to Roy D. Holt, April 14, 1930, Holt Papers.
4. Edmonds Travis interview. Travis claimed early Austin residents believed Grinninger's death occurred after a neighbor's horse was cut up by the barbed fence. As a result of that incident, a Black man paid the price with his life for a crime someone else committed. According to Mr. Travis's story, Grinninger's fence stood for many years near where Austin built the Palms School.
5. *State Gazette* (Austin), June 26, 1862.
6. Frank Brown, *Annals of Travis County and the City of Austin*, typescript, Austin History Center, Austin Public Library; Barkley, *History of Travis County*, 93. The Travis County Commissioners Court Records show Dr. Rentfro had been exempt from service in the Confederacy because there was a need in Travis County.
7. Brown, *Annals of Travis County*. When this murder incident and trial occurred, the Civil War had begun. The jury found in their verdict that the defendant (slave) was property owned by William H. Lount. The slave's owner made no attempt to evade or escape the execution of the law. The jury found the defendant valued at $1,000, and their finding entitled the executed slave's owner to be partially compensated for the loss of his property.
8. McCallum and McCallum, *Wire That Fenced*, 75; Holt Papers. Holt interviewed Texas Ranger Walter M. Robertson, an elderly gentleman, in 1928. Robinson remembered Grinninger. He had seen the farmer's fence and witnessed the hanging of his murderer. Ranger Robertson's father, Dr. Joseph W. Robertson, knew John Grinninger and had been his doctor.
9. McCallum and McCallum, *Wire That Fenced*, 75; W. P. Webb to R. D. Holt, January 7, 1929, Holt Papers. Dr. Webb's first wife, Jane Elizabeth Oliphant Webb, served as the ninth president of the Daughters of the Republic of Texas.
10. In 1969 the State Historical Survey Committee erected a marker commemorating the Grinninger Fence. The marker was located on the trail along Lady Bird Lake in Austin but has been removed. The city's staff says the marker will be replaced on completion of a construction project.

Notes for Chapter 2

1. Forrestine Haney Kothmann and Constance Kothmann Kuhlmann, *The Kothmanns of Texas 1845–1871*, 3rd ed. (Austin: Firm Foundation Publishing House, 1972), 64. Fritz Kothmann's fence builders were Schumaker Stein, Joseph Stendebach, Julius Burghardt, Otto Kollet, John Klossig, Saegner and William Kammelah, and a Mr. Koehler; Grace Heyman Davenport, "Fences in Mason County," *Edwards Plateau Historian*, vol. 8 (1983–1989): 77–79.
2. McCallum and McCallum, *Wire That Fenced*, 209; Walter Prescott Webb, *The Great Plains* (Boston: Ginn and Company, 1931), 291–92. The small town of Bois d'Arc in North Texas became the county seat of Fannin County in 1843. In 1844 the town was renamed Bonham, for James Bonham, a defender of the Alamo.
3. Jane Clements Monday and Frances Brannen Vick, *Petra's Legacy: The South Texas Ranching Empire of Petra Vela and Mifflin Kenedy* (College Station: Texas A&M University Press, 2007), 165, 203, 285; Nueces County Historical Society, *The History of Nueces County* (Austin: Jenkins Publishing, 1972), 90–91; Henry D. McCallum, "Barbed Wire in Texas," *Southwestern Historical Quarterly* 61, no. 2 (October 1957): 210; Tom Lea, *The King Ranch*, 2 vols. (Boston: Little, Brown, 1981), 2:299; J. Frank Dobie, *A Vaquero of the Brush Country* (Dallas: Southwest Press, 1929), 117–18.
4. Lea, *King Ranch*, 1:299, 303.
5. Keith Guthrie, "Coleman-Fulton Pasture Company," in Tyler, *New Handbook of Texas*, 2:203.
6. McClure, "History," 2–3.
7. McCallum and McCallum, *Wire That Fenced*, 52–53.
8. Jesse S. James, *Early United States Barbed Wire Patents* (Maywood, CA: Jesse S. James, 1966), 6–8; McCallum and McCallum, *Wire That Fenced*, 29; Reviel Netz, *Barbed Wire: An Ecology of Modernity* (Middletown, CT: Wesleyan University Press, 2004), 24–25. Rose was one of the first to note that by causing pain a fence could create the habit of avoidance.
9. McCallum and McCallum, *Wire That Fenced*, 44–46; Cox, *Historical and Biographical Record*, 500–503.
10. McCallum and McCallum, *Wire That Fenced*, 75–84. The McCallums present an excellent description of the barbed wire litigation that ended in the US Supreme Court.
11. McCallum and McCallum, *Wire That Fenced*, 65.
12. Cox, *Historical and Biographical Record*, 500–503; Webb, *Great Plains*, 291–92; McCallum and McCallum, *Wire That Fenced*, 108.

13. Cox, *Historical and Biographical Record*, 500–503; McCallum and McCallum, *Wire That Fenced*, 162. Initially, Shanghai Pierce was a staunch opponent of barbed wire, but he used it years later and fenced his ranch and the land of his New York banker and partner, Augustus Kountze; Dobie, *Vaquero of the Brush Country*, 111–12. Screwworm flies attack wounds on animals and lay their eggs, which turn into larva that eat flesh and eventually kill the animal. The US Department of Agriculture announced their screwworm eradication program as a success in 1959, and the screwworm fly no longer destroys livestock in Texas.
14. Cox, *Historical and Biographical Record*, 500–503; H. Allen Anderson, "John F. Evans," in Tyler, *New Handbook of Texas*, 2:905; Seymour V. Connor, "Isaac L. Ellwood," in Tyler, *New Handbook of Texas*, 2:836. John Evans and Sanborn's partner Judson Warner formed a corporation in later years and purchased twenty-three sections of land in what is now Donley County. Evans adopted and filed the Spade Brand used on their cattle and afterward was given the nickname of "Spade" Evans. John Evans was without question a significant contributor to the success of Sanborn and Warner's sale of barbed wire in Texas in their early years. After Isaac Ellwood sold his barbed wire business, he decided to invest in Texas land and cattle and in 1888 bought the Spade Ranch and its cattle as one of his investments.
15. Roy D. Holt, "The Introduction of Barbed Wire in Texas and the Fence Cutting War," *West Texas Historical Association Yearbook*, vol. 6 (June 1930): 73; Cox, *Historical and Biographical Record*, 500–503; Barkley, *History of Travis County*, 144. A note in an Austin newspaper claimed Tips Hardware was the first to sell barbed wire in Austin. Edward Tips and his brother Walter owned a hardware store on Congress Avenue in 1872.
16. *San Antonio Daily Herald*, November 19, 1875.
17. In 1880, five years after Norton & Dentz became Glidden dealers, Sanborn and Warner filed a lawsuit against this company for an unauthorized assignment of $1,586, which defaulted. The Bexar County Court issued a judgment in favor of Norton & Dentz. Henry Sanborn appealed the case to the Texas Supreme Court, which in April 1883 heard Case No. 4814, *Sanborn & Warner vs. Norton & Dentz*. The court reversed and remanded the lower court's decision; Webb, *Great Plains*, 309–10; Holt, "Introduction of Barbed Wire," 73; B. B. Paddock, *Twentieth Century History and Biographical Record of North and West Texas*, 2 vols. (Chicago: Lewis Publishing, 1902–1906), 1:302–04; Chuck Parsons, *Captain Jack Helm: Victim of Texas Reconstruction Violence* (Denton: University of North Texas Press, 2018), 55–59.

18. Bob Chamblee, "The Glidden Barbed Wire Fence," *Barbed Wire Collector* 35, no. 2 (January–February 2018). The April 1885 issue of *Farm Implement News* reported the Glidden and Ellwood Company had grown, with their main building six hundred feet in length, sixty feet wide, and two stories tall. Inside, two hundred automatic machines were making Glidden barbed wire. Wooden spools were manufactured in another building, and there was a building for manufacturing paint, all aligned, with a continuous frontage of eight hundred feet. There was a warehouse for discharging and receiving freight, with a railroad through the center. Also in this building were vats with paint heated by steam, for dipping and painting the wire. The capacity of the shops was about ten rail car loads of finished barbed wire every ten hours.
19. It is probable that John Gates was selling moonshine wire and not Glidden wire when he visited Richardson's hardware store. Moonshine wire was barbed wire manufactured that violated US patents.
20. W. H. Richardson to Walter Prescott Webb, August 28, 1928, in Webb, *Great Plains*, 311–12.
21. Lloyd Wendt and Herman Kogan, *Bet a Million! The Story of John W. Gates* (Indianapolis: Bobbs-Merrill Company, 1948), 48–49; Joanne S. Liu, *Barbed Wire: The Fence That Changed the West* (Missoula: Mountain Press Publishing, 2009), 44–48.
22. McCallum and McCallum, *Wire That Fenced*, 68–73; today, the John Gates barbed wire show has been accepted by many as history, but no documentation of his San Antonio barbed wire show has been found by this author. The dates of Gates's arrival and the show range from 1871 to 1883, depending on which story is read. Wendt and Kogan's biography, *Bet a Million!*, gives the date of the barbed wire show as 1877, saying it was held in San Antonio's Military Plaza. The earliest version and probable origin of the barbed wire carnival story is from E. M. Kingsbury, "John W. Gates: The Forgetful Man," *Everybody's Magazine* 10, no. 1 (January–June 1904): 82. This article is prefaced by the following remark: "Theogony Not History ... Around him, as around other gods and demigods and heroes, creepers of myth and lichens of legend have grown." Apart from Gates's San Antonio barbed wire show, there is clear documentation that John W. Gates manufactured and sold moonshine barbed wire, much of which came to Texas. Years later Gates and Ellwood formed the American Steel and Wire Company, which monopolized the barbed wire industry and eventually manufactured 96 percent of the barbed wire produced in the United States.
23. Paul H. Carlson, *Empire Builder in the Texas Panhandle: William Henry Bush* (College Station: Texas A&M University Press, 1996), 22; *Galveston Daily News*, June 16, 1884.

24. Webb, *Great Plains*, 295; *Galveston Daily News*, September 1, 1883; Paddock, *Twentieth Century History*, 1:304–5; Carlson, *Empire Builder*, relates how in 1881 Sanborn entered into a partnership with his old retired friend Joseph Glidden. They purchased land in the Texas Panhandle and established the Frying Pan Ranch in Potter and Randall Counties. Sanborn built a four-strand barbed wire fence using cedar fence posts cut on their land and fenced about 250,000 acres. The wire used was a special order, number 9 gauge, heavy galvanized barbed wire, much more massive than most fence wire used at the time. Sanborn planned to profit from the cattle business and demonstrate for Texas cattlemen the value of barbed wire fence. He succeeded beyond belief. Sanborn was plowing his money into land and purchased another ranch in Clay County to fatten yearling calves. Later, in 1893, he platted a townsite on Potter County land—Amarillo, the county seat of Potter, located on the Frying Pan Ranch—and today Sanborn is known as the father of Amarillo.
25. Holt Papers. There are numerous advertisements found in various early issues of the *Galveston Daily News* and other prominent Texas newspapers; Hagemeier, *Barbed Wire*, xvii.
26. Lyn Ellen Bennett, "The Politics of Barbed Wire," paper presented at the Western Political Science Association Annual Meeting, Portland, OR, March 23, 2012; McClure, "History," 32.
27. "60 Years Ago They Didn't Want Fences," *San Saba News*, August 17, 1939; Wayne Guard, "The Fence Cutters," *Southwestern Historical Quarterly* 51, no. 1 (July 1947): 3; Holt, "Introduction of Barbed Wire," 73.
28. Bennett, "Politics of Barbed Wire"; Texas Industrial Resources, "Introducing Barbed Wire in Texas," *Frontier Times* 9, no. 2 (November 1931): 91.

Notes for Chapter 3

1. Miller, *Public Lands*, vii; Aldon S. Long and Berte R. Haigh, "Land Appropriations for Education," in Tyler, *New Handbook of Texas*, 4:54–55; Jerry Sadler, *History of Texas Land*, (Austin: Texas General Land Office, 1961), 18–19; H. Leslie Evans, "New York and Texas Land Company," in Tyler, *New Handbook of Texas*, 4:1007; Texas General Land Office, *History of Texas Lands*, revised March 18, 2018, http://www.glo.Texas.gov.
2. Long and Haigh, "Land Appropriations for Education"; Texas General Land Office, *History of Texas Lands*; the *Marlin Ball* as quoted in *Galveston Daily News*, December 24, 1882.

3. *Fort Worth Daily Gazette*, January 18, 1884. Senator Alexander W. Terrell's Speech before the called session of the Eighteenth Texas Legislature; Mary Jayne Walsh, "Jesse Lincoln Driskill," in Tyler, *New Handbook of Texas*, 2:704.
4. Sadler, *History of Texas Land*, 18–19; *Report of State Land Board to the Nineteenth Legislature, January 1, 1885* (Austin: E. W. Swindells, State Printer, 1885), 5. The State Land Board was abolished in 1887, and sale and leasing of public land was placed in the hands of the Commissioner of the General Land Office.
5. J. Frank Dobie, *The Longhorns* (Boston: Little, Brown, 1941), 7; Edward Everett Dale, *The Range Cattle Industry: Ranching on the Great Plains from 1865 to 1925*, new ed. (Norman: University of Oklahoma Press, 1960), 24–30; Frank Goodwin, *Lone Star Land: Twentieth Century Texas in Perspective* (New York: Alfred A. Knopf, 1955), 95–99.
6. Don Worcester, *The Chisholm Trail, High Road of the Cattle Kingdom* (Lincoln: University of Nebraska Press, Amon Carter Museum, 1981), 143–44.
7. Dale, *Range Cattle Industry*, 33–35.
8. Dale, *Range Cattle Industry*, 114; Lawrence M. Woods, *British Gentlemen in the Wild West: The Era of the Intensely English Cowboy* (New York: Free Press, a division of MacMillan, 1989) 117–19; J. Evetts Haley, *The XIT Ranch of Texas and the Early Days on the Llano Estacado* (Norman: University of Oklahoma Press, 1967), 88.
9. Chris Emmett, *Shanghai Pierce: A Fair Likeness* (Norman: University of Oklahoma Press, 1953), 162–63, 136–137; Worcester, *Chisholm Trail*, 144.
10. Worcester, *Chisholm Trail*, 82; Wood, *British Gentlemen in the Wild West*, 102.
11. Monday and Vick, *Petra's Legacy*, 280.
12. Wood, *British Gentlemen*, 118.
13. Dale, *Range Cattle Industry*, 80.
14. Estelle Tinkler, *Archibald John Writes the Rocking Chair Ranche Letters* (Burnet, TX: Eakin Press, 1979), 1–4; Estelle D. Tinkler, "Last Days of the Rocking Chair Ranche," *Panhandle Plains Historical Review*, no. 15 (1942): 76–81.
15. Tinkler, *Archibald John*, 7–10.
16. Tinkler, *Archibald John*, 47–48, 159–165. The London management spent large sums of money on this ranch operation before acknowledging they had a problem. They asked the Texas Rangers for help, and Corporal W. J. L. Sullivan of Company B and Jeff Madkins moved to the ranch. They found nothing to substantiate claims of theft by the nesters in the area. They discovered that J. John Drew, the comanager of the ranch, would ship

a trainload of cattle to Kansas City and report only a single car of cattle sold by the company. The indifferent, unknowing Archie signed his name as comanager to every report and was as guilty under the law as Drew. John Drew was fired and went into the ranching business for himself. Ranger Captain G. W. Arrington was hired by London Management to take over the ranch and dispose of the company's assets. The Rocking Chair Ranch was deeded over to the Continental Land Cattle Company, and its British ownership came to an end in 1893.

17. William Curry Holden, "Matador Ranch," in Tyler, *New Handbook of Texas*, 4:554–55.
18. *Barber County Index* (Medicine Lodge, KS), June 1, 1883; *Galveston Daily News*, June 4, 1883; Gary Kraisinger and Margaret Kraisinger, *The Western Trail, 1874–1897: Its Rise, Collapse, and Revival* (Newton, KS: Mennonite Press, 2014), 147; *San Antonio Express*, October 17, 1931. George W. Saunders, president of the Old Time Trail Drivers Association, told the *San Antonio Express* that fences caused drovers big problems, requiring shipment by rail of cattle from different parts of Texas to get around the barbed wire. Trail driving was coming to an end, and in late 1884 Texas cattlemen employed former Texas Congressman Upton to go to Washington, DC, and lobby Congress to create a cattle trail through the west and southwest to avoid barbed wire.
19. B. Byron Price and Frederick W. Rathjen, *Amarillo and the Texas Panhandle* (Northridge, CA: Windsor Publications, 1986), 57.
20. Holt, "Introduction of Barbed Wire into Texas and the Fence Cutting Wars," *West Texas Historical Association Yearbook*, no. 4 (1928): 84.
21. H. P. Starkweather to Roy D. Holt, October 4, 1929, Holt Papers. Horace P. Starkweather, an accountant, came to Texas from Ohio, took up ranching, and was ranching cattle and sheep in Coleman County. He had forty miles of fence cut in 1883. He sent a letter to Governor Ireland and received a letter back saying, "Kill or Capture." Starkweather was one of many ranchers the fence cutters broke financially. He recovered over the years and was a respected and prominent citizen of Coleman County. He became the president of Coleman's Farmer State Bank.
22. W. H. King, *Report of the Adjutant-General of the State of Texas, December 1884* (Austin: State Printing Office, D & D Asylum, 1884), 14–22.
23. *San Marcos Free Press*, January 10, 1884.
24. *Austin Statesman*, December 22, 1883; *Fort Worth Daily Gazette*, June 10, 1884. The Fort Worth and the Galveston papers were in constant competition and never missed an opportunity to get a lick in on the other.

Notes for Chapter 4

1. Marvin E. Fenoglio, ed., *The Story of Montague County, Texas: Its Past and Present* (Montague, TX: Montague County Historical Commission, 1989), 7; Lois Paschal, "The Frontier History of Jack County" (master's thesis, Midwestern University, 1974), 106.
2. Donald E. Worcester, "Chisholm Trail," in Tyler, *New Handbook of Texas*, 2:89.
3. Carrie J. Crouch, *A History of Young County, Texas* (Austin: Texas State Historical Association, 1956), 45; Paschal, "Frontier History of Jack County," 60. Crouch and Paschal relate the Indian atrocities suffered in the Red River Country and the Warren Wagon Train Massacre, which brought federal action that ended the frequent raids.
4. Cox, *Historical and Biographical Record*, 500–503.
5. Cox, *Historical and Biographical Record*, 501–2. The spring of 1887, Sanborn returned to Clay County and purchased 17,337 acres of prime land located in the fork of the Little Wichita and Red Rivers.
6. Crouch, *History of Young County*, 127–28; Paschal, "Frontier History of Jack County," 112; Williams Charles Taylor, *A History of Clay County* (Austin: Jenkins Publishing, 1989), 82–85. Both Keyser and Ikard suffered heavy losses from the Texas tick fever, of which little was known at the time and to which imported cattle were not immune. One of the cows in Ikard's herd that died of the disease was purchased from the royal herd of England and bore the brand of Queen Victoria. The cow was reported to have cost Ikard $1,125. In years that followed, Ikard became the president of the Texas Hereford Breeders Association.
7. Paschal, "Frontier History of Jack County," 121; Taylor, *History of Clay County*, 83–87.
8. Lucile Glasgow, "Museum Memories," *Clay County Leader* (Henrietta, TX), December 18, 2014; United States Federal Census 1880, Precinct 4, Clay County Texas; "George Cooper Wright," Find A Grave, accessed January 25, 2015, https://www.findagrave.com/memorial/31421184/george-cooper-wright; Sammy Tise, *Texas County Sheriffs* (Albuquerque: Oakwood Printing, 1989), 103.
9. Dale, *Range Cattle Industry*, 112. Many cattlemen refused to bid against each other on land leases where their fellow cattlemen held unofficial range rights on the land in question. The land leasing of the state would cause another crisis over the next few years, with cattlemen going head-to-head with the state government. The Texas State Land Board recognized this lack of bidding as collusion between the cattlemen and raised the lease price to eight cents an acre for unwatered land and twenty cents an acre for watered land. The matter ended up in court, and the state lost.

10. Wayne Gard, *The Chisholm Trail* (Norman: University of Oklahoma Press, 1954), 254; Charles Goodnight to R. D. Holt, 1927, Holt Papers.
11. *Fort Worth Daily Gazette*, September 1, 1883. Mr. McCombs, interviewed in Dallas, described big cattle owners fencing large tracts that they had purchased and some tracts they had not purchased. They also let their cattle graze the common land, then moved their stock in on their wire fenced range for the winter, excluding the nesters. "The latter swear they will not tolerate this and demand common free range for all."
12. Cox, *Historical and Biographical Record*, 647.
13. Katherine Christian Douthitt, ed., *Romance and Dim Trails: A History of Clay County* (Dallas: William T. Tardy, 1938), 273.
14. Lucian Walton Parrish, "An Economic History of Clay County" (master's thesis, University of Texas, 1909), 35–36; Cox, *Historical and Biographical Record*, 647.
15. Douthitt, *Romance and Dim Trails*, 132–33.
16. Taylor, *History of Clay County*, 85; W. C. Kimbrough, "The Frontier Background of Clay County," *West Texas Historical Association Yearbook*, no. 18 (1942): 129
17. *Fort Worth Daily Gazette*, September 23, 1883; THE *Daily Gazette* reported the fence cutting incidents and mentioned several that occurred on Red River Land and Cattle Company's land. Their story was first printed in the *Jacksboro (TX) Citizen*.
18. *Albany (TX) Echo*, September 8, 1883. The description of this incident and stories passed down by local tradition leads the author to believe that this incident occurred when cutters were destroying G. H. Gowan's fence several miles' distance from Henrietta, the Clay County seat.
19. Holt Papers.
20. *Fort Worth Daily Gazette*, September 28, 1883; Will Smith, ed., *Members of the Texas Legislature, 1846–1962* (Austin: Fifty-Seventh Texas Legislature, 1962), 114; Roy D. Holt Papers.
21. Holt Papers. The community of Antelope is located in the northwest corner of Jack County, about a mile from Clay County.
22. Holt Papers; Douthitt, *Romance and Dim Trails*, 132.
23. *Clarksville Standard*, October 12, 1883.
24. Douthitt, *Romance and Dim Trails*, 45; Lida Roe, "Notes from 1993 Tour of West Clay County and Windthorst"; Lucille Lowman Glasgow, ed., *It Used to Be That Way: Remembered Bits of Clay County History* (Henrietta: Clay County Historical Society Inc., 1992) 24; United States Federal Census, 1880, Precinct 4, Jack County, Texas; United States Federal Census, 1920, Lebanon, Laclede, Missouri; "Linton M. Cutter," Find a Grave, accessed June 9, 2014, https://www.findagrave.com/memorial/22566072/linton-m-cutter.

25. Taylor, *History of Clay County*, 154.
26. Taylor, *History of Clay County*, 91; Cox, *Historical and Biographical Record y*, 647; Parrish, "Economic History of Clay County," 36; *Fort Worth Daily Gazette*, March 1, 1892. There are indications that the assets of the Red River Land and Cattle Company sold off over an extended period. As late as 1892, the *Fort Worth Daily Gazette* reported that fifty head of their horses and ranch implements were sold at a sheriff's sale, bringing $885.
27. Cox, *Historical and Biographical Record*, 647
28. *Galveston Daily News*, January 22, 1884; *Fort Worth Daily Gazette*, September 25, 1883; Brian Hart, "Newport," in Tyler, *New Handbook of Texas*, 4:999. Newport is located near the southeastern border of Clay County across the Jack County line. It was established in 1872 and called Bear Hill. In 1878 the town opened a post office and changed its name to Newport.
29. H. Allen Anderson, "William Buford Plemons," in Tyler, *New Handbook of Texas*, 5:239. William Buford Plemons was born in Alabama, fought for the South in the Civil War, and was present at Lee's surrender at Appomattox. He came to Texas, was admitted to the bar in 1872, and practiced at Henrietta in Clay County. He was elected Clay County judge in 1876, serving two terms. He moved to the Texas Panhandle area in 1886 and served as the first county judge of Potter County. Plemons gained fame as an aggressive criminal defense attorney, served as district judge of the Forty-Seventh Judicial District in 1890, and served in the Texas legislature.
30. *Fort Worth Daily Gazette*, September 25, 1883; *Dallas Weekly Herald*, September 27, 1883. The resolution adopted at the Henriette meeting by community leaders appears to acknowledge there were problems with the Red River Land and Cattle Company fencing lands they did not own or lease. No mention of the issue is found in the newspaper articles but is noted in the resolution.
31. *Galveston Daily News*, October 6, 1883.
32. W. H. King, *Report of the Adjutant General of the State of Texas, December 1883* (Austin: E.W. Swindells, State Printer, 1883), 23.
33. *Fort Worth Daily Gazette*, November 28, 1883; Holt Papers.
34. G. W. Cox, *Pioneer Sketches* (1911; repr., Montague, TX: Montague Historical Commission, 1958), 34–35; Marvin F. London, *Indian Raids in Montague County* (Saint Jo, TX: S. J. T. Printers, n.d.), 49–50.
35. *San Antonio Light*, January 29, 1884; Joe Harris was active in the North Texas Cattle Raisers Association. He was on the association's committee in 1883 that drafted and passed a resolution calling for members to provide necessary public highways and provide gates where

roads cross through pastures. This decision subjected any member refusing to abide by the resolution to suspension from the North Texas Cattle Raisers Association. Details of the cattlemen's meeting and resolution are found in the *Fort Worth Daily Gazette*, November 14, 1883.

36. *San Antonio Light*, January 21, 1884; *Fort Worth Daily Gazette*, December 31, 1883, February 5, 1884, February 9, 1884.
37. Clay County Memorial, Henrietta Jail Museum Collection, Clay County, Texas.
38. *Galveston Daily News*, January 22, 1884; 1880 United States Federal Census, Precinct 4, Clay County Texas; Douthitt, *Romance and Dim Trails*, 201; Jim Wheat, "Postmasters & Post Offices of Texas, 1846–1930," www.rootsweb.ancestry.com/~txpost/postmasters.html; Record of Appointment of Postmasters, 1832–Sept. 30, 1971, National Archives and Records Administrations, Washington, DC (NARA).
39. *Galveston Daily News*, January 22, 1884; Donald R. Graves, "Fence Cutting in Texas, 1883–1885" (master thesis, Texas Western College of the University of Texas, 1962), 48; Holt Papers.
40. Cecil O. Harper Jr., "Before They Were Populists: Politics and Politicians in Jack County, 1884–1892" *West Texas Historical Association Yearbook*, no. 53 (1977): 106–11; Ralph Smith, "The Farmers' Alliance in Texas, 1875–1900: A Revolt Against Bourbon and Bourgeois Democracy," *Southwestern Historical Quarterly*, no. 48 (July 1944–April 1945): 346–51. When William Garvin was elected Jack County treasurer, he served as president of the State Farmers' Alliance, but the alliance refused to inject politics into their program; Tise, *Texas County Sheriffs*, 277; *Canadian Free Press*, June 20, 1888. The paper reported that there had been a family feud between Jack County Sheriff J. D. Rains and W. W. Terrell that festered for months. On June 14 Raines and Terrell's quarrel resulted in a fistfight. Terrell was unarmed, went to his home nearby, and picked up a .45 six-shooter. Sheriff Rains and his son Pressly went to a livery stable and picked up a Winchester and their revolvers. The men returned, and the firing commenced near the southwest corner of the Jacksboro Courthouse. Terrell was shot in his left arm and through both thighs. When he fell, he fired the last two rounds from his six-shooter, killing the sheriff and his son.

Notes for Chapter 5

1. T. R. Havins, "The Passing of the Frontier in Brown County," *West Texas Historical Association Yearbook*, no. 8 (June 1932): 43–45; William Carroll Shive, "The Coggins Brothers" (master's thesis, Texas Technology University, 1974), 8–21.
2. Shive, "Coggins Brothers," 115.

3. Leroy Wise, "Brown County from 1856 to 1870," *Frontier Times* 3, no. 5 (February 1926): 44–46.
4. "The Passing of a Pioneer," *Brownwood Banner Bulletin*, December 10, 1925.
5. T. C. Smith Jr., *From the Memories of Men* (Brownwood, TX: Moore Printing, 1980), 27.
6. Cox, *Historical and Biographical Record*, 473.
7. "'Morg' Baugh of Brownwood," *Frontier Times* 23, no. 12 (September 1946): 232–34.
8. W. C. Holden, "Immigration and Settlement in West Texas," *West Texas Historical Association Yearbook*, no. 5 (June 1929): 74–75; McCallum and McCallum, *Wire That Fenced*, 65.
9. W. C. Holden, "Robert Cypret Parrack, Buffalo Hunter, and Fence Cutter," *West Texas Historical Association Yearbook*, vol. 21, (October 1945): 29–49; Havins, "Passing of the Frontier," 44.
10. Holden, "Robert Cypret Parrack," 29–33; Wayne Gard, *The Great Buffalo Hunt* (New York: Alfred A. Knopf, 1959), 191; Fred R. Mullins, "Robert Cypret Parrack: Pioneer Plainsman," (master's thesis, Texas Technological University, 1946), 18, 29–30.
11. Holden, "Robert Cypret Parrack," 44; Barbara Thompson Cox, *Baughs of Brown County, Texas, & Related Lines: Cox, Windham, McInnis* (Lafayette, CA: published by the author, 2000), 9.
12. 1880 United States Federal Census, Brown County Texas, Byrd's Store; "Sarah Jane Williams Lovel," Find a Grave, accessed February 21, 2025. Sarah Jane Williams married G. W. Lovell and had three children, Frank, Jane, and Georgia Ann. G. W. Lowell died in 1857. Sarah, with her mother and other family members, came to Brown County, where she married her brother-in-law David Frank Lovell and had two more children, James B. Lovell and Sue Ellen; Rachel Jenkins, "Byrd, Texas," in Tyler, *New Handbook of Texas*, 1:866. Byrds Store was opened by Martin H. Byrd in 1874 and became a post office in 1877. By the year 1884, the Byrd community prospered, with a population of seventy-five. There were two churches, a school, a cotton gin, and a grist and sawmill. The village was a center for freighting cotton and pecans and a center for cattle trades.
13. John M. Johnson, "Thrifty, Texas," in Tyler, *New Handbook of Texas*, 6:485. Thrifty was a short distance west of Byrd's Store. The community had initially been named Jim Ned and had a post office. In 1880 the post office name was changed to Thrifty. There was a community school, a cotton gin, a freight line, a saloon, and a hotel. Jim Mullins and Doctor Allen established the Mullen-Allen Mercantile Business as a ranch supply center for the surrounding area. The severe drought

that lasted to 1887, and the extension of the Gulf, Colorado and Santa Fe Railroad to Brownwood, led to the end of Thrifty as a trade center; J. W. Baines, *Biennial Report of the Secretary of State of Texas, 1884*, (Austin: State Printing Office, D & D Asylum, 1884). James B. Lovell had a sister and three half-siblings. One of the half-sisters was Georgia Ann Lowell. Georgia Ann married Asa (Ace) Samuel Mathews in 1875.

14. Cox Babb Family Tree of Martin County, Texas, Ancestry.com; 1870 United States Federal Census, Brown County, Texas.
15. Bill O'Neal, *Lampasas, 1855–1895: Biography of a Frontier Texas Town* (Waco: Eakin Press, 2012), 194–96; Roy D. Holt, "The Farmers' Alliance," Holt Papers; Bob Alexander, *Rawhide Ranger, Ira Aten: Enforcing Law on the Texas Frontier* (Denton: University of North Texas Press, 2011), 110
16. *Austin Weekly Statesman*, December 20, 1883; Roy D. Holt "The Land League," Holt Papers.
17. James T. Padgitt, "Colonel William H. Day," *Southwestern Historical Quarterly* 53, no.4 (April 1950): 347; Lee Mobley to Roy D. Holt, November 17, 1927, Holt Papers.
18. Padgitt, "William H. Day," 347; Shive, "Coggins Brothers," 80.
19. *San Saba News*, August 17, 1939. The contemporary newspaper cites San Saba's early ranchers' concerns with barbed wire coming to Texas and the commissioners court's action.
20. T. R. Havins, *Something About Brown: A History of Brown County, Texas*. (Brownwood, TX: Banner Printing, 1958), 36; Padgitt, "William H. Day," 354.
21. Shive, " Coggins Brothers," 83.
22. The rails burned were probably fence staves or pickets used as substitute blinders. Blinders were wood panels or boards required by the state's first fence law to be placed on barbed wire fence. A wooded board was required between the top strand of barbed wire and the next lower strand. The blinders were for livestock to see, to keep them from running into the fence and being cut by the barbs. Rails were often hung on fences and substituted for the board panel.
23. Havins, *Something About Brown*, 36–37; *Galveston Daily News*, January 15, 1884; Cox, *Baughs of Brown County*, 2–9.
24. *Austin Weekly Statesman*, November 15, 1883; Roy D. Holt, "Brown County," Holt Papers.
25. Roy D. Holt, Holt Papers. Holt cites the November 19, 1883, *Fort Worth Daily Gazette*; *Austin Democratic Statesman*, November 23, 1883; *Galveston Daily News*, November 28, 1883.
26. *Fort Worth Daily Gazette*, January 18, 1884.

27. *Galveston Daily News*, November 28, 1883.
28. *Austin Weekly Statesman*, November 15, 1883; Brown County Museum of History, http://browncountyhistory.org, accessed June 2015. The Brown County Courthouse and jail burned in 1880, and the county moved its offices to temporary quarters in a building on North Fisk Street.
29. Havins, *Something About Brown*, 37; *Austin Democratic Statesman*, December 9, 1883; *Fort Worth Daily Gazette*, January 18, 1884; *Austin Weekly Statesman*, December 13, 1883; Shive, "Coggins Brothers," 80–81. A resolution sent to the legislature by Brown County citizens mentions a school burned by cutters. This school may have been on the Coggins land and burned after it was closed.
30. *Fort Worth Daily Gazette*, December 20, 1883.
31. John Henry Brown, *Indian Wars and Pioneers of Texas* (L. E. Daniell, 1890; republished with new material, Austin: State House Press, 1988), 154–56.
32. *Fort Worth Daily Gazette*, December 20, 1883. The Fort Worth paper quoted the Brownwood Bulletin.
33. Alexander, *Rawhide Ranger*, 112; Havins, *Something About Brown*, 37.
34. Havins, "Passing of the Frontier," 42; Havins, *Something about Brown*, 38; Holt Papers.
35. *Fort Worth Daily Gazette*, December 20, 1883. The *Gazette* published the story from the *Brownwood Banner* and also a letter from a traveler who was in Brownwood and witnessed the event.
36. *Austin Weekly Statesman*, December 13, 1883; Havins, *Something about Brown*, 38; Havins, "Passing of the Frontier," 42; Roy D. Holt, "The Old-time Cowboy's Yellow Slicker," Holt Papers. The Fish Brand yellow slickers were manufactured in Gloucester, Massachusetts, at a factory that supplied seagoing fishermen with oilskins for decades before being adopted by the cowboys. The Fish Brand slickers were always yellow and designed to cover the cowboy from chin to toe when horseback. The seat of the yellow slicker was cut out in a swallow forked fashion, to cover the cantle of the saddle, and buttoned in the front. It tightened at the wrist and had inside sleeves that kept out rain; *Austin Weekly Statesman*, December 13, 1883.
37. *Austin Weekly Statesman*, January 31, 1884.

Notes for Chapter 6

1. *Runnels County Ledger* (Ballinger, TX), "T. L. Odom Orbituary," April 9, 1897; August Santleben, *A Texas Pioneer* (New York: Neale Publishing, 1910), 253; Ann Pate, *Fort Chadbourne: A Military Post, a Family Heritage* (Bronte, TX: Fort Chadbourne Foundation, 2010),

218; Garland Richards, interview by the author, March 7, 2013 (hereafter cited as Richards interview). Garland Richards is the great-great-grandson of T. L. Odom.
2. J. Marvin Hunter, ed., *The Trail Drivers of Texas*, 2nd rev. ed. (Nashville: Cokesbury Press, 1925), 661; Jewell E. Pritchett, *From the Top of Old Hayrick: A Narrative History of Coke County* (Abilene, TX: Pritchett, 1980), 23; *History of the Cattlemen of Texas*. (Dallas: Johnson printing and Advertising, 1914; repr.; Austin: Texas State Historical Association in Cooperation with the University of Texas, 1991), 263.
3. Pate, *Fort Chadbourne*, 212–13; Frank W. Johnson, *A History of Texas and Texans* (Chicago: American Historical Society, 1914), 1145; Charlsie Poe, *Runnels Is My County* (San Antonio: Naylor, 1970), 5; Ruth Cooper, *The Organization of Runnels County* (Ballinger, TX: Runnels County Historical Commission, 2014); Robert W. Stephens, *Bullets and Buckshot in Texas* (Dallas: pub. by author, 2002), 216–17.
4. Pate, *Fort Chadbourne*, 213–29; Poe, *Runnels Is My County*, 4–7. Poe notes the legislature created Runnels County in 1858, and Fort Chadbourne was considered part of Runnels County. The county was surveyed in 1886, and Fort Chadbourne was just west and over the county line in what is now Coke County; Jerry Lackey, "From Fort to Ranch: An Interesting Tale," *San Angelo Standard Times*, September 12, 2009; Pate, *Fort Chadbourne*, 213.
5. Katharyn Duff, *Abilene on Cat Claw Creek* (Abilene, TX: Abilene Reporter News, 1969), 89; Smith, *Members of the Texas Legislature*, 114; *Fort Worth Daily Gazette*, March 2, 1883.
6. Pate, *Fort Chadbourne*, 218–21; Grayson Family Papers, 1835–1959, Dolph Briscoe Center for American History, University of Texas at Austin.
7. Leonard Glenn Smith, "A History of Runnels County, Texas, 1683–1960" (master's thesis, Trinity University, 1963), 31; Donald H. Biggers, "From Cattle Range to Cotton Patch," *Frontier Times* 21, no. 5 (February 1944): 203; Clifford R. Caldwell, *Robert Kelsey Wylie, Forgotten Cattle King of Texas* (pub. by author, 2013), 57.
8. Richards interview; Poe, *Runnels Is My Country*, 10. T. L. Odom's fence wasn't the first fence cut in Runnels County. Two Englishmen, Adam T. Brown and W. G. Rusk, owned the first land that suffered fence cutting. They purchased a large tract of land, moved in, and set up a ranching operation on the east side of Runnels County. Their ranch and pasture fenced extended into Coleman County. It was reported fence cutters came and in one night and cut their fences into shoestring-size pieces.

9. Robert M. Utley, *Lone Star Justice: The First Century of the Texas Rangers* (New York: Oxford University Press, 2002), 235; Frank W. Jenkins, *The History of Runnels County* (San Angelo: San Angelo Genealogical and Historical Society, 2004), 14; Richards interview.
10. *San Antonio Light*, December 24, 1883.
11. Pate, *Fort Chadbourne*, 223; Runnels County District Court Records, Cause Number 40, May 9, 1884, District Clerk's Office, Ballinger, TX. The note threatening Odom, found in the case papers, was evidence when the fence cutters were tried in the February 1886 term of Runnels County District Court; Fran Lomas, "Mrs. Frank Lomas," *Stalking Kin, San Angelo Genealogical and Historical Society* 3, no. 2 (2003): 58. L. B. Harris and his son-in-law Eugene Cartledge were founders of Robert Lee, which replaced Hayrick as the county seat of Coke County; *Fort Worth Daily Gazette*, December 18, 1883
12. *San Antonio Express*, January 9, 1884.
13. Holt Papers.
14. *San Antonio Express*, January 1, 1884; *Houston Post*, January 11, 1884.
15. O'Neal, *Lampasas*, 194–95; Alexander, *Rawhide Ranger*, 110.
16. *Fort Worth Daily Gazette*, January 16, 1884; Holt Papers.
17. *Fort Worth Daily Gazette*, January 11, 1884.
18. *Galveston Daily News*, January 11, 1884.
19. *Galveston Daily News*, January 11, 1884; Dora Neill Raymond, *Captain Lee Hall of Texas* (Norman: University of Oklahoma Press, 1940), 191, 208–10; Craig H. Roell, "William Henry Crain," in Tyler, *New Handbook of Texas*, 2:387–88. William Henry Crain was born in Galveston and studied law with the firm of Stockdale and Procter in Indianola. He was elected district attorney in the Twenty-Third Judicial District in 1882, serving until 1876, when he was elected to the Texas Senate. Crain moved to Cuero, resigned his state office, and was elected to the Forty-Ninth US Congress. He served until his death in 1896.
20. *Brenham Weekly Banner*, January 17, 1884; *Fort Worth Daily Gazette*, January 20, 1884. Before the special session began there were other cattlemen's associations that were making their voices heard. The Cattle Raisers Association of Northwest Texas suffered fence cutting problems but passed a resolution calling on its members to place gates on public roads. Those who refused were to be suspended from the association. In South Texas the Guadalupe and San Antonio Rivers Stock Association offered a reward for arrest and conviction of a fence cutter and supported legislation making the killing of a fence cutter justifiable homicide.
21. Thomas W. Cutrer, "George Washington Jones," in Tyler, *New Handbook of Texas*, 3:982. George W. Jones came to Texas with his parents

in 1848, and the family settled on the Colorado River below the town of Bastrop. There he read law and was admitted to the bar in 1851. He was elected Bastrop County's district attorney in 1856 and during this period shot and killed a man in the street in Bastrop. He joined the Confederacy and rose to the rank of lieutenant colonel in the 17th Texas Infantry. Jones was elected to the US Congress in 1878 and ran for governor against John Ireland in 1882 and 1884. He lost both races.
22. *Galveston Daily News*, December 21, 1883. At the end of the published interview with Newel, the Galveston paper made the following qualifying statement: "The foregoing is not the exact dialogue that in fact occurred, but it is nearly correct. The party was in town Saturday, and Monday last, and he is perhaps one of the gang that has been destroying the fences in Bastrop County. It is evident he is a person of some considerable information, but his language would indicate him to be very illiterate. Such men are very dangerous leaders. When they have heard the governor's message on fence cutting now in preparation, they will sing a different tune."
23. Holt Papers.
24. Holt Papers; *San Antonio Light*, January 15, 1884. It appears that A. M. Taylor was replaced by R. C. Foster of Grayson County later in the session; Will Lambert, *Pocket Directory of the Eighteenth Legislature of Texas* (Austin: Deffenbaugh & Company, 1883), 2–8.
25. *Brenham (TX) Weekly Banner*, January 17, 1884.
26. *Austin Weekly Statesman*, January 24, 1884.
27. *Brenham Weekly Banner*, January 17, 1887.
28. *Austin Weekly Statesman*, January 24, 1884, citing the *Dallas Herald*.
29. *Fort Worth Daily Gazette*, January 12, 1884. Martin's bill appears to have initially had Senator Barnett Gibbs as a cosponsor. Several newspapers refer to the senate bill as the Gibbs Bill; C. E. Lee, "The Fence Cutting War in Texas," *Frontier Times* 8, no. 10 (July 1931): 468–69.
30. *Austin Weekly Statesman*, January 23, 1884; *Galveston Daily News*, January 16, 1884; Holt Papers.
31. "The Rag-Tag and Bob-Tail Hell Hounds of Texas," *Fort Worth Daily Gazette*, January 29, 1884.
32. *General Laws of The State of Texas Passed at the Special Session of the Eighteenth Legislature Convened at the City of Austin January 8, 1884, and Adjourned February 6, 1884* (Austin: E. W. Swindells, State Printer, 1884), 18–68.

Notes for Chapter 7

1. Utley, *Lone Star Justice*, 235; Roy Davis Holt Papers.
2. William Carlton to Adjutant General W. R. King, March 12, 1884, Adjutant General Correspondence (AGC), Texas State Library and

Notes for Chapter 7   321

   Archives Commission, Austin (TSLAC). The letter was a report to the adjutant general on the fence cutting investigation; *San Antonio Light*, December 24, 1883.
3. Carlton to King, March 12, 1884, AGC. Frank C Barnes, *Cartridges of the World*, ed. Mic L. McPherson, 9th ed., rev. and expanded (Iola, WI: Krause Publications, 2000), 144; Doug Dukes, *Firearms of the Texas Rangers: From the Frontier Era to the Modern Age* (Denton: University of North Texas Press, 2020), 224. The cartridge Detective Carlton found appears to have been for a Winchester's Model 1876 rifle, which had recently come on the market. This new lever-action rifle was chambered for a new cartridge, the 45-75, and this bottle-neck shape cartridge was to duplicate the power of the old 45-70 cartridge used in breach-loading Sharp rifles. Some Rangers later carried the Model 1876 chambered for the 45-75, and the Canadian Northwest Mounted Police adopted and used the rifle and cartridge for twenty-seven years. Texas Ranger Captain Patrick Dolan ordered one of the new rifles, then comments of Joe Petmecky, an Austin gunsmith, convinced him to drop the order. Petmecky claimed the rifle often had breach failure, saying, "They shoot out behind nearly as often as before."
4. Carlton to King, March 12, 1884, AGC.
5. Barnes, *Cartridges of the World*, 144; Nolan County US Census, enumerated June 22, 1880. John M. Aston is shown as a stockman and John Warren listed as a herdsman living with the Aston family; San Saba County US Census, enumerated July 21, 1870. Earlier years, John Aston was listed as farming in San Saba County.
6. Carlton to King, March 29, 1884, AGC.
7. Carlton to King, March 29, 1884, AGC.
8. Carlton to King, March 29, 1884, AGC.
9. Carlton to King, March 29, 1884, AGC. Wagon Tire Creek is located in the northwest corner of Runnels County and east of Fort Chadbourne. The creek drains into Oak Creek about six miles south of the Odom's Ranch headquarters at Fort Chadbourne; Runnels County District Court Criminal Records, Book I; during the second fence cutting trials on December 2, 1884, James Goutcher, A. E. Goutcher, and S. R. Goutcher were called and bonded as defense witnesses for Dow Hylton in Cause No. 40.
10. Carlton to King, March 29, 1884, AGC.
11. William Carlton to King, March 29, 1884, AGC.
12. *San Saba County History, 1856–2001*, vol. 2 (San Saba, TX: San Saba Historical Commission, 2002), 179–80; Masonic Records of Membership, Texas Masonic Grand Lodge Library and Museum, Waco, Texas; US Census, San Saba County, TX, July 1870.

13. US Census Nolan County, TX, 1880
14. Benjamin Warren's Frontier Forces Discharge, February 10, 1885, Fort Chadbourne Museum, Bronte, TX. The discharge document notes Warren was mustered into Ranger service on April 18, 1884.
15. Carlton to King, March 29, 1884, AGC; Captain Samuel A. McMurry and his Ranger Company B were stationed at Coleman.
16. Alma Ward Hamrick, *The Call of the San Saba: A History of San Saba*, 2nd ed. (Austin: San Felipe Press, 1969), 101; Ross J. Cox Sr., *The Texas Rangers and the San Saba Mob* (San Saba, TX: C&S Farm Press, 2005), 6.
17. *San Saba County History*, 2:178–79. John William's Ranger Company was in Williamson County from April 10, 1858, to June 16, 1859, before joining the Confederate Army, 2:178–79; Hamrick, *Call of the San Saba*, 211–12. McMillin's Company was created under Governor Edward Clark to fight Indians during the Civil War, and N. D. McMillin served as captain of Company E at Camp San Saba.
18. Lloyd C. Pyle, "History of Nolan County to 1900" (master's thesis, East Texas State Teachers College, 1937), 134.
19. Nolan County Commissioners Court Minutes, vol. II, February 14, 1884, County Clerk's Office, Sweetwater, TX; the Sweetwater and Runnels City Road Commissioners District No. 3, Road Precinct No. 1 was bounded as follows: Beginning at a point about one and a half miles north of Ballard Springs on the Sweetwater and Fort Concho Road, thence Southeast by Hackberry Springs to head of Fish Creek and thence down said Creek to the southeast corner of Nolan County. Precinct No. 1 includes all public roads within the boundaries described above. Men named in the court order for road work and then named in indictments for fence cutting soon afterward were W. J. Wood, John Ford, Mack Boyett, Dow Hylton, Riley Hylton, Dave Farley, Nimrod Franks.
20. Runnels County District Court Records; Odom's fences were cut February 23 and April 9, 1884, as noted in indictments in Runnels County District Court Records.
21. Runnels County Criminal Records, vol. I, and indictments in Runnels County District Court Files; *Galveston Daily News*, February 24, 1885. Elisha Hylton acknowledged in court proceedings later (Formwalt v. State of Texas, Case No. 5087) that he had been under indictment for cattle stealing.
22. Runnels County District Court Records, Indictments; C.W. Boyett v. The State of Texas, Case No. 2266, Texas Court of Appeals, December 15, 1887.

23. Utley, *Lone Star Justice*, 235. After the special session of the legislature, on March 6 Adjutant General King assigned temporary command of the entire Frontier Battalion to Ranger Captain George Baylor stationed in Ysleta, Texas. Baylor was charged with deploying Ranger companies to assist local authorities and to support the commercial detectives working on fence cutting problems; *Austin Weekly Statesman*, May 22, 1884; Pyle, "History of Nolan County," 136; Peter R. Rose, *The Reckoning: The Triumph of Order on the Texas Frontier* (Lubbock: Texas Tech University Press, 2012), 66–69. Captain George Baylor's Runnels County roundup of fence cutter may have expected to replicate Major John B. Jones's Kimble County outlaw roundup of 1877, but it didn't. The Kimble County roundup captured forty-one suspects, including the sheriff and county judge.
24. Runnels County District Court Criminal Minutes, vol. I, and case papers. Sheriff Dick Ware signed the documents when the fence cutters secured a bond to leave jail. Ware was elected the first sheriff of Mitchell County, winning the office by one vote. During his career he served as a sheriff, Texas Ranger, and US marshal, and in later years he was a prominent cattleman. Dick Ware was one of the Rangers in the shootout with the Sam Bass Gang in Round Rock.
25. C. W. Boyett vs. State of Texas, Case 2266, Texas Court of Appeals.
26. Poe, *Runnels Is My County*, 11. In 1884 Fort Chadbourne's population was twenty-five, with a postmaster, a justice of the peace, a general store, and a semiweekly stage run to Buffalo Gap. Four Odoms were listed as residents: T. L. Odom and sons Garland, Lee, and C. W.; E. L. Yeats and Hooper Shelton, *History of Nolan County, Texas* (Sweetwater, TX: Shelton Press), 210; C. W. Boyett vs. State of Texas, Case 2266, Texas Court of Appeals.
27. J. M. Formwalt et al. vs. E. Hylton, Case 5807, Texas Supreme Court.
28. Runnels County District Court Records. On December 2, 1884, the fence cutter cases were brought to trial in Runnels City the second time but were continued by agreement of the state and fence cutters.
29. C. W. Boyett vs. State of Texas, Case 2266, Texas Court of Appeals.
30. Royston C. Crane Sr. Papers, Southwest Collection / Special Collections Library, Texas Tech University, Lubbock. R. C. Crane and R. A. Ragland formed a partnership and established a law office and abstract firm in Sweetwater. Crane practiced law for many years and was a founding member of the West Texas Historical Association, serving as president from 1925 to 1948.
31. Crane Papers.
32. Crane Papers.

33. C. W. Boyett vs. The State of Texas, Case 1891, habeas corpus appeal.
34. C. W. Boyett vs. The State of Texas, Case 1891, habeas corpus appeal.
35. Nolan County Commissioners Court Minutes, vol. II, February 12, 1885, May 11, 1885; Odom to King, AGC.
36. Nolan County Commissioners Court Minutes, vol. II, May 13, 1885, 224–25; the County Commissioners Court minutes noted payment of criminal trial fees three dollars each for W. J. Wood, Neal and Mack Boyett, and Dow Hylton in cases filed by the state of Texas and disposed of in the April term of 1885. No Nolan County District Court Criminal Records for the 1800s were found. Staff in the Nolan County District Clerk's Office advised that the old criminal records were destroyed many years ago, probably in 1900; C. W. Boyett vs. State of Texas, Case No. 1891, habeas corpus appeal, Texas Court of Appeals, October 14, 1885; *Galveston Daily News*, February 24, 1885.
37. *Galveston Daily News*, July 9, 1885.
38. *Galveston Daily News*, July 9, 1885.
39. *Galveston Daily News*, July 14, 1885.
40. Robert K. DeArment, *George Scarborough: The Life and Death of a Lawman on the Closing Frontier* (Norman: University of Oklahoma Press, 1992), 34–37. Earlier in 1885 Sheriff Scarborough had secured extradition papers, traveled to New Mexico Territory, and chased down A. J. Williams, finally capturing him by shooting his horse. Williams was returned to Texas by Scarborough and imprisoned in Sweetwater's rock jail because it was considered more secure than the jail in Jones County. On October 15, 1887, two years after the attempted jailbreak in Sweetwater, Sheriff Scarborough killed A. J. Williams in a shootout in Haskell, Texas; *Galveston Daily News*, July 14, 1885.
41. *Galveston Daily News*, November 20, 1885.
42. Boyett vs. State of Texas, Case No. 2266, capital murder, Texas Court of Appeals.
43. *Fort Worth Daily Gazette*, January 5, 1886.
44. *Fort Worth Daily Gazette*, April 19, 20, 1886. During the time of the trial, Judge Thomas B. Wheeler was the Texas lieutenant governor–elect.
45. Formwalt vs. State of Texas, Case No. 5807, Texas Supreme Court.
46. *Fort Worth Daily Gazette*, December 19, 20, 1886; C. W. Boyett vs. State of Texas, Tyler Term, Case No. 2266, Texas Court of Appeals, December 15, 1887.
47. Convict Registers, vols. 1998/038-138–1998/038-176, Texas Department of Criminal Justice, Archives and Information Services Division, TSLAC; Convict and Conduct Registers, 1875–1945, vols. 1998/038-177, 1998/038-236, TSLAC.

48. Baines, *Biennial Report*; Nolan County Commissioners Court Minutes, November 10, 1884; Boyett vs. the State of Texas, Case No. 1891, Texas State Court of Appeals.
49. William R. Hunt, "Hylton, Texas," in Tyler, *New Handbook of Texas*, 3:809.
50. Runnels County District Court Records.
51. Runnels County District Court Records; Smith, "History of Runnels County," 33.
52. Pate, *Fort Chadbourne*, 227; US Census, Nolan County Texas, enumerated June 25, 1900.

Notes for Chapter 8

1. *General Laws, Special Session of the Eighteenth Legislature*; Edmund Thornton Miller, *A Financial History of Texas*, Bulletin of the University of Texas 37 (Austin: University of Texas, 1916), 253. Adjutant General King was conservative with the public's funds, and state records reflect only $16,500 of the special $50,000 appropriation for rewards and detectives was spent. Ranger pay was a pittance compared to what commercial detectives cost, and it appears Rangers rather than commercial detectives were paid and sent to work undercover in the hot spots.
2. Jim Ned Creek begins in Taylor County and runs southeast across Callahan and Coleman Counties into Brown County. There it flows into Lake Brownwood, which covers what was once the Baugh's property. The stream was named for Jim Ned, a Delaware Indian chief who served as a scout for the early Texas militia.
3. Frontier Battalion Correspondence, TSLAC; Robert W. Stephens, *Captain George H. Schmitt Texas Ranger* (Dallas: pub. by author, n.d.), 120
4. A. E. Kramer to Adjutant General W. H. King, AGC; Utley, *Lone Star Justice*, 235.
5. Kramer to King, February 19, 1884, AGC.
6. Kramer to King, February 27, 1884, AGC.
7. King, *Report of the Adjutant General, December 1884*, 14.
8. Gillespie to Quartermaster Johnson, June 18, 1884, AGC; Texas County Tax Rolls, 1846–1910, Brown County, Texas, 1883, TSLAC; National Park Services, US Civil War Soldiers, 1861–1865, Ancestry.com. Tax records indicate J. B. Scoggin came to Texas and acquired property in Brown County after the Civil War. Record of his Civil War service shows Scoggin served the South as a private in the 19th Regiment, Arkansas Infantry. His duty as a Confederate soldier may have cost him his arm.

9. Gillespie to King, March 12, 1884, AGC.
10. Vallin to King, March 9, 1884, AGC.
11. Monthly Return, Company E, Frontier Battalion, March 30, 1884, TSLAC.
12. Gillespie to Johnson, June 18, 1884, AGC.
13. Company D Monthly Return, Frontier Battalion, February 29, 1884, TSLAC; Graves, "Fence Cutting in Texas," 66–67.
14. Graves, "Fence Cutting in Texas," 67.
15. W. J. Bradley to John O. Johnson, July 18, 1884, AGC. Bluffton was northeast of the town of Llano and a stage stop. Lake Buchanan now covers the site of the old community; Company D Monthly Return, Frontier Battalion, February 29, 1884, TSLAC. In February undercover men W. Bradley, A. Himmel, and Thomas G. Martin had been placed on special duty without pay in Ranger Company D and carried on Captain Sieker's Company D monthly return. The three men were enlisted in early February and played a role in the capture of three fence cutters at Green Lake in Edwards County. W. J. Bradley and A. Himmel then began work in Brown County.
16. Ranger Ira Aten came to Brown later, and he certainly wasn't a rookie. Aten's Rangering days are described in his letters and are in his biography by Bob Alexander, *Rawhide Ranger*, which relates much of Aten's story on detective work among fence cutters.
17. William W. Collier to Roy D. Holt, January 11, 1928, Holt Papers; Colliers work in Brown preceded Ira Aten's work there; Alexander, *Rawhide Ranger*, 49.
18. Gillespie to King, April 23, 1884, AGC, Brown County Tax Roll, 1884, 1885, 1886, and 1887, Texas County Tax Rolls, 1846–1910, FamilySearch.org. J. O. Copeland was first assessed taxes in Brown County in 1884 and again in 1885, 1886, and 1887. Copeland probably arrived in Brown County in 1883, or possibly earlier.
19. Alexander, *Ira Aten*, 112; Texas Adjutant General Service Records, 1836–1935, TSLAC.
20. Hall Family Tree and Duncan Family Tree, Ancestry.com.
21. The 14th Infantry fought in the bloody battle of Jenkins Ferry, where one of the Texans reported half of his company was killed. The 14th Infantry also took part in the Red River Campaign in Louisiana and stopped General Nathaniel Banks's advance toward Texas. Copeland's unit was active in battles at both Pleasant Hill and Pea Ridge.
22. Confederate Pension Application, 1899–1975, Collection CPA16526, Roll 270, TSLAC. On filing the application they asked Joab's widow, What was your husband's full name? She states on the application, "His

name was Joab Copeland, but after leaving the Service, he assumed the initials, J. O. Copeland."
23. Lisa C. Maxwell, "Falls County, Texas," in Tyler, *New Handbook of Texas*, 2:942. The Texas legislature created Falls County in 1850, with its early settlers migrating from Mississippi, Tennessee, and Alabama. These emigrants brought their slaves with them. Falls County had 1,716 slaves in 1860, making up 47% of the county population. Cattle and cotton were the significant parts of the county's economy through sheep, and wool was becoming important. In 1860 farmers harvested 2,030 bales of cotton and sheared 17,500 pounds of wool.
24. Find a Grave Memorial, https://www.findagrave.com, accessed June 30, 2017; Texas County Tax Rolls, 1846–1910, Falls County, Falls County Tax Assessments for 1870, 1873, 1874, 1875, 1876, 1877, and 1879, FamilySearch.org; Joab Jacob "Joe" Copeland (1847–1915), Masonic Grand Lodge Library and Museum.
25. *Austin Weekly Statesman*, November 15, 1883.
26. Monthly return, Company E, Frontier Battalion, May 1884, TSLAC; Havins, *Something About Brown*, 37; Texas Ranger Service Records, TSLAC.
27. Utley, *Lone Star Justice*, 235. Following the special legislative session, Adjutant General Wilburn King placed George W. Baylor in temporary command of the Frontier Battalion. Baylor's mission was to deploy Ranger companies to assist detectives and local authorities statewide to stop fence cutting; monthly return, Company E, Frontier Battalion, July 1884, TSLAC. Ranger Benjamin Warren, a detached member of Gillespie's Company E, was working undercover among fence cutters in Runnels County. Warren presented damning evidence to the district court's grand jury with details and names of the fence cutters. The grand jury handed down indictments for fourteen fence cutters. Captain George W. Baylor showed up in Fort Chadbourne with support of Rangers from Companies B and E. The fence-cutter roundup began on July 8th. Corporal Cartwright with six Company E Rangers assisted Lieutenant Platt of Company B in arresting eight of the indicted fence cutters.
28. Monthly return, Company E, Frontier Battalion, July 1884, TSLAC; *Austin Weekly Statesman*, April 10, 1884.
29. DeArment, *George Scarborough*, 26; Company E Monthly Return, December 1884, TSLAC; Holt Papers, Southwest Collection Texas Tech University, Lubbock; Smith, *Memories of Men*, 29.
30. Darrell Debo, ed., *Burnet County History*, Burnet County Historical Commission, vol. 2 (Austin: Eakins Press, 2002), 20; *General Laws, Special Session of the Eighteenth Legislature*.

31. *Coleman (TX) Democrat-Voice*, February 25, 1910. Obituary published for J. C. Randolph in a resolution from the Coleman County bar; Baines, *Biennial Report*.
32. Havins, *Something About Brown*, 38–39; monthly return, Company E Frontier Battalion, February 1885, TSLAC; *General Laws, Session of the Eighteenth Legislature*. The second indictment delivered on Lovell was a charge of conspiracy for fence cutting, such charge recently being added to the penal code during the 18th Legislature Special Session.
33. Darren L. Ivey, *The Texas Rangers: A Registry and History* (Jefferson, NC: McFarland, 2010), 171; Sieker to King, February 28, 1884, AGC; Bob Alexander and Donaly E. Brice, *Texas Rangers: Lives, Legends, and Legacy* (Denton: University of North Texas Press, 2017), 326; Tise, *Texas County Sheriffs*, 65. In 1887 James T. Gillespie's Ranger Company E was disbanded because of reduced state appropriations. Gillespie was then elected the first sheriff of Brewster County, reelected, and served until his death in 1890.
34. *Fort Worth Daily Gazette*, April 6, 1886. Two men named Joe Griffiths lived in the area at the time of the newspaper's report, but both men lived well beyond the year of the shooting described in the Fort Worth newspaper. A man named John Griffith wanted for murder in Karnes County was arrested in Brown County by Ranger George Schmitt the year after the shooting. He may have been a relative to the man killed by Nat Perry; Havins, *Something about Brown*, 39.
35. Adjutant General's Service Records, William Scott, TSLAC; Capt. Joseph Shely to W. H. King, January 5, 1884, AGC. Shely telegraphed a message reporting that Scott and Deputy Sheriff Elder arrested three fence cutters in the act of cutting a fence.
36. Scott to Sieker, July 23, 1886, AGC.
37. The story of the Conner family of outlaws and Ranger Company F ends in a bloody encounter. The battle is described in Paul Spellman's *Captain J. A. Brooks: Texas Ranger* (Denton: University of North Texas Press, 2007); and William Warren Sterling's *Trials and Trails of a Texas Ranger* (1959, repr., Norman: University of Oklahoma Press, 1969).
38. Monthly return, Company F, Frontier Battalion, September 1886, TSLAC; Sarah Ellen Davidge, "Texas Rangers Were Rough and Ready Fighters," *Frontier Times* 13, no. 2 (November 1935): 125–29. Sara Davidge interviewed the elderly J. Allen Newton, who served as a Ranger under Scott in Company F. In the interview Newton located the site of Scott's camp on Lev Baugh's ranch. Newton said Baugh told the Rangers if they wanted meat, to kill any animal with the LEV brand; J. Allen Newton, Adjutant General Service Records, TSLAC. Newton

mustered into Ranger Company F on March 1, 1887, as the Rangers prepared to leave Brown County for duty on their second trip to East Texas; Havins, *Something About Brown*, 39. Havins says the Rangers went into camp on Baugh's land, but gives their arrival in November. Scott's monthly return shows Company F arrived in Brown County the last day of September 1886.

39. Monthly return, Company F, Frontier Battalion, October 31, 1886, TSLAC; George Schmitt to Sieker, March 31, 1887, AGC; Sergeant Brooks and Private Putz were in federal court in Arkansas on murder charges that following a shooting in Indian Territory.
40. Frontier Battalion Records, 1883–1935, TSLAC.
41. Alexander, *Rawhide Ranger*, 364n52.
42. Harold D. Jobes, "Seeking Reparation for the Murder of Johann Wolfgang Braeutigam," paper presented at the fall meeting of the Edwards Plateau Historical Association, Harper, Texas, October 30, 2019; Alexander, *Rawhide Ranger*, 99, 108.
43. Alexander, *Rawhide Ranger*, 108–14; *Austin Weekly Statesman*, September 15, 1883. The *Statesman* gives a good description of Brown County businesses with location of the Coggin Bank and mention of Henry Ford.
44. Alexander, *Rawhide Ranger*, 124.
45. Alexander, *Rawhide Ranger*, 115–18; Ira Aten, "Six and One-Half Years in the Ranger Service: Memoirs of Sergeant Ira Aten, Sergeant Company D, Texas Rangers," *Frontier Times* 22, no. 5 (February 1945): 129–30; King to Scott, Letter Press Book, July 28, 1886, to May 4, 1887, TSLAC.
46. Smith, *Memories of Men*, 29–30; Havins, "Passing of the Frontier," 49. Havins cites an interview with W. M. Baugh on April 24, 1930.
47. Stephens, *Bullets and Buckshot*, 101–2; J. A. Brooks and 19-year-old Ranger Henry Putz were sent to the Indian Territory in May of 1886 to capture thieves that stole a string of mules. Brooks, Putz, and Thomas R. Knight, an Indian agent, tried to arrest Albert St. John, a fugitive from justice. In a struggle St. John was shot and killed. The three lawmen were indicted for premeditated murder in federal court at Fort Smith, Arkansas. They were placed in jail with their trial set for November by Judge Isaac Parker. The judge granted a continuance; they were released, then tried in March of 1887. Henry Putz was discharged from Ranger service on May 31, 1886. Brooks was discharged on July 11, 1887, after he, Putz, and Knight were found guilty of manslaughter. All three men eventually received a presidential pardon; records of the Texas Volunteer Guard, Adjutant General Circular No. 8, TSLAC. Captain J. A. Brooks filed a form (Adjutant General Circular No. 8), the purpose being to

make a record of engagements of officers of the Texas Volunteer Guard. Brooks mailed the form to the adjutant general's office from Alice, Texas, November 9, 1900. In a section describing his past engagements he said, "I was with Capt. Scott during the fence cutting trouble in Brown County but was not present when the fence cutters were killed." Brooks wasn't a participant in the fence cutter shootout the night of November 9, 1886. Ira Aten was sent back to Brown County by Adjutant General King at the request of Scott and was a participant in the fence line shootout. Ed Caldwell and T. S. Crowder, both members of Company F, were absent on detached service when the battle on the Baugh Ranch occurred; Nannie Nichols, interviewed by author, Fredericksburg, Texas, June 1963. Nannie's husband, Newton A. Nichols, rancher, friend and occasional deputy sheriff, served under James Moore's brothers, Kerr County Sheriff John Tarleton Moore. John Moore had been a Ranger in Company D and served as Kerr County sheriff for many years. Newt heard John Moore's stories of James's shootout with fence cutters and his brother's death in East Texas. When his brother was killed, the family recovered his firearms, saddle, and horse named Streak from Hemphill. They kept the horse, a sorrel gelding with a blaze face, until the horse died of old age.

48. Monthly return, Company F, Frontier Battalion, November 1886, TSLAC. Scott's neat handwritten "Record of Scout" is filed with his November monthly return and describes the shootout on the fence line; *Fort Worth Daily Gazette*, December 9, 1886; Smith, *Memories of Men*, 29. Smith interviewed Ed Chandler, the son of William Chandler, one of the first settlers in Brown County. Ed Chandler told Smith, "The Rangers called for the four men to surrender. Jim Lovell, one of the fence cutters, jerked his pistol and fired. When he shot, you know what happened."

49. Havins, " Passing of the Frontier," 47; Havins, *Something About Brown*, 39.

50. Smith, *Memories of Men*, 29. Smith offers details about the fence cutter plans and the trap set to catch them. His source, Ed Chandler told him, "Nineteen wirecutters were due to come the night we laid the trap. Four of them came way ahead of time and began to destroy the fence. We kept waiting for the others. Perhaps they had grown suspicious."

51. Monthly return, Company F, Frontier Battalion, November 1886, TSLAC.

52. Monthly return, Company F, Frontier Battalion, December 1886, TSL; Frontier Battalion Correspondence, Gillespie to Sieker, December 12, 1886, TSLAC.

53. Monthly return, Company F, Frontier Battalion, February 1887, TSLAC; *Galveston Daily News*, September 1, 1886.
54. Monthly return, Company F, Frontier Battalion, February 1887, TSLAC.
55. Havins, *Something About Brown*, 40; monthly return, Company F, Frontier Battalion, March 1887, TSLAC.

Notes for Chapter 9

1. Stephens, *George H. Schmitt*, 19–25.
2. Monthly return, Co. C, Frontier Battalion, March 1887, TSLAC.
3. Scott to Sieker, March 20, 1887, AGC.
4. Schmitt to King, April 13, 1887, AGC; State of Texas v. Robert Parrack, Cause no. 1338, Brown County District Court Indictment, sent on change of venue to Bell County and found in District Court Records in Bell County, Texas.
5. Schmitt to Sieker, April 21, 1887, AGC.
6. Monthly return, Co. C, Frontier Battalion, April 1887, TSLAC; Schmitt to King, April 30, 1887, AGC; Schmitt to Sieker, May 19, 27, and 31, 1887, AGC; Stephens, *George H. Schmitt*, 206–7, 209, 244. There were problems in Karnes County and the patience of Adjutant General Wilburn Kings reached an end. In 1887 budgetary constraints called for a reduction in the Frontier Battalion. Captain H. Schmitt's Ranger Company C was disbanded on November 30, 1887, and Captain Schmitt's career with the Frontier Battalion ended.
7. State of Texas v. Robert Parrack, Cause No. 1337, assault to murder indictment from the Brown County District Court. The indictment was sent from Brown to Bell County District Court on change of venue and is found in District Court Records, Bell County, Texas.
8. Bell County District Court Records, vol. 2, Bell County Criminal Minutes and Case Papers, Cause 3354. The assault to murder indictment from Brown County lists Bud Copeland, Lewis McCord, and Pete Shephard as witnesses. Young James, the oldest son of J. O. Copeland, was nicknamed Bud. James would have been 4 or 5 years old when Copeland was shot; Scott to King, February 14, 1887, AGC.
9. *Galveston Daily News*, July 19, 1887; Bell County District Court Records have three indictments with case records for assault with intent to murder Joe Copeland sent from Brown to Bell County District Court on change of venue. The newspaper's statement of three attempts on Copeland's life in three weeks was an error. Court records show indictments for three attempts to assassinate Copeland in April, June, and July of 1887. District court's records of one of

the assault cases show Copeland identified his assailants as Robert Parrack and Ace Mathews.
10. Spellman, *J. A. Brooks*, 45–50; Paul N. Spellman, *Captain John H. Rogers: Texas Ranger* (Denton: University of North Texas Press, 2003), 46–54; Sterling, *Trials and Trails*, 310–11; J. A Brooks and John H. Rogers wore scars and physical impairments from this gun battle for the rest of their life but went on with their Ranger careers. Brooks and Rogers with John Hughes and Bill McDonald are considered the Four Great Captains by Ranger historians; Nannie Nichols, interview by author, June 1963. James Moore's body was reinterred and given a Christian burial by his family in the Hemphill Cemetery.
11. Spellman, *J. A. Brooks*, 52; Stephens, *Bullets and Buckshot*, 102; monthly return, Co. F, Frontier Battalion, July 1887, TSLAC.
12. Monthly return, Co. F, Frontier Battalion, August 1887, TSLAC.
13. Monthly return, Co. F, Frontier Battalion, September 1887, TSLAC; J. O. Copeland, Texas Ranger Service Records, Frontier Battalion, TSLAC; some believe J. O. Copeland and his family had been under the protection of the Baugh brothers. There was a strong bond between Copeland and the Baughs, but nothing was found to substantiate Copeland's protection by the Baughs.
14. Monthly return, Co. F, Frontier Battalion, September 1887, TSLAC. Ira Aten to Roy D. Holt, January 25, 1928, Holt Papers. In a letter to R. D. Holt, Ira Aten, referring to the fence cutters, said that every time he attended court at Brownwood, "They tried to get me."
15. Stephens, *Bullets and Buckshot*, 105–6; monthly return, Co. F, Frontier Battalion, September 1887, TSLAC.
16. Monthly return, Co. F, Frontier Battalion, November 1887, TSLAC.
17. Monthly return, Co. F, Frontier Battalion, January 1888, TSLAC.
18. Monthly return, Co. F, Frontier Battalion, March 1888, TSLAC.
19. Frontier Battalion Special Orders, 1874 to 1899, "Special Order No. 126," April 1888, TSLAC.
20. Bell County District Court Minutes, and Case Papers; Havins, *Something About Brown*, 40; *Coleman Democrat-Voice*, February 25, 1910. The Coleman newspaper published a resolution and obituary for J. C. Randolph. Randolph was a 28-year-old Coleman attorney when elected judge of the Thirty-Fifth Judicial District. He served only one two-year term, then choose to not run for reelection; Secretary of State, *Biennial Report of the Secretary of State, 1888* (Austin: State Printing Office, 1888), 14. J. O. Woodard, the newly elected district attorney, was also from Coleman County.
21. *Brenham Daily Banner*, October 7, 1887; Havins, "Passing of the Frontier," 46–47.

22. Bell County District Court Criminal Minutes, January 17, 1888; the Texas Code of Criminal Procedures in effect at that time provided that "if a district or county attorney prosecuting a felony case represents in writing to the district court, that by reason of existing combinations or influences in favor of the accused, or on account of lawless conditions of affairs in the county, a fair and impartial trial as between the accused and the state cannot be safely and speedily had, or whenever he shall represent that the life of the prisoner, or any witnesses, would be jeopardized by a trial in the county in which the case is pending, the judge shall hear proof in relation thereto, and if satisfied that such representation is well-founded and that the ends of public justice will be subserved thereby, he shall order a change of venue to the county in his own or in an adjoining District," (Article 577, Texas Code of Criminal Procedure).There are no provisions as to the duties of the court to which the case has been transferred. However, Article 439 provides: "When a cause has been improvidently transferred to a court which has no jurisdiction of the same, the court to which it has been transferred shall order it to be retransferred to the proper court, and the same proceedings shall be had as in the original transfer." In reviewing Bell County's district court records, the court did not provide reasons that it didn't have jurisdiction. It may have been insufficient or improper paperwork, faulty indictments, or such, which would not legally bring the cases before the court. Apparently, cases were sent from Brown with defective indictments, with missing papers, insufficient evidence, and lacking necessary witnesses to prosecute the cases.
23. Havins, *Something About Brown*, 40; Bell County District Court's criminal minutes and district court case records. Eight cases were found which were returned by Judge Randolph to Bell County and later placed on the Bell County District Court's docket.
24. Bell County District Court Records, vol. 1, vol. 2, Criminal Minutes and Case Papers, Cause no. 3024, 3203, 3204, 3255, and 3256.
25. Bell County District Court Records, vol. 2, Bell County Criminal Minutes and Case Papers. Cause no. 3201, 3353; Ira Aten to Roy D. Holt, January 11, 1928, Holt Papers.
26. No reason for their absence from court was found in the court records. Bell County District Court Records, vol. 2. Bell County Criminal Minutes and Case Papers. Cause no. 3348; Alexander, *Rawhide Ranger*, 117–18, 365n58. Ira Aten moved the stolen horses to Huling's ranch in Lampasas.
27. Ira Aten to R. D. Holt, January 25, 1928, Holt Papers; Alexander, *Rawhide Ranger*, 115–16. J. O. Copeland, posing as Aten's uncle, help plant the young Ranger on the farm with Robert Parrack and family for undercover work. Although staying for only a short time, Aten gathered

enough evidence to get Robert Parrack indicted in Brown County for crimes besides fence cutting; Aten to Sieker, June 11, 1887, AGC.

28. Bell County District Court Records, vol. 2, Bell County Criminal Minutes and Case Papers, Cause 3348; Alexander, *Rawhide Ranger*, 117, 365n58; J. Marvin Hunter, "Fence Cutting Days in Texas," *Frontier Times* 16, no. 10 (July 1939): 443–44; J. Marvin Hunter, "Fence Cutting in Brown County," *Frontier Times* 22, no. 5 (February 1945): 129–30. In the two Hunter publications Aten describes the horse theft; Bell County District Court Records vol. 2, Bell County Criminal Minutes and Case Papers. Cause no. 3350. During the 1870s and '80s, the Texas Court of Criminal Appeals was noted for nitpicking and overturning lower court rulings. Judge Blackburn appears to have had this foremost on his mind and was cautious as he tried the cases delivered to his court on a change of venue from Brown County.

29. Bell County District Court Records vol. 2, Bell County Criminal Minutes and Case Papers. Cause No. 3350; Alexander, *Ira Aten*, 117. Aten rode with the fence cutters killing and butchering rancher's cattle, then distributing the meat among the cutters families. Butchered stolen cattle may have been the issue or stolen cattle may have been taken from the county. Details are not in the court records.

30. Bell County District Court Records, vol. 2, Bell County Criminal Minutes and Case Papers. Indictment 1348; Cause, 3354. J. O. Copeland, Bud Copeland, Lewis McClure, and Pete Shepard are on the indictment as witnesses. Bud (James Copeland), Joe's son, would have been too young to testify.

31. Schmitt to Sieker, April 21, 1887, AGC; Bell County District Court Records, Cause no. 3351, February 13, 1890; Tise, *Texas County Sheriffs*, 70.

32. Bell County District Court Records, Cause no. 3351, vol. 2, Bell County Criminal Minutes and Case Papers, January 14, 1889. An attachment demanding Copeland's presence as a state witness in District Court at Belton was sent to the Coleman County's sheriff asking that Copeland be delivered to Bell County District Court. There followed a witness reimbursement form signed by J. O. Copeland and approved by Judge Blackburn showing Copeland traveled to the Bell County District Court from his Coleman residence, five miles west of Santa Anna in Coleman County. Copeland received three cents a mile for travel from his residence, to and from Belton, Texas, for a total of 310 miles in this instance. The Coggin brothers' massive ranching interests extended into Coleman County. The author believes Copeland was employed by the Coggins after he was discharge from Ranger Company F.

33. Bell County District Court Records, vol. 2, Bell County Criminal Minutes and Case Papers. Attorneys John E. Bell and C. H. Jenkins represented Bob Parrack in the Bell County trials. Jenkins, a prominent Brownwood lawyer, served in the Thirtieth and Thirty-First Texas Legislature representing Brown and Coleman Counties, and later was associate justice of the Third Court of Appeals in Austin. In 1893 John E. Bell argued the J. J. Ferguson vs. The State of Texas case before the Texas Court of Criminal Appeals. One of the points for the appeal was a continuance denied for witnesses in a horse theft case. District Judge Willian Allison in this Llano County horse stealing case overruled the defense's motion for continuance to bring in four witnesses. The defense asked for a retrial and the judge overruled the motion for retrial. The case was appealed, then reversed and remanded by the Texas Court of Criminal Appeals.
34. Bell County District Court Records, vol. 2, Bell County Criminal Minutes and Case Papers, Indictment 1337, Cause 3199, and Cause 3351.
35. Bell County District Court Records, vol. 2, Bell County Criminal Minutes and Case Papers, Cause no. 3351.
36. Bell County District Court Records, vol. 2, Bell County Criminal Minutes and Case Papers, Cause no. 3351.
37. Bell County District Court Records, vol. 2, Bell County Criminal Minutes and Case Papers, Cause no. 3351. The indictment in the Bell County District Court Records has a note written across the front stating, "We the jury find the defendant not guilty, signed by T. W. [Heron] Jury Foreman."
38. Bell County District Court Records, vol. 2, Bell County Criminal Minutes and Case Papers, Cause no. 3200; Cause no. 3352.
39. Bell County District Court Records, vol. 2, Bell County Criminal Minutes and Case Papers, Cause 3354.
40. Havins, *Something About Brown*, 38; Bell County District Court Records, vol. 2, Bell County Criminal Minutes and Case Papers.
41. *Biennial Report of the Secretary of State 1888*; *Coleman Democrat-Voice*, February 25, 1910; Tise, *Texas County Sheriffs*, 70.
42. Holden, "Robert Cypret Parrack," 47–49; Gard, *Great Buffalo Hunt*, 304; Mullins, "Robert Cypret," 50–53; 1910 Federal Census, Plains, Chaves, New Mexico; Lubbock, Texas City Directory 1933, United States City Directories, 1822–1989, Ancestry.com; Find a Grave.com.
43. Joab Jacob (J. O. and Joe) Copeland, Hall Family Tree, Ancestry.com; a family descendant says J. O. built a boarding house in Temple, Texas, that he and his wife Laura managed.; J. O. Copeland, Certificate of

Death, Texas State Board of Health, Register 6868; 1900 US Federal Census, Justice Precinct 4, Falls, Texas; James P. Copeland, Texas State Department of Health, Bureau of Vital Statistics, File No. 04247, Certificate of Death, Kerr County, January 18, 1967. James P. Copeland, the oldest son of Joab and Mary Christene Scarborough, died of natural causes in the Kerrville State Hospital at the age of 84 years.

Notes for Chapter 10

1. Harry Hubert, "The First Barbed Wire Fence in Coleman County," *Frontier Times* 1, no.10 (July 1924); Roy D. Holt, "Fence Cutting in Coleman County," no date, Holt Papers. Holt was born and raised in Coleman County and confirmed Mann was the first user of barbed wire in the county. Holt said Mann was attempting to comply with the state of Texas's General Law of 1879 and had elm poles hung between the top two strands of the barbed wire fence as blinds. The first Texas statute relating to the new barbed wire was passed in 1879 and required boards (blinds) be hung between the fence's top two wires. These blinds were for livestock to see and to keep stock from running into the fence. Holt suggests the rails or poles Mann was using were probably a substitute for board blinds.
2. Padgitt, "William H. Day," 358; Daniel P. Green, "Mountain City, Texas," in Tyler, *New Handbook of Texas*, 4:861.
3. Padgitt, "William H. Day," 352; Tula Townsend Wyatt, *Historical Markers in Hays County, 1907–1976* (Austin: Hays County Historical Commission, 1977), 165; Walsh, "Jesse Lincoln Driskill," in Tyler, *New Handbook of Texas*, 2:704. In the spring of 1888, a late blizzard blew into the northern plains, killing off one of Driskill's large herds of cattle. Financial problems followed, and Driskill sold the hotel. Soon afterward, in 1890, Jesse died of a stroke.
4. Padgitt, "William H. Day," 352–54; Hunter, *Trail Drivers of Texas*, 872.
5. Padgitt, "William H. Day," 353–58; Jane Padgitt, "William Henry Day," in *A History of Coleman County and Its People*, vol. 1, by Coleman County Historical Commission (San Angelo: Anchor Publishing, 1984), 558–56.
6. Padgitt, "William H. Day," 358–59; Steve Wemlinger, "Ohio Steel Barb Fence Co," *Barbed Wire Collector* 35, no. 3 (March/April 2018): 9–11. When the first barbed wires were manufactured, they were usually coated with a black paint and not galvanized. Galvanizing came later. The manufacturers would dip rolls of the barbed wire in black paint for protection against the elements. The Ohio Steel Barb Fence Company was incorporated in 1876. They advertised their barbed wire in 1877, saying: "For a year past we have been using every means in our power

sparing neither time nor expense, to obtain rustproof coverings for our barbed wire that would not be affected by the weather. . . . We have tried black varnish, Japans, coal tar, galvanizing's, etc. etc.. We are now covering our wire with Red Rust Proof Paint." The barbed wire William Day purchased in Austin was painted red, and his bright red fence was an eye-catcher. Several years ago, Dale Duggan of Runnels County gave the author a link of barbed wire for his collection that came from the old Day Ranch. This old wire was rusted, and no paint remained. On checking this particular piece of wire in references, I discovered it was patented by John C. Merrill in 1876 and matched the wire in the Ohio fence company's advertisement. The Ohio Steel Barbed Fence Company manufactured the red wire using one of Merrill's patents. William Day red barbed wire was made in Cleveland, Ohio, shipped to Austin, and sold by one of the town's merchants.

7. Padgitt, "William H. Day," 353–58, 365.
8. Padgitt, "William H. Day," 362–66; Gene M. Gressley, *Bankers and Cattlemen* (Lincoln: University of Nebraska Press, 1971), 174.
9. Mabel Day, Adm'x etc. vs. R.Y. Cross et al., Case No. 4731, Supreme Court of Texas 1883, vol. 59.
10. Mabel Day, Adm'x etc. vs. R.Y. Cross et al., Case No. 4731, Supreme Court of Texas 1883, vol. 59.
11. Gressley, *Bankers and Cattlemen*, 176; *Fort Worth Daily Gazette*, July 24, 1883. The Fort Worth newspaper reported that Mrs. Mabel Day of Austin has leased her seventy-thousand-acre ranch and sold half of her cattle for $100,000.
12. James T Padgitt, "Mrs. Mabel Day and the Fence Cutters," *West Texas Historical Association Yearbook*, no. 26 (October 1950), 53.
13. *Fort Worth Daily Gazette*, November 7, 1883.
14. Padgitt, "Mrs. Mabel Day," 56–57, 65
15. Padgitt, "Mrs. Mabel Day," 57
16. Padgitt, "Mrs. Mabel Day," 66; monthly return, Co. F, Frontier Battalion, January 31, 1888, TSLAC.
17. Padgitt, "Mrs. Mabel Day," 58; Holt, "Fence Cutting in Coleman County"; Tise, *Texas County Sheriffs*, 107. Benjamin H. Pittman was one of Coleman's more popular sheriffs. He came to Coleman in 1875, served on the county's first grand jury, and was later elected sheriff on November 2, 1880. Pittman was reelected and served two terms. He was elected county clerk in 1890 and served three terms.
18. Holt, "Fence Cutting in Coleman County."
19. Holt, "Fence Cutting in Coleman County." Hemp fiber in those days was used to manufacture rope, and every cattleman carried a hemp rope on his saddle to rope livestock with.

20. B. B. Paddock, *A History of Central and West Texas*, vol. 1 (Chicago: Lewis Publishing, 1911), 332–33; Charles Wayland Towns, *Shepard's Empire* (Norman: University of Oklahoma Press, 1945), 138–39.
21. Hubert, "First Barbed Wire Fence," 16; Holt, "Fence Cutting in Coleman County"; Towns, *Shepherd's Empire*. Scab or scabies is a parasitic disease that infects sheep, causing their loss of weight, ruining the wool, and maybe eventually causing the death of the animal. The early sheepmen treated scabies parasite by dipping the sheep in a water dip made with sulfur and lye, or some used a dip of strong tobacco mixed with corrosive sublimate; Paddock, *History*, 333.
22. Holt, "Fence Cutting in Coleman County." Other large Coleman County ranchers of note who suffered fence cutting were J. L. Vaughn, L. L. Shields, R. S. Bowen, and C. J. Dibrell. Small ranchers and farms suffered too; like the large landowner, they also lost their fences. By the time the special legislative session took up fence cutting in 1884, almost all of the fences in Coleman County were already down.
23. *Galveston Daily News*, November 3, 1883. The paper didn't name the owners of the large pastures; the tracts referred to may have been owned by Horace Starkweather, Mabel Day, or J. L. Vaughan, all located in south Coleman County.
24. Padgitt, "Mrs. Mabel Day," 60–61; *Galveston Daily News*, November 3, 1883; King, *Report of the Adjutant General, December 1883*, 23–29.
25. *Galveston Daily News*, September 19, 1883.
26. Padgitt, "Mrs. Mabel Day," 63; Hubert, "First Barbed Wire Fence," 16.
27. Padgitt, "Mrs. Mabel Day," 64–66.
28. Gressley, *Bankers and Cattlemen*, 177.
29. *Fort Worth Daily Gazette*, April 26, 1885, September 20, 1885.
30. Elvis E. Fleming, *Captain Joseph C. Lea: From Confederate Guerrilla to New Mexico Patriarch* (Las Cruces, NM: Yucca Tree Press, 2002), 144–47; Gressley, *Bankers and Cattlemen*, 177.

Notes for Chapter 11

1. Ross McSwain, *The Texas Sheep and Goat Raisers Association: A History of Service to The Industry* (San Angelo: Anchor Publishing Company, 1996), 7–14; Lem Jones, *Angora Goats Then and Now: 1849 to 1995* (Austin: Nortex Press, 1995), 4–6; Paul H. Carlson, *Texas Woollybacks: The Range Sheep and Goat Industry* (College Station: Texas A&M Press, 1982), 36–39.
2. Edith Black Winslow, *In Those Days: Memories of the Edwards Plateau* (San Antonio: Naylor, 1950), 10; Frank S. Gray, *Pioneering in Southwest Texas* (Austin: Steck, 1954), 81–84; Grace King et al., *From*

Notes for Chapter 11

Muskets to Mohair: The History of Old Fort Terrett (Waco: Texian Press 1992), 142–45.
3. Sieker to Adj. Gen. W. H. King from Camp Leona, Uvalde County, August 8, 1884, AGC; Frank S. Gray, *Pioneering in Southwest Texas* (Austin: Steck, 1949), 83.
4. Rocksprings Women's Club Historical Committee, *A History of Edwards County* (San Angelo: Anchor Publishing, 1984), 346–47.
5. Rocksprings Women's Club, *History of Edwards County*, 347. In 2008, while visiting Green Lake on the Greer Ranch, the author found rusted remnants of the brothers' Glidden fence wire, joining a fallen rock fence probably built by Mexican shepherds before the Greers arrived in Edwards County.
6. Monthly return, Company D, Frontier Battalion, February 29, 1884; Sieker to King, August 8, 1884, AGC.
7. Monthly return, Company D, Frontier Battalion, July 31, 1884.
8. Baird, report of scout to Green Lake, August 8, 1884, AGC; P. C. Baird, "The Fight at Green Lake Water Hole," *Frontier Times* 3, no. 6 (March 1926): 33.
9. Baird, "Fight at Green Lake," 33.
10. Baird, report of scout to Green Lake, August 8, 1884, AGC.
11. Baird, report of scout to Green Lake, August 8, 1884, AGC.
12. Green B. Greer to Governor Ireland, July 30, 1884, AGC; Baird later explained Baker's problem. He had placed a .45 Colt pistol cartridge in his .44-caliber Winchester rifle.
13. Tom Dragoo, interview by Mrs. Eugene Mayes, August 5, 1947, cited in Rocksprings Women's Club, *History of Edwards County*, 54–55.
14. Baird, report of scout to Green Lake, August 8, 1884, AGC; Baird, "Fight at Green Lake," 35.
15. Baird, report of scout to Green Lake, August 8, 1884, AGC; Green Berry Greer to Governor Ireland, July 30, 1884, AGC; Dragoo interview by Mayes, in *History of Edwards County*, 54.
16. Baird, "Fight at Green Lake," 35–36.
17. Frederica Burt Wyatt, interview by the author, May 2008, Junction, Texas; Baird, "Fight at Green Lake," 36.
18. Baird to Sieker, telegram, August 8, 1884, AGC.
19. Baird, "Fight at Green Lake" 36.
20. Dragoo interview by Mayes, in *History of Edwards County*, 54.
21. Baird, "Fight at Green Lake," 37; 1880 US Census, Runnels County. Census data for the Tillery family shows William Tillery was 9 years old in 1880. Dr. James B. Hays, medical doctor and Brown County historian, believed it was William's older brother James Tillery, a well digger, who was killed in the shootout with Bill Turner.

22. 1880 US Census, Runnels County. Chuck Parsons and Donaly E. Brice, *Texas Ranger N. O. Reynolds, the Intrepid* (Honolulu: Talei Publishers, 2005), 121–22, 286. After their capture on November 11, 1883, Dee Bailey and his brother James were taken from the Comanche jail and lynched. Dee's wife came to Comanche with her small son to post bond for her husband, but on arrival found he and his brother had just been hanged. The citizens of the community cut the two men down, dressed them nicely, and put them in coffins. Dee's wife then took the bodies back to Coryell County for burial.
23. Mrs. C. D. Bruce, "Gillett vs. Dublins and Potters," in Kimble County Historical Survey Committee, *Recorded Landmarks of Kimble County* (Junction, TX: Kimble County Historical Survey Committee, 1971), 200–202; Baird, "Fight at Green Lake," 36; the author's grandfather, Harry Douglas (Doug) Jobes, lived on his father's preempted ranch on the South Llano River. The Dublin and Potter families were their neighbors. Ranger James B. Gillett killed Dick Dublin on the Potter family homestead. Doug Jobes said that Bailey, the fence cutter killed at Green Lake, lived on the South Llano and ran with the Dublin Boys before the gang was broken up.
24. Sieker to King, August 21, 1884, AGC.
25. Sieker to King, August 21, 1884, AGC. The author believes that Burton and Dodson were leaders of the cattlemen's group Captain L. P. Sieker refers to as the North and South Llano Fence Cutter Association.
26. G. B. Greer to Sieker, August 26, 1884, AGC. Daniel W. Roberts had been captain of Ranger Company D and retired from the Ranger service in the fall of 1882. He had operated out of Kimble, Mason, and Menard Counties and worked Edwards County and counties west. Before retiring he was stationed in Uvalde County, adjoining Edwards County. Roberts knew the people and the country and was probably a friend of the Greer brothers.
27. G. B. and W. J. Greer to Adj. Gen. King, mailed from Junction City Post Office, August 26, 1884, AGC.
28. Frank Jones to King, September 6, 1884, AGC.
29. Frank Jones to King, September 6, 1884, AGC.
30. Jones to King, sent from Samuel Warllick's General Merchandise Store in Fort McKavett, September 13, 1884, AGC; Sieker to G. B. Greer, March 6. 1885, Quartermaster Correspondence, TSL.
31. Jones to King, September 26, 1884, AGC.
32. Sieker to King, September 30, 1884, AGC. When the state created Edwards County in 1883, Bullhead became the county seat, and it was the county seat at the time of the shootout. Later Bullhead changed its name to Vance, and then later that portion of Edwards was split off

and became Real County. Rocksprings became the new county seat of Edwards County in 1891. But at the time of the Green Lake shootout, the town didn't exist. Rock Springs was only several seeping springs and a water hole used by stockmen.

33. J. Marvin Hunter in *Trail Drivers of Texas* notes that Joe Burton drove cattle to Newton, Kansas, in 1871, and as early as 1869, John Burton joined with Billie Campbell and Dan Phillips in driving three herds to Abilene, Kansas. The Burtons were prominent cattlemen; John Burton to Cousin D. Eisha Burton from Kimble County, August 2, 1884, ADJ; D. Eisha Burton to Governor John Ireland from Kyle, Texas, August 9, 1884, transmitting the letter from Cousin John Burton in Kimble County, AGC; Barbara Donaldson Althaus, "Fergus Kyle," in Tyler, *New Handbook of Texas*, 3:1172.
34. Sieker to King, August 8, 1884, AGC.
35. Baird, "Fight at Green Lake," 37; American Local History Network, USGenNet, accessed May 12, 2009, http://www.usgennet.org/usa/az/state/pioneers_of_tonto_basin.htm.
36. In 1958 Edwards County Rancher Johnny Whitworth showed the author a large cave on his ranch. He related the cave history, describing it as an outlaw hideout in the 1880s. Details of this discussion were not recorded, and few details are remembered. Tom Dragoo was a former owner of the Whitworth Ranch.
37. Allan A. Stovall, *Pioneer Days in the Breaks of the Balcones: A Regional History* (Austin: Firm Foundation Publishing, 1967), 257; Tise, *Texas County Sheriffs*, 503. The young Ranger Searce Baylor and Sheriff Henry Baylor were sons of John R. Baylor, the Confederate officer, Indian fighter, and rancher. John Baylor had established a large ranch on the Nueces River in Uvalde County south of Edwards County in 1878.
38. *Roanoke (AL) Leader*, January 10, 1923; Baird, "Fight at Green Lake," 37.
39. Bob Alexander, *Bad Company and Burnt Powder: Justice and Injustice in the Old Southwest* (Denton: University of North Texas Press, 2014), 163–73. Alexander writes a noteworthy chapter describing the exploits of P. C. Baird, a little-known Ranger and Mason County sheriff.
40. Rocksprings Women's Club, *History of Edwards County*, 347.

Notes for Chapter 12

1. Ruben E. Ochoa, "Castroville," in Tyler, *New Handbook of Texas*, 1:1024.
2. Luke Gournay, *Texas Boundaries: Evolution of the State's Counties* (Texas A&M University Press, 1959), 56. In 1892 the Southern Pacific Railroad tried to get Castroville to pay a bonus for routing their rail

line through the community but Castroville refused. The new line was routed south of town through Hondo. Hondo then became the new county seat of Medina.

3. Ruben E. Ochoa, "Medina County," in Tyler, *New Handbook of Texas*, 4:602–4; Chuck Parsons and Gary P. Fitterer, *Captain C. B. McKinney: The Law in South Texas* (Wolf City, TX: Henington Publishing, 1993), 27–46.

4. J. Marvin Hunter, *Pioneer History of Bandera County: 75 Years of Intrepid History* (Bandera, TX: Hunter Printing House, 1922), 54–55; Tise, *Texas County Sheriffs*, 369.

5. Hunter, *Trail Drivers of Texas*, 322; *San Antonio Light*, May 19, 1885; Paddock, *Twentieth Century History*, 173–74.

6. *San Antonio Light*, August 31, 1885; Tise, *Texas County Sheriffs*, 369; *Dallas Weekly Herald*, October 19, 1882; Robert Ernst, *Deadly Affrays: The Violent Deaths of the United States Marshals* (Avon, IN: Scarletmask Enterprises, 2006), 262–64; on February 21, 1885, US Marshal Hal Gosling was killed in the line of duty and was replaced by Sidney Jackson. Ferdinand Niggli continued as deputy US marshal under Jackson.

7. Tise, *Texas County Sheriffs*, 369. Years after the bitter fence cutting politics settled, Ney was elected and served four terms, retired, then came back and served four more terms; *Dallas Times Herald*, December 16, 1883.

8. *San Antonio Herald*, November 19, 1875. In 1880 Sanborn and Warner filed a suit against Norton and Dentz for an assignment of $1,586. The Bexar County court issued a judgment in favor of Norton and Dentz. Henry Sanborn appealed the case to the Texas State Supreme Court, which in April 1883 heard Case No. 4814, Sanborn and Warner vs. Norton and Dentz. They reversed and remanded the lower court decision; Castroville *Quill*, as quoted in the *Texas Wool Journal* (San Antonio), December 9, 1882; *Fort Worth Daily Gazette*, March 19, 1884.

9. *San Marcos Free Press*, January 10, 1884; *San Antonio Light*, January 23, 1886. The *Light* reported W. A. Wallace, known as Big Foot, was living in Medina County in 1886. In Wallace's last years of life, he lived in northeast Frio County at the Big Foot community, which was named for him. He died in 1899, and today his grave and monument are in the Texas State Cemetery in Austin. Over the years many historians and folklorists have written about Big Foot Wallace's exploits, but no one has picked up on his fence-cutting experiences.

10. Raymond, *Captain Lee Hall*, 191. By 1883 the Dull Ranch grew to an estimated four hundred thousand acres and pastured about twelve

thousand head of cattle and six thousand sheep; J. C. Newton, Pioneer of Frio County, to Roy D. Holt, Holt Papers; Hunter, *Trail Drivers of Texas*, 159, 686; *Galveston Daily News*, November 23, 1883; *Fort Worth Daily Gazette*, February 3, 1884; Wayne Gard, *Frontier Justice* (Norman: University of Oklahoma Press, 1949), 109.
11. *Galveston Daily News*, November 5, 1883.
12. *Galveston Daily News*, November 5, 1883; *San Antonio Light*, December 5, 1883.
13. Ernst, *Deadly Affrays*, 262. Harrington Lee "Hal" Gosling, an attorney, came to Castroville from Tennessee in 1878, practiced law, and published an early newspaper, the *Castroville Quill*. He was active in politics and considered a possible candidate for Congress. President Chester A. Arthur nominated Gosling US marshal for the Western District of Texas. Gosling was confirmed May 22, 1882.
14. *San Antonio Light*, December 15, 1883.
15. *San Antonio Light*, December 15, 1883.
16. *Fort Worth Daily Gazette*, December 20, 1883.
17. *Galveston Daily News*, December 16, 1883; *Dallas Daily Herald*, December 16, 1883.
18. *Fort Worth Daily Gazette*, December 29, 1883.
19. E. C. DeMontel, "Charles S. DeMontel," in Tyler, *New Handbook of Texas*, vol. 2, 591. Edmund DeMontel was the son of Charles and Justine DeMontel. Edmond's father, Charles, guided Henry Castro's German and French immigrants from Port Lavaca to their new home and settlement of Castroville when they arrived in Texas. Charles DeMontel's surname name was originally Scheidemontel but changed soon after arriving in Texas. When Sheriff William Foster stepped down as sheriff, his chief deputy, George Brown, entered the race for Medina County sheriff with the strong support of Ferdinand Niggli and the law-and-order group. Brown was defeated.
20. *San Antonio Express*, March 11, 1884; *Austin Weekly Statesman*, March 6, 1884. The description and details about the fence cutter's organization were passed to the newspapers by detective R. S. Davis.
21. Frontier Battalion, Texas Adjutant General Service Records, 1836–1935, TSLAC. As early as January 12, 1883, Detective Davis was provided a train pass signed by Lieutenant Joseph Shely and signed off on by Adjutant General King for travel from San Antonio to Hondo City; *San Antonio Light*, May 19, 1885. In May 1985 R. S. Davis filed a lawsuit in Bexar County District Court against ten prominent cattlemen and Ferdinand Niggli for $10,000. These individuals were the law-and-order group and presumably his employer.

22. *Fort Worth Daily Gazette*, February 3, 1884; *Galveston Daily News*, November 5, 1883.
23. *Fort Worth Daily Gazette*, February 3, 1884. Not mentioned in the newspapers is that a frequent cause of the fence cutting in counties across the state were barbed wire fences with no gates built across roads.
24. *San Antonio Light*, February 20, 1884; *San Antonio Express*, March 11, 1884.
25. Lula Blair Ellis, "Another Frontier Episode," *Frontier Times* 10, no. 6 (March 1933): 157–59. After fleeing Castroville Davis arrived in San Antonio and was mustered into the Frontier Battalion, Ranger Company F, as a private by Lieutenant Joseph Shely; *San Antonio Express*, March 11, 1884; *San Antonio Light*, May 19, 1885; Texas Adjutant General Service Records, 1836–1935, Frontier Battalion, TSLAC.
26. Ellis, "Another Frontier Episode," 259; *Austin Weekly Statesman*, March 6, 1884.
27. *Austin Weekly Statesman*, March 6, 1884.
28. *San Antonio Light*, February 28, 1884; *Austin Weekly Statesman*, March 6, 1884. Both newspapers reported thirteen cutters were delivered to Castroville and jailed, but only ten men were named in the papers.
29. *Fort Worth Daily Gazette*, March 2, 1884; *Bastrop (TX) Advertiser*, March 8, 1884.
30. *San Antonio Express*, March 11, 1884. What little information is known about the fence cutter's organization was provided by Detective Robert Davis and published in the newspapers; Texas Adjutant General Service Records 1836–1935, TSLAC. R. S. Davis was mustered into Lieutenant Joseph Shely's Company F, Frontier Battalion March 1, 1884, as a private. Davis served two years and was honorably discharged from Company F, February 28, 1886, by Lieutenant William Scott, the new company commander. No record of Davis returning to Castroville following his detective work has been found.
31. *Fort Worth Daily Gazette*, February 27, 1884; *Galveston Daily News*, March 11, 1884. The special legislative session met on January 8 and adjourned on February 6, 1884. When the legislature adjourned, fence cutting and pasture burning were made a felony punishable with mandatory penitentiary time. Before the enactment of this legislation, destroying a fence was only a misdemeanor offense. Lieutenant Joseph Shely was promoted to captain of Ranger Company F on March 1, 1884.
32. *Medina County News*, as reported in the *San Antonio Light*, March 15, 1884.
33. *San Antonio Light*, April 14, 1884.
34. *Omaha (NE) Daily Bee*, April 18, 1884; *Fort Worth Daily Gazette*, April 28, 1884; *The Democrat* (McKinney, TX), April 24, 1884.

35. *San Antonio Light*, April 30, 1884. There is no record of who arrested Wallace, but the fence cutter element had connections in San Antonio. A later incident would point to Fred Bader, a San Antonio constable.
36. *San Antonio Light*, June 10, 1884, and October 30, 1883; O. C. Fisher, *King Fisher: His Life and Times* (Norman: University of Oklahoma Press, 1966), 114–18, 144; G. R. Williamson, *Texas Pistoleers: The True Story of Ben Thompson and King Fisher* (Charleston, SC: History Press, 2010), 158; O. C. Fisher, *The Texas Heritage of the Fishers and Clarks* (Salado, TX: Anson Jones Press, 1963), 55–58; Chuck Parsons and Thomas C. Bicknell, *King Fisher: The Short Life and Elusive Legend of a Texas Desperado* (Denton: University of North Texas Press, 2022), 133–35. King Fisher came to Austin with Medina's officials after the legislature adjourned to attend a meeting and legal briefing on the new fence-cutting laws just passed. Later in the day, he was returning home on the train traveling with Ben Thompson, who was going to San Antonio. King made the fatal mistake of staying over in San Antonio with Thompson.
37. *Runnels County Record* (Ballinger, TX), November 8, 1884, as quoted in *Hunters Frontier Times* 18, no. 5 (February 1941): 244.
38. *San Antonio Light*, November 12, 1884.
39. Gary P. Fitterer, "F. Thumm, Der Revolverheld Von Deutschland," *Quarterly of the National Association and Center for Outlaw and Lawman History* 14, no. 3–4 (1990): 23–26; United States Federal Census, Mason County, Texas Precinct 4, enumerated June 18, 1880; David Johnson, *The Mason County Hoo Doo War, 1874–1902* (Denton: University of North Texas Press, 2006), 225; *Denison Daily News*, August 11, 1878.
40. *Reports of Cases Argued and Adjudged in the Court of Appeals of Texas During the Entire Tyler Term 1887*, reported by Jackson & Jackson, vol. 24 (St. Louis, MO: Gilbert Book, 1888), Case No. 2351, F. Thumm vs. the State of Texas (hereafter cited as Thumm vs. State of Texas); *San Antonio Light*, August 26, 1885.
41. Thumm vs. State of Texas.
42. *San Antonio Light*, May 19, 1885. Davis alleged in his lawsuit, "wicked and lawless persons disregarded the rights of the defendants and other stockmen and cut and destroyed their fences. An organization consisting of two bands of over forty fence cutters was formed in Medina County. Such was their influence in the counties where the defendants lived, and it was impossible to learn who the desperados that cut and destroyed fences were. It was dangerous even to bring them to punishment. The defendants in order to preserve their property and with Medina Sheriff Foster resolved to employ detectives to ferret out

fence cutters." He was employed on January 25, 1884, and said his duties were arduous and extreme. Davis said he assumed the role of a criminal, stayed with the fence cutters for twenty-eight days, and was discovered to be a detective. He said he would have been killed but made his escape and gave information that led to the conviction of the fence cutters.

43. *San Antonio Light*, August 26, 1885.
44. *San Antonio Daily Express*, September 1 and 27, 1885; *San Antonio Light*, August 26 and 31, 1885; Fitterer, "F. Thumm, Der Revolverheld," 25.
45. *San Antonio Light*, August 26 and 31, 1885; Ernst, *Deadly Affrays*, 262–63.
46. *San Antonio Light*, August 26 and 31, 1885.
47. Bradford Boehme, communications with author during January and February of 2021. Bradford is Frank Seekatz's great, great-grandson; Medina County District Court indictment number 1036, Medina District Court for Aggravated Assault and Battery against F. Thumm, issued October 10, 1885. Witnesses on the indictment are F. P Seekatz and Joe Jungman; capias for F. Thumm's arrest issued from Medina District Court, dated October 10, 1885; copy of handwritten charge to the jury by the Medina County district judge and other documents provided by Bradford Boehme. Outcome of the trial on F. Thumm's aggravated assault and battery charge was not found, but it is presumed the jury refused to return a true bill.
48. *San Antonio Light*, October 10, 1885.
49. Ernst, *Deadly Affrays*, 262–63; *San Antonio Daily Light*, November 4, 1886; *Fort Worth Daily Gazette*, January 29, 1888.
50. US Census, Fayette County, Texas, 1880; *Brenham Banner*, January 19 and February 9, 1882. John Hildebrand's father, Wm. H. Hildebrand, was a farmer and then a merchant in Fayette County. John worked with his father as a merchant while reading law to become a lawyer. John then assumed the editor's job with the *La Grange Journal* in 1882. The following month he married Miss Jennie (Virginia) McDaniels of Columbus.
51. Fitterer, "F. Thumm, Der Revolverheld," 25–27; *Fort Worth Daily Gazette*, June 23, 1887; *Southwestern Reporter*, vol. 31, permanent ed., December 23, 1895, 916. J. W. Hildebrand was deeded land on June 5, 1884, in Medina County.
52. Martin O. Noonan, "Hondo, Texas," in Tyler, *New Handbook of Texas* vol. 3, 681. Following an election in 1892, Castroville was displaced as Medina's County seat by the town of Hondo. Medina County's new courthouse in Hondo was built in 1893 on a lot donated by the railroad

that had bypassed Castroville; Thumm vs. State of Texas; *Fort Worth Daily Gazette*, June 23, 1887.
53. Thumm vs. State of Texas.
54. *Austin Weekly Statesman*, June 2, 1887.
55. *Fort Worth Daily Gazette*, June 25, 1887; Thumm vs. State of Texas.
56. *Austin Weekly Statesman*, June 30, 1887.
57. *The Standard* (Clarksville, TX), July 14, 1887.
58. *Austin Weekly Statesman*, July 14, 1887.
59. Thumm vs. State of Texas; Doug Duke, *Ben Thompson: Iron Marshal of Austin* (Austin,: pub. by author, 2010), 38; William M. "Buck" Walton, the Austin attorney who defended Frederick Thumm, had earlier been Ben Thompson's defense attorney and years later wrote a biography of Ben Thompson; *Sherman Daily Register*, October 20, 1887.
60. *Fort Worth Daily Gazette*, January 29, 1888; Thumm vs. State of Texas.
61. Ernst, *Deadly Affrays*, 263–64.
62. *Dallas Times Herald*, May 12, 1887.
63. *Brenham Weekly Banner*, February 9 and 16, 1888. Joseph Ney was the lineal descendant of the famous Marshal Ney of France, who led Napoleon's march across the Alps; Tice, *Texas County Sheriffs*, 369.

Notes for Chapter 13

1. *Austin Weekly Democratic Statesman*, April 5, 1883; the 1880 US Census records list most of the stockholders as farmers and residents of Missouri. Stockholder George E. Wittich was a prominent Kansas City mining and real estate investor and founded the Missouri & Mexico Mining Company in Old Mexico; *Milam (TN) Exchange*, April 14, 1883.
2. 1880 US Census, Walnut Grove, Greene, Missouri; Douthitt, *Romance and Dim Trails*, 90–91, 182–83, 279; Military Service of Soldiers Who Fought in Confederate Organizations, compiled 1903–1927, documenting the period 1861–1865, Catalog ID: 586957; Record Group 109; Roll 90, NARA; Frank J. Douthitt of Henrietta, Texas, telephone interview by author, December 1, 2014. Nancy Douthitt was a strong woman and a good mother. Nancy Douthitt lived a long productive life in Clay County, and her grave is in the Riverland Cemetery.
3. Douthitt, *Romance and Dim Trails*, 97.
4. 1880 US Census, Precinct 1, Clay County, Texas.
5. 1880 US Census, Precinct 1, Clay County, Texas.
6. It appears that Lewis Smith purchased the tract of land from Jackson Haley, with what was referred to as a contract for deed. Haley was simultaneously making payment to Angelina County on this land Lewis purchased. When Haley defaulted on his payments, the county

repossessed the property. Consequently, Lewis's purchase with Haley was for naught. Under a contract for deed, the buyer doesn't receive an actual deed until a specified part of the sale price is paid, which may occur years from the contract date. In the interim, if the seller fails to pay taxes or make his mortgage payments and defaults, his buyer may suffer severe legal complications. Although Lewis later received a quitclaim deed from Mrs. Haley, the deed was of no benefit. Angelina County had already foreclosed this land. The land and any money Lewis may have paid Haley was lost; Tennessee State Marriage Records, 1780–2002, Tennessee State Library and Archives, Nashville Tennessee. Mrs. N. R. Haley returned to Tennessee, where she married Thomas Marley in Roane County, December 23, 1885; *Fort Worth Daily Gazette*, September 13, 1886.

7. Although the Clay County Land & Cattle Company was investing in cattle, court actions in later years cited in newspapers indicate that the company was also involved in land speculation; *Fort Worth Daily Gazette*, September 17, 1886.
8. Dock Thompson, Cause 483, September 15, 1886, Clay County District Clerks Office, Henrietta, Texas (hereafter cited as Thompson Cause 483).
9. The improvement that Butcher referred to was probably the remains of the old Haley House and corrals; *Fort Worth Daily Gazette*, July 13, 1886.
10. Thompson Cause 483; *Fort Worth Daily Gazette*, July 13, 1886.
11. 1880 US Census, Precinct 1, Clay County, Texas; *Galveston Daily News*, July 8, 1886.
12. Thompson Cause 483; *Fort Worth Daily Gazette*, July 13, 1886.
13. *Fort Worth Daily Gazette*, July 13, 1886; *History of Henrietta and Clay County*, n.d. This document resides in the Clay County Historical Commission Collection. William Weddington was one of Clay County's early pioneers. The town of Cambridge in Clay County was established east of Henrietta in 1873, and in 1876 the US government built a telegraph line from Cambridge to Fort Sill in the Indian Territory. Weddington was their telegraph operator; Thompson Cause 483; *Fort Worth Daily Gazette*, July 14, 1886.
14. *Fort Worth Daily Gazette*, July 13, 1886.
15. Thompson Cause 483; *Fort Worth Daily Gazette*, July 10 and 13, 1886.
16. *Fort Worth Daily Gazette*, July 13, 1886; Douthitt, *Romance, and Dim Trails*, 124.
17. *Fort Worth Daily Gazette*, July 10, 1886.
18. *Fort Worth Daily Gazette*, July 13, 1886.

19. *Fort Worth Daily Gazette*, July 8, 1886; Lucille Glasgow and Leda Roe, Clay County Historical Commission; *Iola (KS) Register*, July 8, 1886.
20. *Fort Worth Daily Gazette*, 14 July 1886; Ibid. 17 Sept. 1886; Clay County District Court Records, District Clerks Office. Thompson Cause 481, Cause 482 and Cause 483. Dawson Cause 475, Cause 476, Cause 477. Douthitt Cause 478, Cause 479, Cause 480.
21. Clay County District Court Records, District Clerks Office, Thompson Cause 481, Cause 482, and Cause 483.
22. 1880 US Census Records, Precinct 1, Clay County, Texas; 1900 US Census Records, Justice Precinct 1, Brown County, Texas; B. F. Thompson, Certificate of Death, April 29, 1939, Bangs, Brown County, Texas, Bureau of Vital Statistics, Texas State Department of Health, Austin.
23. District Court Records, Clay County District Clerks Office; *Fort Worth Daily Gazette*, August 26, 1887; *Wise County Messenger* (Decatur, TX), August 27, 1887, September 3 and 10, 1887.
24. *Wise County Messenger*, February 11, 18, and 25 1888.
25. *Wise County Messenger*, March 3, 1888.
26. 1870 US Census Records, Precinct 5, Collins County, Texas; Sterling Dawson, Certificate of Death, January 4, 1931, Potter County, Bureau of Vital Statistics, Texas State Department of Health; "Sterling Dawson," Find a Grave Memorial #47421897, accessed September 8, 2014, https://www.findagrave.com/memorial/47421897/sterling-dawson.
27. Gary L. Brown, *The Legend of Dollie Douthitt*, accessed March 2, 2018, http://www.brownlaw-ok.com/enidhistory/articles/douthitt.pdf; *Fort Worth Daily Gazette*, September 15, 1891.
28. *Enid (OK) Events*, April 28, 1904; *Noble (OK) Weekly Journal*, November 10, 1904; "James Taylor Douthitt," Find a Grave Memorial #59835532, accessed November 8, 2014, https://www.findagrave.com/memorial/59835532/james-taylor-douthitt.

Notes for Chapter 14

1. John M. Winslow, interview by the author, Menard, Texas, December 2, 2001.
2. Davenport, "Fences in Mason County," 77. There was little concern about rock fences affecting free range grazing. Rock fences were built by farmers or stockmen who owned the land, and most pastures or fields were small; very few were large. During the heat of the barbed wire wars, however, there were cases where rock fences were pushed over. Like the destruction of rail fences, this action was part of the angry protest against massive barbed wire fencing.

3. Gray, *Pioneering in Southwest Texas*, 84–85; John M. Winslow, interview by the author, London Texas, October 6, 2001. John Miller Winslow, known as Judge Winslow to Menard residents and friends, was the grandson of Col. William Black of Fort McKavett. Judge Winslow was a prominent citizen of Menard and a founding member of the Edwards Plateau Historical Association; King, *From Muskets to Mohair*, 132, 142, 147, 197; Paul H. Carlson, *Texas Woollybacks*, 105.
4. John M. Winslow, interview by author, London, Texas, October 6, 2001; James Callan to R. D. Holt, January 30, 1928, Holt Papers; the author's family ranch south of Menard in Kimble County had rolls of old Buckthorn barbed wire stacked behind the barn. In years past sheep and goat ranchers replaced barbed wire with the new net wire (then then known as wolf-proof wire), and this aged barbed wire had been rolled up and replaced.
5. Earmarks were used on both cattle and hogs, but hogs were not branded as were cattle. Earmarks were another means for owners to identify their animals. Like brands, earmarks usually had a name. There were crops, slopes, splits, swallow-forks, underbits, overbits, and others. For example, the overbit was a V-shaped notch in the upper ear, made by doubling the ear and cutting out a small V-shaped notch in the top. The underbit was the same but on the underpart of the ear. There are many variations of these earmarks, and they are still used today. When a rancher records his brand at the county courthouse, he usually also records his earmark. For more information on brands and marks, see Manfred R. Wolfenstine, *The Manual of Brands and Marks* (Norman: University of Oklahoma, 1970).
6. Poe, *Runnells Is My County*, 99; Davenport, "Fences In Mason County," 79.
7. Gournay, *Texas Boundaries*, 80–85. The town of Menardville was laid out in 1858. It wasn't organized until 1871, and Menardville became the county seat that year. When the Fort Worth and Rio Grande Railroad laid track through the town in 1910, citizens of Menardville shortened the town name to Menard to facilitate painting the name on their signs; John Warren Hunter, "The First Fence Cutting Case at Menard," *Frontier Times* 5, no. 2 (November 1927): 62–63.
8. Theophilus Parvin, MD, ed., *The Western Journal of Medicine*, vol. 4 (Cincinnati: Robert Clarke & Company 1869), 257; *Mooney & Morrison's General Directory of the City of Austin, Texas, 1877–1878* (Houston: Mooney & Morrison, 1877), 100; Jake Landers and Alicia Brown, "Dr. Eber Green Dorr: First Doctor and Veterinarian in Menardville," *Menard (TX) News and Messenger*, February 16, 2012;

Notes for Chapter 14   351

Roger (Jake) Q. Landers, PhD., long time Menard County resident and historian, interview by author, May 4, 2019.

9. Hunter, "First Fence Cutting," 62; Sheriff Richard R. "Dick" Russell began his lawman career as a Ranger in Company D with Captain Dan Roberts. Russel was elected sheriff of Menard County in 1886 and was later reelected, serving ten years.
10. Hunter, "First Fence Cutting," 62; Grand Jury Indictment, November Term 1887, District Court Records, Menard, Texas.
11. John M. Winslow, interview by author, Menard, Texas, December 2, 2001. John Winslow's father was on the jury that handed down the verdict in the fence cutter trial.
12. Albert W. H. Moursund (aka A. W. Moursund Sr.) emigrated from Norway to the US in 1869 and settled in Texas on the advice of his family physician, who believed the moderate climate would benefit his poor health. In 1874 he acquired a license to practice law, built a home in Blanco, Texas, and married. In 1883 the Moursund family and three sons relocated to nearby Fredericksburg, Texas, where the elder Moursund set up a law practice in partnership with pioneer lawyer and judge A. O. Cooley. During his career, in addition to practicing law, A. W. Moursund Sr. served as a county judge, Texas legislator, district attorney, and district judge; Smith, *Members of the Texas Legislature*, 113.
13. Hunter, "First Fence Cutting," 63.
14. *San Saba News*, December 9, 1887; Hunter, "First Fence Cutting," 63.
15. Criminal Record Book, November Term 1887, Menard County District Court.
16. Criminal Record Book, November Term 1887, Menard County District Court; it is recorded in the minutes of the Menard County Criminal Court Proceedings that on November 14, District Attorney Walters appeared before the court and read into the record "prosecuting the pleas of the state and the sheriff by order of the court brought the defendant E. Goodin with the open court who on a former day of this term of the court to wit: on November 9, 1887, has been tried and convicted of the crime of fence cutting by a jury of Menard County Texas. . . . It is, therefore, the order and instruction of the court that the defendant E. Goodin be adjudged guilty of the offense of wantonly and willfully with intent to injure the owner cutting injuring and destroying a part of fence not his own and condemned to hard labor in the State Penitentiary for the term of three years. . . . It is adjudged and ordered, that the said E. Goodin is hereby remanded to the custody of the sheriff of Menard County Texas and from here be taken, by the authorized

agent of the state, and delivered to the superintendent of the Penitentiary of the State of Texas, then to remain for a period of three years."
17. Criminal Record Book, November Term 1887, Menard County District Court.
18. Hunter, "First Fence Cutting," 63; 1910 US Federal Census, San Diego, California, Bonsall Township.
19. 1880 US Federal Census, Burnet County, Texas; 1900 US Federal Census, Burnet County, Texas; 1920 US Federal Census, Travis County, Texas, Austin City; "Eber Green Dorr," Find a Grave Memorial #24488893, accessed February 8, 2008, https://www.findagrave.com/memorial/24488893/eber-green-dorr.
20. *San Saba News*, December 14, 1888.

Notes for Chapter 15

1. Utley, *Lone Star Justice*, 145; Rick Miller, *Texas Ranger John B. Jones and the Frontier Battalion, 1874–1881* (Denton: University of North Texas Press, 2012), 34; after the death of John B. Jones in 1881, his widow Ann Holliday Jones married Austin Senator Alexander W. Terrell. Senator Terrell was a prime mover in the legislative and political battles over fence cutting in the 1884 special legislative session. Henry Jones, father of John B. Jones, was a prominent farmer and rancher and a former state representative. He was active in Navarro County affairs until his death December 26, 1888.
2. Julie G. Miller, "Navarro County," in Tyler, *New Handbook of Texas*, 4:957–58.
3. Roy D. Holt, "Navarro County," Holt Papers.
4. Holt, "Navarro County," Holt Papers.
5. *General Laws, Special Session of the Eighteenth Legislature*; *Galveston Daily News*, February 15, 1884.
6. June Rayfield Welch, *The Texas Governor* (Dallas: GLA Press, 1977), 92–94; Judith Ann Brenner, "Lawrence Sullivan Ross," in Tyler, *New Handbook of Texas*, vol. 5, 688.
7. *Fort Worth Daily Gazette*, April 14, 1887; this incident occurred near Birdville, a prosperous farming community founded in 1841 and named after Captain Jonathan Bird. Birdville was selected by the legislature as the county seat of Tarrant County when the county was organized. Later in 1856 it lost a county seat election to Fort Worth by seven votes.
8. *Fort Worth Daily Gazette*, May 19, 1887.
9. *Fort Worth Daily Gazette*, June 17, 1887.
10. *Fort Worth Daily Gazette*, July 19, 1887.
11. *Fort Worth Daily Gazette*, July 7, 1887.

12. *Fort Worth Daily Gazette*, November 19, 1887; Gard, *Frontier Justice*, 115–16; Henry Jones, a prominent farmer and rancher, old Indian fighter and former state representative, was father of John B. Jones. His son died July 19, 1881.
13. Miller, *Ranger John B. Jones*, 34; Frederick Wilkins, *The Law Comes to Texas: The Texas Rangers, 1870–1901* (Austin: State House Press, 1999), 278–79; *Report of the Adjutant General of the State of Texas, December 1888* (Austin: State Printing Office, 1889).
14. Walter Prescott Webb, *The Texas Rangers: A Century of Frontier Defense* 2nd ed. (Austin: University of Texas Press, 1965), 428.
15. John Hughes to L. P. Sieker, June 13, 1888, AGC.
16. *Fort Worth Daily Gazette*, March 30, 1887, December 4, 1887; Webb, *Texas Rangers*, 434.
17. Aten, "Six and One-Half Years," 131.
18. Aten, "Six and One-Half Years," 131. In Aten's memoirs, published by Hunter, he describes Jim King as a fiddling fool who drew a crowd of listeners anywhere he broke out his fiddle. Referring to Navarro fence cutter dances, Aten said Jim King would play the violin for their dances at night. "We were having a great time at these dances, but not catching many fence cutters."
19. Nelson Ross, "Free Grass vs. Fences," *Navarro County Scroll*, 1967.
20. *Fort Worth Daily Gazette*, June 20, 1888; Ross, "Free Grass vs. Fences"; Harold Preece, *Lone Star Man Ira Aten: Last of the Old Texas Rangers* (New York: Hastings House, 1960), 162.
21. Alexander, *Rawhide Ranger*, 150–52. Aten's frustration was boiling as he penned this letter to his old boss. In March he threatened to resign from the Battalion.
22. Alexander, *Rawhide Ranger*, 153; Aten, "Six and One-Half Years," 131.
23. Aten, "Six and One-Half Years," 131; James K. Greer, *Bois d'Arc to Barb'd Wire: Ken Cary, Southwestern Frontier Born* (Dallas: Dealey and Low, 1936), 403; the prominent stockmen Aten was referring to were the old Indian fighter Buck Barry and T. C. Frost of Civil War fame, not District Judge Samuel L. Frost.
24. Aten to Sieker, August 31, 1888, AGC.
25. Aten to Sieker, August 31, 1888, AGC.
26. Aten, "Six and One-Half Years," 132
27. Webb, *Texas Rangers*, 434.
28. Webb, *Texas Rangers*, 434, September 17, 1888; anarchists exploded a dynamite bomb in a group of policemen during a demonstration in Chicago, Illinois, in 1886. This Chicago incident was referred to as the

Haymarket Affair and made the front page of newspapers across the nation.
29. Aten, "Six and One-Half Years," 131–32.
30. Aten to Sieker, October 8, 1888, AGC; Webb, *Texas Rangers*, 436. Dr. Prescott Webb points out that Aten spells dynamite correctly in this letter. Webb surmises that he had in fact bought dynamite and discovered he had been spelling the word wrong. This time he used the correct spelling.
31. Bruce C. Nelson, *Beyond the Martyrs: A Social History of Chicago Anarchists, 1870–1900* (New Brunswick: Rutgers University Press, 1988), 188–89; "Rioting and Bloodshed in the Streets of Chicago," *New York Times*, May 5, 1886.
32. Aten to Sieker, October 1, 1888, AGC.
33. Aten, "Six and One-Half Years," 130–32. Inconsistencies are found in Ira Aten's memoirs and the Ranger records in the Texas State Archives. This might be expected, as Aten wrote his memoirs more than fifty years after his work in Navarro County.
34. *Fort Worth Daily Gazette*, December 10, 1886. The story printed in the *Daily Gazette* was a spoof, and the writer of the letter signed off with the name K. Lamity. The subject of this letter, Mr. Wrenn, claimed to have sold the bombs to pasture men, but no record has been found of such sale, use of, or explosion of an Angel Maker on a fence line. But such a bomb was manufactured by an anarchist in Chicago and used in the Haymarket Incident. The only Texas record found of a similar explosive device being used to protect a barbed wire fence is Ira Aten's dynamite boom, as he called it.
35. Stephens, *Bullets and Buckshot*, 117–19; Mike Cox, "Range King," *Texas Escape Online Magazine*, October 8, 2003, http://www.texas-escapes.com/MikeCoxTexasTales/155LifeNMurderOfTexasRanger-JamesWKing.htm.
36. Alexander, *Rawhide Ranger*, 312–22. Alexander's *Rawhide Ranger* is a biography of a Ranger whose long career had more than his share of fence cutting assignments. Alexander's research is exceptional, and he tells a good story.

Notes for the Epilogue

1. *Galveston Daily News*, September 1, 1883.
2. *Fort Worth Daily Gazette*, January 29, 1884.
3. Miller, *Financial History of Texas*, 241; Smith, *Members of the Texas Legislature*, 221, 231.
4. Dan W. Roberts, *Rangers and Sovereignty* (San Antonio: Wood Printing & Engraving, 1914), 161.

5. *Galveston Daily News*, November 20, 1883 (copied from the *Marlin Ball*).
6. Miller, *Financial History of Texas*, 241.
7. Olivier Razac, *Barbed Wire: A Political History*, trans. Jonathan Kneight (New York: New Press, 2002), 37–41, 55–58.
8. "State Capitol Highlights," *Junction (TX) Eagle*, November 2, 2022.
9. Hagemeier, *Barbed Wire*; the Houston County Sheriff's Office reported a property known as the Old Lively Property on the west side of FM 3316 had its fence cut, allowing cattle to get into the roadway. The boundary fence of this property was cut several times the past year. A $3,000 reward was offered for information leading to the arrest and conviction of the person responsible for the cutting. Sharon Raissi, "$3,000 Reward Offered for Information About Person Who Cut Fence, Let Cattle Roam," June 30, 2023, https://www.ketk.com/news/local-news/3000-reward-offered-for-information-about-person-who-cut-fence-let-cattle-roam/.

Notes for Appendix 1

1. *Brenham Weekly Banner*, January 10, 1884.

Bibliography

Archives, Libraries, and Museums

Archives of the Big Bend. Bryan Wildenthal Memorial Library, Sul Ross State University, Alpine, Texas.

Austin History Center. Austin Public Library.

Bell County District Court Records. District Clerk's Office, Belton, Texas.

Brownwood Public Library, Brownwood, Texas.
  Local History and Genealogy Branch

Bureau of Vital Statistics, Texas State Department of Health, Austin.

Clay County 1890 Jail Museum–Historical Center, Henrietta, Texas.

Clay County District Court Records. Clay County District Clerk's Office, Henrietta, Texas.

Devil's Rope Museum, McClain, Texas.

Fort Chadbourne Foundation, Coke County, Texas.

Fort Chadbourne Museum, Bronte, Texas.

Grayson Family Papers, 1835–1959. Dolph Briscoe Center for American History, University of Texas at Austin.

Henrietta Jail Museum Collection, Clay County, Texas.

Historical Society for Southeast New Mexico Archives, Roswell.

Libraries Special Collections, University of Texas at San Antonio.

Mason County Historical Commission, Mason, Texas.

Masonic Records of Membership. Masonic Grand Lodge Library and Museum of Texas, Waco.

Menard County District Court Records. District Clerk's Office, Menard, Texas.

National Archives and Records Administrations, Washington, DC.

Nolan County Commissioners Court Records. County Clerk's Office, Sweetwater, Texas.

Panhandle-Plains Historical Museum, Canyon, Texas.

Pioneer City County Museum, Sweetwater, Texas.

Runnels County District Court Records. District Clerk's Office, Ballinger, Texas.

Southwest Collection / Special Collection Library, Texas Tech University, Lubbock.
  Roy Davis Holt Papers
  Royston C. Crane Sr. Papers

Tennessee State Marriage Records, 1780–2002. Tennessee State Library and Archives, Nashville.
Texas Ranger Hall of Fame and Museum, Waco, Texas.
Texas State Library and Archives Commission, Austin.
    Confederate Pension Applications, 1899–1975
    Frontier Battalion Correspondence
    Frontier Battalion Monthly Returns
    Governor's Correspondence (John Ireland)
    Stephen H. Daren Collection
    Texas Adjutant General Correspondence
    Texas Adjutant General Service Records, 1836–1935
    Texas Convict and Conduct Registers, 1875–1945
    Texas County Tax Rolls, 1846–1910
    Texas Department of Criminal Justice, Archives and Information Services Division
    Texas Ranger Service Records
    Texas Volunteer Guard
    W. R. King Letter Press Book
Texas State Preservation Board, Austin.
West Texas Collection, Angelo State University, San Angelo, Texas.
Western History Collections, University of Oklahoma Libraries, Norman.

Primary Sources

Baines, J. W. *Biennial Report of the Secretary of State of Texas, 1884*. Austin: State Printing Office, D & D Asylum, 1884.
Brown, John Henry. *Indian Wars and Pioneers of Texas*. L. E. Daniell, 1890. Republished with new material, Austin: State House Press, 1988.
Gammel, Hans Peter Nielson. *The Laws of Texas, 1822–1897*. Austin: Gammel Book, 1898.
General Laws of the State of Texas Passed at the Special Session of the Eighteenth Legislature Convened at the City of Austin January 8, 1884, and Adjourned February 6, 1884. Austin: E. W. Swindells, State Printer, 1883.
James, Will S. *27 Years a Maverick, or Life on a Texas Range*. 1893. Reprint, Austin: Steck Vaughn, 1968.
Journal of the House of Representatives, State of Texas, Called Session of the Eighteenth Legislature, January 8, 1884. Austin: E. W. Swindells, State Printer, 1884.
King, W. H. *Report of the Adjutant General of the State of Texas, December 1883*. Austin: E. W. Swindells, State Printer, 1883.
King, W. H. *Report of the Adjutant General of the State of Texas, December 1884*. Austin: State Printing Office, D & D Asylum, 1884.

Lambert, Will. *Pocket Directory of the Eighteenth Legislature of Texas.* Austin: Deffenbaugh & Company, 1883.
Mooney & Morrison's General Directory of the City of Austin, Texas, 1877–1878. Houston: Mooney & Morrison, 1877.
Nimmo, Joseph, Jr. *Report in Regard to the Cattle Business of the United States.* Washington, DC: Government Printing Office, 1885.
Report of the Adjutant General of the State of Texas, December 1888. Austin: State Printing Office, 1889.
Report of State Land Board to the Nineteenth Legislature, January 1, 1885. Austin: E. W. Swindells, State Printer, 1885.
Reports of Cases Argued and Adjudged in the Court of Appeals of Texas During the Entire Tyler Term 1887. Reported by Jackson & Jackson, vol. 24. St. Louis, MO: Gilbert Book, 1888.
Secretary of State. *Biennial Report of the Secretary of State, 1888.* Austin: State Printing Office, 1888.
Washburn & Moen Manufacturing Company. *The Fence Problem in the United States as Related to General Husbandry and Sheep Raising.* Worchester, MA, 1882.

Books

Alexander, Bob. *Bad Company and Burnt Powder: Justice and Injustice in the Old Southwest.* Denton: University of North Texas Press, 2014.
Alexander, Bob. *Rawhide Ranger, Ira Aten: Enforcing Law on the Texas Frontier.* Denton: University of North Texas Press, 2011.
Alexander, Bob. *Winchester Warriors: Texas Rangers of Company D, 1874–1901.* Denton: University of North Texas Press, 2009.
Alexander, Bob, and Donaly E. Brice. *Texas Rangers: Lives, Legends, and Legacy.* Denton: University of North Texas Press, 2017.
Barkley, Mary Starr. *History of Travis County and Austin, 1839–1899.* 2nd ed. Austin: Steck, 1967.
Barnes, Frank C. *Cartridges of the World.* Edited by Mic L. McPherson. 9th ed., rev. and expanded. Iola, WI: Krause, 2000.
Brown, John Henry. *Indian Wars and Pioneers of Texas.* Austin: State House Press, 1988.
Caldwell, Clifford R. *Robert Kelsey Wylie: Forgotten Cattle King of Texas.* Published by the author, 2013.
Caldwell, Clifford R., and Ron DeLord. *Texas Lawmen, 1835–1899.* Charleston: Historic Press, 2011.
Carlson, Paul H. *Empire Builder in the Texas Panhandle: William Henry Bush.* College Station: Texas A&M University Press, 1996.
Carlson, Paul H. *Texas Woollybacks: The Range Sheep and Goat Industry.* College Station: Texas A&M Press, 1982.

Clarke, Mary Whatley. *A Century of Cow Business*. Fort Worth: Texas and Southwest Texas Cattle Raisers Association, 1976.

Clifton, Robert T. *Barbs, Prongs, Prickers and Stickers*. Norman: University of Oklahoma Press, 1973.

Cooper, Ruth. *The Organization of Runnels County*. Ballinger, TX: Runnels County Historical Commission, 2014.

Cox, Barbara Thompson. *Baughs of Brown County, Texas, & Related Lines: Cox, Windham, McInnis*. Lafayette, CA: published by the author, 2000.

Cox, G. W. *Pioneer Sketches*. 1911. Reprint, Montague, TX: Montague County Historical Commission, 1958.

Cox, James. *Historical and Biographical Record of the Cattle Industry and the Cattlemen of Texas and Adjacent Territory*. St. Louis: Woodward & Tiernan Printing, 1895.

Cox, Mike. *The Texas Rangers*. Vol. 1, *Wearing the Cinco Peso, 1821–1900*. New York: Tom Doherty Associates, 2008.

Cox, Ross J., Sr. *The Texas Rangers and the San Saba Mob*. San Saba, TX: C&S Farm Press, 2005.

Crouch Carrie J. *A History of Young County, Texas*. Austin: Texas State Historical Association, 1956.

Dale, Edward Everett. *The Range Cattle Industry: Ranching on the Great Plains, from 1865 to 1925*. New ed. Norman: University of Oklahoma Press, 1960.

DeArment, Robert K. *George Scarborough: The Life and Death of a Lawman on the Closing Frontier*. Norman: University of Oklahoma Press, 1992.

Debo, Darrell, ed. *Burnet County History: A Texas Pioneer History, 1847–1979*. 2 vols. Austin: Eakins Press, 2002.

Dobie, J. Frank *The Longhorns*. Boston: Little, Brown, 1941.

Dobie, J. Frank. *A Vaquero of the Brush Country*. Dallas: Southwest Press, 1929.

Douthitt, Katherine Christian, ed. *Romance and Dim Trails: A History of Clay County*. Dallas: William T. Tardy, 1938.

DuCoin, Candice. *Lawmen on the Texas Frontier: Rangers and Sheriffs*. Round Rock, TX: Riata Books, 2007.

Duff, Katharyn. *Abilene on Cat Claw Creek*. Abilene, TX: Abilene Reporter News, 1969.

Duke, Cordia Sloan, and Joe B. Frantz. *6000 Miles of Fence: Life on the XIT*. Austin: University of Texas Press, 1992.

Dukes, Doug. *Ben Thompson: Iron Marshal of Austin*. Austin: published by the author, 2010.

Dukes, Doug. *Firearms of the Texas Rangers: From the Frontier Era to the Modern Age*. Denton: University of North Texas Press, 2020.

Emmett, Chris. *Shanghai Pierce: A Fair Likeness*. Norman: University of Oklahoma Press, 1953.

Bibliography

Ernst, Robert. *Deadly Affrays: The Violent Deaths of the United States Marshals*. Avon, IN: Scarletmask Enterprises, 2006.
Fenoglio, Marvin E., ed. *The Story of Montague County, Texas: Its Past and Present*. Montague, TX: Montague County Historical Commission, 1989.
Fisher, O. C. *Cactus Jack*. Waco: Texian Press, 1978.
Fisher, O. C. *It Occurred in Kimble*. Houston: Anson Jones Press, 1937.
Fisher, O. C. *King Fisher: His Life and Times*. Norman: University of Oklahoma Press, 1966.
Fisher, O. C. *The Texas Heritage of the Fishers and Clarks*. Salado, TX: Anson Jones Press, 1963.
Fleming, Elvis E. *Captain Joseph C. Lea: From Confederate Guerrilla to New Mexico Patriarch*. Las Cruces, NM: Yucca Tree Press, 2002.
Gard, Wayne. *Frontier Justice*. Norman: University of Oklahoma Press, 1949.
Gard, Wayne. *The Chisholm Trail*. Norman: University of Oklahoma Press, 1954.
Gard, Wayne. *The Great Buffalo Hunt*. New York: Alfred A. Knopf, 1959.
Giles, Bascom, and Curtis Bishop. *Lots of Land*. Austin: Steck, 1949.
Glasgow, Lucille Lowman, ed. *It Used to Be That Way: Remembered Bits of Clay County History*. Henrietta, TX: Clay County Historical Society, 1992.
Glover, Jack. *The "Bobbed Wire" Bible*, no. 4. Sunset, TX: Cow Puddle Press, 1996.
Goodwin, Frank. *Lone Star Land: Twentieth Century Texas in Perspective*. New York: Alfred A. Knopf, 1955.
Gournay, Luke. *Texas Boundaries: Evolution of the State's Counties*. College Station: Texas A&M University Press, 1995.
Gray, Frank S. *Pioneering in Southwest Texas*. Austin: Steck, 1949.
Greer, James K. *Bois d'Arc to Barb'd Wire: Ken Cary, Southwestern Frontier Born*. Dallas: Dealey and Low, 1936.
Gressley, Gene M. *Bankers and Cattlemen*. Lincoln: University of Nebraska Press, 1971.
Hagemeier, Harold L. *Barbed Wire Identification Encyclopedia*. 5th ed. Kearney, NE: Morris Publishing, 2010.
Haley, J. Evetts. *Charles Goodnight: Cowman and Plainsman*. Boston: Houghton Mifflin, 1936.
Haley, J. Evetts. *The XIT Ranch of Texas and the Early Days on the Llano Estacado*. Norman: University of Oklahoma Press, 1967.
Hamrick, Alma Ward. *The Call of the San Saba: A History of San Saba*. 2nd ed. Austin: San Felipe Press, 1969.
Havins, Thomas R. *Something About Brown: A History of Brown County, Texas*. Brownwood, TX: Banner Printing, 1958.

History of the Cattlemen of Texas. Dallas: Johnson Printing and Advertising, 1914. Reprint, Austin: Texas State Historical Association in Cooperation with the University of Texas, 1991.

Holden, William Curry. *The Espuela Land and Cattle Company.* Austin: Texas State Historical Association, 1970.

Huckabay, Ida Lasater. *Ninety-Four Years in Jack County, 1854–1948.* Austin: Steck, 1949.

Hunter, J. Marvin. *Pioneer History of Bandera County: 75 Years of Intrepid History.* Bandera, TX: Hunter Printing House, 1922.

Hunter, J. Marvin, ed. *The Trail Drivers of Texas.* 2nd rev. ed. Nashville: Cokesbury Press, 1925.

Ivey, Darren L. *The Texas Rangers: A Registry and History.* Jefferson, NC: McFarland, 1970.

James, Jesse S. *Early United States Barbed Wire Patents.* Maywood, CA: Jesse S. James, 1966.

Jenkins, Frank W. *The History of Runnels County.* San Angelo: San Angelo Genealogical and Historical Society, 2004.

Johnson, David. *The Mason County Hoo Doo War, 1874–1902.* Denton: University of North Texas Press, 2006.

Johnson, Frank W. *A History of Texas and Texans.* Chicago: American Historical Society, 1914.

Jones, Lem. *Angora Goats Then and Now: 1849 to 1995.* Austin: Nortex Press, 1995.

Kimble County Historical Survey Committee. *Recorded Landmarks of Kimble County.* Junction, TX: Kimble County Historical Survey Committee, 1971.

King, Grace, Sherwood Noel McGuigan, and Gem Meacham. *From Muskets to Mohair: The History of Old Fort Terrett.* Waco: Texian Press, 1992.

Kothmann, Forrestine Haney, and Constance Kothmann Kuhlmann. *The Kothmanns of Texas, 1845–1871.* 3rd ed. Austin: Firm Foundation Publishing House, 1972.

Kraisinger, Gary, and Margaret Kraisinger. *The Western Cattle Trail, 1874–1897: Its Rise, Collapse, and Revival.* Newton, KS: Mennonite Press, 2014.

Kraisinger, Gary, and Margaret Kraisinger. *The Western: The Greatest Texas Cattle Trail, 1874–1886.* Newton, KS: Mennonite Press, 2004.

Lea, Tom. *The King Ranch.* 2 vols. Boston; Little, Brown, 1981.

Liu, Joanne S. *Barbed Wire: The Fence That Changed the West.* Missoula, MT: Mountain Press Publishing, 2009.

London, Marvin F. *Indian Raids in Montague County.* Saint Jo, TX: S. J. T. Printers, 1977.

McCallum, Henry D., and Francis T. McCallum. *The Wire That Fenced the West.* Norman: University of Oklahoma Press, 1965.

Bibliography

McSwain, Ross. *The Texas Sheep and Goat Raisers Association: A History of Service to the Industry*. San Angelo: Anchor Publishing, 1996.

Miller, Edmund Thornton. *A Financial History of Texas*. Bulletin of the University of Texas 37. Austin: University of Texas, 1916.

Miller, Rick. *Texas Ranger John B. Jones and the Frontier Battalion, 1874–1881*. Denton: University of North Texas Press, 2012.

Miller, Thomas Lloyd. *The Public Lands of Texas, 1519–1970*. Norman: University of Oklahoma Press, 1972.

Monday, Jane Clements, and Frances Brannen Vick. *Petra's Legacy: The South Texas Ranching Empire of Petra Vela and Mifflin Kenedy*. College Station: Texas A&M University Press, 2007.

Monday, Travis. *Best of the Museum Musings*. Vol. 2. Sweetwater, TX: Lulu Enterprises, 2004.

Montague County Historical Commission. *The Story of Montague County Texas: Its Past and Present*. Montague, TX: Curtis Media, 1989.

Nelson, Bruce C. *Beyond the Martyrs: A Social History of Chicago Anarchists, 1870–1900*. New Brunswick: Rutgers University Press, 1988.

Netz, Reviel. *Barbed Wire: An Ecology of Modernity*. Middletown, CT: Wesleyan University Press, 2004.

Nueces County Historical Society. *The History of Nueces County*. Austin: Jenkins Publishing, 1972.

O'Neal, Bill. *Lampasas, 1855–1895: Biography of a Frontier Texas Town*. Waco: Eakin Press, 2012.

Paddock, B. B. *A History of Central and West Texas*. Vol. 1. Chicago: Lewis Publishing, 1911.

Paddock, B. B. *A Twentieth Century History and Biographical Record of North and West Texas*. 2 vols. Chicago: Lewis Publishing, 1902–1906.

Parsons, Chuck. *Captain Jack Helm: Victim of Texas Reconstruction Violence*. Denton: University of North Texas Press, 2018.

Parsons, Chuck, and Thomas C. Bicknell. *King Fisher: The Short Life and Elusive Legend of a Texas Desperado*. Denton: University of North Texas Press, 2022.

Parsons, Chuck, and Donaly E. Brice. *Texas Ranger N. O. Reynolds, the Intrepid*. Honolulu: Talei Publishers, 2005.

Parsons, Chuck, and Gary P. Fitterer. *Captain C. B. McKinney: The Law in South Texas*. Wolfe City, TX: Henington Publishing, 1993.

Parvin, Theophilus, ed. *The Western Journal of Medicine*. Vol. 4. Cincinnati: Robert Clarke, 1869.

Pate, Ann. *Fort Chadbourne: A Military Post, a Family Heritage*. Bronte, TX: Fort Chadbourne Foundation, 2010.

Poe, Charlsie. *Runnels Is My County*. San Antonio: Naylor, 1970.

Preece, Harold. *Lone Star Man Ira Aten: Last of the Old Texas Rangers*. New York: Hastings House, 1960.

Price, B. Byron, and Frederick W. Rathjen. *Amarillo and the Texas Panhandle.* Northridge, CA: Windsor Publications, 1986.

Pritchett, Jewell E. *From the Top of Old Hayrick: A Narrative History of Coke County.* Abilene, TX: Pritchett, 1980.

Raymond, Dora Neil. *Captain Lee Hall of Texas.* Norman: University of Oklahoma Press, 1940.

Razac, Oliver. *Barbed Wire: A Political History.* Translated by Jonathan Kneight. New York: New Press, 2002

Roberts, Dan W. *Rangers and Sovereignty.* San Antonio: Wood Printing & Engraving, 1914.

Rocksprings Women's Club Historical Committee. *A History of Edwards County.* San Angelo: Anchor Publishing, 1984.

Rose Peter R. *The Reckoning: The Triumph of Order on the Texas Frontier.* Lubbock: Texas Tech University Press, 2012

Sadler, Jerry. *History of Texas Land.* Austin: Texas General Land Office, 1961.

San Saba County History, 1856–2001. Vol. 2. San Saba, TX: San Saba Historical Commission, 2002.

Santleben, August. *A Texas Pioneer.* New York: Neale Publishing, 1910.

Skaggs, Jimmy M. *The Cattle Trailing Industry: Between Supply and Demand, 1866–1890.* Lawrence: University Press of Kansas, 1973.

Smith, Will L., ed. *Members of the Texas Legislature, 1846–1962.* Austin: Fifty-Seventh Texas Legislature, 1962.

Smith, T. C., Jr. *From the Memories of Men.* Brownwood, TX: Moore Printing, 1980.

Spaw, Patsy McDonald, ed. *The Texas Senate.* Vol. 2, *Civil War to the Eve of Reform, 1861–1889.* Collage Station: Texas A&M University Press, 1999.

Spellman, Paul N. *Captain J. A. Brooks: Texas Ranger.* Denton: University of North Texas Press, 2007.

Spellman, Paul N. *Captain John H. Rogers: Texas Ranger.* Denton: University of North Texas Press, 2003.

Stephens, Robert W. *Bullets and Buckshot in Texas.* Dallas: published by the author, 2002.

Stephens, Robert W. *Captain George H. Schmitt, Texas Ranger.* Dallas: published by the author, n.d.

Stephens, Robert W. *Texas Rangers Sketches.* Dallas: published by the author, 1972.

Sterling, William Warren. *Trials and Trails of a Texas Ranger.* 1959. Reprint, Norman: University of Oklahoma Press, 1969.

Stovall, Allen A. *The Nueces Head Water Country.* San Antonio: Naylor, 1959.

Bibliography

Stovall, Allen A. *Pioneer Days in the Break of the Balcones: A Regional History*. Austin: Firm Foundation, 1967.

Taylor, Williams Charles. *A History of Clay County*. Austin: Jenkins Publishing, 1989.

Tinkler, Estelle. *Archibald John Writes the Rocking Chair Ranche Letters*. Burnet, TX: Eakin Press, 1979.

Tise, Sammy. *Texas County Sheriffs*. Albuquerque: Oakwood Printing, 1989.

Towns, Charles Wayland. *Shepard's Empire*. Norman: University of Oklahoma Press, 1945.

Twentieth Century History of Southwest Texas. Vol. 2. Chicago: Lewis Publishing, 1907.

Tyler, Ron C., ed. *The New Handbook of Texas*. 6 vols. Austin: Texas State Historical Association, 1996.

Utley, Robert M. *Lone Star Justice: The First Century of the Texas Rangers*. New York: Oxford University Press, 2002.

Walton, William M. *The Life and Adventures of Ben Thompson: A Famous Texan*. Austin: Steck. 1956.

Webb, Walter Prescott. *The Great Plains*. New York: Ginn and Company, 1931.

Webb, Walter Prescott. *The Texas Rangers: A Century of Frontier Defense*. 2nd ed. Austin: University of Texas Press, 1965.

Welch, June Rayfield. *The Texas Governor*. Dallas: GLA Press, 1977.

Wellman, Paul I. *The Trampling Herd: The Story of the Cattle Range in America*. New York: Carrick and Evans, 1939.

Wendt, Lloyd, and Herman Kogan. *Bet a Million! The Story of John W. Gates*. Indianapolis: Bobbs-Merril, 1948.

Wilkins, Frederick. *The Law Comes to Texas: The Texas Rangers, 1870–1901*. Austin: State House Press, 1999.

Williams, Docia Schultz. *The History and Mystery of the Menger Hotel*. Lanham, MD: Republic of Texas Press, 2000.

Williamson, G. R. *The Texas Pistoleers: The True Story of Ben Thompson and King Fisher*. Charleston, SC: History Press. 2010.

Winslow, Edith Black. *In Those Days: Memoirs of the Edwards Plateau*. San Antonio: Naylor, 1950.

Wolfenstine, Manfred R. *The Manual of Brands and Marks*. Norman: University of Oklahoma Press, 1970.

Woods, Lawrence M. *British Gentlemen in the Wild West: The Era of the Intensely English Cowboy*. New York: Free Press, 1989.

Worcester, Don. *The Chisholm Trail: High Road of the Cattle Kingdom*. Lincoln: University Of Nebraska Press, Amon Carter Museum, 1981.

Wyatt, Tulia Townsend. *Historical Markers in Hays County, 1907–1976*. Austin: Hays County Historical Commission, 1977.

Yeats, E. L., and Hooper Shelton. *History of Nolan County, Texas*. Sweetwater, TX: Shelton Press, 1975.

Articles, Chapters, and Papers

Althaus, Barbara Donaldson. "Fergus Kyle." In Tyler, *New Handbook of Texas*, vol. 3.

Anderson, H. Allen. "John F. Evans." In Tyler, *New Handbook of Texas*, vol. 2.

Anderson, H. Allen. "William Buford Plemons." In Tyler, *New Handbook of Texas*, vol. 5.

Ashburn, Sam. "Cattle Battles on the Edwards Plateau in 1884." *Frontier Times* 9, no. 6 (March 1932).

Aten, Ira. "Fence-Cutting Days in Texas." *Frontier Times* 16, no.10 (July 1939).

Aten, Ira. "Six and One-Half Years in Ranger Service: Memoirs of Ira Aten, Sergeant Co. D, Texas Rangers." *Frontier Times* 22, no. 7 (April 1945): 129–30.

Baird P. C. "The Fight at Green Lake Water Hole." *Frontier Times* 3, no. 6 (March 1926): 33–37.

Bennett, Lyn Ellen. "The Politics of Barbed Wire." Paper presented at the Western Political Science Association Annual Meeting, Portland, OR, March 23, 2012.

Biggers, Donald H. "From Cattle Range to Cotton Patch." *Frontier Times* 21, no. 5 (February 1944): 203.

Brenner, Judith Ann. "Lawrence Sullivan Ross." In Tyler, *New Handbook of Texas*, vol. 5.

Brownwood Banner. "'Morg' Baugh of Brownwood." *Frontier Times* 23, no. 12 (September 1946).

Chamblee, Bob. "The Glidden Barbed Wire Fence." *Barbed Wire Collector* 35, no. 2 (January–February 2018).

Conger, Roger N. "Fencing in McLennan County, Texas." *Southwestern Historical Quarterly*, no. 59 (October 1955).

Connor, Seymour V. "Isaac L. Ellwood." In Tyler, *New Handbook of Texas*, vol. 2.

Cutrer, Thomas W. "George Washington Jones." In Tyler, *New Handbook of Texas*, vol. 3.

Davenport, Grace Heyman. "Fences in Mason County." *Edwards Plateau Historian*, vol. 7 (1978–1982): 77–79.

Davidge, Sarah Ellen. "Texas Rangers Were Rough and Ready Fighters." *Frontier Times* 13, no. 2 (November 1935): 125–29.

DeMontel, E. C. "Charles S. DeMontel." In Tyler, *New Handbook of Texas*, vol. 2.

Ellis, Lula Blair. "Another Frontier Episode." *Frontier Times* 10, no. 6 (March 1933): 157–59.

Evans, H. Leslie. "New York and Texas Land Company." In Tyler, *New Handbook of Texas*, vol. 4.

Evans, J. D. Evans. "Fence Cutters' War." *Clay County Historical Society*, August 11, 2013.

Fitterer, Gary P. "F. Thumm. Der Revolverheld Von Deutschland." *Quarterly of the National Association and Center for Outlaw and Lawman History* 14, no. 3–4 (1990): 23–26; 15, no. 1 (1991).

Gard, Wayne. "The Fence Cutters." *Southwestern Historical Quarterly* 51, no. 1 (July 1947): 1–15.

Green, Daniel P. "Mountain City, Texas." In Tyler, *New Handbook of Texas*, vol. 4.

Guthrie, Keith. "Coleman-Fulton Pasture Company." In Tyler, *New Handbook of Texas*, vol. 2.

Harper, Cecil O., Jr. "Before They Were Populists: Politics and Politicians in Jack County, 1884–1892." *West Texas Historical Association Yearbook*, no. 53 (1977): 106–20.

Hart, Brian. "Newport." In Tyler, *New Handbook of Texas*, vol. 4.

Havins, T. R. "The Passing of the Frontier in Brown County." *West Texas Historical Association Yearbook*, no. 8 (June 1932): 43–50.

Havins, T. R. "Sheepman-Cattleman Antagonism on the Texas Frontier." *West Texas Historical Association Yearbook*, no. 18 (June 1942).

Holden, William Curry. "Immigration and Settlement in West Texas." *West Texas Historical Association Yearbook*, no. 5 (June 1929): 72–94.

Holden, William Curry. "Matador Ranch." In Tyler, *New Handbook of Texas*, vol. 4.

Holden, William Curry. "Robert Cypret Parrack: Buffalo Hunter and Fence Cutter." *West Texas Historical Association Yearbook*, no 21 (October 1945): 29–49.

Holden, William Curry. "West Texas Droughts." *Southwest Historical Quarterly*, no 32 (October 1928): 103–23.

Holt, Roy D. "The Introduction of Barbed Wire into Texas and the Fence Cutting War." *West Texas Historical Association Yearbook*, no. 6 (June 1930): 65–79.

Holt, Roy D. "The Saga of Barbed Wire in Tom Green County." *West Texas Historical Association Yearbook*, no. 4 (1928): 32–49.

Hubert, Harry. "The First Barbed Wire Fence in Coleman County." *Frontier Times* 1, no. 10 (July 1924).

Hunt, William R. "Hylton, Texas." In Tyler *New Handbook of Texas*, vol. 3.

Hunter, J. Marvin. "Fence Cutting in Brown County." *Frontier Times* 22, no. 5 (February 1945): 129–30.

Hunter, J. Marvin. "Fence Cutting Days in Texas." *Frontier Times* 16, no. 10 (July 1939): 443–44.

Hunter, John Warren. "The First Fence Cutting Case at Menard." *Frontier Times* 5, no. 2 (November 1927): 62–63.

Jenkins, Rachel. "Byrd, Texas." In Tyler, *New Handbook of Texas*, vol. 1.

Jobes, Harold D. "Seeking Reparation for the Murder of Johann Wolfgang Braeutigam." Paper presented at the fall meeting of the Edwards Plateau Historical Association, Harper, Texas, October 30, 2019.

Johnson, John M. "Thrifty, Texas." In Tyler, *New Handbook of Texas*, vol. 6.

Kimbrough, W. C. "The Frontier Background of Clay County." *West Texas Historical Association Yearbook*, no. 18 (1942): 116–31.

Kingsbury, E. M. "John W. Gates: The Forgetful Man." *Everybody's Magazine* 10, no. 1 (January–June 1904): 82.

Lackey, Jerry. "From Fort to Ranch: An Interesting Tale." *San Angelo Standard Times*, September 12, 2009.

Lee, C. E. "The Fence Cutting War in Texas." *Frontier Times* 8, no. 10 (July 1931): 468–69.

Lomas, Fran. "Mrs. Frank Lomas." *Stalking Kin, San Angelo Genealogical and Historical Society* 3, no. 2 (2003): 58.

Long, Aldon S., and Berte R. Haigh. "Land Appropriations for Education." In Tyler, *New Handbook of Texas*, vol. 4.

Maxwell, Lisa C. "Falls County, Texas." In Tyler, *New Handbook of Texas*, vol. 2.

McCallum, Henry D. "Barbed Wire in Texas." *Southwestern Historical Quarterly* 61, no. 2 (October 1957): 207–19.

McClure, C. Boone. "History of the Manufacture of Barbed Wire." *Panhandle Plains Historical Review*, vol. 31 (1958): 1–114.

Miller, Julie G. "Navarro County." In Tyler, *New Handbook of Texas*, vol. 4.

Mitchell, Glynn. "The Coggin Ranch." *Edwards Plateau Historian*, vol. 6 (1974–1977).

"'Morg' Baugh of Brownwood." *Frontier Times* 23, no. 12 (September 1946): 232–34.

Noonan, Martin O. "Hondo, Texas." In Tyler, *New Handbook of Texas* vol. 3.

Ochoa, Ruben E. "Castroville." In Tyler, *New Handbook of Texas*, vol. 1.

Ochoa, Ruben E. "Medina County." In Tyler, *New Handbook of Texas*, vol. 4.

Padgitt, James T. "Colonel William H. Day: Texas Ranchman." *Southwest Historical Quarterly* 53, no. 4 (April 1950): 347–66.

Padgitt, James T. "Day Ranch and Neighboring Ranches." *Edwards Plateau Historian*, vol. 6 (1974–1977).

Padgitt, James T. "Mrs. Mabel Day and the Fence Cutters." *West Texas Historical Association Yearbook*, no. 26 (October 1950).

Padgitt, Jane. "William Henry Day." In *A History of Coleman County and Its People*, vol. 1, by Coleman County Historical Commission. San Angelo: Anchor Publishing, 1984.

Roell, Craig H. "William Henry Crain." In Tyler, *New Handbook of Texas*, vol. 2.

Rose, Evelyn. "Glen Canyon Ties to the Nobel Prize." *Glen Park News, Paper of the Glen Park Association*, Winter 2007/2008.

Ross, Nelson. "Free Grass vs. Fences." *Navarro County Scroll*, 1967.

Smith, Glenn. "Fence Cutting and Stage Robbing in Runnels County." *West Texas Historical Association Yearbook*, vol. 41 (October 1965).

Smith, Ralph. "The Farmers' Alliance in Texas, 1875–1900: A Revolt Against Bourbon and Bourgeois Democracy." *Southwestern Historical Quarterly*, no. 48 (July 1944–April 1945): 346–69.

Stenholm, Charles W. "Recognition of Fort Chadbourne, Coke County Texas." *Congressional Record*, July 10, 2001.

Texas Industrial Resources. "Introducing Barbed Wire in Texas." *Frontier Times* 9, no. 2 (November 1931): 91.

Thompson, Theronne. "Fort Buffalo Springs, Texas Border Post." *West Texas Historical Association Yearbook*, vol. 36 (1960).

Tinkler, Estelle D. "Last Days of the Rocking Chair Ranche." *Panhandle Plains Historical Review*, no. 15 (1942): 76–81.

Walsh, Mary Jayne. "Jesse Lincoln Driskill." In Tyler, *New Handbook of Texas*, vol. 2.

Wemlinger, Steve. "Ohio Steel Barbed Fence Co." *Barbed Wire Collector* 35, no. 3 (March/April 2018): 9–11.

Wise, Leroy. "Brown County from 1856 to 1870." *Frontier Times* 3, no. 5 (February 1926): 44–47.

Wolfgang, Otto. "How the Wild West Was Fenced In." *The Cattleman*, March 2001.

Worcester, Donald E. "Chisholm Trail." In Tyler, *New Handbook of Texas*, vol. 2.

Theses

Graves, Donald R. "Fence Cutting in Texas, 1883–1885." Master's thesis, Texas Western College of the University of Texas, 1962.

Mullins Fred R. "Robert Cypret: Pioneer Plainsman." Master's thesis, Texas Technological University, 1946.

Parrish, Lucian Walton. "An Economic History of Clay County." Master's thesis, University of Texas, 1909.

Paschal, Lois. "The Frontier History of Jack County." Master's thesis, Midwestern University, 1974.

Pyle, Lloyd C. "History of Nolan County to 1900." Master's thesis, East Texas State Teachers College, 1937.
Shive, Carroll William. "The Coggins Brothers." Master's thesis, Texas Tech University, 1974.
Smith, Leonard Glenn. "A History of Runnels County, Texas, 1683–1960." Master's thesis, Trinity University, 1963.
Smith, Maggie Ruhamah (Ruie). "The Administration of Governor John Ireland, 1883-1887." Master's thesis, University of Texas, Austin, 1934.

Newspapers
Austin Democratic Statesman
Austin Statesman
Austin Weekly Statesman
Albany (TX) Echo
Barber County Index (Medicine Lodge, KS)
Bastrop (TX) Advertiser
Brenham (TX) Weekly Banner
Bronte Enterprise
Brownwood Banner Bulletin
Canadian Free Press
Clarksville Standard
Clay County Leader (Henrietta, TX)
Coleman (TX) Democrat-Voice
Dallas Herald
Dallas Times Herald
Dallas Weekly Herald
The Democrat (McKinney, TX)
Denison Daily News
Enid (OK) Events
Fort Worth Daily Gazette
Galveston Daily News
Glen Park News
Iola (KS) Register
Jacksboro (TX) Citizen
Junction (TX) Eagle
Llano News
Menard (TX) News and Messenger
Milam (TN) Exchange
New York Times
Noble (OK) Weekly Journal
Omaha (NE) Daily Bee
Roanoke (LA) Leader

Runnels County Ledger (Ballinger, TX)
Runnels County Record (Ballinger, TX)
San Angelo Standard Times
San Antonio Daily Express
San Antonio Express
San Antonio Light
San Marcos Free Press
San Saba News
Sherman Daily Register
State Gazette (Austin)
The Standard (Clarksville, TX)
Texas Wool Journal (San Antonio)
Wise County Messenger (Decatur, TX)

Index

A

Abilene, KS, 42, 68, 175
Abilene, TX, 83, 85, 114, 118, 123, 137
Adams, J. O., 81
Adams, William Nelson, 76, 78–80, 129, 143, 147–49, 157, 167, 171, 286
Albany, TX, 41, 50, 205
Albert, Charles, 270
Albin, B. F., 49
Allen, N. J., 113
Allen, R. T., 64
Ames, J. R., 113
Angelina County, TX, 243–45
Armistead, W. T., 98
Aston, John, 107, 109–11
Aten, Ira, 143–47, 158, 163–66, 265, 273–84
Austin, 3–9, 19–20, 29–30, 56, 58–59, 85–92, 97–98, 104–5, 114, 130–34, 149–50, 152–53, 158, 174–78, 187, 204, 236–37, 271–75, 277–80, 282
Avery, Willis, 86
Aycock, K., 29

B

Bader, August, 221, 226
Bader, Emil, 218, 221–23, 226
Bader, Fred, 226
Bailey, Dee, 200
Bailey, James, 200
Bailey, John (a.k.a. John Mason), 200
Baird, TX, 123, 142
Baird, Phillip C., 196–99, 203–6
Baker brothers, 270
Baker, O. D., 197, 201, 205
Baker, Sam, 23
Baker, W. W., 197–99, 205
Ballinger, TX, 83, 157, 160, 258

373

Bangs, TX, 252
barbed wire, 4–5, 8–9, 11–25, 29, 33, 35–36, 41–45, 70–71, 82–83, 85,
    104–6, 173–74, 177, 190, 210–11, 256–57, 285–86, 288–91
  fences, 21–22, 24–25, 35, 37, 44–47, 83, 185–86, 188, 207, 244, 246,
    255, 257–60, 266–67, 287–90
  patents, 8, 16, 18, 291
  sales, 16, 19, 21, 23, 43–44, 67
barbed wire war, 5, 104, 185–86, 207, 218, 229, 285–87, 289–91
Bardwell, H. G., 119–22
Barrett, L. C., 252
Barron, James B., 6
Barron, Julia, 180
Bastrop County, TX, 87, 174
Baugh, David, 65, 72
Baugh, Harvey J., 66
Baugh, Levin "Lev," 65–66, 70, 72–73, 76–77, 135, 142, 145–46, 161
Baugh, Pencey, 72
Baugh, Powell, 65
Baugh, Washington Morgan "Morg," 65–67, 76, 128, 138, 145–49, 151,
    153, 164, 166
Baugh brothers, 65, 67, 72–73, 76–77, 128, 133–35, 139, 142, 144, 146–47,
    153–54, 158, 165–66
Baugh Ranch, 133, 160
  fence line, 73, 134–35, 145, 149, 157, 170–71
Baylor, George W., 114, 116–17, 123–24
Baylor, Henry W., 205
Baylor, Searce, 205
Bee County, xiii, 21
Beetz, Anton, 230–32
Belcher, John, 43, 286
Bell, John E., 166–70
Bell County, TX, 159, 161–67, 170–72
Belton, TX, 144, 162, 174
Benavides, Carlos, 185
Benavides, Santo, 185
Berry, Buck, 277
Bexar County, TX, 81–82, 208–9, 214, 229, 231, 233
Biediger, Stephen, 220, 229
Biry, Jacob, 220
Black, William Leslie, 194, 256
Blackburn, William A., 138, 161–62, 165–66, 168–70
Blue Devils of the West, 207, 217–18, 223, 228

Index 375

Bluffton, TX, 134
Boerne, TX, 229, 237–38
Bohl, Joseph, 220, 230
Bolinger, Henry, 168, 170
Bonflie, Henry, 220
Booth, J. M., 54, 181, 187, 190–91
Bosque County, TX, 270
Bowie, TX, 54
Boyett, Cornelius W. "Neil," 106–7, 109–10, 112–15, 119–25
Boyett, Mack, 109, 114, 119
Boyett brothers, 119
Bradford, M. M., 199
Bradly, W. J., 134
Braeutigam, Johann Wolfgang, 143
Bratton, Will, 250
Brewer, E. J., 72
Brisbin, James S., 32
Brooks, James A., 142, 145, 148–49, 156, 158–60
Brown, A. O., 106
Brown, Frank, 7
Brown, George W., 218, 228–29, 232
Brown, John Henry, 77
Brown, Owen, 95
Brown, W. F., 63
Brown County, TX, 63–65, 67–80, 127–31, 133–45, 148–52, 154–55, 157–66, 170–72, 228, 252, 257, 283, 286–87
Brownfield, J. C., 115
Browning, J. N., 83
Browning, W. H., 138, 162
Brownsville, TX, 176
Brownwood, TX, 63–64, 66, 68–69, 71–80, 129, 131–32, 134, 137–40, 142–50, 152, 154–55, 157–58, 162, 164, 167
Brunson, James, 204
Brunson, John, 196–98, 204
Buffalo Gap, TX, 107, 109, 115
Buffalo Springs, TX, 44, 48, 58–60
Burch, Charley, 47
Burghardt, Schumaker, 12
Burnet County, TX, 139, 259, 262
Burnett, John, 164
Burnett, W. D., 218, 220, 223
Burns, John, 134

Burt, James W., 199
Burton, D. Elisha, 203–4
Burton, Henry, 196–98, 201, 203
Burton, Joe, 201–3
Burton, John, 203
Butcher, Alice E., 242
Butcher, Nathaniel, 242
Butler, J. W., 48, 52–54
Butler, John Calvin, 205
Butler, W. A., 147
Byrd, Shep, 150, 161–63

C

Callahan County, TX, 123, 142, 149
Camp Colorado, TX, 173, 175–76, 178
Canyon, TX, 171
Carie, Joseph, 209, 229
Carleton and Chandler (law firm), 8
Carlton, William, 105–11, 125
Carmichael, Frank, 158–59
Carmichael, Jim, 145, 147
Carpenter, J. C., 43
Carter, C. L. "Kit," 43
Cartwright, L. F., 137, 139
Castro, Henri, 208
Castro County, TX, 208, 210, 284
Castroville, TX, 208–11, 213, 218–26, 228–29, 231–37
cattle, 19–20, 24–25, 27, 30–31, 33, 36–37, 42–43, 45–49, 53–54, 63–68, 81–85, 89–90, 92–93, 171–72, 174–81, 183–86, 188–91, 216–17, 285, 288–91
  business, 30, 33, 48, 64, 66–67, 69, 75, 99, 175, 209
  grazing, 42–43, 68, 82–83, 110, 176, 179, 204, 287
  operations, 43, 64, 72, 179, 288, 290
  stealing, 108, 114, 131, 134, 151, 154, 159, 166, 209–10, 218, 223, 288–89
  thieves, 45, 65, 73, 112, 140, 157, 159, 183, 210, 284, 288
cattlemen, 18–19, 21–22, 30–31, 42–48, 53–54, 57–58, 65, 69, 76–77, 81–83, 88, 90–91, 179–80, 194–95, 256–58, 266, 289–90
Causey brothers, 68
Central Texas, 42, 174, 258
Chandler, W., 63

Index

Cherokee County, TX, 124
Chicago, 8, 127, 132, 186, 279, 281
Childs, N. B., 242
Chisum, John, 64
Cisco, TX, 156–57
Civil War, 13–14, 18–19, 21, 31–32, 41, 44, 64–65, 67, 69, 191, 193, 208–9, 265–66, 268
Clarksville, TX, 52, 95
Clay County, TX, xiii, 37, 41–45, 47–61, 70, 84, 86, 187, 241–47, 249–53, 285–86
Clay County Land & Cattle Company, 242–44, 246, 252–53
Cleburne, TX, 95, 269
Clements, Israel, 63
Cleveland, J. S., 78, 158, 177, 182
Cobb, Ben, 47, 59
Cobb, W. F. (Babe), 47
Cobb brothers, 47, 51
Cobb Land and Cattle Company, 47, 53
Coggin, Modie J., 75
Coggin, Samuel R., 63, 75
Coggin brothers, 75
Coke, Richard, 266
Coke County, TX, 82, 84–85
Coleman County, TX, 37, 70–71, 121–22, 124, 131, 144, 151, 154, 167, 172–73, 175–77, 179, 181, 183–90, 192
Coleman, Mathis, and Fulton Cattle Company, 13, 21
Coleman, Redmond "Bud," 120, 122
Collier, Wesley, 143
Collier, William W., 135
Collingsworth County, TX, 34
Collins, Frank, 7, 246–47, 249–50, 253
Collins, N. G., 98
Collins, Thomas C., 7
Collins County, TX, 98, 242, 246, 253
Comal County, TX, 152
Comanche (Indians), 43, 63–65, 67
Comanche County, TX, 65, 67, 84, 134, 200
Comanchero, 64
Concho County, TX, 83, 149, 159, 177, 179–80, 183
Conkle, A., 34
Conner, Alfie, 141
Conner, Bill, 156

Conner family, 141, 150, 156
Conner Gang, 155, 160
Conover, W. H., 242
Cooke County, TX, 55, 57–58
Cooper, G. A., 109
Cooper Wright, George, 44–45, 250
Copeland, Bud, 155
Copeland, Florena, 172
Copeland, James, 135
Copeland, Joab (J. O., Joe), 113, 135–36, 144–48, 151, 153–55, 157–61, 163–69, 172, 216
Copeland, John, 216
Copeland, Laura Christine (Scarborough), 136, 158, 172
Corsicana, TX, 266, 272–74, 277, 280
Coryell County, TX, 200
Cotton, J. S., 113
Cotulla, TX, 152, 210
Crain, William Henry, 88–91
Crane, Rayston C., 117–18
Creech, E., 195
Creech, J. D., 195
Crosby County, TX, 171, 253
Cross, G. W., 166
Cross, R. Y., 180
Cross Cut, TX, 70
Crouch, B. L., 209, 229
Crouse, J. A., 242
Cuero, TX, 90
Curry, Emmitt, 248–50

D

Dallas, TX, 20, 23–24, 43, 96, 150, 280, 282
Dannheim, Caroline, 227
Davis, R. A., 270
Davis, Robert, 219, 221, 223, 229
Dawson, Sterling, 242, 246, 248–53
Day, Jesse, 30, 174–75, 177, 179–80
Day, Nancy Elizabeth, 175
Day, Sarah Logan, 174, 177
Day, Tommye Mabel (Doss), 176–81, 183–84, 189–92

Index

Day, William Henry, 30, 71, 174–81, 189, 191
Day, Willie Mabel, 192
Day Ranch Company, 177, 179–81, 184–85, 187, 189–92
De Morse, Charles, 52
Decatur, TX, 20, 42, 54, 252–53
Delk, Eli, 245–46
Delta County, TX, 95–96
DeMontel, Charles, 208, 218
DeMontel, Edmund (Ed), 218, 222
Denison, TX, 19, 175–76, 178
Devine, T. J., 213–14
Devine, TX, 212–13
DeWitt County, TX, 88
Dinwiddie, Charles, 44–45
Dodge City, Kansas, 176
Dorr, Eber Green, 259, 262
Dorr, Hadley, 259
Doss, William, 178, 187, 189, 191
Douthitt, Ambrose, 242
Douthitt, James Taylor (Tack), 242, 244–54
Douthitt, Joseph W. (Joe), 242
Douthitt, Lee Morris (Dink), 242
Douthitt, Nancy (Smith), 242–43, 252
Douthitt, Smithy, 242
Douthitt brothers, 242, 244, 253–54
Dragoo, E. A., 199
Dragoo, Tom, 193, 198, 200, 205
Drew, J. John, 34
Driskill, Bud, 86
Driskill, J. W., 74
Driskill, Jesse Lincoln, 30, 175, 177, 179–80
Driskill Hotel, 30, 175
Drummond, C. J., 8, 35
Dublin, Dell, 200–201
Dublin, Dick, 200–201
Dublin, James, 201
Dublin, Jim, 200–201
Dull brothers, 209
Dull Ranch, 90, 209–10, 212. *See also* Hall Ranch
Dully, Olise, 221
Duval County, TX, 98

E

Earl, Arch, 268
Earl, J. P., 243
Earp, Bill, 170
Earp, James, 68
Earp, Mary, 68, 170
East Texas, 98–99, 136, 141, 150–52, 160
Eastland County, TX, 168, 170
Eaton, Squire, 139
Eddleman, James, 170
Eddleman, R. W., 164, 170
Eddleman, Ruben, 168
Edwards County, TX, 159, 193–97, 199–206
Eighteenth Texas Legislature, 30, 56, 84, 104, 127, 138, 226, 261, 267
El Paso, TX, 43
Ellison, John, 220
Ellison, Sam, 220
Ellwood, Isaac, xi, 8, 15–18, 21–23, 25
Emma, TX, 171
Evans, John F. (Spade), 19–20
Evolution of barbed wire and cattle industry, 27–29

F

Falls County, TX, 96, 136, 158, 172
Fannin County, TX, 12
Fannintown (Joy), TX, 48
Farley, Dave, 114
farmers, 12, 14–16, 18–20, 42–46, 48, 54–55, 57, 59–61, 65, 67, 151–71, 185, 187–89, 208, 243
Faulkner, B. F., 269
fence cutting, 1, 79, 99, 107–8, 140, 145, 151, 187, 204, 273, 283
   cases, 58, 117, 132, 140, 157, 163, 165, 224–25, 227, 271
   charges, 150, 159, 163
   indictments, 113–16, 120, 122–23, 125, 130–31, 139–40, 157, 159–61, 163–64, 166, 168–71, 224–25, 232–33, 236–37, 262
   law, 33, 81, 100–104, 226
   trial, 2, 117–18, 260–61, 263
   war, 54, 70, 72, 185, 192, 208, 219, 239, 241, 256, 290
Ferris, J. H., 250–51
Finger, Joe, 228

Index 381

Fish Brand Slickers, 63, 79
Fish Creek, 83–84, 106–13, 115–17, 120, 122
Fish Creek Gang, 84, 108, 111, 113
Fisher, King, 226
Fisher County, TX, 24, 226
Fitterer, Gary, 233
Ford, Henry, 78, 131, 143–44
Formwalt, Coke H., 82
Formwalt, John McEwen, 82–83, 107, 116–17, 123–24
Fort Bend County, TX, 176, 284
Fort Chadbourne, TX, 82, 98, 105–8, 110–11, 114–15, 117, 119, 126, 137
Fort Concho, TX, 64, 68
Fort Graham, TX, 269
Fort Griffin, TX, 173
Fort McKavett, TX, 194, 203, 205, 255–56, 262
Fort Sill, OK, 43
Fort Sumner, NM, 42
Fort Terrett, TX, 194–95, 256
Fort Worth, TX, 48, 50, 52, 54, 57, 71, 73, 118, 122–23, 191, 216, 218, 268–69, 283–84, 286
Foster, John R., 242
Foster, William Burl, 239
Fowler, J. H., 63
Franks, Nimrod, 114
Franks, Thomas, 114
Fredericksburg, TX, 81, 143, 175, 261
free grazing, 29–30, 36–37, 46, 48, 71, 82, 194, 256, 266, 285, 290
French, James, 23, 208, 226
Frio County, TX, 37, 152, 208–9, 211–13, 223, 229
Frost, B. L., 55
Frost, Samuel, 271–73
Frost, T. C., 277

G

Gaines, J. D., 198–99
Gainesville, TX, 19, 57–58
Galveston, TX, 73, 136, 208, 286
Gates, John Warne, 21–24, 100, 291
Gibbs, Barnett, 96
Gilbert, John T., 144, 164–65
Gillespie, James T. (J. T.), 111, 114, 129, 131–33, 135, 137–39

Gillespie County, TX, 255
Gillett, James, 201
Glidden, Joseph Farwell, 15–24, 33, 43–44, 285
Glidden Barbed Wire, 8, 20
Glidden patents, 8–9, 15–18
Glidden wire, 15–17, 20, 22–24, 33, 43, 177, 211, 257, 285, 291
Goche, J. M. (Goutcher), 109–10
Gonzales County, TX, 106, 108, 223
Goodin, Elisha, 255, 258–62
Goodin, Nathaniel, 260
Goodnight, Charles, 42, 46, 64
Goodrum, S. R., 177–79
Gordon, Albion, 57
Gordon, Giles J., 57
Gosling, Hal, 210, 213–14, 227
Gowan, G. H., 49
Graham, George T., 74
Graves, Amos, 168, 214, 231
Gray, Ike, 141
Green, Bill, 134, 157, 200
Green, Joseph, 195, 202, 206
Green, William, 150, 157, 161–63
Green Lake, 193–206
Greer, Green Berry (G. B.), 195, 197, 199, 206
Greer, Ida Jane Armstrong, 206
Greer, William Joseph, 195, 199, 202, 206
Grice, Frank, 213
Griffin, Thomas, 270
Griffith, Joe, 86, 140
Grinninger, John, 4–9, 14
Guadalupe County, TX, 152
Guyle, Joe, 269

H

Haggerman, Frank, 200
Haggerman, Fred, 200
Haish, Jacob, x, xi, 8–9, 15–17
Haley, Jackson M., 243
Haley, Nancy R., 243
Halff, M., 213
Halff, Sol, 214

Index

Hall, Lee, 90, 209–10, 212, 229
Hall Ranch, 209. *See also* Dull Ranch
Halse, John, 171
Halsell, Glenn, 43
Hamilton County, TX, 65, 263
Handley, R. W., 55–56
Hanna, David, 64
Hanna, James, 64
Hanna, John, 64
Hanna, R. M., 64
Hanscomb, Alfred E., 113–14
Harris, Abner, 262
Harris, Frank, 200
Harris, Jack, 55, 200, 238
Harris, Joe, 55, 57–58
Harris, Leasial B., 85
Harris, Maggie, 242
Harris Ranch, 85
Harrison, S. B., 47
Harry, James, 142–43, 145, 152
Hart, Dorothy "Dollie," 253
Hartung, Julius, 221
Hartung, Louis, 221
Hathaway, J. W., 113
Havins, T. R., 147–48, 162
Hayes, Tom, 189
Hays, Jack, 208
Hays County, TX, 30, 174–75, 211
Hazelwood, R. R., 251
Helena, TX, 154
Helm, Jack, 21
Hemphill, Mark, 196–97, 201, 203, 205
Hemphill, TX, 141, 155–56
Henderson, Lemuel, 199, 265
Henrietta, TX, 42–43, 45, 48–52, 54–55, 57–58, 241–43, 246, 250–51, 253
herd law, 70, 87–89, 91, 98, 104
Hildebrand, John William, 233–38
Hill County, TX, 238, 265, 267, 269
Hill Country, 294
Himmel, A., 133
Hocker, J. M., 180
Hogan, J. H., 159

Hogan, Wilbur Fisk, 59–60
Hogg, James S., 61, 104
Holden, Margaret, 205
Holmes, Henry N., 228
Holt, J. M., 269
Holt, Roy D., 164
Hoog, Peter, 231
Hooper, Baz, 139, 171
Hopkins, J. M., 242
horses, 11–12, 18–19, 34–36, 57, 65–66, 68, 102–3, 144–47, 152–53, 159, 164–66, 174–75, 178, 195–99, 201, 248–50
Houston, Frank, 47, 51–52, 71, 137
Houston, TX, 23, 51–52, 71, 137, 285
Howard, G. S., 160, 164
Howard, H. P., 213
Hubbard, A. G., 95, 267
Hubbert, Eppie, 110, 126
Hudman, J. M., 55
Huffman, W. A., 24
Hughes, John R., 160, 272–73, 284
Huling, Proctor H., 165
Hunt, W. G., 85
Hunt, William D., 14
Hunter, Warren, 176, 262, 282
Hutzler, August, 221
Hylton, Dow, 109, 113, 116–17, 125–26, 191
Hylton, Elisha, 112, 115–17, 123, 125
Hylton, Riley, 109, 113, 116–17, 119, 125

I

Ikard, William Sude, 43–44
Indian Territory, 35, 42, 45, 54, 145, 156, 158, 246–47, 253
Indians, 4, 42–43, 57, 64–67, 212, 271, 287
Ireland, John, 38–39, 50, 56–57, 60, 80, 84–87, 89, 181–82, 187, 190, 194, 197, 203–4, 267–68, 286

J

Jack County, TX, 42, 47, 49, 51, 53, 55–56, 58, 60–61
Jaybirds–Wood Peckers feud, 284
Jenkins, Charles H., 78, 167

Index

Johnson, Charles, 139, 146, 149, 168, 170–71
Johnson County, TX, 95, 269
Johnson, Frank, 139, 149–50, 171
Johnson, James, 178
Johnson, J. M., 68
Johnson, Jeff, 139, 171
Johnson, John O., 134
Johnston, W. C., 120
Jones, B. T., 55
Jones, Bob, 220
Jones County, TX, 121–22, 138
Jones, Frank, 134, 202–3, 273
Jones, George W., 87, 92, 289
Jones, Henry, 220, 266, 270
Jones, J. C., 173
Jones, John B., 255, 266, 271
Jones, Johnny, 184
Jones, N. P., 113
Jones, Newt, 53
Jones, Thomas W., 164
Joy (Fannintown), TX, 48
Junction, TX, 199, 202–3
Jungman, Joe, 232

K

Kammellah, Kohler, 12
Kammellah, Saeger, 12
Kammellah, William, 12
Kampmann, J. H., 213
Karm, George, 212–13
Karnes County, TX, 141, 154
Kauffman County, TX, 275
Kelly, Michael, 14, 24
Kemp, August, 234
Kemp, Joseph, 234–36
Kendall County, TX, 229, 237–38
Kenedy, Mifflin, 13, 34
Kennedy, William, 116, 119, 122–25
Kerrville, TX, 204
Ketchum, Pete, 218, 222
Kimble County, TX, 200, 202–3, 255, 257

King, Jim, 273, 275–76, 280, 284
King, Richard, 13
King, Wilburn H., 105, 111–12, 114, 129, 131–35, 137, 140–43, 149–54, 158, 184, 187–90, 201–3, 271, 273, 278–82
Kingsbury, W. H., 270
Kinnebrew, J. D., 79
Knight, Thomas, 156, 158
Kollet, Otto, 12
Kothmann, Heinrich Friedrich (Fritz), 11–12
Kountze, Augustus, 33
Kramer, A. E., 128–29, 131–33
Kyle, TX, 204

L

Laman, Joseph, 211
Lamar, Mirabeau, 3
Lamb family, 45
Lampasas County, TX, 37, 70, 87, 143–44, 149, 165
Landigan, John, 196
Lane, E. R., 209, 229
LaSalle County, TX, 223
Lea, Joseph, 191–92
Lee, Brooks W., 63, 65
Lehman, Joe, 228
Leslie, Jesse W., 228
Lester, W. S., 1, 118
Lewis, Jake, 139, 171
Lewis, Nat, 231, 244, 247
Lindsey, J. C., 49
Lindsey, N. R., 84
Litburu, Brown, 220
Litburu brothers, 223
Live Oak County, TX, 21
livestock, 3, 5, 11, 14, 24–25, 30–31, 63–64, 67, 101–2, 208–9, 212, 217–18, 285, 287–89
  grazing, 24, 48, 97, 104, 195
Llano County, TX, 65, 134, 202
Lockhart, L. P., 12, 255
Loring, Fred, 231
Louisiana, 13, 136, 141, 174–75
Lount, George, 6–8

Lount, W. R., 6
Lovell, David Franklin, 69
Lovell, Frank, 165
Lovell, Georgia Ann, 69
Lovell, James, B. 69, 139, 146–48, 165, 171
Lovell, Sarah Jane, 69
Lovell, Sue Ellen, 69
Loving, James, 43
Loving, Oliver, 42–43
Loyal Valley, TX, 12
Luckett, Henry H., 82
Lucy, J. E., 90–91
Lytle, John T., 34, 209–10, 229
Lytle, William (Bill), 209, 242

M

Mahoney, George W., 184–85
Majoribanks, Archibald John (Archie), 34–35
Mangold, Jacob, 220
Mann, Clark, 70, 173
Mann, William H., 12
Marsh, John J., 194, 256
Martin, J. A., 96
Martin, William, 74
Mason County, TX, 11–12, 110, 134, 136, 175, 195–203, 205–6, 227–28, 255–56, 258
Massey, William, 159
Mathews, Asa Samuel (Ace), 69, 139, 148, 155, 157, 161–62, 170
Mathews, Bob, 139, 157, 171
Mathews, John, 69, 139, 146–47, 149, 157, 160, 163, 171
Maverick, Mary, 82
Maverick, Samuel A., 82
Mayes, William, 78
McCall, S. R., 113
McCloud, J. L., 79, 246, 248–49, 252–53
McClure, Lewis, 155
McConnell, W. D. R., 160
McCoy, Joseph, 42
McCullough, A. D., 79
McCullough County, TX, 83, 131, 134, 149, 183
McCullough, Henry, 64

McCutcheon, John, 108
McDaniels, Thomas, 209, 229
McDonald, Bill, 160
McGraw, Sammy, 47
McLennan County, TX, 124, 268–69
McMillin, N. D., 112
McMullen County, TX, 90, 209, 212
McMurry, Samuel, 56, 107–8, 114, 187, 250
Medina County, TX, 207–12, 218–19, 222–29, 232–39, 286
Menard County, TX, 131, 134, 206, 255–60, 262–63
Menardville, TX, 258–62
Meny, Frank, 231
Mercer, A. S., 54
Meriwether, William H., ix
Merriman, James E., 232
Mesquite Ranch (Coggin brothers), 71, 76
Mexia, TX, 21, 273–75
Miles County, TX, 67, 186
Millhartz, August, 220
Millhartz, Joe, 220
Mills County, TX, 165
Mineola, TX, 141
Missouri, 19, 47, 51–53, 67–68, 176, 195, 206, 241–42, 253
Mitchell County, TX, 115, 123
Mitchell, W. A., 197, 205
Mobley, Lee, 70
Montague County, TX, 42, 47, 57–58, 286
Moody, R. E., 119
Moon, William, 175
Moore, J. M., 24
Moore, James, 141, 145, 156
Morris, Bob, 218, 220
Moursund, A. W., 260–63
Munday, E. B., 252
Murchison, Flora, 259

N

Nail, Sam, 221
Nance, Ezekiel, 175
Navarro County, TX, 265–84
Neal, F. K., 170

Index

New Braunfels, TX, 152
Newel, Theodore F., 91–92, 94
Newport, TX, 48, 54
Ney, Joseph, 211, 239
Nichols, A. J., 113
Niggli, Ferdinand (Ferd), 210–11, 218–22, 226, 228–33, 235, 239
Nolan County, TX, 1, 24, 106–7, 110–12, 114–20, 122–23, 125–26, 137
North Texas, 12, 19, 23, 41–44, 56, 60, 70, 84, 182, 187, 241
North-Central Texas, 265, 271
Numant, Louis, 220

O

O'Connor, Tomas, 30
Odom, Cyrus, 108
Odom, Garland G., 81–82, 107, 109, 113, 116–17, 123–24
Odom, Lucinda, 82
Odom, Thomas Lawson (T. L.), 1–2, 81–86, 98–99, 105–7, 109–11, 113–14, 116–19, 137, 286
O-D Ranch (Odom family), 82–85, 113, 115
Oliphant, W. J., 8
Orange, TX, 205
Overall, R. H., 185

P

Paint Rock, TX, 178
Park, W. N., 236
Parks, Claiborne, 75
Parks, William C., 64
Parrack, Robert Cypret (Bob), 67–69, 134, 139, 144–45, 147, 150, 155, 157, 163–72
Parrish, Lucien Walton, 53
Paschal, Thomas M., 224, 232, 237
pasture, 13, 36–38, 51–52, 54–57, 59–60, 71–72, 74, 101–2, 137–38, 182, 186–88, 211–13, 217, 267–68, 270, 277–79
Patton, C. D., 113
Pearce, Y. A., 171
Pearsall, 223
Pendleton, Abraham, 189–90
Perry, J. M., 70, 166
Perry, Nat A., 140, 166–67, 171

Phillips, Jim, 159
Pierce, Abel, 18
Pingenot, Cleste, 235
Pinkerton, Allen, 132
Pinkerton Detective Agency, 127–28, 132
Pittman, Ben, 183–84
Plemons, Judge William B., 54–56
Port Arthur, TX, 23
Postoak, TX, 48, 55, 57
Potter County, TX, 253
Powell, C. F., 1, 118
Pratt, Andrew, 109
Premier Ranch, 12, 255–56
Price, Tom, 159, 263
Prospect, TX, 48, 53
Province, George, 270
Putz, Henry, 142, 145, 156, 158

Q

Quihi, TX, 231

R

Rains, John D., 61
Randolph, J. C., 139–40, 161–62, 164, 171
Rathbone, Rufe, 221
Red River, 37, 41–42, 44
Red River Country, 35, 42, 44, 46, 61, 241, 285
Red River County, TX, 95
Red River Land and Cattle Company, 47–49, 51–55, 59
Reeves County, TX, 140
Refugio County, TX, 30
Rentfro, Dr., 6–7
Reynolds, H. H., 163, 200
Rhein, Peter, 220
Rialto, Pedro, 159
Richardson, W. H., 21–22
Richland, TX, 272, 274–76, 278
Robbins, William, 86
Roberts, William Amos, 69, 139, 146–48, 171, 266, 287
Robertson, Walter M., 8

Index

Robinson, D. S., 232
Rocking Chair Ranch, 34–35
Rockport, TX, 13–14
Rogers, John, 145, 156–57, 159–60
Rogers, Robert, 165
Rogers, Thomas, 165
Rose, Henry M., 14
Ross, Laurence Sullivan, 124, 149–50, 158, 268–71, 273, 278, 282, 284
Runnels County, 1–2, 82–84, 105–6, 110–11, 113–18, 123–26, 137, 149, 157–58, 227, 286
Runnels, TX, 82, 84
Runnels, Wood, 147, 149, 157
Russell, Richard R., 260
Russell, S. R., 270
Ryan, Andy, 246, 248

S

S barb wire, 15–16, 24
Sabine County, TX, 141–42, 150, 152–53, 155
San Angelo, TX, 157, 159, 184, 206
San Antonio, TX, 20–22, 81, 205, 208, 210–11, 213, 216, 221–28, 230–31, 233, 237–39, 283, 285
San Patricio County, TX, 21
San Saba County, TX, 11, 24, 107, 110–12, 140, 149, 151, 154
Sanborn, Henry B., 17–25, 33, 43–44, 67, 211, 285
Sanylin, J. W., 126
Sanzenberger, Chris, 49
Sayre, Ephraim, 181
Scarborough, George, 122, 138
Schmitt, George H., 142–43, 151–54, 166–67
Schorp, Joseph, 212, 220
Schorp, Louis, 212
Scoggin, J. D., 131
Scott, S. F., 242
Scott, William, 127, 141–43, 145–53, 155–60, 164, 184
Scruggin, J. B. (Scoggin), 78
Scurry County, TX, 124
Seabaugh, Charles, 216
Sedberry, J. M., 137, 139
Seekatz, Frank, 232
Sellman, Richard, 149

Sellman, Tom, 149
Sheffield, W. F., 137
Shelby County, TX, 69
Shely, Joseph, 218–19, 222–23, 226, 229
Shephard, Pete, 155
Sherman, TX, 19–20, 23, 43, 176, 242
Sherman, William Tecumseh, 43
Sherwood, Bink, 47
Sherwood, Samuel E., 46
Sieker, Lamartine (Lamar), 134, 141, 165–66, 194, 196, 201, 203, 271–72, 274, 282
Simmons, Jesse, 206
Simmons, John, 206
Simms, Billy, 178, 226
Skates, J. R., 209, 229
Skidmore, Frank, 21
Slaughter, C. C., 43
Slaughter, G. W., 64
Slover, W. A., 55–56
Smadler, Lee, 200
Smith, Clair, 250
Smith, Elmer, 243, 247–49, 252
Smith, James M. (Jim), 243, 249, 251–52
Smith, Lewis C., 243–50
Smith, Lucien B., 14
Smith, Nancy J., 243
Smith family, 243–44, 246–53
  home, 243–44, 246
smooth wire, 12–15, 20–21
  fence, 14–15, 20
Sneed, Joseph, 136
Sneed, Thomas, 7
South Llano River, 195, 200–202
South Texas, 18, 20–21, 30, 34–36, 81–83, 88, 90–91, 128, 142, 211–12, 284–85
Sparkman, L. C., 252
Speed, James, 209, 229
Speed, Stephen, 209, 229
Spencer, Early W., 34
St. John, Albert, 156, 158
stake-and-rider fence, 3, 11
Starkweather, Horace R., 185–86

Index 393

Steele, L. W., 119
Stewart, A. J., 113
Stine, P. M., 252
Stine, Vincent, 252
Story, L. J., 24
Story, W. J., 213
Sutton, George (a.k.a. George Baker), 106–9, 111, 113–14, 194, 197–99
Swan, Allen K., 50, 58, 84
Sweetwater, TX, 1, 105–25

T

Tarr, William, 180–81
Tarrant County, 242, 268
Taylor County, TX, 36, 82, 95, 107, 109–11, 115, 123, 132, 137, 203, 242
Taylorville (Taylor), TX, 36
Templeton, J. A., 252
Tennessee, 85, 110, 135, 174, 243
Terrell, Alexander W., 4, 7, 30, 87, 97–98, 269–70
Terrell, J. W., 269–70
Terrell, W. W., 61
Texas Land and Cattle Company, 34
Texas legislature, 30, 32, 41, 45, 56, 185, 190, 194–95, 260, 266, 271, 286, 288. *See also* Eighteenth Texas Legislature
Texas Panhandle, 32, 34, 83, 171, 284, 290
Texas Rangers, 38, 56–57, 90, 107–8, 111–12, 114–17, 124–25, 128–31, 133–35, 137, 139–43, 145–58, 160, 170–71, 187, 195–205, 209–10, 222–23, 265–83, 286–87
  Company A, 114, 271
  Company B, 56, 107, 114, 131, 187, 190,
  Company C, 142–43, 151–52, 154, 271
  Company D, 143, 183, 195–96, 206, 272–74, 284
  Company E, 1, 111, 114, 128, 131–32, 137–40, 271
  Company F, 136, 141–43, 152–53, 155–60, 184, 223
  Frontier Battalion, 83, 90, 111, 114, 116, 141, 158, 160, 266, 271, 274
  Special Rangers, 153, 203, 206
Thompson, B. F. "Dock," 174, 246, 248, 250–52
Thompson, Ben, 5, 90, 226, 238
Thompson, Charles, 248–50
Thompson, Pete, 114–15
Thompson, W. S., 214
Thompson, William, 90, 114

Thrifty, TX, 69, 160, 162
Thuken, George, 236
Thumm, Christopher Friedrich (Fritz), 227–39
Thurman, Jesse, 205
Tillery, William, 200
Todd, George W., 228
Tom Green County, TX, 157, 159–60
Tomerlin, Martin, 220
Tompkins, R. V., 23
Toyah, TX, 140
Travis County, TX, 9, 86, 110, 180
Treadwell, William, 142–43, 145, 152, 156
Trickham, TX, 189
Tuckness, Charles, 161, 163
Turner, Jack, 198, 200
Turner, William, 200

U

Uvalde, TX, 143, 199, 205, 226, 273
Uvalde County, TX, 143, 196, 205, 226, 272, 280, 284

V

Vallin, T. N., 128, 132–33
Van Zandt County, TX, 270
Vance, R. M., 222
Vernon, TX, 142

W

Waco, TX, 23, 174, 268, 272–73
Waelder, Jacob, 213
Waggoner, D. W., 64
Waggoner, John, 64
Wahlburg, Theodore, 228
Walker, A., 136, 269
Wallace, William A. (Big Foot), 211–12, 287
Wallace, Willis R., 218–20, 222, 224–27, 233, 236
Waller, Edwin, 3–6
Walters, G. W., 160, 261
Walton, William M., 237

Index 395

Warner, Judson, 18–20, 22–25, 43
Warren, Benjamin Goodin, 1–2, 105, 107, 110–15, 117–23, 125–26, 137
Warren, Elizabeth Owen, 110
Warren, Eppie, 126
Warren, Henry Clay, 43, 112
Warren, Jefferson, 110
Warren, John, 107, 110–11, 115
Warren, Joseph, 111–13, 115
Warren, Vollie Ann, 112
Washburn & Moen Manufacturing Company, 8–9, 16–17, 21–25
Washburn, Charles Francis, 8–9, 16–17, 21–25
Washington County, TX, 65, 135–36
Weakley, Joseph, 78
Weathered, William, 150
Weatherford, TX, 43, 156, 269
Webb, John A., 20
Webb, Walter Prescott, 8, 12, 20
Webber, Joseph, 221
Wentworth, P. H., 194, 256–57
Wernette, Charles, 230
Wernette, Joseph, 221
West, C. S., 7
West, Hezekiah P. (Ki), 271–74
West Texas, 66, 118, 140, 244
Wharton County, TX, 18
Wheat, Ira L., 196, 200, 204
Wheeler, Ellen M., 18
Wheeler County, TX, 34
Wheeler, Thomas B., 113–16, 123–24
Whipple, B. F., 242
White, George, 181
White, Nub, 47
Whitney, TX, 269
Wichita Falls, TX, 27, 35–36
Wilhelm, John, 257
Williams, A. J., 122
Williams, John, 65
Williams, Lee, 247
Williams, W. J., 121, 247
Williamson County, TX, 86, 132
Wilson, George J., 209, 229
Wilson, J., 159

Wilson, Robert B., 160, 164
Wilson, Samuel A., 238
Wilson, Stanford, 47
Wilson County, TX, 160
Winter, A. V., 177, 251
Wise County, TX, 252–53
Wittich, George, 242
Wood, Henry, 195
Wood, William J., 114–15, 117, 119–20
Woodard, J. O., 139–40, 161
Woods, S. H., 74, 122–23
Worsham, William Benjamin, 43, 48
Wortham, TX, 275
Wrenn, F. K., 283–84
Wright, George Cooper, 44–45, 250–51
Wylie, Robert K., 82–84

X

XIT Ranch, 32, 284

Y

Yardley, James, 114
Yardley, William, 114
Young County, TX, 42–45